Cosmopolitan Elites and the Making of Globality

Histories of Internationalism

Series Editors: Jessica Reinisch, Reader in Modern History at Birkbeck, University of London, UK and David Brydan, Lecturer of 20th Century History and International Relations at King's College London, UK.

Editorial Board:
Tomoko Akami, Australian National University, Australia
Martin Conway, University of Oxford, UK
Adom Getachew, University of Chicago, USA
Sandrine Kott, University of Geneva, Switzerland
Stephen Legg, University of Nottingham, UK
Su Lin Lewis, University of Bristol, UK
Erez Manela, Harvard University, USA
Samuel Moyn, Yale University, USA
Alanna O'Malley, Leiden University, The Netherlands
Kiran Patel, Ludwig Maximilian University Munich, Germany
Tehila Sasson, Emory University, USA
Frank Trentmann, Birkbeck University, USA
Heidi Tworek, University of British Columbia, Canada

This new book series features cutting-edge research on the history of international cooperation and internationalizing ambitions in the modern world. Providing an intellectual home for research into the many guises of internationalism, its titles draw on methods and insights from political, social, cultural, economic and intellectual history. It showcases a rapidly expanding scholarship which has begun to transform our understanding of internationalism.

Cutting across established academic fields such as European, World, International and Global History, the series will critically examine historical perceptions of geography, regions, centres, peripheries, borderlands and connections across space in the history of internationalism. It will include both monographs and edited volumes that shed new light on local and global contexts for international projects; the impact of class, race and gender on international aspirations; the roles played by a variety of international organizations and institutions; and the hopes, fears, tensions and conflicts underlying them.

The series is published in association with Birkbeck's Centre for the Study of Internationalism.

Published:
Organizing the 20th-Century World,
ed. by Karen Gram-Skjoldager, Haakon Andreas Ikonomou and Torsten Kahlert
Placing Internationalism: International Conferences and the Making of the Modern World,
ed. by Stephen Legg, Mike Heffernan, Jake Hodder and Benjamin Thorpe
Inventing the Third World: In Search of Freedom for the Postwar Global South,
ed. by Jeremy Adelman and Gyan Prakash
Internationalists in European History: Rethinking the Twentieth Century,
ed. by Jessica Reinsich and David Brydan
International Cooperation in Cold War Europe,
Daniel Stinsky
Socialist Internationalism and the Gritty Politics of the Particular,
ed. by Kristin Roth-Ey
Relief and Rehabilitation for a Postwar World,
ed. by Samantha K. Knapton and Katherine Rossy
Dismantling the League of Nations: The Quiet Death of an International Organization, 1945-8, Jane Mumby

Forthcoming:
Informing Interwar Internationalism: The Information Strategies of the League of Nations, Emil Eiby Seidenfaden
Socialism, Internationalism, and Development in the Third World: Envisioning Modernity in the Era of Decolonization, ed. by Su Lin Lewis and Nana Osei-Opare
Dam Internationalism: Rethinking Power, Expertise and Technology in the Twentieth Century, ed. by Vincent Lagendijk and Frederik Schulze

Cosmopolitan Elites and the Making of Globality

M. N. Roy and Fellow Anti-Colonial, Communist and Humanist Intellectuals, c. 1915–1960

Leonie Wolters

BLOOMSBURY ACADEMIC
LONDON • NEW YORK • OXFORD • NEW DELHI • SYDNEY

BLOOMSBURY ACADEMIC
Bloomsbury Publishing Plc, 50 Bedford Square, London, WC1B 3DP, UK
Bloomsbury Publishing Inc, 1385 Broadway, New York, NY 10018, USA
Bloomsbury Publishing Ireland, 29 Earlsfort Terrace, Dublin 2, D02 AY28, Ireland

BLOOMSBURY, BLOOMSBURY ACADEMIC and the Diana logo are trademarks of
Bloomsbury Publishing Plc

First published in Great Britain 2024
This paperback editon published in 2025

Copyright © Leonie Wolters, 2024

Leonie Wolters has asserted her right under the Copyright, Designs and Patents Act, 1988,
to be identified as Author of this work.

For legal purposes the Acknowledgements on p. x constitute
an extension of this copyright page.

Series design by Tjaša Krivec
Cover image by Joshua Waleson

All rights reserved. No part of this publication may be: i) reproduced or transmitted in
any form, electronic or mechanical, including photocopying, recording or by means of
any information storage or retrieval system without prior permission in writing from the
publishers; or ii) used or reproduced in any way for the training, development or operation
of artificial intelligence (AI) technologies, including generative AI technologies. The rights
holders expressly reserve this publication from the text and data mining exception as per
Article 4(3) of the Digital Single Market Directive (EU) 2019/790.

Bloomsbury Publishing Plc does not have any control over, or responsibility for,
any third-party websites referred to or in this book. All internet addresses given in
this book were correct at the time of going to press. The author and publisher regret
any inconvenience caused if addresses have changed or sites have ceased to exist,
but can accept no responsibility for any such changes.

A catalogue record for this book is available from the British Library.

A catalog record for this book is available from the Library of Congress.

ISBN: HB: 978-1-3503-7315-0
PB: 978-1-3503-7318-1
ePDF: 978-1-3503-7316-7
eBook: 978-1-3503-7317-4

Series: Histories of Internationalism

Typeset by Integra Software Services Pvt. Ltd.

For product safety related questions contact productsafety@bloomsbury.com.

To find out more about our authors and books visit www.bloomsbury.com
and sign up for our newsletters.

Contents

List of figures	viii
Acknowledgements	x
Introduction: Distinguished cosmopolitanism and the making of globality	1
1 Cosmopolitan clubs – Making a vagrant elite	17
2 Foreign bodies – The making of a cosmopolitan persona	61
3 We are the world – Bengali actors on world stages	105
4 Human resources – Opportunities for objective outsiders	143
5 A flat earth – Assertions of equivalence	181
The face of the global	217
Bibliography	229
Index	254

List of figures

1.1 Interior of Mexico City nightclub 'M. N. Roy,' photography by Ramiro Chaves, 2011 — 18

2.1 Delegates to the Second Congress of the Comintern at the Uritsky Palace in Petrograd. Niday Picture Library / Alamy Stock Photo — 67

3.1 Isaak Brodsky. Lenin's speech on the Second World Congress of the Comintern. 1924. State Historical Museum — 105

3.2 Manabendra Nath Roy by Isaak Brodsky, 1920 — 126

To the giants and the dwarves

Acknowledgements

A wise old man once told me that the most important part of writing anything at all was the part where we ask others for help. Throughout the many years it took to complete this book, I spent a great deal of time figuring out what the questions might be with which I could ask for help. It is a testimony to their patience and resourcefulness that so many people have managed to support me – especially when it came to finding out what the question was to begin with.

Over the years, I have benefited enormously from the ideas and suggestions of Margrit Pernau and the members of the South Asia and Beyond Colloquium, Sebastian Conrad and the Graduate School of Global Intellectual History, Camilla Bertoni, Valeska Huber, Sebastian Gottschalk, Valerian Rodrigues, Aditya Nigam, Kris Manjapra, Mauricio Tenorio and an anonymous graduate student of his, Jitumani Sharma, N. D. Pancholi, Roy Carton, Riet Hofstede, Frank Ankersmit and Itamar Ben-Ami.

I especially want to thank Charlotte Piepenbrock, Lisa Hellman, Soheb Niazi, Katie Dumm, Irene Thomas Mkama and Daniel Kolland for their help.

Lastly, I am grateful to my family. They all are experts at providing a sense of perspective, whether as a consultant, an artist or an architect.

Introduction: Distinguished cosmopolitanism and the making of globality

Each of the volumes of the *Selected Works of M. N. Roy* has a world map printed on the insides of its covers. On this map, the itinerary travelled between 1915 and 1930 by the Indian anti-colonial revolutionary, international communist and humanist thinker Manabendra Nath Roy (1887–1954) is traced in a red line. It goes from India to Indonesia, the Philippines, Japan and China, back to Japan and on to the United States, from its West Coast to its East Coast, to Mexico, Cuba, Spain, Italy and Switzerland, via Germany and Finland to Western Russia, Central Asia, China, back to Russia, Germany, France and Italy and via Baghdad back to India.[1] Something appealing is communicated through the medium of lines drawn across a map, associating a single individual with an overwhelming array of places. It is as though before they found out about Roy's thoughts, readers needed to know that they came from a man who knew the world.

Maps are popular aesthetic objects, not only as book covers for works in global history, but on living room walls, in textile design and beyond. With their familiar lines, they suggest 'the world,' or a collection of more or less faraway places, which can be connected to a sense of importance tinged with adventure and the unknown, or knowledge and science. This book argues that much like maps, individual human beings also could communicate an idea of the wider world. That ability had great political significance during the first half of the twentieth century, when ideologies such as communism, fascism and various nationalisms vied for global domination.[2] In the propaganda efforts that went

---

[1] Sibnarayan Ray, *Selected Works of M. N. Roy: Volume I – 1917 – 1922* (Oxford; Delhi: Oxford University Press, 1987); Sibnarayan Ray, *Selected Works of M. N. Roy: Volume II – 1923 – 1927* (Oxford; Delhi: Oxford University Press, 1988); Sibnarayan Ray, *Selected Works of M. N. Roy: Volume III – 1927 – 1932* (Oxford; Delhi: Oxford University Press, 1990).

[2] Sebastian Conrad, Dominic Sachsenmaier, 'Introduction: Competing Visions of World Order; Global Moments and Movements, 1880s–1930s', in *Competing Visions of World Order; Global Moments and Movements, 1880s–1930s*, ed. Sebastian Conrad, Dominic Sachsenmaier (New York: Palgrave Macmillan, 2007), 7–11; for the universal claims of Hindu nationalism, see Sugata Bose, *A Hundred Horizons; The Indian Ocean in the Age of Global Empire* (Cambridge, MA: Harvard University Press, 2006), 31–2.

with this competition, particular individuals could give weight to an ideology's claim that its tenets held true around the world. They played the role of acceptable outsiders for those who worked to see their ideologies extended to new places, thereby rendering the ideology less parochial.

M. N. Roy is the central example of such a character in this book. His world-spanning image was a key aspect of his reputation.[3] It meant that those looking to engage with the world at large could feasibly find it with the help of just one man. This impression helped Roy to quickly rise through the ranks of the Communist International between 1920 and 1928, hobnobbing and publicly disagreeing with Vladimir Lenin, without much experience in socialist politics prior to that. He also became a household name in all-India politics during the 1930s and 1940s, mentioned alongside figures such as Jawaharlal Nehru, even though he did not have a large political following. At the dawn of the Cold War age, Roy headed a small humanist organization in India, which was quickly taken seriously by the US Rockefeller and Ford foundations, and allowed Roy to become a founding member of the International Humanist and Ethical Union, headed by former UNESCO president Julian Huxley. In the present day, Roy's humanist organization is still active in the field of human rights, drawing on universal ideas in order to fight instances of injustice in India.

Roy's presence in international organizations is reflected in his significant presence in the field of global history.[4] Accordingly, uncovering the mechanisms that helped him to speak for the world on various stages does not only shed a new light on the workings of international organizations, but it also has lessons to offer for global history: there, a similar mechanism is often at work, according to which an actor from outside that which is already familiar – often the

---

[3] In a national Indian context, by contrast, he has been labelled a 'failure' in terms of political leadership, as well as largely 'forgotten' in its historiography. Sudipta Kaviraj, 'The Heteronomous Radicalism of M. N. Roy', in *Political Thought in Modern India*, ed. Thomas Pantham, Kenneth L. Deutsch (New Delhi: Sage Publications, 1986), 214; Kris Manjapra, *M. N. Roy; Marxism and Colonial Cosmopolitanism* (London; New York; Delhi: Routledge, 2010), xiii–xxiv; Ali Raza, *Revolutionary Pasts: Communist Internationalism in Colonial India* (Cambridge: Cambridge University Press, 2020), 5–6.

[4] See for example Brigitte Studer, *Reisende der Weltrevolution: Eine Globalgeschichte der Kommunistischen Internationale* (Berlin: Suhrkamp, 2020); Timothy Harper, *Underground Asia Global Revolutionaries and the Assault on Empire* (London: Allen Lane, 2020); Isabel Huacuja Alonso, 'M. N. Roy and the Mexican Revolution: How a Militant Indian Nationalist Became an International Communist', *South Asia: Journal of South Asian Studies* 40, no. 3 (2017): 517–30; Michael Goebel, 'Geopolitics, Transnational Solidarity or Diaspora Nationalism? The Global Career of M. N. Roy, 1915–1930', *European Review of History: Revue Européenne D'histoire* 21, no. 4 (2014): 485–99.

West – offers something known as the global.⁵ This book deconstructs such claims by carefully investigating the basis on which they are made, thereby unpicking tacit assumptions about the relationships between mobility, cosmopolitanism and the global.

Historians have elaborated on the highly specific interests that went into various map-making projects, which have both shaped the way maps look as well as the notion of the world that they are able to portray.⁶ Similarly, those who were able to represent the world were very specific people, and their ability to do so was as much determined by themselves as by their social circles, the gendered, classed and racial landscapes they acted in and the ideologies they lent their voices to. As much as mobility played a role in this ability for the way in which it made people present in places where they seemed unfamiliar, as well as providing them with experience of many places, most of the millions of migrants whose mobility shaped the twentieth century did not belong to the small elite Roy was a member of.⁷ It was Roy's cosmopolitan reputation, rather than mobility plain and simple, that brought opportunities and political influence. This reputation was not a straightforward product of mobility, but made by the practices that went alongside it in the social circles Roy formed a part of. Their members shared and accepted an intellectual authority resting on a self-conscious foreignness or cosmopolitanism that they cultivated through social practices and in writing. While Roy's qualities were shared by a range of intellectuals playing similar roles, he was still unusual among them because of the variety of places and ideologies of the milieus connected through and by him.

The circles that provide focus to this book had members from Asia, Europe and North America, and were politically largely leftist – although the book includes exceptions, as the ability to cross boundaries and to make this boundary-crossing into a central aspect of one's reputation is part of the cosmopolitanism under scrutiny. The book portrays chameleons, clandestines

---

⁵ Duncan Bell, 'Making and Taking Worlds', in *Global Intellectual History* (New York: Columbia University Press, 2013), 255.
⁶ Simon Schaffer, 'Introduction', in *Aesthetics of Universal Knowledge*, ed. Simon Schaffer, John Tresch, Pasquale Gagliardi (Cham: Palgrave Macmillan, 2017), 14; Andy Hahnemann, *Texturen des Globalen: Geopolitik und Populäre Literatur in der Zwischenkriegszeit, 1918–1939* (Heidelberg: Winter, 2010); James R. Akerman, ed., *The Imperial Map: Cartography and the Mastery of Empire* (London; Chicago: University of Chicago Press, 2009).
⁷ Adam McKeown, 'Global Migration, 1846-1940', *Journal of World History* 15, no. 2 (2004): 155–89.

and converts, including ideologically varied Indian revolutionaries such as the anarchist M. P. T. Acharya (1887–1954) who single-handedly made the syndicalist International Working Man's Association more global by joining it in 1922; communist revolutionaries such as the Indonesian Tan Malaka (1897–1949), who ran for Dutch parliament on a communist ticket in 1922, making its elections suddenly about the wider world; as well as humanist intellectuals such as the Austrian-born monk and anthropologist Leopold Fischer/Swami Agehananda Bharati (1923–91), whose very adopted name communicated his homelessness. What these individuals shared with one another, as well as many more of the heterogeneous personalities from Roy's networks who feature in the book, was a privileged and actively cultivated cosmopolitanism, allowing them to both represent the world for specific audiences, and also claim to understand it on a higher level. They could recognize one another as fellow cosmopolitans, regardless of their differences, and functioned as a particular kind of precarious elite.

Distinguished cosmopolitanism

The focus on mobile lives in global intellectual history exists for a reason, as it would be impossible to study the interaction of ideas over distances without looking at the movement of people and things. What this book adds to the picture is that the mobility of individuals is not merely an innocent analytical category, but that it could be a consciously cultivated part of a public persona, which could play a more or less immediate role in the opportunities open to its owner during their lifetime. Analytically, cosmopolitanism revolves around a love of difference, or emphasis on chosen affiliations rather than received ones, meaning notions of difference and movement are key to its meaning.[8] While a great deal has been written about cosmopolitanism as a concept, historical investigations of the phenomenon are more rare.[9] What

---

[8] Kwame Appiah, *Cosmopolitanism; Ethics in a World of Strangers* (London: Allen Lane, 2006), xv; Leela Gandhi, *Affective Communities Anticolonial Thought, Fin-De-Siècle Radicalism, and the Politics of Friendship* (Durham: Duke University Press, 2006), 7–10.

[9] Glenda Sluga and Julia Horne, 'Cosmopolitanism: Its Pasts and Practices', *Journal of World History* 21, no. 3 (2010): 369; 'Introduction', Bernhard Gissibl, Isabella Löhr, *Bessere Welten: Kosmopolitismus in Den Geschichtswissenschaften* (Frankfurt; New York: Campus, 2017), 20; for the early modern period, See Felicia Gottmann, ed., *Commercial Cosmopolitanism?: Cross-Cultural Objects, Spaces, and Institutions in the Early Modern World. Political Economies of Capitalism, 1600–1850* (London; New York: Routledge, 2021).

is more, historians have justly criticized cosmopolitanism as Eurocentric,[10] referring exclusively to elite,[11] anglophone actors, to the detriment of other kinds of cosmopolitans.[12] This book uses this critique in order to reverse its perspective onto an elite, anglophone, often Eurocentric set of cosmopolitans in order to bring out their specificities as well as the way in which these specificities were hidden and allowed them to – more or less convincingly – speak for and about the world.[13] The book characterizes this specific type of cosmopolitanism as a 'distinguished' cosmopolitanism, because it was characterized by distance, it was cultivated, and it was 'smooth,' meaning it was aimed at easily surmounting the potential difficulties of encounters between different people and ideas.[14] While mobility was to an extent a prerequisite for coming into contact with what was experienced as different, it was at least as much shaped by subsequent cultivation through sociability and writing. Cosmopolitanism as an asset thus mainly came into its own once someone had reached a modicum of stability.

Distinguished cosmopolitanism was characterized as much by distance from its direct environment as it was by its affiliations. This book does not use cosmopolitanism as a singularly positive notion, focusing instead on its blind spots and omissions. Neither is cosmopolitanism used as a quantitative term, suggesting cosmopolitan actors were more connected than non-cosmopolitan ones. Rather, the cosmopolitan actors in these pages were often connected to other cosmopolitan actors, and less so to more settled ones. This means distinguished cosmopolitanism is a counterpoint to what has been influentially labelled a 'rooted' or 'vernacular' cosmopolitanism.[15] This notion has proved popular with historians who caution against an over-emphasis on mobile actors,[16] but this misses the fact that sometimes, cosmopolitans stuck to

---

[10] Homi K. Bhabha, *The Location of Culture* (Abingdon: Routledge, 2004), ix–xxv; Walter D. Mignolo, 'The Many Faces of Cosmo-Polis: Border Thinking and Critical Cosmopolitanism', *Public Culture* 12, no. 3 (2000): 721–48.

[11] Raza, *Revolutionary Pasts*, 64.

[12] Nile Green, 'The Waves of Heterotopia: Toward a Vernacular Intellectual History of the Indian Ocean', *The American Historical Review* 123, no. 3 (2018): 846–74.

[13] For the connection between cosmopolitanism and universality, see: Daniel Chernilo, 'There Is No Cosmopolitanism without Universalism', in *Routledge International Handbook of Cosmopolitanism Studies*, ed. Gerard Delanty (London; New York: Routledge, 2018), 30–42.

[14] Smooth is used in contradistinction to Anna Lowenhaupt Tsing's idea of 'friction' as 'the grip of encounter.' Anna Lowenhaupt Tsing, *Friction: An Ethnography of Global Connection* (Princeton: Princeton University Press, 2011), 5.

[15] Kwame Appiah, *The Ethics of Identity* (Princeton: Princeton University Press, 2010), 213–50; Bhabha, *Location of Culture*, xvi–xvii; Sidney G. Tarrow, *Strangers at the Gates: Movements and States in Contentious Politics* (Cambridge: Cambridge University Press, 2012), 183–6.

[16] See for example Antje Dietze, Katja Naumann, 'Revisiting Transnational Actors from a Spatial Perspective', *European Review of History: Revue Européenne D'histoire* 25, nos. 3–4 (2018): 416.

circles of their own that possessed a degree of separateness from their direct environments.

The notion of rooted cosmopolitanism has been a necessary corrective to the antisemitic conception of 'rootless cosmopolitans,' prevalent in the 1930s and 1940s among proponents of Nazism and, to an extent, Stalinism.[17] Rather than returning to some conception of cosmopolitanism as free-floating and unlinked to any material reality, distinguished cosmopolitanism emphasizes the specific connections of actors who to many audiences *seemed* to float above the ordinary world. It investigates how and why certain cosmopolitans could give off the impression of being connected to the world at large, and what practices went into creating this impression. A distinctly cosmopolitan reputation could be seized upon in a positive sense in order to celebrate intellectual independence and flexibility, and in a negative sense as evidence of opportunism or a lack of loyalty. In the case of M. N. Roy and the Indian revolutionary Har Dayal (1884–1939) – who formed the revolutionary *Ghadar* movement in California in 1913, their variegated lives meant that at one time they were persecuted by the British Empire and counted among its dangerous enemies, at other times they lent it their support.[18] The constantly changing affiliations of US radical, Indian independence activist and communist Agnes Smedley (1892–1950) were such that in an autobiographical text, she found herself on the outside of not just parts of the world but the planet overall, floating through space.[19] For all three, a lifetime of great political upheaval meant that the chosen way to navigate it changed – a course of action that could only be recognized by an insightful, independent observer.

Cosmopolitanism could also bring distinction when it was an asset for either work opportunities, social standing or political clout. This recalls the anthropological notion of 'spiralists' whose upward mobility within professional organizations was linked to their geographic mobility.[20] In order to have geographic instability become a positive marker, it was cultivated into a distinguished cosmopolitanism, in no small part through writing practices that thematized the close relationship between an individual and the wider world. M. N. Roy as well as the Asian revolutionaries, US radicals, European

---

[17] James Loeffler, *Rooted Cosmopolitans: Jews and Human Rights in the Twentieth Century* (New Haven: Yale University Press, 2018), xv.
[18] See Chapter 4.
[19] See Chapter 2.
[20] William Watson, 'Social Mobility and Social Class in Industrial Communities', in *Closed Systems and Open Minds*, ed. Max Gluckman (Edinburgh: Oliver and Boyd, 1964), 147–51.

communists and various humanists among his circles produced a great deal of writing about their own lives.[21] According to Javed Majeed, travel writing by South Asian anti-colonial intellectuals was an inherently political act, as they claimed their own subjecthood as travellers, against a colonial establishment that viewed them as immobile natives who could merely be travelled *to*.[22] In Roy's circles, their writing mingled with that of other mobile actors remembering their journeys and encounters, in ways that often paid a great deal of attention to first impressions and the textures of life in various places. This involved thick descriptions of appearances, food and drink, clothing and ways of living together. In creating themselves and each other as mobile characters, they created both their circles and the world as a particular kind of place.[23] Distinguished cosmopolitan writing could stylize a fraught life on the move into a glamorous and even narrative in a way that made their author seem light-hearted (and -footed) and their path to have been rather smooth. It was this smoothness that lent itself so well to the propaganda efforts of universalizing ideologies.

Practising difference

Moving beyond theoretical expositions of cosmopolitanism, the book goes into the shared practices that constituted distinguished cosmopolitanism. These practices were to an extent necessitated by a mobile life, partly lived under clandestine conditions and persecution. They also made up the social world that distinguished cosmopolitans shared, from which many others were excluded. On top of that, they formed a subject of cosmopolitan reflection and performance in published and unpublished writing – a shared practice in its own right – and contributed to a cosmopolitan public persona.

Practice theory is useful in order to connect the social circles of distinguished cosmopolitans to the ways in which these shaped their members. It does so without reducing human activity to either an account of individual intentions and interests, or to a function of complying with or deviating from social

---

[21] On Asian revolutionaries and South Asian anti-colonialists, see Harper, *Underground Asia*, xxix.
[22] Javed Majeed, *Autobiography, Travel and Postnational Identity; Gandhi, Nehru and Iqbal* (Houndmills: Palgrave Macmillan, 2007), 10–16.
[23] See Doreen Massey, *For Space* (London: Sage, 2005), 81–9; 177–95; Doreen Massey, *Space, Place, and Gender* (Minneapolis: University of Minnesota Press, 1994), 1–16.

norms.[24] Instead, Pierre Bourdieu's notion of the habitus provides the notion of an 'inner construction map' of their milieu that shaped the way they lived and the way in which they conceived of the desirable qualities in life.[25] On top of that, there were shared practices that more actively cultivated a cosmopolitan persona in practices that can be called performative.[26] Practice theory draws attention to the shared notion of the desirability of this persona. Remaining in the practice-oriented vocabulary of Bourdieu, symbolic cosmopolitan capital could be exchanged for financial, social or political capital.[27] Lastly, practice theory allows to take into account the emotional dimensions of practices.[28] Emotions could provide the glue between small in-groups of cosmopolitans, at the same time creating distance from the emotional regimes of their places of origin. This meant that within their shared places, an emotional style had currency that was much more specific than emotional regimes as they have been considered for cultures in various parts of the world.[29] Feelings of distinguished cosmopolitans strongly related to their itinerancy, as they marked the temporariness of their connections.[30] The nostalgia this engendered played a key role in the shared practice of committing their memories to paper. More generally, feelings were a part of the distinction of a cosmopolitan character in what can be called a distant emotional style.[31] Much of the cosmopolitan writing under scrutiny was markedly emotional, spanning the range between the crafting of affiliations in one direction and distances in another.

Cosmopolitan practices revolved around defining, using, making and unmaking differences between people. By the twentieth century, the world

---

[24] Theodore R. Schatzki, 'Introduction: Practice Theory', in *The Practice Turn in Contemporary Theory*, ed. Karin Cetina Knorr, Theodore R. Schatzki, Eike von Savigny (London: Routledge, 2000), 12; Andreas Reckwitz, 'Toward a Theory of Social Practices: A Development in Culturalist Theorizing', *European Journal of Social Theory* 5, no. 2 (2002): 249.

[25] Michael Vester, *Soziale Milieus Im Gesellschaftlichen Strukturwandel: Zwischen Integration Und Ausgrenzung* (Köln: Bund-Verlag, 1993), 88.

[26] Erving Goffman, *The Presentation of Self in Everyday Life* (New York: Doubleday, 1959), 1–14.

[27] Pierre Bourdieu, 'The Forms of Capital', in *Readings in Economic Sociology*, ed. Nicole Woolsey Biggart (Oxford: Blackwell, 2008), 280–91.

[28] Monique Scheer, 'Are Emotions A Kind of Practice (And Is That What Makes Them Have a History)? A Bourdieuvian Approach to Understanding Emotion', *History and Theory: Studies in the Philosophy of History* 51, no. 2 (2012): 217.

[29] See for example Margrit Pernau, 'Studying Emotions in South Asia', *South Asian history and Culture* 12, nos. 2–3 (2021): 118.

[30] Tobias Becker, 'History and Nostalgia: Historicizing a Multifaceted Emotion', in *Intimations of Nostalgia: Multidisciplinary Explorations of an Enduring Emotion*, ed. Michael Hviid Jacobsen (Bristol: Bristol University Press, 2022), 52–69.

[31] Benno Gammerl, 'Emotional Styles – Concepts and Challenges', *Rethinking History* 16, no. 2 (2012): 161–75.

could be seen as a limited range of options, such as various kinds of national dress, formalized religions and human races, which all belonged to a defined collection, rather than an infinite range of the unknown.³² Such articulation of differences meant that certain kinds were fetishized and sought after, in ways that could create opportunities as well as limitations for those who could supply them. They created a persona or a habitus that was called upon to supply a sought-after difference to the table, but that could also help an individual to claim an expertise of difference more generally; instead of only delivering what was desired, a distinguished cosmopolitan could claim an expertise in difference in order to redefine where the boundaries of difference and sameness lied. Beyond that, one could even argue that what seemed different was in fact the same, dissolving all difference.³³ This last line of argument was what could allow for the claim to not just represent a different part of the world, but the world in general.

During the twentieth century, racial difference was a key difference that could be met with hostility or fetishization. Various anti-Asian exclusion acts were instituted at the end of the nineteenth and early twentieth centuries, as Asian migration to the British Empire's white Dominions as well as the United States had grown and anti-colonial activities were on the rise, an increasing number of exclusive laws saw to keep Asian people out.³⁴ Among Indian anti-colonial revolutionaries who travelled to North America in the early twentieth century, racial discrimination often was a fundamental and politicizing experience. It played a role in bringing together the Punjabi labourers and the Bengali students who formed the *Ghadar* movement in 1913,³⁵ and intellectuals such as Lala Lajpat Rai (1865–1928), Benoy Kumar Sarkar (1887–1949) and Taraknath Das (1884–1958) wrote extensively about the racial segregation and violence they

---

[32] Christopher Alan Bayly, *The Birth of the Modern World, 1780-1914: Global Connections and Comparisons* (Malden, MA; Oxford; Carlton: Blackwell Publishing, 2004), 2.

[33] Similar to what Christopher Hill has labelled 'generalising universalization,' where ideas are universalized without allowing for variation of their content between different contexts. Christopher L. Hill, 'Conceptual Universalization in the Transnational Nineteenth Century', in *Global Intellectual History*, ed. Samuel Moyn, Andrew Sartori (New York: Columbia University Press, 2016), 150–2.

[34] Adam McKeown, *Melancholy Order: Asian Migration and the Globalization of Borders* (New York: Columbia University Press, 2008); Renisa Mawani, 'From Migrants to Revolutionaries: The Komagata Maru's 1914 "Middle Passage"', in *Viapolitics; Borders, Migration, and the Power of Locomotion*, ed. William Walters, Charles Heller, Lorenzo Pezzani (Durham: Duke University Press, 2022), 60–1.

[35] Maia Ramnath, *Haj to Utopia: How the Ghadar Movement Charted Global Radicalism and Attempted to Overthrow the British Empire* (Berkeley: University of California Press, 2011), 22.

witnessed in US cities, linking it to the bane of the imperialist system.[36] M. N. Roy's writings, in contrast, did not mention him experiencing discrimination in the United States at all; where they mentioned racial inequalities it was with reference to US attitudes towards Black people.[37] More than that, in his published texts, racial bias was never something that had any effect on himself. While racial exclusion was certainly something Roy encountered, particularly in marrying a white woman in the United States during the late 1910s,[38] he did not make it a part of his public persona. In a social field determined by difference, he increasingly characterized himself as above it.

In cases where racial difference was fetishized, Roy equally portrayed himself as immune – as well as laughing at the ways of those in its thralls. Among culturally and politically experimentalist circles in the United States and Europe, racial difference could be imbued with a more positive, desirable meaning because of the spiritualist faith of theosophy. This had been concocted in the United States in the late nineteenth century by fusing orientalist knowledge of Asian religions with mysticism and Christian esotericism, and became influential in experimental circles in Europe, North America and India, where many of its followers joined the cause of Indian nationalism.[39] The spiritual teachings of theosophy had done a lot to affect desires surrounding brown-skinned men in the early twentieth century, suggesting they were spiritual, enlightened beings.[40] Yet, a sensual desire for exotic brown bodies was never far off, and professions of purity and holiness were as common as rhapsodizing on the beauty of Indian men.[41] As a noticeable intellectual influence in many of the experimental circles Roy formed a part

---

[36] Clemens Six, 'Challenging the Grammar of Difference: Benoy Kumar Sarkar, Global Mobility and Anti-Imperialism Around the First World War', *European Review of History = Revue européene d'histoire* 25, nos. 3-4 (2018): 436–7; Neilesh Bose, 'Taraknath Das: A Global Biography', in *South Asian Migrations in Global History: Labor, Law, and Wayward Lives*, ed. Neilesh Bose (New York: Bloomsbury Academic, 2021), 168.

[37] M. N. Roy, *Memoirs* (Bombay, New Delhi, Calcutta, Madras: Allied Publishers, 1964), 32.

[38] See Chapter 1.

[39] Significantly, the British socialist and feminist Annie Besant (1847–1933) was one of the leaders of the theosophical movement, as well as the president of the Indian National Congress in 1917. Peter Washington, *Madame Blavatsky's Baboon; A History of the Mystics, Mediums and Misfits Who Brought Spiritualism to America* (New York: Schocken Books, 1995), 105–7;124–7.

[40] The '… dominant tendency of many British theosophists …' was '… to look for a Mahatma [saint] in every Indian member they encountered.' Joy Dixon, *Divine Feminine: Theosophy and Feminism in England* (Baltimore: Johns Hopkins University Press, 2001), 30.

[41] Rajbir Singh Judge, 'Dusky Countenances: Ambivalent Bodies and Desires in the Theosophical Society', *Journal of the History of Sexuality* 27, no. 2 (2018): 264–93; On the role of white women in the theosophical movement, see Kumari Jayawardena, *The White Woman's Other Burden: Western Women and South Asia during British Colonial Rule* (New York: Routledge, 1995), 107–74.

of, perceptions of him and other Indian men were certainly affected by theosophical ideas. Roy and the author Dhan Gopal Mukerji (1890–1936) would come to vehemently resist all of its assumptions of cultural difference and Indian mysticism, and to gleefully make fun of anyone who professed otherwise.

Roy would come to resist any notion of particularity at all – in a highly particular way. Over the course of his time back in India, from 1930 until his death in 1954, he positioned himself, and was characterized, as a universal or Renaissance man.[42] Roy's professed model for a universal man was Leonardo da Vinci rather than a Bengali intellectual with an encyclopaedic mind, of which many examples exist.[43] Even more specifically, his idea of the Italian Renaissance and its celebration of the creative individual was something he drew from the Swiss historian Jacob Burckhardt's *The Civilisation of the Renaissance in Italy* (1860).[44] Yet, at the same time, Roy's facility with universal thinking drew on anti-colonial Bengali thought,[45] Marxist dialectics, the exercise of applying specific ideas to Mexican, Indian, Chinese, British and other contexts, as well as the strength of conviction that his own presence had had on audiences far and wide.[46] Smooth, anglophone, elitist versions of the global possessed highly particular cosmopolitan histories, excluding much more than they included.

Sticking to the itinerary

This book uses M. N. Roy's life as a site, meaning his itinerary limits the scope of the study. It also means that the book explicates how Roy's itinerary created him as a specific kind of cosmopolitanism, and how the cosmopolitan practices

---

[42] Roy's fellow humanist G. D. Parikh (1915–76), for example, remembered him as such in the 1960s, surmising: 'He was unique in the universality of his experience.' G. D. Parikh, 'Introduction' in Roy, *Memoirs*, viii;v.
[43] Examples of these characters ranged far and wide; the religious reformer Rammohun Roy (1772–1833) was celebrated as a Renaissance man by philosophy professor Brajendranath Seal (1864–1938), while the latter was labelled just that by journalist and author Nirad Chaudhuri (1897–1999), who evidenced encyclopedic knowledge of his own. David Kopf, *The Brahmo Samaj and the Shaping of the Modern Indian Mind* (Princeton: Princeton University Press, 1979), 63; Nirad Chaudhuri, *Autobiography of an Unknown Indian* (Mumbai: Jaico Publishing House, 2016), 368–9.
[44] Roy's *Reason, Romanticism and Revolution* drew liberally from Burckhardt's magnum opus, of which the second part was devoted to 'The Development of the Individual.' On Burckhardt's influential account, see Tony Davies, *Humanism* (London: Routledge, 1997), 16–17.
[45] Manjapra, *M. N. Roy*, 12–17.
[46] See Chapter 5.

he engaged in along his way, together with many others, created his itinerary as a cosmopolitan asset in turn. This perspective, in which mobility is both a fact and a resource, allows for close scrutiny of a mechanism of ideological globalization by which individuals could convincingly represent the world. The book does not take the approach of connecting the macro of the global to the micro of the individual with reference to the relation of these scales.[47] Instead, it conceives of the global as argument, recovering practices that allowed for universal arguments to be made more or less convincing by highly specific individuals, engaging in equally specific practices.[48] A life is where this personal dimension of impersonal thought systems becomes visible, especially so in the life of M. N. Roy. So this book does not offer a new biography of M. N. Roy, but rather brings into view several cosmopolitan milieus connected to him in which cosmopolitan personae were made and had value, as they provided support for global thinking and acting.[49] The focus on this particular actor allows for close scrutiny of the strategies intellectuals could deploy to gain legitimacy as cosmopolitan figures across a range of places, networks, ideologies and time. Without exaggerating continuities, this allows for gaining a grip on what was necessarily an in-between phenomenon, existing between places, as well as between the shifting sands of various ideologies, whose boundaries only crystallized with time.

Limiting the study with reference to an individual rather than a geographical area, organization or ideology means the practices and networks brought into view transcend such limits, and that the specific kind of cosmopolitanism comes into view as an asset in several different ones. It includes locations within the South Asian part of the British Empire, but also outside of it, in East Asia, the United States, Mexico, Western Europe and Soviet Russia – markedly

---

[47] Christian G. De Vito, 'History without Scale: The Micro-Spatial Perspective', *Past & Present* 242, no. Supplement_14 (2019): 348–72.
[48] Where the global focuses '… on enunciations of universality, on attempts to cognitively encompass a given world (of whatever physical scale).' Bell, 'Making and Taking Worlds', 257.
[49] Several are available: Manjapra, *M. N. Roy*. Written by Roy's political associates are the five-volume Sibnarayan Ray, *In Freedom's Quest: A Study of the Life and Works of M. N. Roy, Volume 1 (1887–1922)* (Calcutta: Minerva Associates Publications, 1998); Sibnarayan Ray, *In Freedom's Quest: A Study of the Life and Works of M. N. Roy, Volume Two: The Comintern Years (1922–1927)* (Calcutta: Minerva Associates Publications, 2002); Sibnarayan Ray, *In Freedom's Quest: A Study of the Life and Works of M. N. Roy, Volume Three: Against the Current (1928–1939)* (Calcutta: Minerva Associates Publications, 2005); Sibnarayan Ray, *In Freedom's Quest: A Study of the Life and Works of M. N. Roy, Volume Four, Part One: From Anti-Fascist War to Radical Humanism (1940–1946)* (Calcutta: Minerva Associates Publications, 2007); Sibnarayan Ray, *In Freedom's Quest: A Study of the Life and Works of M. N. Roy, Volume Four, Part Two: From Anti-Fascist War to Radical Humanism (1947–1954)* (Calcutta: Minerva Associates Publications, 2007).

excluding Britain. The long time window of a lifetime means that the personal dynamics of intellectual globalization are considered both before, during and after the Interwar Period, which has often been labelled as the high point of such individually driven internationalism.[50] With specific reference to the life of M. N. Roy, it means the study goes beyond the era he is mostly known for, as the '… ultimate celebrity of Bengali Marxism.'[51] Thereby, the role of cosmopolitan capital and universal argument are investigated far beyond the communist realm. It was at work both before Roy was a well-known figure while he was in the United States and Mexico, as well as once he returned to India in 1930 and his worldly past was one of his main assets in gaining political influence, as well as a new kind of international standing in humanist circles.

Structure of the book

The first two chapters of the book go into the practices that went into the making of distinguished cosmopolitans, where Chapter 1 focuses on the social aspects thereof and Chapter 2 zooms in on the body and its transformation into an image or even icon of cosmopolitanism. The three chapters after each develop a field of application for the 'capital' that their cosmopolitanism provided Roy and his peers and rivals with, ranging from representation to providing general expertise, and lastly, engaging in the practice of translation.

Chapter 1, *Cosmopolitan Clubs*, departs from the exclusive night club named El M. N. Roy in Mexico City, which is based in the house where the historical M. N. Roy lived between 1917 and 1919. It uses the nightclub as a metaphor for the places that M. N. Roy frequented during his lifetime and that were just as exclusive. By zooming in on these places, the chapter introduces a wide range of characters and paints a picture of a diffuse yet particular and highly elitist social world. The chapter explicates which social practices were an important factor in making these places both cosmopolitan and exclusive. These included food and drink, language, ways of making a living as well as engaging in interracial relationships. In addition, it included the subject of birth control – both as a

---

[50] See for example Ali Raza, Franziska Roy, Benjamin Zachariah, eds., *The Internationalist Moment: South Asia, Worlds and World Views, 1917–39* (Los Angeles: Sage, 2015).

[51] Andrew Sartori, *Bengal in Global Concept History; Culturalism in the Age of Capital* (Chicago: University of Chicago Press, 2008), 225.

practice, easily scandalizing others, and as a subject of expertise for thinkers used to considering global population as a whole.

Chapter 2, *Foreign Bodies*, argues that there was a personal, corporeal side to the making of universal arguments. The associations various audiences in Europe and North America made with regards to Roy, a brown-skinned, tall, imposing Indian intellectual, were important ingredients in the reputation he built and the life it enabled him to lead. The chapter goes into the social and performative practices that did not only allow foreigners to become acceptable, but that turned them into recognizable cosmopolitans and made them desirable. These shared practices included the use of aliases and name changes, using sartorial disguises as well as a concern with the cultural and political implications of dress, as well as a range of writing practices that linked an individual to the world at large. These practices included advice literature, prison memoirs recalling free-roaming days, as well as writings that tried to sell the social capital of acquaintance with political figures known the world over, and even appearing in works of fiction.

Chapter 3, *We Are the World*, addresses the value of distinguished cosmopolitans in acts of international representation. It delves into the particular prowess of Bengali intellectuals to appear on world stages – and to make these stages worldly by their appearance. It discovers a lineage for the political career of Roy and other leftist intellectuals in the lives of Swami Vivekananda, Philosophy professor Brajendranath Seal as well as the poet Rabindranath Tagore. While Roy's politics were unlike those of these men, the techniques used to represent the world and to claim to speak for large parts of the world's population were highly similar. This is shown by a close reading of world stages Roy appeared on: from the Second World Congress of the Communist International held in 1920 in St. Petersburg (then Petrograd) and Moscow, to his work on behalf of the International Communist Opposition in the 1930s and the founding of the International Humanist Ethical Union in Amsterdam in 1952. All these organizations made universal claims of their own, and counting Roy among their ranks made their membership more universal.

Chapter 4, *Human Resources*, inquires into the matter of staffing in the business of changing the world. It complements Chapter 3 by delving into the roles that existed for cosmopolitan actors beyond that of political spectacle. Among Roy's circles, many seized upon their outsiderhood to proudly consider themselves exiles and therefore intellectually independent. They also found ways to have their expertise in difference earn them a living abroad: as translators, language teachers, academics or journalists. More enduringly, they had the status of 'professional revolutionaries' who travelled from country to country in order to ignite the revolution everywhere, or even as 'development experts' who sought to eradicate poverty around the world. When these roles are kept apart because of their differing politics, their similarities are missed. Taken together, they are viewed as 'professional outsiders' whose value to an organization lay in their distance from it, providing a perspective that included more than could be seen from inside.

Chapter 5, *A Flat Earth*, takes a closer look at Roy's written output – and contrasts his arguments with those of his cosmopolitan peers. About ninety years before Thomas L. Friedman wrote that the world is flat, M. N. Roy was able to convince certain audiences that there were no meaningful differences between Europe, North America and Asia. Over time, he argued racial mixing had the same benefits in Latin America as it had done in ancient India in 1919; explained that the Bengali *bhadralok* ('gentlefolk') were the same as Marx' working-class in 1923; and elucidated that German, Italian and Indian nationalism were all expressions of the same global fascist force in 1945. The chapter situates Roy among his peers who were often highly critical of his sweeping statements, but argues that they were a particular kind of translation, which, rather than diagnosing two contexts as different and engaging in an act of translation to cover the space between them, assumed that two distinct places were already more similar than they looked. The chapter widens the field of how we can think of translations, as well as offering a way to understand some of Roy's more baffling writings as a key part of his habitus.

Taking a biographical approach, yet not writing a biography, captures a subject that is both theoretical and human. Zooming in on one man allows for a granular understanding of what it is a single, highly particular person could be used for when it comes to ideologies claiming universal validity; conversely, it allows for individual agency to remain in focus, supporting, subverting and potentially unmaking the universalizing causes it was enlisted to. M. N. Roy was highly unusual but not singular. Situating him into the social circles he shared with others shows how a precarious political elite cultivated a cosmopolitan reputation that allowed them to be taken seriously when speaking on behalf of and about the whole world, even though – or because – they were in many ways outsiders in the places where they operated. By carefully considering the social and performative practices that turned them into credible cosmopolitans, the book uncovers the exclusive basis on which the universal claims of world-changing ideologies were made.

1

Cosmopolitan clubs – Making a vagrant elite

In the early 2010s, a new Mexico City night club was named after the man who had occupied its premises almost a century before: the Indian founder of the Communist Party of Mexico, M. N. Roy (1887–1954). Welcoming the stylish addition to the international club scene, the journal *dezeen* gushed over the M. N. Roy's interior design with copper and basalt tiles, timbre-lined walls and a glass mezzanine. Yet, one of its readers wondered if '… the founder of the communist party of Mexico would be rolling in his grave if he could see his name attached to a private dance club for the haute culture of Mexico city to drink and dance all night, in his old house no less. Times change I guess.'[1] Few historians doubt the reality of change, and yet there exists a remarkable parallel between the house with the address Mérida 186 in the late 1910s and the 2010s: not just anyone could get in.

In 2012, *Time Out* Mexico City highlighted how difficult it was to gain entrance into the M. N. Roy. If one was not on the guest list, knew the cross-dressing bouncer or paid for a membership, one had to join the long queue for a small security camera that judged if one possessed the ephemeral qualities granting entrance – qualities rarely found.[2] A 2017 Facebook review of the M. N. Roy shed light on what some of those qualities might be: 'Terrible experience. Arrived with 6 expats and 3 Mexican Nationals. They let the expats inside and they did not let our Mexican friends enter.'[3] Back in the 1910s, the eponymous M. N. Roy may have felt a spark of recognition when it came to a restrictive door policy, as there would similarly have been more foreign than Mexican guests in

---

[1] Amy Frearson, 'M.N.ROY by Emmanuel Picault and Ludwig Godefroy', *Dezeen*. 15 July 2011. Accessed 15 May 2020, https://www.dezeen.com/2011/07/15/m-n-roy-by-emmanuel-picault-and-ludwig-godefroy/.
[2] Paola Del Castillo, 'M. N. Roy', *Time Out Mexico*, 19 March 2012. Accessed 15 May 2020, https://www.timeoutmexico.mx/ciudad-de-mexico/nocturna/m-n-roy.
[3] Andrew McDermott, 2017. 'Terrible Experience', *Review of M. N. Roy*, Facebook. 16 December 2017. Accessed 15 May 2020, https://tinyurl.com/y878ojyt.

Figure 1.1 Interior of Mexico City nightclub 'M. N. Roy,' photography by Ramiro Chaves, 2011.

the house. The group who often congregated there consisted largely of a group of counter-cultural US socialists who were avoiding being drafted into the First World War.[4] Roy came to refer to these people as '... a small cosmopolitan community of free human beings.'[5] Notwithstanding their shared ideal of global proletarian revolution, the circles Roy moved in during his life lived on three continents mostly consisted of other cosmopolitans like himself.

As a metaphor for a chosen association rather than a given one, a club is apt for the social circles that M. N. Roy formed a part of during his lifetime.[6] These were spread across many continents but involved shared practices and lifestyles. This meant that however dispersed in space circles were, there was a sense of coherence in who had access to them and who did not. Circles were located in specific locations, made up of the people in them, but also of sets of shared practices common there – and these practices shaped their members in turn. The chapter will give a rundown of the cosmopolitan circles brought into view by the itinerary of M. N. Roy, and introduce their members. It shows that circles were made up less by ideological uniformity – however important ideology was to their members – and goes into the social practices that gave them cohesion instead. These included practices involving shared tastes and blind spots, around the themes of food, drink and language. A second complex of practices revolves around relationships, love, sex and violence, as well as family and birth control – all involving the making of affiliative ties, practices and themes also involving animosities and even violence. Overall, a distinguished cosmopolitan sociability was made up as much of distinction and exclusion as it was of association and affiliation.

Cosmopolitan clubs

There were several cosmopolitan circles along the itinerary M. N. Roy travelled during his lifetime. Their members moved between them and beyond, sharing friendships and animosities. In Tokyo, an integrative space had been found and further enhanced by the Indian revolutionary Rash Behari Bose (1887–1945) at a European-style bakery called Nakamuraya. Bose found refuge there after fleeing India because he had made an attempt on the life of its viceroy in 1912.

---

[4] Dan La Botz, 'American "Slackers" in the Mexican Revolution: International Proletarian Politics in the Midst of a National Revolution', *The Americas* 62, no. 4 (2006).
[5] Roy, *Memoirs*, 165.
[6] On filiation and affiliation, see Gandhi, *Affective Communities*, 7–10.

Nakamuraya was run by the culturally influential and Christian, Soma family, who held literary salons, and welcomed Bose into their family when he married Tosiko Soma (1898–1925) in 1918. In Tokyo, Bose laid the foundation of the Indian National Army, with which the much better known Subhas Chandra Bose (1897–1945, no relation) planned to take India during the Second World War.[7] Rash Behari Bose would also welcome the Pan-Islamic Bolshevist Maulana Mohamed Barakatullah (1854–1927) and the Pan-Asianist Mahendra Pratap (1886–1979) to Tokyo at various points in time. Like many Indian revolutionaries, including Roy and many others, both cooperated with Imperial Germany during the First World War, and looked to the young Soviet Union for support, as well as working among Indian communities in North America. One bakery could be a stepping stone for attempts to create vastly different future worlds.

In the United States, Ramakrishna Missions as well as universities were integrative spaces for Indian revolutionaries. Dhan Gopal Mukerji (1890–1936), the brother of one of Roy's fellow revolutionaries in Bengal,[8] had used the San Francisco Ramakrishna Mission as a stepping stone to establish himself in California,[9] and the Mission in New York was the base from which the well-known nationalist politician Lala Lajpat Rai established himself in exile, between 1917 and 1920.[10] There, Rai financially supported Roy and his first wife Evelyn Trent (later Roy/Jones, 1892–1970), and mentored Agnes Smedley (1892–1950), who would become a leading member in the Indian movement in both the United States and Europe, as well as an international birth control activist.[11] Stanford University in Palo Alto, California, became a meeting place when the intellectually eclectic revolutionary Har Dayal (1884–1939) was hired as a lecturer by Stanford's president, the ichthyologist and eugenicist David Starr Jordan (1851–1931), in 1912.[12] Jordan wrote an introduction to the novel *Rajani: Songs of the Night* (1916) that Dhan Gopal Mukerji wrote after he had become a Stanford student. Har Dayal was a connective figure between white female students, notably Agnes Smedley, and male Indian revolutionaries; he in fact

---

[7] Joseph Mcquade, 'The New Asia of Rash Behari Bose: India, Japan, and the Limits of the International, 1912–1945', *Journal of World History* 27, no. 4 (2016): 641–67.
[8] Gordon Chang, 'The Life and Death of Dhan Gopal Mukerji', in *Caste and Outcast*, ed. Dhan Gopal Mukerji (Stanford: Stanford University Press, 2002), 9.
[9] Chang, 'The Life and Death of Dhan Gopal Mukerji', 7.
[10] Babli Sinha, 'Dissensus, Education and Lala Lajpat Rai's Encounter with W.E.B. DuBois', *South Asian History and Culture* 6, no. 4 (2015): 462.
[11] Roy, *M. N. Roy*, 17; Ruth Price, *The Lives of Agnes Smedley* (New York: Oxford University Press, 2005), 57–97.
[12] Lulu Miller, *Why Fish Don't Exist: A Story of Loss, Love, and the Hidden Order of Life* (New York: Simon & Schuster, 2020), 127–40.

recruited female students as message runners, since they drew far less attention than men when they engaged in 'covert work.'[13] In this space of meetings, it was that Evelyn Trent met Roy, and that her fellow Stanford student Ethel Ray Dugan (1888–1966) met Dhan Gopal Mukerji.[14]

In Mexico City, Roy's luxurious living quarters were a meeting space for all kinds of exiles, for a time even including an elderly Prussian professor in linguistics, who had been pushed out of Asia by the First World War and was '… blatantly reactionary to the core …' as well as prone to declamating odes to the German emperor.[15] There were also a few other Indian revolutionaries such as Herambalal Gupta (1884–1950) and Sailendranath Ghose (?–?), who would go unmentioned in Roy's recollections. Beyond the confines of Roy's home, cosmopolitans met at a Chinese restaurant called Fat Sing, a 'little hole-in-the-wall restaurant on Dolores Street,' according to the radical US journalist Carleton Beals (1893–1979), who devoted a considerable part of his 1938 memoirs to the amorous and artistic exploits of the 'Fat Singers': a 'rough-neck group' of poets, journalists, painters and anarchists – whom he counted himself among.[16] This group included New York radical journalist Charles Phillips (1895–1989) and birth control propagandist and spiritualist Linn Gale (1892–1940).[17] After the Russian Revolution, they would be joined by an emissary of the brand-new Communist International: Mikhail Gruzenberg, better known under the alias of Borodin (1884–1951). Save for the bilingual Mexican politician and writer José Vasconcelos (1889–1959), who provided many foreign radicals with jobs, there was a dearth of Mexican intellectuals among them.[18] While Mexican intellectuals knew of Roy living in their capital, Roy did not know of them as that would have involved '… living wholly the cultural life of the city – not just the city as a temporary site for international radical networking.'[19] Roy stuck out as an Indian in Mexico, but to him, fellow foreigners were more present in the composition of his life there.

---

[13] Price, *The Lives of Agnes Smedley*, 43.
[14] Sachidananda Mohanty, *Cosmopolitan Modernity in Early 20th-Century India* (Boca Raton, FL: Routledge, 2018), 148.
[15] Roy, *Memoirs*, 82.
[16] Carleton Beals, *Glass Houses: Ten Years of Free-Lancing* (Philadelphia: J. B. Lippincott, 1938), 31.
[17] In New York, Gale had gotten into legal trouble for receiving birth control material in the mail, which amounted to 'using the mails for illegal purposes.' Gale left New York for Mexico City in 1918, where he published *Gale's Magazine* that continued to publish on birth control, socialism and spirituality. La Botz, 'American "Slackers" in the Mexican Revolution', 574.
[18] Vasconcelos would go on to become Secretary of Education and rector of the National Autonomous University of Mexico. Mauricio Tenorio-Trillo, *I Speak of the City: Mexico City at the Turn of the Twentieth Century* (Chicago: University of Chicago Press, 2013), 115;120.
[19] Ibid., 120.

Different practices were acceptable for those within a cosmopolitan bubble than those without; notably for women. Unlike most other women in Mexico City, they could go out at night and maintain their respectability.[20] Evelyn Roy proved a keen observer of her own separateness from the society she found herself in. In 1919, she published a series of articles named *Mexico and Her People*, in which foreigners in Mexico chose to remain in their isolated bubbles:

> The foreigner lives in Mexico, but is not of it. His life is a round of business and festivity, lived in a concentric circle, within, and yet apart from Mexican life itself. Each colony, be it Spanish, French, English, German or American, is a perfect reproduction if its own national life, transplanted to an exotic soil, whose natural opportunities for getting rich quick, its cheap living and cheap labor permit its members to indulge in an excessive luxury never enjoyed by them in their own countries.[21]

In her articles, Evelyn developed the idea that unlike the foreigners criticized in her piece, she and her allies were a different, better kind of foreigners. Because there was a problem the other kind had in common: 'At bottom of this ill-concealed intolerance is racial prejudice, which makes the European and North American feel in his heart that the Mexicans, not being altogether of the godlike Aryan race, are destined to be the hewers of wood and drawers of water for those that unquestionably are.'[22] While Evelyn was aware of the separateness of the lives of expats and Mexicans, she maintained that the important difference between her group and others was that of racial prejudice. It was important for US radicals in Mexico to uphold their difference from what was seen as the norm in the imperialist North. One of Evelyn's and Roy's associates in Mexico City, the US socialist Charles Phillips, put it as such in his memoirs: 'Gringos were resented and hated in Mexico. But we were gringos with a difference.'[23] Distinguished cosmopolitans could find superiority in their foreignness as they set it apart from those of other foreigners.

In Soviet Russia, Roy mingled with additional US radicals who had been recruited to the Comintern, such as Jay Lovestone (1897–1990), Bertram Wolfe (1896–1977), Luis Fraina (1892–1953) and John Reed (1887–1920). The space where foreign delegates lived and met was the Hotel Lux in Moscow, where exclusivity of access was formalized, as only those with the right piece of paper

---

[20] Ibid., 123.
[21] Evelyn Trent-Roy, 'Mexico and Her People Chapter VII', *El Heraldo de México*, 3 November 1919.
[22] Ibid.
[23] Charles Shipman, *It Had to Be Revolution; Memoirs of an American Radical* (Ithaca; London: Cornell University Press, 1993), 116.

could enter there. The Hotel was the subject of a 1978 sensationalist novel by the Austrian communist Ruth von Mayenburg, who lived there from 1938 until 1945. She labelled the hotel as '... the shared residence of the Comintern, [...] the flophouse of the headquarters of the world revolution.'[24] Apart from the Lux, the University of the Toilers of the East (KUTV) was founded in 1921 to instruct revolutionaries from various parts of Asia in the methods of communist revolutionary struggle. Well-known revolutionaries who taught or studied at the KUTV were the Vietnamese Ho Chi-Minh, who then still used the name of Nguyen Ai Quoc (1890-1969), the Japanese Sen Katayama (1859-1933) and the Indonesian Ibrahim Datuk Tan Malaka (1897-1949). The US journalist Ernestine Evans (1889-1971), who visited Russia in 1921, observed a class taught by Evelyn Roy. It was described as having

> ... consisted in [her] reading aloud in English to eighteen Indian boys chapters from Raymond William Postgate's *Revolutions from 1789-1906*. [...] A Korean who had attached himself to the class nodded sleepily from time to time. The girl read on in a fresh, eager voice. The boys asked a few questions about library cards. The class was over.[25]

Even though Evans moved in leftist and suffragist circles, some puzzlement at the efficacy of Evelyn Roy's political work is palpable in her writing. Meaningful contact between teacher and student remained a vague possibility, but was thoroughly questioned in this portrait of a non-committal, almost ritualistic scene.

Berlin had been a space of connections between various anti-British anti-colonialists and Imperial Germany during the First World War, and both Virendranath Chattopadhyaya (1880-1937) and Har Dayal had been central figures in this collaboration. In a later characterization of Indian revolutionaries in Berlin, Har Dayal emphasized their disconnection from what he by then considered essential to their efforts: 'They do not know much about their national literature and history. They are denationalised and demoralised through the influence of their unnatural environment. Their whole life is a hothouse growth.'[26] Groups of people who could be seen as out of place would not disappear from Berlin with the end of the First World War, as the city was

---

[24] Ruth von Mayenburg, *Hotel Lux* (Frankfurt am Main: Ullstein, 1981), 16. Original: '... das Gemeinschaftshaus der Komintern, [...] das Absteigquartier [sic] des Hauptquartiers der Weltrevolution.
[25] Quoted in Ramnath, *Haj to Utopia*, 143.
[26] Har Dayal, *Forty-Four Months in Germany and Turkey; February 1915 to October 1918* (London: P. S. King & Son, 1920), 70.

the home of the largest communist party outside of Russia and became a hub for international communism in the interwar period.[27] At the Comintern's Western European Bureau (WES), Roy worked alongside Tan Malaka, Sen Katayama and the Dutch communist Henk Sneevliet (1883–1942).[28]

An important Berlin space for 'fringe' or 'oppositional' communists – as Roy became over time – was the Malik Verlag.[29] There, Roy met Louise Geissler (1899–1973), with whom he travelled to China between 1926 and 1927, as well as the 'red orientalist' August Thalheimer (1884–1948).[30] A final Berlin space was an apartment owned by communist propagandist Willi Münzenberg (1889–1940),[31] which was used to put up visitors from Moscow, as well as Indian revolutionaries such as Roy. Geissler and Roy lived there for a while, and often invited communist Ellen Gottschalk (1904–60) with her former partner, before Gottschalk became Roy's second wife in 1936.[32] The Münzenberg apartment was situated in the same building as the Institute for Sexual Science, which was linked to the German Birth Control Committee – a cause Münzenberg had been brought to by Agnes Smedley. The combination of causes meant that '… any visitor moved in the midst of the sexual images and artefacts that cluttered the building.'[33] It seems safe to assume these would have alienated many potential visitors. These spaces only existed for brief moments of time, as both the Institute for Sexual Science and the Malik publishing house did not survive the rise to power of the Nazis in 1933, when each of their stock of books was publicly burnt.[34]

---

[27] Nathanael Kuck, 'Anti-Colonialism in a Post-Imperial Environment – The Case of Berlin, 1914–33', *Journal of Contemporary History* 49, no. 1 (2014): 134–59.

[28] Kris Manjapra, 'Communist Internationalism and Transcolonial Recognition', in *Cosmopolitan Thought Zones: South Asia and the Global Circulation of Ideas*, ed. Sugata Bose, Kris Manjapra (New York: Palgrave Macmillan, 2010), 166.

[29] Its unusual name was a result of a joke: during the First World War, the founder convinced the censorship authorities he needed a publishing permit in order to publish the novel 'Der Malik,' arguing that the meaning of its Turkish title 'The Prince' meant it was concerned with an ally of the German Emperor. In 1927, the founder contentedly reminisced that 'malik' did not only mean 'prince,' but also signified the head of a band of thieves ('Räuberhauptmann'). H. D. Müller, 'Der Malik-Verlag Als Vermittler Der Jungen Sowjetliteratur in Deutschland 1919–1933', *Zeitschrift Für Slawistik* 7, no. 5 (1962): 721.

[30] Daniel Brückenhaus, *Policing Transnational Protest: Liberal Imperialism and the Surveillance of Anticolonialists in Europe, 1905–1945* (New York: Oxford University Press, 2017), 115.

[31] Sean McMeekin, *The Red Millionaire: A Political Biography of Willi Münzenberg, Moscow's Secret Propaganda Tsar in the West* (New Haven: Yale University Press, 2005), 1–4.

[32] Evelyn and Roy had split in 1925. Sibnarayan Ray, *Selected Works of M. N. Roy; Volume III 1927–1932* (Delhi: Oxford University Press, 1990), 12.

[33] Veronika Fuechtner, 'Agnes Smedley between Berlin, Bombay, and Beijing: Sexology, Communism, and National Independence', in *A Global History of Sexual Science, 1880–1960*, ed. Veronika Fuechtner, Ryan M. Jones, Douglas E. Haynes (Oakland, CA: University of California Press, 2017), 411–12.

[34] Müller, 'Der Malik-Verlag', 737; Ralf Dose, *Magnus Hirschfeld: The Origins of the Gay Liberation Movement* (New York: Monthly Review Press, 2014), 65.

A small cosmopolitan community could even be found in war-threatened, cholera-plagued revolutionary Wuhan in China's Hubei province in 1927, a year that would be disastrous for communists there. In the apartment Borodin and his wife Fanya Borodin (?-?) shared, they were visited by a 'coterie' of Chinese, Russian, American, English, Indian and Indo-Chinese admirers. Among them was the radical US journalist Rayna Prohme (1894–1927), whose letters from Wuhan described the Borodins' living situation and the quick changes between deprivation an luxury that might occur:

> ... down in Canton [they] had barn-like quarters in a former barracks. Now they have the entire third floor of a big building, with thick carpets, deep chairs and, strangely, Reuben's [sic] Madonna – also September Morn – on the walls. September Morn, I assure you, is discarded and sits with her face to the wall. But Mary and Jesus smile down on all comers.[35]

Prohme's own apartment too '... became a sanctuary for anyone in Wuhan who spoke English, whatever their ideology.' The salon involved drinking, discussions of literature, and one attendant recalled it '... more like an excited lot of college freshmen than a real revolution complete with blood.'[36] To an extent, foreign visitors and correspondents were more likely to be protected from bloodshed than others, as there was an interest in having them produce – good – publicity. Yet, the life people like Prohme lived was not an easy one, and she died of illness the same year.[37]

In India, a cosmopolitan group of people gathered around Roy and Ellen, including the trade unionists Maniben Kara (1905–79), V. B. Karnik (1903–85) and Tayab Shaikh (?-?). In 1946, they established a philosophical institute at the Roys' home in Dehradun, a town just North of Delhi, called the Indian Renaissance Institute. There they ran discussion groups with the engineer Sushil Dey (?-?), journalist and Progressive Writer Sudhindranath Dutta (1901–60), doctor Indumati Parikh (1918–2004), university lecturer Sibnarayan Ray (1921–2008), one-time member of the Communist Party of Great Britain Philip Spratt (1902–71),[38] and film producer, writer and director

---

[35] Quoted in Baruch Hirson, Arthur Knodel, *Reporting the Chinese Revolution: The Letters of Rayna Prohme* (London: Pluto Press, 2007), 63.
[36] Quoted in Dan Jacobs, *Borodin, Stalin's Man in China* (Cambridge: Harvard University Press, 1981), 260–1.
[37] Hirson, Knodel, *Reporting the Chinese Revolution*, 11.
[38] Spratt had been one of those convicted at the highly publicized Meerut Conspiracy Case of 1924. Carolien Stolte, 'Introduction The Meerut Conspiracy Case in Comparative and International Perspective', *Comparative Studies of South Asia, Africa and the Middle East* 33, no. 3 (2013): 310.

J. B. H. Wadia (1901–86),[39] as well as his brother, the director Homi Wadia and the latter's wife, 'stunt queen' Fearless Nadia, the Australia-born Mary Evans (1908–96).[40] While the name of the institute could have referred to the Bengal Renaissance of the nineteenth century, signifying a period of cultural innovation,[41] the model was exclusively Western European, as it was based on the Malik publishing house, and the much more famous Frankfurt Institute.[42] The Renaissance Institute attracted academic guests, among them anthropology lecturer and Hindu monk Swami Agehananda Bharati (1923–91) (born in Austria as Leopold Fischer), and the US South Asianist and development consultant Richard Park (1920–80).[43] The sociability practised at the institute, which itself was a space that mixed the personal with the political, would be written about by many of them.[44]

Ideological variation

Even though the above individuals largely shared a leftist politics, it is not the case that different ideologies were confined to different places.[45] A range of intellectuals who became parts of rightist experiments can easily be found among Roy's circles. Regardless of the fact that the racial hierarchy envisioned by fascists was an obvious hindrance to connections between Indian revolutionaries and European activists, fascist models proved popular for a range of revolutionaries.

---

[39] J. B. H. Wadia produced pro-war documentaries and tried to move his Wadia Movietone toward producing social melodramas rather than the stunt films it would become famous for. Rosie Thomas, *Bombay before Bollywood: Film City Fantasies* (Albany: State University of New York Press, 2013), 100.

[40] Dorothee Wenner, *Zorros blonde Schwester: Das Leben der indischen Kinolegende Fearless Nadia* (Berlin: Ullstein, 1999), 194–6. Rosie Thomas has described Fearless Nadia as starring Fearless Nadia, born in Australia as Mary Evans, a whip-cracking white Australian woman fighting for justice, fusing the genres of the 'Hollywood stunt queen' and 'the legendary Indian warrior woman.' Thomas, *Bombay before Bollywood*, 107.

[41] While the idea of national renewal and re-discovery in the present had gained currency during the late nineteenth and early twentieth centuries, implying a golden age of Hindu knowledge and culture in the past, a subsequent period of decline and stagnation under Mughal rule, the phrase 'Bengal Renaissance' was not popularized until the 1940s, through the work of historians Susobhan Sarkar and Sir Jadunath Sarkar. Brian A. Hatcher, 'Great Men Waking: Paradigms in the Historiography of the Bengal Renaissance', in *Bengal: Rethinking History: Essays on Historiography*, ed. Sekhar Bandyopadhyay (Delhi: Manohar, 2001), 147–8.

[42] M. N. Roy, *Letters from Jail* (Dehradun: Renaissance, 1943), 176–7.

[43] *The Radical Humanist*, 5 April 1953, 158.

[44] '… for was not home also the centre of a movement?' S. H. Vatsayayan, 'The Roys of "Roshan Bagh"', in *The World Her Village; Selected Writings and Letters of Ellen Roy*, ed. Sibnarayan Ray (Dehradun: Indian Renaissance Institute, 1979), 93.

[45] A similar argument is made for interwar Paris in Michael Goebel, *Anti-imperial Metropolis: Interwar Paris and the Seeds of Third World Nationalism* (New York, NY: Cambridge University Press, 2015), 1–20.

Italy had for a longer time been considered a source of inspiration for nation-building, and Germany had been an anti-British partner during the First World War. So when Taraknath Das published several texts where he considered fascist models from Europe as a potential blueprint for India once he was a lecturer at New York's Columbia University, this was not entirely unusual.[46] Creating practical alliances was rarer, but not entirely impossible. While 1933 meant the end of most anti-colonial activities in Berlin, this was not true for all. Chempakaraman Pillai (1891–1934) had been a leading member of the Berlin-based Indian Independence Committee, sponsored by the German government since 1914. Pillai was later connected to several right-wing parties, holding speeches at their gatherings and attending the high-profile 1933 funeral of Albrecht von Graefe-Goldebee, who had founded two extreme-right parties.[47] In Roy's memoirs, Pillai is remembered fondly, if as a 'diehard nationalist' who had no patience for his newly communist colleagues. Regardless of political differences, there is a sense of kindred spirits in the passages devoted to Pillai, by comparison to whom most other Indian revolutionaries seemed lacking – Roy noted Pillai's perfect German and French with approval, as well as noting Pillai's pride on being the only non-white member of a Pan-German organization.[48] Affiliations and fondness did not fall neatly along ideological lines.

That is not to say Nazism was not a threat to much of Berlin cosmopolitan life, especially when foreigners present were considered racially other and inferior. Even privileged cosmopolitans could be in danger, as foreigners were regularly attacked. The well-connected Pillai, for example, died under unclear circumstances in 1934, and there were many Indians who felt Berlin at this time was not safe for them and left.[49] Still, the lives of two other Indian revolutionaries suggest that ties with the Nazi regime were, under particular circumstances, possible, even if they looked unlikely initially. Revolutionary A. C. N. Nambiar (1896–1986) was arrested, beaten and held for several weeks by paramilitary Nazi troops in 1933, who terrorized both leftists and 'non-Aryans' in Germany. He was only released because of persistent pressure from the British Government –

---

[46] Maria Framke, 'Shopping Ideologies for Independent India? Taraknath Das's Engagement with Italian Fascism and German National Socialism', *Itinerario* 40, no. 1 (2016): 55–81.
[47] Heike Liebau, 'Historische Ideale und Vorstellungen von Authentizität: Chempakaraman Pillai und die Geschichte der indischen Unabhängigkeitsbewegung', in *Geschichte als Ressource: Politische Dimensionen historischer Authentizität*, ed. Barbara Christophe, Christoph Kohl, Heike Liebau (Berlin: Klaus Schwarz Verlag, 2011), 249.
[48] Roy, *Memoirs*, 201.
[49] Brückenhaus, *Policing Transnational Protest*, 180–2.

even though its agents had pursued revolutionaries like himself in their own right – as well as his own publications in Indian newspapers.[50] Their connections to states and publics abroad could be a reason for cosmopolitans to stay alive, as almost any regime had a need to enhance its reputation abroad.

The best-known Indian politician liaising with the Nazis was Subhas Chandra Bose, who also played a role in keeping Indians there out of harm's way. In 1942, he founded the Free India Centre in Berlin, and sought to convince Indians in Europe and Asia to fight against British Imperialism.[51] Nambiar was an old friend of Bose's but had initially fled Nazism to Prague, then Paris, and once the Germans invaded there too, Marseille. Bose convinced Nambiar to return to Berlin to help his propaganda work there. When Bose left for Japan in 1943, where he would rely on the help of Rash Behari Bose, Nambiar remained virtually in charge in Berlin, and went on to become India's first ambassador to West Germany in 1947.[52] Even a movement so hostile to cultural and racial difference as a murderous fascist regime had some sensitivity to foreign propaganda and its image abroad, meaning it had a use for foreign agents who could spread its messaging to wider audiences.

Among a camp that would come to define itself as antithetical to fascism, communism, there were certain cosmopolitans too who blurred the lines between them more easily. There was Roy's fellow Comintern emissary to China, the French Jacques Doriot (1898–1945), whom Roy would still remember as '... one of the few people who measured up to my standard' in 1934, and send his greetings: '... I often think of him – in many connections, the Cabaret at Hankow, for example.'[53] Then there was the Italian Nicola Bombacci (1879–1945), who appeared next to Roy in a widely distributed photograph of delegates to the 1920 World Congress of the Comintern,[54] and would later feature in an even more iconic image: the 1945 photograph that documents the body of the Italian dictator Benito Mussolini suspended from the roof of a Milan petrol station. It shows four other corpses hanging from the rafters, including that of Bombacci.[55] After the Second World War, Roy's Indian journal *The Marxian Way* printed an

---

[50] Ibid., 169. On the isolation of foreign correspondents in the Third Reich more generally, see Norman Domeier, *Weltöffentlichkeit und Diktatur: Die amerikanischen Auslandskorrespondenten im 'Dritten Reich,'* (Göttingen: Wallstein Verlag, 2021).
[51] Sugata Bose, *His Majesty's Opponent* (Cambridge: Harvard University Press, 2011), 206.
[52] Brückenhaus, *Policing Transnational Protest*, 191–7, 209.
[53] Roy, *Letters from Jail*, 92;85.
[54] See Chapter 2, page 67 (Figure 2.1).
[55] Bombacci had never seen a contradiction between the socialism of Mussolini and that of Lenin. Arrigo Pettaco, *Il comunista in camicia negra: Bombacci, tra Lenin e Mussolini* (Milano: Mondadori, 1996), 115.

article by the French thinker Jules Monnerot (1909–95),[56] a communist from Martinique whose post-Second World War writing on communism as a 'secular religion' was a stepping stone in his path towards membership of the arguably fascist Front National in 1989.[57] Certain connections and a shared cosmopolitan credibility could persist even where ideological affiliations shifted. Specific places were shared by those who found themselves abroad without many local contacts, and shared a mode of life, even if their paths would diverge again. Only after paths had diverged would a sense of a coherent ideological identity be constructed – retrospectively. Connecting highly specific sites in various cities highlights the thinness of the networks they point to, as they were not merely sites of new affiliations, but also of exclusion. In a way, the exclusivity of their sociability was what enabled a degree of commonality between them, more so than a uniformity in the belief systems of their members.

A precarious elite

The exclusivity of shared spaces along Roy's itinerary was captured in the sense of exceptionality with which they were remembered by their members. Exceptionality easily became superiority in a range of ways: through associations with established elites; the ennobling qualities of suffering and surviving dangerous situations; the sheer unusualness of the life courses lived or, as the next section will delve into, a shared sense of cosmopolitan good taste. The elite sociability of the circles Roy formed a part of was characteristic of a privileged, anglophone, leftist set, which travellers who were otherwise inclined nevertheless occasionally moved in and out of. It was shaped by the presence and proximity of other Indian revolutionaries, but also to an extent distinct from it. On the one hand, there were less privileged Indian revolutionaries, whose experiences abroad were characterized by harshness and discrimination.[58] Such experiences were not highlighted, even if they were present, in Roy's circles. Their sociability was also oppositional to the style of mobility that more established figures, Gandhi in particular, would come to cultivate. That has been called one of 'simplicity', in the sense that it entailed the pairing down a household to such an extent that it could be travelled with.[59] It was also

---

[56] *The Marxian Way*, Vol. III, No. 1, 1947–8, 16.
[57] Dan Stone, 'The Uses and Abuses of "secular Religion": Jules Monnerot's Path from Communism to Fascism', *History of European Ideas* 37, no. 4 (2011): 465.
[58] Raza, *Revolutionary Pasts*, 64.
[59] Majeed, *Autobiography, Travel and Postnational Identity*, 23.

true for Roy's circles that no great deal of possessions could be accumulated, and yet Gandhian style formed a counterpoint to the sociability Roy would practise and write about.[60] Yet, the influence of Gandhi and other established figures on the Indian movement abroad was often palpable, and divisions never entirely stable, even if contrasts mattered a great deal.[61] An additional element of elite sociability was that shaped by the Comintern, which allowed for a both risky and comfortable lifestyle. Certain assignments required staying in expensive hotels, and travelling in luxurious ways such as in chauffeured cars, or by aeroplane.[62] Within Roy's circles, a combination of privilege and precarity was at play, complicated by various ways of recollecting such lives.

Luxury and hardships were both among shared experiences, but in for example the recollections of the anarchist M. P. T. Acharya, suffering played a large role. In his autobiographical writings, travel was hard, as their protagonist always lacked money and felt great shame at 'pestering' several people for funds when he was penniless in Paris.[63] In an episode where Acharya sought to travel to Morocco to join the fight of the Berbers from the Rif mountains against the Spanish, he ended up stranded in Tangiers, without the means to travel on.[64] In stark opposition to Acharya's reminiscences, Roy's writing about his years on the move professed to experiencing to some discomfort clandestinely travelling from Japan to the United States,[65] but in general they portrayed their protagonist as one to life on the run with ease. Alone in Mexico City, a bag of gold pesos quickly landed in his lap, with unspecified origins.[66] Freshly landed in Europe, he explored a glitzy Spanish seaside resort with a Mexican diplomat and his French wife.[67] Barely installed in his luxury hotel in Berlin, he witnessed the 1920 Kapp Putsch from his window.[68]

At the time they were writing these memoirs, both Acharya and Roy were struggling as returned revolutionaries in India. Not many of the Indian

---

[60] Kris Manjapra, 'The Impossible Intimacies of M N Roy', *Postcolonial Studies* 16, no. 2 (2013): 169–84.
[61] For Vivekananda and Tagore, see Chapter 3.
[62] David Mayer, 'Leo Katz (1892–1954): Viele Welten in einer Welt', in *Globale Lebensläufe; Menschen als Akteure im weltgeschichtlichen Geschehen*, ed. Bernd Hausberger (Wien: Mandelbaum Verlag, 2006), 244–5.
[63] M. P. T. Acharya, *Reminiscences of an Indian Revolutionary* (New Delhi: Amol Publications, 1991), 80.
[64] Ibid., 32.
[65] Stowed away with another revolutionary from British India, with the boots of police inspectors looking for them making stomping right above their heads, the protagonist's condition only came truly precarious when his fellow stowaway wet himself in fear. Roy, *Memoirs*, 16.
[66] Ibid., 71–2.
[67] Ibid., 228–9.
[68] Ibid., 269–70.

revolutionaries who had been Roy's peers and competitors abroad ended up returning to India for good. When they did, their nationalist credentials and itinerant past were an asset to them, but often they also struggled to find a place for themselves again. Once the anarchist Acharya returned to India, he was supported by the income of his wife Russian Magda Nachman Acharya, a painter. When this fell away after her death in 1951 he wrote to friends abroad to support him because he feared he might die from malnutrition.[69] Pandurang Khankhoje (1884–1967) had become a respected agricultural scientist in Mexico, but went back to India in 1954, where he offered his services to the independent government but was rejected. He ended up being supported by his Belgian wife Jeanne Sindic (1889–1951), feeling 'out of place' and 'unappreciated' until his death in 1967.[70] Roy's life in India would also be full of struggles where much of his work relied on his second wife Ellen Gottschalk, and together they were far from wealthy.[71] Yet, Roy's Indian Renaissance Institute was characterized by '… frugality that went side by side with generosity, an almost ascetic regimen was combined with good living …'.[72] Minor differences such as tastes and the degree of attention paid to them could set apart one group of cosmopolitans from another, even if they went through quite similar experiences.

Certain elements of the sociability Roy and his peers cultivated and immortalized in their writings could be notably elitist, particularly considering their political claims. In their milieu, people associated themselves intellectually with the proletariat; the journal many of his friends in Mexico City had worked for in New York was called *The Masses*,[73] and the journal Roy would publish from Europe with Comintern money was initially called *The Masses of India*.[74] In many self-narratives, however, a small circle of international friends and figureheads loomed far larger than the working class, which rather featured as a figure of speech. In the words of Swami Agehananda: 'If I ever attended an elitist house in India – or for that matter, anywhere – it was at 13 Mohini Road [the Indian Renaissance Institute]. Karl Marx did not like workers and

---

[69] Ole Birk Laursen, 'M. P. T. Acharya: A Revolutionary, an Agitator, a Writer' *We Are Anarchists: Essays on Anarchism, Pacifism, and the Indian Independence Movement, 1923–1953*, ed. M. P. T. Acharya (Edinburgh, Scotland: AK Press, 2019), 32.
[70] Daniel Carrasco, 'From British Colonial Subject to Mexican 'Naturalizado': Pandurang Khankhoje's Life beyond the Reach of Imperial Power (1924–1954)', in *South Asian Migrations in Global History: Labor, Law, and Wayward Lives*, ed. Neilesh Bose (New York: Bloomsbury Academic, 2021), 192–3.
[71] Laursen, 'M. P. T. Acharya', 101–3.
[72] Vatsayayan, 'The Roys of "Roshan Bagh"', 93.
[73] Jeremy McCarter, *Young Radicals: In the War for American Ideals* (New York: Random House, 2017), 157–60.
[74] *The Masses by M. N. Roy*, 1925 and 1926, Rare Journals 302–303, P. C. Joshi Archives, Jawaharlal Nehru University, Delhi, India (hence PCJ).

people personally, though he wrote about them. Neither did Roy and Ellen.'[75] Agehananda's recollections were fond, and full of the relishing of paradoxes, but this elitism was clearly reflected in Roy's own writing during that period.

In Roy's recollections of Mexico, written during the 1950s, he much exaggerated the bond between himself and its president Venustiano Carranza (1859–1920), explaining their mutual understanding with reference to their being upper class and upper caste, sharing a sense of '*noblesse oblige:*'

> Carranza personified the Christian culture of the European Middle Ages, which seems to have appealed to the *Brahmanical* tradition of intellectual aristocracy. My socialist conscience struggled hard to deny to myself the empirical truth that, while I felt at home in the company of a feudal aristocrat, the uncouth comrades never ceased to embarrass me.[76]

After the fact, Roy much exaggerated the closeness between him and Carranza,[77] which fit a narrative in which he had been close to a small minority of somehow aristocratic men and women. Even within the Communist International, Roy fondly remembered his 'chum' Lola, a nobleman's daughter who worked as an interpreter, as well as the Mozart-loving diplomat Georgy Chicherin (1872–1936),[78] calling the latter: '… the picture of a highly cultured European gentleman, so very conscious of the nobility of his inner self as made him oblivious of his physical appearance.'[79] Even in the lack of attention to one's appearance, Roy's could find a mark of distinction, especially when it flouted more established norms of good taste – and at the same time drew on them. Roy came up with a vaguely Marxist explanation for why it was that he had felt so drawn to aristocrats of various stripes: '… I felt that an aristocrat, intellectually emancipated from the prejudices of his class, might be a more disinterested and culturally more Dionysian revolutionary than the most passionately class-conscious proletarian.'[80] Even though the gist of his narrative was an awkward one, Roy's closeness to elite figures and subtle understanding of their appearances, styles and tastes would become a mainstay of his writing.

---

[75] Agehananda Bharati, 'Cats, Brunches and the Open Society – Memories of Mohini Road', in *The World Her Village; Selected Writings and Letters of Ellen Roy*, ed. Sibnarayan Ray (Dehradun: Indian Renaissance Institute, 1979), 103.
[76] Roy, *Memoirs*, 163.
[77] In his autobiography, Roy claimed that it was President Carranza who provided him with a passport with which to travel to Russia. According to Mauricio Tenorio this was not the case, but it was a US-Mexican communist called José Allen who provided both Roy and Evelyn with passports. Tenorio, *I Speak of the City*, 275.
[78] Ludmila Thomas, *Georgi Tschitscherin: "Ich Hatte Die Revolution Und Mozart"* (Berlin: Dietz, 2012).
[79] Roy, *Memoirs*, 356–8; 323.
[80] Ibid., 165.

In good taste

One complex of shared practices characterizing Roy's circles revolved around direct ways to bodily connect with and experience new spaces: food, drink and language. Such practices also allowed for the display of one's ability to keenly select from different options on offer, exercising a capacity for exercising good taste – and lamenting its absence in others. Some of the most basic features of cosmopolitan sociability consisted of the meals people shared, as both immediate practices creating affiliation and exclusion, and a topos for cosmopolitan reflection. In one example where food played a large role in the making of a cosmopolitan place, Rash Behari Bose's integration into Japanese society was tied up with a European-style bakery that provided different cuisines to its patrons, from the innovative patisserie it was known for in the 1910s to the curry that was introduced by Bose. One historian writes that rather than for his politics, Bose is mainly remembered in Japan for his curry recipe.[81]

Food was also an important way to highlight the strangeness of one's surroundings – as well as one's own affiliations to this strangeness. In the letters Rayna Prohme wrote from Wuhan, she mused on the '… strange noises and strange speech and strange things going on down in the streets and strange clothes and strange things to eat, and I watch it all in a rather detached way and haven't yet come out of the stage of wondering what the devil it is all about.' She also emphasized the immediacy of this strangeness meeting her sense, adding that:

> I can't avoid hearing it and smelling it. I'm doing the second right now. I'm near the street and there is strange food engendering just outside. Good food, I think it must be. One can never know for Chinese food in China is poison to the foreigner. It really is dangerous. As unsanitary a country as can be imagined. But I like it even so.[82]

This uncircumventable strangeness was highlighted as not just unpleasant but dangerous to Prohme – specifically to foreigners like herself. Yet, her conclusion that she likes it *even so* highlights her own commitment to this cosmopolitan life she has chosen, and sets her apart from other foreigners who have not done so. Prohme's letters also dwell on the drinking culture that exists among foreigners

---

[81] Eri Hotta, 'Rash Behari Bose and His Japanese Supporters: An Insight into Anti-Colonial Nationalism and Pan-Asianism', *Interventions* 8, no. 1 (2006): 123;119.
[82] Quoted in Hirson, Knodel, *Reporting the Chinese Revolution*, 25–6.

in China, citing this as rather a shared foreign occupation: 'You have to drink if you play at all with the foreigners here, for there are so few diversions. [...] Or else they play bridge. Or else drink.'[83] Her letters make clear that her lifestyle was characterized by both food practices that sought affiliation with the local diet – while pointing out its strangeness and even potential threat, and drinking practices that set cosmopolitans apart – while uttering judgement for them doing so. In both instances, she exercised her own cosmopolitan tastes and distinguished them.

Colonial conditions, revolutions, wars and imprisonment meant that food could be a vital subject for reflection – because of its absence. Famine was a vital political subject for those seeking to expose the inhumanity of colonial rule. When Taraknath Das, for example, started the publication *Free Hindusthan* in Canada in 1907, he would make the toll of famines under colonial rule into one of the recurring arguments for the necessity of freedom for India.[84] And when Roy began to publish in Mexico City, a 1919 article elaborated on the theme of Indian starvation and the lack of awareness of it among North American socialists. Published in the English-language *Gale's Magazine*, entitled 'Hunger and Revolution in India,' it baulked at the colonial silencing.[85] Navigating between famine as a key political subject and the display of shared cosmopolitan tastes could involve many silences and marked contrasts.

There existed a clear lack of food in war-struck Russia when Roy first came there in 1920, which he would recall in his memoirs, with a sense of embarrassment.[86] Yet, delegates to the Comintern Congress had lived comfortably, as part of their job was to report positively on developments after the revolution. This was damningly recalled by the Russian revolutionary writer Victor Serge (Victor Kibalchich, 1890–1947), who underlined Moscow's 1920 '… starvation-rations, its arrests, its sordid prison-episodes, its backstage racketeering …' and contrasted this with the life of international communists there:

> Sumptuously fed amidst universal misery (although, it is true, too many rotten eggs turned up at meal-times), shepherded from museums to model nurseries, the representatives of international Socialism seemed to react like holiday-makers or tourists within our poor Republic, flayed and bleeding with the siege.[87]

---

[83] *Ibid.*, 36.
[84] Bose, 'Taraknath Das', 161–3.
[85] M. N. Roy, 'Hunger and Revolution in India', *The Call*, 18 September 1919, Marxists Internet Archive https://www.marxists.org/archive/roy/1919/09/18.htm
[86] Roy, *Memoirs*, 352, 559.
[87] Victor Serge, *Memoirs of a Revolutionary* (London: Oxford University Press, 1963), 100.

Keeping foreign delegates reasonably well fed and healthy was a priority for the Comintern organizers; US delegate John Reed (1887–1920) had died of typhus while in Moscow, which prompted Leon Trotsky (1879–1940) to write an internal memo warning his colleagues that if more foreign delegates would perish, no new ones would come.[88] As dangerous as visiting a country where war and famine raged was, the Comintern did not want to let this taint Soviet Russia's external image. So while many cosmopolitan actors lived through different kinds of hardships, to an extent there was an interest in protecting them therefrom.

The years during which Roy produced many of his cosmopolitan reflections were marked by deprivation of both himself and then millions of people in India. Food played a large role in Roy's memories of more mobile days while behind bars, deprived of sustaining meals. To Ellen Gottschalk, he confessed to his day-dreams of being sent a cheese by Henk Sneevliet, knowing full well this was out of the question: 'I wish he would send me one of those fascinating red balls with golden interior and piquant taste. Only, it won't reach my watering mouth, even if he did send it.'[89] He even recommended Ellen would go visit their Dutch friends, being of the unusual opinion that some of the best food was to be had there: 'It is splendid, you know! In my opinion, the best thing in the world, being a combination of French fineness and German solidity.'[90] Food was a way to both make places cosmopolitan and qualify oneself as such – even under dire circumstances. In another letter from prison, Roy fondly remembered the drinks poured by fellow members of the communist crème de la crème in the bars of 1920s Berlin, and judged their choices: 'Did Heinz[91] choose a good bottle at Kempinsky's?[92] But the boor! Did he order red wine for dinner? A German who prefers Burgundy to Rhine should be charged of Hochverrat (High Treason)!'[93] Including a little polyglot, German flourish, wine became a subject that did not only situate Roy apart from Gandhist ideas of purity, and in close proximity to European communists, but showed that he could play with each of their codes of what counted as good fare – and had better taste than both.

During the 1940s, famine again became a major political theme in India, as a devastating famine laid waste to Bengal in 1943 and killed an estimated

---

[88] Alexander Vatlin, *Das Jahr 1920: Der Zweite Kongress der Kommunistischen Internationale* (Berlin: BasisDruck, 2019), 117; 128.
[89] Roy, *Letters from Jail*, 83.
[90] Ibid., 73.
[91] A reference to Heinrich Brandler (1881–1967), a founding member of the Communist Party of Germany who was expelled from the Communist International at the same time as Roy, and formed the Communist Party of Germany (Opposition) and the International Communist Opposition.
[92] A hotel on Berlin's then fashionable street Kurfürstendamm.
[93] Roy, *Letters from Jail*, 12.

3 million people.[94] Then, no flaming political tract, accusing those with blood on their hands, was dedicated to it by Roy.[95] As opposed to the 1919 text Roy had published in Mexico City, his general take was that people were not starving because of an injustice, but because there were too many people.[96] In 1947, Partition violence meant that millions of people were suddenly fleeing their homes in what had become India and Pakistan. With channels of supply disturbed, food scarcity touched Roy's own life.[97] Yet, the violence that caused it did not assume a central role in Roy's writing of the time, and while they recalled some deprivation in their own lives, this was tinged with more nostalgia and details of the specific dishes and drinks they had shared.

At the Indian Renaissance Institute, one of the main subjects for recollections seems to have been the particular nature of the brunches served. Richard Park diligently sourced '... forbidden beef – really undercut of buffalo ...' chocolates, pork, '... and a bottle of something if the price was not astronomical ...' which was then referred to as 'Marshall Aid.'[98] According to Swami Agehananda, these were: '... all things I had been craving for in my unconscious mind – cream, coffee, bacon, cheese; and then we had drinks till late, late at night.'[99] Agehananda's public admittance of enjoying the fare was so unusual for a Hindu monk that he added he had been a 'fanatical vegetarian' when he was younger but was enlightened mostly by Roy to see that he has been wrong: 'The protagonists of vegetarianism, Hindu, or occidental orientalizing cranks, have no arguments which will stand critical analysis.'[100] This dietary opposition came in view against both mainstream society and family; when Roy's brother visited, Agehananda reported his wife to have been so dismayed at the lack of

---

[94] Amartya Sen, *Poverty and Famines: An Essay on Entitlement and Deprivation* (Oxford: Oxford University Press, 1983), 52–85.

[95] Instead, the famine was referred to in two pragmatic, planning-related publications: the *People's Plan for the Economic Development of India* (1944) and *Indian Labour and Post-War Reconstruction* (1943). Both texts emphasized the importance of increasing food production in a post-war India, with the *Plan* including the need to limit population growth. M. N. Roy, *Indian Labour and Post-War Reconstruction* (Lucknow: Bhargava Printing Works, 1943); B. N. Banerjee, G. D. Parikh, V. M. Tarkunde, *People's Plan for Economic Development of India* (Delhi: Indian Federation of Labour, 1944), 15.

[96] On population control, see below.

[97] 'The bakers, butchers, vegetable vendors, egg and fruit sellers, were all Mussalmans. Their places have not been taken by new aspirants, or by amateurs who can do nothing but sell worthless goods at 3 or 4 times their price.' Letter from M. N. Roy to Philip Spratt, 13 October 1947, Philip Spratt Correspondence, Catalogue 70: M. N. Roy Papers, Section 1, NMML.

[98] Richard L. Park, 'Ellen Roy: A Personal Profile', in *The World Her Village; Selected Writings and Letters of Ellen Roy*, ed. Sibnarayan Ray (Dehradun: Indian Renaissance Institute, 1979), 65.

[99] Swami Agehananda Bharati, *The Ochre Robe* (London: George Allen & Unwin, 1961), 185.

[100] *Ibid.*, 186.

food she considered proper that she cried.[101] Radical humanists were well aware that the food they shared and relished among themselves set them apart from others.

Especially drink featured regularly as a way to convey their opposition to Hindu religiosity. Radical humanist J. B. H. Wadia wrote that this had clear implications for political possibilities: 'Everyone knew that Roy cherished good wine and it was one of the reasons for his unpopularity in [the Indian National Congress] ...,' but also made it clear that he had no such hang-ups himself. Instead, he fondly remembered a concoction labelled 'Roy's Cocktail,': '... after the fashion of European blenders of repute whose names are associated with their respective recipes.[...] It was a treat to watch him at his expertise as he blended the wines with flourishes which would have been the envy of many a "patrons" in Europe.'[102] Food and drink did not only stand for opposition to Gandhist orthodoxy, but in reflecting on their nature those engaging in this sociability could show an understanding of the importance – or lack thereof – of rules surrounding food betraying a higher level of sophistication than their political opponents. So not only did certain food practices exclude those with less or differently cosmopolitan credentials, it also portrayed their practitioners as having a keen sense of what mattered and what was good.

In Roy's memoirs, giving up rules of Brahmanic purity played an important part in his becoming 'sophisticated,' 'modern' or 'cosmopolitan,' as he described himself in the 1950s. Roy's *Memoirs* were full of instances where wine was woven into the narrative of his rise to becoming an internationally known communist with friends and enemies in high places, including learning to enjoy wine as a luxury, an episode on Borodin ordering Rhine wine in Mexico, French wine illicitly being drunk in post-revolutionary Leningrad under conditions of famine, or champagne flowing into the Moskva river from a mansion that had been occupied by revolutionaries.[103] He even saw wine as a directly enabling element in creating a shared lifestyle between people from different places, allowing them to share not merely places, but feelings:

> People from different parts of the world, but pursuing the same ideal, met on these occasions as human beings and allowed their emotions to run riot, without any conventional or ideological inhibitions. Naturally, wine played a very important part on such occasions. Nothing else breaks down artificially built

---

[101] Bharati, 'Cats, Brunches, and the Open Society', 103.
[102] J. B. H. Wadia, *M. N. Roy, the Man – an Incomplete Royana* (Bombay: Popular Prakashan, 1983).
[103] Roy, *Memoirs*, 139; 186; 308; 560.

up inhibitions so completely and enables even the most affected and pompous individuals to be their natural selves.[104]

Sharing drinks in places where few other people partook set cosmopolitans apart from their direct surroundings. On top of that, Roy and some other cosmopolitans were largely insulated from famine when it got close. Their connections or propagandistic value meant that they might be spared the harsher realities of the places in which they were present. In a general sense, this meant that the kind of cosmopolitan life under scrutiny in these pages was often characterized by proximity to danger – which regularly became threatening – but nevertheless, to various extents, benefited from insulation from its all too dire consequences.

Language

Another insulating feature of cosmopolitan sociability that is mostly written about as a connective one is that of language; polyglossy is one of the most remarked upon practical aspects of itinerant lives.[105] For example, the poet Harindranath Chattopadhyaya (1898–1990) noted of his brother Chatto that he spoke sixteen languages,[106] and Von Mayenberg's description of Moscow's Hotel Lux paints its picture by writing that '… dozens of languages were spoken, and used to politicize, conspire, discuss – and at times to remain silent in agony.'[107] Similarly, accounts of the Indian Renaissance Institute dwell on the fact that English and German were the main languages spoken there.[108] What is sometimes overlooked about the working of languages, however, are its capacities for exclusion as opposed to affiliation.[109] Equally, while the requirements of international organizing make the use of different languages – particularly English, in Roy's contexts – a necessity, making language a part of one's public persona also went beyond such necessities.

There were pressures at work in the cosmopolitan contexts Roy had been working in that caused English to be the most widely used language, even

---

[104] *Ibid.*, 559.
[105] See for example Benedict Anderson's 'true, hard internationalism of the polyglot.' Benedict Anderson, *Under Three Flags: Anarchism and the Colonial Imagination* (London: Verso, 2005), 5.
[106] Shompa Lahiri, *Indian Mobilities in the West : 1900–1947 ; Gender, Performance, Embodiment* (New York: Palgrave, 2010).
[107] Von Mayenburg, *Hotel Lux*, 17. Original: 'Unter dem Dach des Lux wurde in Dutzenden von Sprachen gesprochen, politisiert, konspiriert, diskutiert – und bisweilen halber Agonie geschwiegen.'
[108] Ray, *In Freedom's Quest: Vol. 3, 1*, 62.
[109] This aspect is referred to in Jürgen Osterhammel, *Unfabling the East: The Enlightenment's Encounter with Asia* (Princeton, NJ: Princeton University Press, 2018), 117.

if many of those present would have preferred to use another one. Among Comintern delegates, for example, English was one of the major languages used – even though there existed objections against it. At the 1920 World Congress, the US delegation requested English to be added to the official Comintern languages of Russian, German and French – only to be rebuked by the Presidium, possibly because the several Anglophone delegations represented strains of anarchy and syndicalism that were quite far removed from Bolshevism. Yet, because some Anglophone delegates did not speak other languages and had to be involved in the discussions, English ended up being used nevertheless.[110] In addition, when Comintern delegates were sent to China during the 1920s, they were generally selected on the basis of the strength of their English.[111] The practice of using English was almost always controversial, yet hard to avoid for other international organizations too. When the Asian Relations Conference took place in New Delhi in 1947, Roy observed how the delegates tried to find an alternative language to English yet had problems agreeing on one.[112] In a report about the conference, he wrote: 'Ninety percent of the delegates wore Western dress and spoke English to be understandably communicated to one another. Nevertheless, on the opening day, almost all the delegates spoke in their national language which had then to be translated into English.'[113] As unnerving as the use of English might be, for organizations with emphatically global aspirations who sought long-range connections, other international languages were too regional by comparison. Possibilities and constraints had been shaped by the British Empire even for those who sought to destroy it, as it had created the option of a monolingual

---

[110] Vatlin, *Das Jahr 1920*, 77–8.

[111] Ishikawa Yoshihiro, *The Formation of the Chinese Communist Party*, trans. Joshua A. Fogel (New York, NY: Columbia University Press, 2012), 96.

[112] As there had been in the Comintern, there were reasons not to use English at the ARC, as well as a practical inability not to. Their reliance on English did bother some of the delegates, and they tried to find a more Asian alternative to use as a common language. A professor of economics at the Hebrew University in Palestine, Alfred Bonne, suggested the development of a new language, modelled on Esperanto – only to have the proposal be immediately criticized by Chinese delegate Wen Yuan Yang, who '… commented sarcastically that Japanese schools had taught Esperanto before the war but there was little proof of such sentiments for humanity flourishing there' Vineet Thakur, 'An Asian Drama: The Asian Relations Conference, 1947', *International History Review* 41, no. 3 (2019): 685. An Indian professor of linguistics, Baburam Saxena, suggested Hindi would be fit for the purpose of a shared Asian language, at least more so than English, whereas several Soviet delegates rather thought of Russian. The discussion proved thorny, and the most likely candidates, Hindi or Russian, inspired fears of cultural imperialism of their own so that in the end English would still be used even if it was only 'for the moment'. Carolien Stolte, '"The Asiatic Hour" New Perspectives on the Asian Relations Conference, New Delhi, 1947', in *The Non-aligned Movement and the Cold War; Delhi – Bandung – Belgrade*, ed. Nataša Mišković, Harald Fischer-Tiné, Nada Boškovska (London; New York: Routledge, 2014), 66.

[113] Quoted in Ray, *In Freedom's Quest: Vol. 4, 2*, 263.

yet international existence mainly for those who spoke English as their only language. In turn, they then exerted pressure for others to use this language as well.

Beyond necessity, the use of language could become a part of one's persona. This becomes amply clear in the biographical work of one of Roy's associates in his later years, Sibnarayan Ray. Ray spent a good part of his intellectual efforts publishing Roy's selected works as well as an exhaustive biography. He did not hide his fondness and admiration for his one-time teacher, and yet judged his political career to have been a failure on Roy's own terms, as: 'Roy never succeeded in reaching the "masses" whose enlightenment and emancipation had been the objectives of his life.'[114] An issue Ray delved into at length in order to illustrate the separation between Roy and the people his politics had been, at least in the abstract, concerned with:

> His alienation was farther accentuated by the fact that Roy, who had mastered and written in five European languages, showed no interest in acquiring command of any Indian vernacular, including his mother tongue Bengali. He spoke and wrote after his return to India exclusively in English which narrowly circumscribed the area of his personal reach. [...] On several occasions he lamented my wasting time in writing in a *patois* like Bengali! On one occasion at a public meeting, he was pressurised by the Calcutta audience to give his speech in Bengali. It was painful to see his very critical analysis of a serious theme stumbling repeatedly over the choice of wrong Bengali words (e.g. *antaric*, cordial, for *antarjatic*, international). His Hindi was no better when he had to address any large meeting of workers affiliated to the IFL.[115] And yet he was a polyglot in full command of five European languages.[116]

A preference for English and German both had to do with Roy's individual circumstances and preferences, the life he lived with his German wife, the efforts to remain in or regain contact with friends and acquaintances abroad, as well as attempts to be a public intellectual in not only one Indian language but in the language used in parts of independent India as well as Pakistan. Yet, cultivating it in a certain way was also a way to clearly affiliate him with certain people instead of others.

With language's potential for inclusion as much as exclusion, it is unsurprising that the most common way to make a living for cosmopolitans was as translators

---

[114] Ray, *In Freedom's Quest: Vol. 4, 2*, 369.
[115] The International Federation of Labour, a trade union. See Chapter 4.
[116] Ray, *In Freedom's Quest: Vol. 4, 2*, 389–90.

and language teachers. As fresh arrivals in Mexico City, Roy and Evelyn made a living teaching English and translating Tagore's poetry. The first was a common occupation for those arriving from the United States in Mexico City then, as it was in various places across the world, with English a crucial international language for business and politics.[117] When Dhan Gopal Mukerji lived in New York in the 1920s, translations were one of the ways in which he supported himself.[118] And in mid-1920s Berlin, both Chatto and Nambiar taught English to Germans and translated articles between the two languages.[119] More specifically, Tagore's popularity after receiving the Nobel Prize in Literature in 1913 created some work opportunities for those knowing Bengali. They could earn money translating poetry, riding on a wave of fascination with the Nobel Prize-winning poet.[120] Evelyn Roy wrote a letter to her mother from Mexico City in which she told her about her efforts translating Tagore's work into Spanish,[121] and Herambalal Gupta would spend the rest of his life in Mexico City, translating Tagore.[122] Language barriers shaped connections that could be made but could also be a source of income.

In a similar but more professional fashion, distinguished cosmopolitans could be employed academically, in subjects that revolved around cultural difference such as linguistics, anthropology and philosophy. Mohamed Barakatullah, for example, was a professor in oriental languages at Tokyo University between 1909 and 1914,[123] whereas Har Dayal taught Indian Philosophy in the United States and Sweden.[124] Bhupendranath Datta (1880–1961), Virendranath Chattopadhyaya and Swami Agehananda made names for themselves as anthropologists in Germany and India, the Soviet Union and the United States, respectively.[125] Chattopadhyaya was particularly mobile and inventive, and when he was struggling to find political partners while stuck in Sweden in 1917–18, he tried to make a living writing and teaching about Indian history, and seems to have

---

[117] Daniela Spenser, *Stumbling Its Way through Mexico: The Early Years of the Communist International* (Tuscaloosa: University of Alabama Press, 2011), 42.
[118] Chang, 'The Life and Death of Dhan Gopal Mukerji', 15.
[119] Ole Birk Laursen, 'Anti-Colonialism, Terrorism and the "Politics of Friendship": Virendranath Chattopadhyaya and the European Anarchist Movement, 1910–1927', *Anarchist Studies* 27, no. 1 (2019): 56.
[120] Mauricio Tenorio has labelled this the 'Tagore moment.' Tenorio, *I Speak of the City*, 262.
[121] Letter from Evelyn Trent to her mother, 19 July 1917, Evelyn Trent Files, Correspondence, Hoover Institution.
[122] Tenorio, *I Speak of the City*, 260–2.
[123] Mohammed Ayub Khan, 'Universal Islam: the Faith and Political Ideologies of Maulana Barakatullah "Bhopali"', *Sikh Formations* 10, no. 1 (2014): 58–60.
[124] Emily C. Brown, *Har Dayal : Hindu Revolutionary and Rationalist* (New Delhi: Manohar, 1976).
[125] On Chattopadhyaya, see Nirode Barooah, *Chatto: The Life and Times of an Indian Anti-imperialist in Europe* (New Delhi: Oxford University Press, 2004), 350.

tried to work for a local translation and communication agency.[126] While still in Berlin, Chatto also attempted a more formal capitalization on his connections abroad, when he set up the Indian News Service and Information Bureau.[127] This too was to an extent a shared cosmopolitan practice. Once Roy had been released from prison and Ellen Gottschalk had joined him in India, their foreign connections represented some of their most important assets. One of their first attempts at making a living involved setting up a press service, writing to friends in the United States to supply them with the journals that would provide them with the material to do so:

> Any material is of greates [sic] importance for us; this land here is so damned far away from everywhere. And then we have started the (see letter head) Press Service from which we hope to make a living […]. For that we entirely depend on informations from abroad.[128]

Since Roy and Elen found themselves far away from 'everywhere,' it was also to everywhere that their contacts abroad presumably offered them access. Connections abroad represented something of value to those who had them, potentially even in a financial sense. The wider field of journalism and publishing as a cosmopolitan way to earn an income is treated in the next chapter.

Relationships

When it came to Indian revolutionaries abroad, women were a rare phenomenon, mobility itself being largely frowned upon in their case.[129] One of the exceptions was Bhikaji Rustom Cama (1861–1936),[130] who had accompanied her husband

---

[126] Henrik Chetan Aspengren, 'Indian Revolutionaries Abroad: Revisiting Their Silent Moments', *Journal of Colonialism & Colonial History* 15, no. 3 (2014): n.a.

[127] Jürgen Dinkel, 'Mecca of Oriental Patriots – Antikolonialismus in Deutschland 1900–1960', in *Weimar und die Welt. Globale Verflechtungen der ersten deutschen Republik*, ed. Dirk van Laak, Christoph Cornelißen (Göttingen: Vandenhoeck & Ruprecht, 2020), 76.

[128] Ellen asked for journals such as New Republic, Living Age, Asia, Foreign Affairs, Amerasia. Letter from Ellen Roy to Jay Lovestone, Bombay, 5 August 1937, Jay Lovestone Correspondence, Catalogue 70: M. N. Roy Paper Section 1, NMML.

[129] Lahiri, *Indian Mobilities in the West*, 34.

[130] Bhikaji Cama (1861–1936), widely known as Madame Cama attended the Second Socialist International's 1907 congress in Stuttgart, where she hoisted the Indian national flag. Another famous exception was Kamaladevi Chattopadhyaya, who travelled the United States in the 1940s. In the 1920s, she married Chatto's brother Harindranath. Ali Raza, Franziska Roy, Benjamin Zachariah, 'The Internationalism of the Moment: South Asia and the Contours of the Interwar World', in *The Internationalist Moment: South Asia, Worlds and World Views, 1917–39*, eds. Ali Raza, and Franziska Roy, Benjamin Zachariah (Los Angeles: Sage, 2015); Lahiri, *Indian Mobilities in the West*, 169–70.

abroad and became a nodal point in networks of Indian revolutionaries and socialist radicals in Paris. In 1912, Cama published an open letter in her Parisian journal *Bande Mataram* that evidenced the wide-spread nature of interracial marriage among her circles. The letter addressed itself to Persian, Egyptian and Indian men, discussing '… the question of marrying foreign wives.' Cama urged her audience against doing so, for political reasons: 'The only way to bring up your fallen countries to a high pitch is the bringing out of your womankind, which is half your population!'[131] The phenomenon of marrying white women was widespread enough for her to publicly comment on it and consider its social and political implications.

Interracial love and marriage could function in the widest sense as a way to create and institute distance from what should be familiar, as well as affiliation to someone different, and thus mark a habitus of a cosmopolitan kind. Marriages of this kind were rare in society at large, but common among Roy's circles, and provided a common thread among otherwise varied people. At their most practical, interracial marriages provided opportunities to settle elsewhere, to integrate, learn a language and at times, to acquire a passport. Relationships between coloured women and white men were a longstanding phenomenon in several colonized spaces, accompanied by evolving anxieties about racial mixing and shifting sexual and legal regimes.[132] In Roy's circles, the common constellation was marriage between brown men and most often white women. This practice was imbued with additional meaning because of its crossing of the global colour line of white supremacy. On a symbolic level, such interracial relationships could be seen as anti-imperialist.[133] After the First World War, more and more such unions began to occur, particularly in spaces away from the colonies, such as the urban milieus under scrutiny here, and particularly on occasions when caste or class mediated the implications of race.[134] Still,

---

[131] Quoted in Maia Ramnath, 'Meeting the Rebel Girl: Anticolonial Solidarity and Interracial Romance,' *The Internationalist Moment; South Asia, Worlds, and World Views 1917-39*, ed. Raza, Ali Roy, Franziska Zachariah, Benjamin (New Delhi: Sage Publications, 2015), 129–30.

[132] Damon Ieremia Salesa, *Racial Crossings* (Oxford: Oxford University Press, 2011), 1–12; Durba Ghosh, *Sex and the Family in Colonial India; The Making of Empire* (Cambridge: Cambridge University Press, 2006), 4–14; Ann Stoler, 'Making Empire Respectable: The Politics of Race and Sexual Morality in 20th-century Colonial Cultures,' *American Ethnologist* 16 (1989): 634–60.

[133] Mrinalini Sinha, *Colonial Masculinity: The 'Manly Englishman' and the 'Effeminate Bengali' in the Late Nineteenth Century* (Manchester: Manchester University Press, 1995), 46–51.

[134] Writing about Asian nationalists in interwar Paris, Michael Goebel has contrasted the rates of marriage to French women between anti-colonial elites and migrant labourers, finding the practice to have been wide-spread among the former, and virtually non-existent, among the latter group. Goebel, *Anti-Imperial Metropolis*, 91–9; On the mediation of race through class, and lower-class

interracial couples of this constellation were rare enough for the practice to be imbued with meaning, and counted as a distinguishing feature of a certain kind of cosmopolitan milieu, where they were not uncommon.

Among communists, interracial marriages almost seem to have been the norm, with many examples of Russian women marrying Indian communists, for example Rosa Fitinghoff (?–?) who married Abani Mukherji (1897–1937); the two of them were founding members of the Communist Party of India founded in Tashkent in 1920, alongside Evelyn and Roy. The painter Magda Nachman married M. P. T. Acharya, and head of the Indonesian section at Moscow's Institute of Anthropology and Ethnography, Lidiya Karunovskaya (1889–1951) married Virendranath Chattopadhyaya after he joined the same institute in 1933. Previously, in Berlin, Chatto had been together with Agnes Smedley. In the early 1960s, the daughter of Josef Stalin, Svetlana Aliluyeva (1926–2011), also known as Lana Peters, would be in a 'common law marriage' with Roy's one-time associate Brajesh Singh (c.1909–1966).[135] Yet, there were other cosmopolitan milieus than the radical, communist and humanist ones Roy belonged to, in which interracial partnerships had a place. Transnational spiritualism, containing tropes of a mystical East and materialist West, allowed for contact between men and women that colonial decency frowned upon. This means that Evelyn Roy and Agnes Smedley had something in common with Swami Vivekananda's companion, the Irish Margaret Noble (1867–1911), more commonly known as Sister Nivedita, as well as Aurobindo Ghosh's partner, the French Mirra Alfassa (1878–1973), generally referred to as 'The Mother.'[136] In both realms, the cosmopolitan affiliations of interracial marriage were a distinguishing feature.

In another ideological realm, interracial marriages occurred as well, but were not equally openly acknowledge or even celebrated. Within the much more

---

white women undermining 'white racial prestige' see a case study of European prostitutes in India. Harald Fischer-Tiné, '"White Women Degrading Themselves to the Lowest Depths" : European Networks of Prostitution and Colonial Anxieties in British India and Ceylon ca. 1880–1914', The Indian Economic & Social History Review 40, no. 2 (June 2003): 163–90; And two cases of upper-class coloured men's relations with white women in the late nineteenth century. Nurfadzilah Yahaya, 'Class, White Women, and Elite Asian Men in British Courts during the Late Nineteenth Century', Journal of Women's History 31, no. 2 (2019): 101–23.

[135] Sanjay Seth, Marxist Theory and Nationalist Politics: The Case of Colonial India (New Delhi: Sage, 1995), 77; Laursen, 'M. P. T. Acharya', 8–9; Barooah, Chatto, 314–20;225–76; Jayawardena, The White Woman's Other Burden, 226.

[136] In a monograph on the roles of white women in colonial South Asia, Kumari Jayawardena has dedicated two parts revolving around their relationships to South Asian men, where Evelyn Roy and Agnes Smedley find themselves grouped alongside Swami Vivekananda's companion, the Irish Margaret Noble (1867–1911) or Sister Nivedita, as well as Aurobindo Ghosh's partner, the French Mirra Alfassa (1878–1973) or 'The Mother.' Jayawardena, The White Woman's Other Burden, 175–220.

limited fascist sphere of connectivity, some possibilities existed for personal affiliations between European women and Indian men. But the 1937 marriage of Subhas Chandra Bose and the Austrian Emilie Schenkl (1910–96), as well as their daughter, were kept a secret from the Indian public during Bose's lifetime.[137] The relationship of A. C. N. Nambiar with the German communist Eva Geissler (1900–91) was not public either, since it resulted in his wife, the revolutionary Suhasini Chattopadhyay (1902–73) leaving him.[138] Yet, ideology-spanning relationships still evidenced a small and shared world; Suhasini Chattopadhyay was Chatto's sister; Eva Geissler's sister Louise was in a relationship with M. N. Roy between 1926 and 1927; and Louise had previously been with Roy's close friend Jay Lovestone.[139] Roy and Nambiar had little in common politically, but during 1929–30 Nambiar and Eva Geissler would visit Roy and Louise at the Münzenberg apartment, 'for relaxation.'[140] Intimate bonds meant that experiences and places could be shared across ideological differences.

Beyond the sphere of the Comintern and those who were at one time involved in it, the complexities of various belongings contained in relationships and their political significance are embodied in the conjugal trajectory of Har Dayal, who was never a communist. When he first left India in 1905, he was perhaps the only man to reason like Madame Cama would like all expatriate Indians to do: his wife Sundar Rani/Dayal (?–?) had travelled with him to England, though her family protested. Consequently, the first year of Har Dayal's stay in England was highly unusual, not being characterized by loneliness and discomfort but by the establishment of a family life.[141] His increasing contact with members of London's revolutionary India House moved Har Dayal to give up his Oxford scholarship, after which Sundar and their first child returned to her family. Har Dayal then for a time explored the ideal of celibacy; in an article for the *Indian Sociologist*, the journal of the famous lawyer and revolutionary Shyamji Krishnavarma (1857–1930), he proposed that revolutionaries, or missionaries as he called them, should live celibate lives in as far as this was possible. 'The Ideal of Renunciation is familiar to every Hindu child. Let missionaries, such as I have

---

[137] Sarmila Bose, 'Love in the Time of War: Subhas Chandra Bose's Journeys to Nazi Germany (1941) and towards the Soviet Union (1945)', *Economic and Political Weekly* 40, no. 3 (2005): 249–56.
[138] Ray, *Selected Works of M. N. Roy*, 11.
[139] Mauricio Tenorio has called the cosmopolitan space occupied by international communists in the 1920s an 'erotic mess.' Tenorio, *I Speak of the City*, 115.
[140] Sibnarayan Ray, 'Introduction', in *The World Her Village: Selected Writings and Letters of Ellen Roy*, ed. Sibnarayan Ray (Dehradun: Indian Renaissance Institute, 1979), 29.
[141] Brown, *Har Dayal*, 20–1.

described above, arise and save the country from despair and destruction.'[142] The role of celibacy in personal and national continence was to receive an important role in the thought of Gandhi, but Har Dayal would continue to explore alternative options in the spaces he shared with other revolutionaries and with communists, regardless of ideological differences.

While Har Dayal was a central figure in the Ghadar movement and taught at Stanford at around 1913, he also became involved with the anarchist International Workers of the World and assumed an interest in women's emancipation. Consequently, he began to acquire a reputation for his support of 'free love', a vague term amounting to sex out of wedlock, causing some of the Indian students he tried to provide with scholarships and accommodation to be put off. According to one of them: 'The Hindi students in America at that time thought that the scholarship holders would have to live according to the wishes of Mr Har Dayal. This is one of the reasons why the scholarship holders did not care to live in the house conducted by Mr Har Dayal.'[143] A love life was not only complicated in a personal sense, but could also complicate political projects.

In the United States, too, Har Dayal caused unease: the Stanford community was scandalized by Har Dayal falling in love with a Swiss student, even though she did not reciprocate his feelings.[144] Stanford University too would prove to be squeamish about his politics, personal or otherwise; Har Dayal's anarchist ideas, and his founding of the 'International-Radical-Communist Anarchist Club' caused him to lose his job.[145] His combinations of incompatibilities would continue until the end of his life. Discredited within the Indian movement after publishing a text that celebrated the British Empire in 1920, Har Dayal retreated to Sweden where he met the philanthropist Agda Erikson (?–?) in 1926. She supported him financially, and they married in England in 1932, even though Har Dayal was still married to Sundar, and would leave his property to her when he died in 1939.[146] Practical circumstances, such as the presence of a wife or her absence, as well as the closeness of the Indian movement in California to US radicals, and Har Dayal's isolation in Sweden would come to shape the way he lived with women but also how he reflected on partnerships. Both in the opportunities and the constraints that existed for Har Dayal during his lifetime,

---

[142] Quoted in *Ibid.*, 31.
[143] Quoted in Benjamin Zachariah, 'A Long, Strange Trip: The Lives in Exile of Har Dayal', *South Asian History and Culture* 4, no. 4 (2013): 579.
[144] Brown, *Har Dayal*, 106.
[145] Zachariah, 'A Long, Strange Trip', 577.
[146] Brown, *Har Dayal*, 238; 270.

relationships were a key shaping factor, all the more so since they contributed to the reputation he had in the eyes of others.

In one of the cosmopolitan places along Roy's itinerary, interracial marriages were rarer than in the others, which supplied the odd example discussed here with powerful political potential. While there were many Indian revolutionaries passing through Japan, interracial marriages there were not common, and Rash Behari Bose's marriage to Tosiko Soma formed an exception. In the way the marriage between Tosiko and Rash Behari was remembered later, we get a glimpse of the role of difference in establishing these bonds of solidarity.

> The Japanese hated all international marriages. They were extremely nationalistic and orthodox at that time. All girls married to Westerners, however rich or kind or intelligent or powerful, were considered the most detestable creatures in the world. The case was worse for the Indian, the Chinese or the Indonesian. [...] She gave up all pleasures in social life to save one black Indian penniless aud threatened with death at every moment! She had to live always as a social outcast. A young and beautiful girl of a rich family [...] who might have married any intelligent and rich youngman of the land, gave up her all for Bose. [...] Tosiko devoted her unique life and soul to the wellbeing of the poor fugitive in exile, nay she devoted her pure, noble lily-like body and spirit, for the love of Great Mother India![147]

This text was published in India in 1954, and while the writer, Georges Ohsawa,[148] highlighted the immense taboo that existed on Japanese women marrying foreign men, particularly Indians, he did so in order to convey the heroic status Tosiko should have within the Indian canon.[149] For emphasis, Ohsawa highlighted the vastness of the racial difference between them as it would have been perceived at the time. In his narrative, Tosiko embodied a pan-Asian solidarity in her sacrifice, which she had not been able to make if Bose had not been quite so different, in such a taboo manner. Ohsawa's account of the

---

[147] George Ohsawa, *Two Great Indians in Japan: Sri Rush Behari Bose and Netaji Subhas Chandra Bose* (Calcutta: Kusa Publications, 1954), 13; 15–16.

[148] Ohsawa's partly French pen name stemmed from his European career spreading the macrobiotic diet. Eva-Maria Schulz, 'Das Leben Eines Menschen Wird Durch Seine Ernährung Bestimmt', *Zeitschrift Für Junge Religionswissenschaft*, no. 1 (2006): 4–5.

[149] According to Naoko Shimazu, there existed a 'two-tiered' conception of race in the Japan of the early twentieth century, where the first divided the world into white, black and yellow races, with Japan sharing a realm with China, Korea and potentially India, although its position was more ambiguous. On the second tier of the nation, Japan stood hierarchically above China and Japan, assuming a leading role in the region. Naoko Shimazu, *Japan, Race and Equality: The Racial Equality Proposal of 1919* (London: Routledge, 1998), 183.

overcoming of the distance created by suffering at the same time brought it into sharp focus. In this way, perceptions of difference were an important ingredient in the establishment of bonds of solidarity, since it was in the overcoming of difference that a bond was made which could be felt to be transformative.

Households

In the itinerary of M. N. Roy, his relationships with several white women co-determined his course, an example of the 'counter domesticities' in which Indian revolutionaries abroad often lived,[150] which was distinct from the 'simplicity' and 'pairing down' of his household that had allowed for Gandhi's mobility.[151] What set Roy apart from this other mobile households was that in most of his published ego-documents, Roy would be silent about his partners and living situation. Roy wrote his memoirs as those of a man who had travelled alone.[152] In reality, however, Evelyn Trent, his wife between 1916 and 1925, lived, travelled and worked with him between those years, in the United States, Mexico, Western Europe and Soviet Russia. Roy's mission to China between 1926 and 1927 was one he undertook alongside the German Louise Geißler, who would even visit him in India in 1930, while he was still on the run from the police.[153] Ellen Gottschalk was a German Jewish woman with US citizenship who had been born in France. Her citizenship was a source of great complications when she had to flee Germany in 1933 and lived in illegality in France.[154] They only ended when she married Roy in 1936 and got an Indian passport. By then, Roy recalled from his first marriage: '… those "white Caucasians" with a mixture of all sorts of blood in their veins, do not take kindly to women marrying "Non-Aryans." You tell them that you do not want to defile their "God's own country,"

---

[150] Lahiri, *Indian Mobilities in the West*, 55.
[151] Majeed, *Autobiography, Travel and Postnational Identity*, 23.
[152] Roy left Evelyn out of his Memoirs to protect her from persecution during the anti-communist McCarthy years in the United States. Evelyn embraced this anonymity, as she wrote to Ellen Roy in 1954, declining to contribute to a memorial volume about M. N. Roy: 'As I wrote you previously, it would seem far better to leave me out of the picture entirely, since so many years have elapsed, all except a very few are entirely unaware of this phase and it is better to leave it that way. Let the past bury its dead. […] I am sorry to disappoint you and I do hope you will understand and forgive me, but judging from his own memoirs, that is the way R. wanted it to be and I am convinced he was right.' Letter from Evelyn Jones to Ellen Roy, 11 July 1954, Evelyn Jones Correspondence, Catalogue 71: M. N. Roy Papers Section II, NMML.
[153] Roy, *Selected Works, Volume III*, 15.
[154] Ray, 'Introduction', in *The World Her Village*, 32.

that you will abandon American citizenship, as soon as you will reach your adopted country.'[155]

Ellen Roy would be included in Roy's later public persona as she engaged in Indian politics, and the correspondence she and Roy had sent between North Indian prison cells and European cities was published by their own publishing house in 1943 – though only the letters Roy had written.[156] One of their colleagues would call the extent to which Ellen made herself subservient to Roy's projects 'spiritual self-immolation'.[157] Whether he was silent about it or turned the relationship into a part of his public persona, political activities, intellectual production and propaganda writing were done by the women by his side as well as himself, meaning Roy's intellectual persona often rested on the work of two people.

White women who married Indians in California, for example Evelyn Trent and Ethel Ray Dugan, committed radical acts through their unions, since an anti-miscegenation statute specifically prohibited marriages between whites and non-whites. Back in the 1910s, certain Indian revolutionaries in California listed both parties as 'caucasian' on the marriage certificate – this was possible as the argument of the Aryan descent of some of India's population was occasionally accepted, in cases the claimant seemed to be sufficiently upper class or caste.[158] After the marriage between Roy and Evelyn ended in 1925, her act would assume added meaning. In personal letters, she emphasized the distance from her direct surroundings her marriage had come with. To Roy, she wrote about their marriage as a marker of her radical politics, at odds with received norms and standards: '… we perhaps experienced a love that was rarer and sweeter for having to do battle against the whole world of ignorance, prejudice, hostility and jealousy.'[159] And to their mutual friend, the Dutch communist Sneevliet, she wrote of her dismay at having been betrayed by her husband, '… this man whom I met and loved because he seemed so immeasurably

---

[155] Roy, *Letters from Jail*, 226.
[156] Roy, *Letters from Jail*.
[157] Ray, 'Introduction', in *The World Her Village*, 18.
[158] Contemporary notions in the United States held that upper-class Indians were Aryans, and the lower classes Dravidians. Several wealthy Indians had proved in US courts that they were white, and could therefore hold citizenship, until the 1923 supreme court case of Bhagat Singh Thing overturned those verdicts. Nico Slate, *Colored Cosmopolitanism: The Shared Struggle for Freedom in the United States and India* (Cambridge: Harvard University Press, 2012), 28–30.
[159] Letter from Evelyn Trent to M. N. Roy, California, 25 December 1926, Roys Correspondence Inventory 362, Archief Henk Sneevliet, IISH.

removed from the degenerate and rotten society of the modern world.'[160] It was his difference from the world she had known, and come to disapprove of, that Evelyn portrayed as attractive about her first husband.

In other letters, however, her own difference from the new environments she moved into with her first husband would come to play a negative role. Being back home, '... among my own people who partly understand and fully trust me without the necessity of living under a constant cloud of fear and suspicion, ...'[161] Evelyn reflected on her nine years spent travelling, living in places where she often did not speak the language, on the run from the police. She concluded: 'I am beginning to be very averse to foreign missionaries – one should work in the country to which one naturally belongs by birth and associations and understanding.'[162] From her own experience, Evelyn generalized to find the way of living and working she had come to know uncommendable. She urged Sneevliet to convince his second, Russian wife, to leave the Netherlands and return to Russia.

> I say this much only because my own experience has taught me that it is very very difficult if not impossible to be either useful or happy in working outside of one's natural environment and among a strange people. [...] She could be very useful in her own country, where so much is needed to be done ...[163]

The differences Evelyn had encountered in her marriage, and then through her marriages, provided spaces for critique; both of her own society, defining her role in opposition to it, and of recognizing the boundaries of her capacities to do so when cut off from it, in places where through lack of knowledge and understanding her work was rendered ineffectual. Even though Evelyn's homecoming had not been voluntary, the sudden change of perspective gave her a new insight into the efficacy of cosmopolitan agents. Her evaluations contained different versions of suffering; on the one hand, the 'world of ignorance [and] prejudice' she had to face in order to marry Roy; on the other, the hardships of living with him, feeling her capacities to be limited in foreign environments. Cosmopolitan affiliations had the ability to integrate people into new groups, but also to exclude them from old ones.

---

[160] Letter from Evelyn Trent to Jack Horner, Chicago, 17 August 1925, Roys Correspondence Inventory 362, Henk Sneevliet Archive, IISH.
[161] Letter from Evelyn Trent to Jack Horner, 19 May 1927, Roys Correspondence Inventory 362, Henk Sneevliet Archive, ISSH.
[162] Letter from Evelyn Trent to Jack Horner, 13 March 1926, Roys Correspondence Inventory 362, Henk Sneevliet Archive, IISH.
[163] *Ibid.*

For Agnes Smedley, her reflections on relationships formed a part of her critique of inherited structures. Of meeting her partner Virendranath Chattopadhyaya in Berlin in 1920, Smedley would come to write:

> When Viren and I began life together, two eras and two cultures met. I was an American working woman, the product of a distorted commercial civilization, he a high caste Indian with a cultivated, labyrinthine Brahmin mind and a British classical education …. His mind was modern, but his emotional roots were in Hinduism and Islam.[164]

Smedley's dwelling on Chatto's difference was clearly written in the vein of critique of her own 'distorted commercial civilization.' Her love for Chattopadhyaya could be seized upon as a demonstrative underlining of that critique. Accompanying her celebration of difference, however, were accounts of the suffering their four-year relationship had entailed. A 1924 letter to Smedley's close friend, the Danish writer Karin Michaëlis (1872–1950), detailed Smedley's unhappiness at having to devote her time to running the Berlin household that was frequented by many Indian revolutionaries, where she had to cook and clean. Apart from these duties taking up so much of her time, Smedley wrote that Chatto begrudged her intellectual productivity, and no longer wanted her to write or practise politics. At its most intimate, the letter revealed Chatto's jealousy of her former relationships: '… he said that he "got leavings from other men"! Now when a man strikes at a woman like that, in view of the fact that he is also "the leavings from other women" it is not only unethical, but it is contrary to all laws of decency and fair play.'[165] The way Smedley made sense of these accusations was to incorporate them into her judgement of patriarchy in general, not just of Indian men.[166] Her efforts to live beyond the rules of her own society led to a confrontation with the seeming universality of its more lamentable structures. Those turned out to be impossible to escape, even for cosmopolitans on the move.

As much as interracial relationships could be made into an aspect of a cosmopolitan persona, they could be used as a smear – if they were engaged in by women. Smedley's relationship to Chatto, and her belief women could have different relationships just as men, invited a lot of criticism in their circles; Roy's recollections of her were harshly judgmental, entailing a mostly fictional list of all

---

[164] Agnes Smedley, *Battle Hymn of China* (New York: A. Knopf, 1943), 14.
[165] Quoted in Barooah, *Chatto*, 238.
[166] Purnima Bose, 'Transnational Resistance and Fictive Truths: Virendranath Chattopadhyaya, Agnes Smedley and the Indian Nationalist Movement', *South Asian History and Culture* 2, no. 4 (2011): 511.

the Indian lovers Smedley was supposed to have had.[167] What seems to be at the root of his aggressive disdain was a 'disastrous sexual encounter' between them in New York in 1917.[168] What transpired exactly is disputed among historians, as the source for their encounter is Smedley's fictionalized autobiography *Daughter of Earth*, in which her character, Marie Rodgers, was raped by an Indian revolutionary called Juan Diaz, who is variously taken to represent Herambalal Gupta, M. N. Roy, or a combination of both.[169] In Smedley's narrative, the rape was part of her critique of the patriarchy in general, not merely in terms of male sexual aggression, but also of her own troubling attraction to it. While in this instance, the attacker was Indian, her analysis linked it to previous experiences of sexual aggression and located their significance in the violence that existed between men and women in general, wherever they were from. Against that background, she espoused sexual freedom as well as the cause of birth control, which would liberate women from the potentially grave consequences of sex, allowing them to freely admit to their desires rather than only being able to feel them in a forced way.[170] Violence is generally absent from the recollections of cosmopolitans, even though they lived through it was clearly present in their lives – with specific dangers a real possibility for women. If violence was written about, it was either intellectualized or made light of.

Not all interracial relationships were recalled as instances of suffering or even violence. After her break with Chatto, Smedley met the Indian communist and later Congress politician Bakar Ali Mirza (1900–?), who had been studying at Oxford. The two were together between 1926 and 1927, but as an Islamic marriage was out of the question for Smedley, Mirza moved to Hyderabad where he married and entered the political scene. In later years, the two corresponded about sexual science, birth control in India, avant-garde theatre, psycho-analysis and the anti-colonial movement. When Smedley went to China in 1928, Mirza wrote: 'Go, Agnes, go to canton [*sic*], and may you be happy. You have written a few pages in my life, in gold, and they will not be forgotten.'[171] Their changing nature was often a feature of cosmopolitan relationships, with members moving along different itineraries, but even that could be seized upon as evidence of the richness of the life that had been shared.

---

[167] Roy, *Memoirs*, 487.
[168] Price, *The Lives of Agnes Smedley*, 60.
[169] Bose, 'Transnational Resistance and Fictive Truths', 514.
[170] Price, *The Lives of Agnes Smedley*, 62.
[171] Quoted in Fuechtner, 'Agnes Smedley between Berlin, Bombay, and Beijing', 416.

In retrospect, the different women involved in Roy's love life were a point of interest for his fellow revolutionaries as they recalled their days in Moscow in Berlin with a mixture of nostalgia and sensual orientalism. Bertram Wolfe, for example, recalled being invited to a New Year's party in Berlin, celebrating the year 1929: 'We were invited to a party at the home of M. N. Roy, at which all the girls seemed to be German blondes, including technical secretaries of the large German delegation in Moscow, and virtually all the men were Indians.'[172] There might have been a degree of jealousy in Wolfe's recollections, as well as nostalgia for a youth riddled with titillating details. Contained in such nostalgia was the transience of cosmopolitan milieus; what had been possible in 1920s Berlin and within an internationalist Comintern became unthinkable in later years.[173] When Louise Geissler reminisced about her love life many years later, she wrote to a friend: 'I "slowed down" in terms of love affairs, [...] I took in my earlier years everything I wanted and [...] I am saturated in every respect.'[174] Life in the 1950s, when many former communists wrote their memoirs, was dull by comparison.[175] Luis Fraina had settled in the United States as Lewis Corey with his Russian wife. In a letter, Roy poked fun at the twee domesticity implied by the stationary his old friend used, which had 'The Coreys' emblazoned across the top.[176] Nostalgia was characteristic in descriptions of a cosmopolitan life that had come and gone, its worldliness elusive in more stable times. Both happy and unhappy recollections, as well as prurient remarks of others' past, were signs of shared places that were no longer there for the aged former revolutionaries who had sensibly settled down.

The settled life Roy and Ellen shared was heavily imbued with domesticity in the way their colleagues and friends wrote about it, and yet, it was in this household that Ellen Roy would be brutally murdered in 1961. The culprits seem to have been teenage thieves – even though there was barely any wealth in the house. The Roys had only seemed affluent.[177] Kris Manjapra has suggested

---

[172] Bertram D. Wolfe, *A Life in Two Centuries: An Autobiography* (New York: Stein & Day, 1981), 446.
[173] A certain licentiousness tied to the feminist current coloured the world of the Cominternians in the 1920s, and disappeared in the 1930s when policies began to urge the formation of large nuclear families. Brigitte Studer, *The Transnational World of the Cominternians* (Hampshire: Palgrave Macmillan, 2015), 46.
[174] Letter from Louise Geissler to Ella Wolfe, 17 November 1964, Bertram Wolfe Files: Collection Number 77029, Box 6, Louise Geissler Correspondence, Hoover.
[175] 'One need only think of the futures of Ella Wolfe and her friends: Ella safe and comfortable in Palo Alto, Evelyn Trent back in the U.S. remarried in a "normal" American life ...' Tenorio, *I Speak of the City*, 130.
[176] Letter from M. N. Roy to Louis Fraina, 20 August 1952, Lewis Corey (Louis Fraina) Correspondence, Catalogue 70: M. N. Roy Papers Section 1, NMML.
[177] Park, 'Ellen Roy', 63.

that Ellen Roy's murder was linked to the '… strangeness of her presence in the eyes of mainstream Hindu society, as a politically-outspoken single widowed European woman in post-independence India.'[178] The circles and contexts where interracial marriages counted as a mark of cosmopolitan richness were thinly spread and unstable. Any change in their composition, such as Roy's death in 1954, could radically alter what was possible and what practices were acceptable since they were insulated from the judgement of those in their direct vicinity. This could be disproportionately risky for women.

Reproduction

Among cosmopolitans, there existed a subject for reflection that connected relationships and their most immediately affiliative outcome: children and family.[179] Matters of population and birth control had been more widely written about by cosmopolitan intellectuals of a radical or humanist orientation.[180] As a country with a large population and occasional famines whose scientists worked in English, India was particularly scrutinized by and accessible to the international community.[181] When the highly controversial book *Mother India*, a sensationalist account of the sexual oppression of India's women was published in 1927 by US author Katherine Mayo, the subject became one many Indian intellectuals abroad felt they had to address. The book's most famous critic was Gandhi, who called it a 'Drain-Inspector's Report.'[182] In a different vein, Dhan Gopal Mukerji weighed in on the issue in a humorous riposte titled *A Son of Mother India Answers* (1928). He labelled Mayo's work a 'pornocracy,' and surmised that the author of *Mother India* '… has detected the root of India's trouble in sex. It is new and startling,'[183] only to quickly point out that this idea was, in fact, an established element in the orientalist repertoire.[184] In a tongue-in-cheek way, Mukerji's book emphasized the affiliative potential of sex. If it really

---

[178] Manjapra, 'Impossible Intimacies of M. N. Roy', 173.
[179] Kris Manjapra referred to Roy's way of life as one in a 'chosen family.' Manjapra, *M. N. Roy*, xii, 137–41.
[180] Alison Bashford, *Global Population: History, Geopolitics, and Life on Earth* (New York: Columbia University Press, 2014), 158.
[181] Bashford, *Global Population*, 211–66; Matthew Connelly, *Fatal Misconception: The Struggle to Control World Population* (Cambridge: Belknap Press of Harvard University Press, 2008), 55–95.
[182] Mrinalini Sinha, *Specters of Mother India: The Global Restructuring of an Empire* (Durham: Duke University Press, 2006), 2.
[183] Dhan Gopal Mukerji, *A Son of Mother India Answers* (Noida, India: Rupa&Co, 1922), 3.
[184] '… if we look at such books as "The Broken Road" and "A Passage to India," and the play "The Green Goddess," we will see in them that all Indians whether Hindu or Moslem suffer from the assumption of the Westerner that the Orientals are sex-addicts.' *Ibid.*, 26.

was sex that was at the root of India's trouble, this was shared between all people on earth. 'Indians need but rejoice. For that makes us as modern as the rest of the world. Nowadays a single touch of sex makes the whole world kin.'[185] At least potentially, sex formed a bridge between all members of the human species. And Mukerji was the sort of light-handed cosmopolitan writer who could breezily reject the accusation that among the world's people, some were doing it wrong.

While in prison, Roy read about the 1935 visit to India of the leading figure of the international birth control movement, Margaret Sanger (1879–1966), a longtime friend and colleague of Agnes Smedley's.[186] The highlight of Sanger's Indian tour was a visit to Gandhi's ashram where she had a long public discussion with the Mahatma, trying to get him to change his belief that abstinence was the only acceptable version of birth control.[187] In his writings, Roy took issue with Gandhi's recommended method of birth control, abstinence, in order to underline his own beliefs about sex: 'Gandhi advises women to resist lustful husbands. [...] But sex-attraction is mutual. Women are no more goddesses than men are animals.'[188] He did not seek to dispel reservations surrounding the subject of sex by considering it a necessary evil in order to enable procreation. 'Gandhi says that the woman has been given a field of life by God, and it is her duty to make use of it. [...] ... if the field of life is a gift of God, why cannot the woman select the seed to be planted on her field, and hire the ploughman to her liking.'[189] Pleasure, in Roy's estimate, was a far nobler principle than family obligations, or any other human reason to procreate. By contrast, he linked the imperative to have large families to openly fascist politics, not only in Germany and Italy, but in India.[190] Such political reservations fit Roy's humanist conviction that the existence of too many people was an inherent problem, pointing to an elitism that limited existence to something exclusive.

Political reservations around the impetus to invite more souls into existence were accompanied by practical projects and personal decisions. Birth control was a shared theme as well as a practice, especially within the Radical Humanist movement, with Dr Indumati Parikh specializing

---

[185] *Ibid.*, 52.
[186] A direct link between Roy and Sanger was made up by Agnes Smedley, who spent her years in New York City were organizing and publicizing for her organization *Friends of Freedom for India* as well as Sanger's *Birth Control Review*. Fuechtner, 'Agnes Smedley between Berlin, Bombay, and Beijing', 400.
[187] Barbara Ramusack, 'Embattled Advocates: The Debate over Birth Control in India, 1920–40', *Journal of Women's History* 1, no. 2 (1989): 50–2.
[188] Roy, *Fragments of a Prisoner's Diary: Volume II*, 16–17.
[189] *Ibid.*, 29.
[190] For global fascism, see Chapter 5.

in family planning and the organization running a development project in Bihar where the subject was given wide attention.[191] But many cosmopolitans qualified the practice as an element in their way of life. Or as a colleague succinctly explained for Ellen Roy: '… revolutionaries of her time did not rear families …'[192] Roy also clearly linked his thinking about global population to his own lifestyle in a rejection of familial bonds and affiliation with people he was not related to.[193] His sparse writings about his own family origins were characterized by emotional detachment and a refusal to fulfil his expected role as an older brother or scion of a priestly family. A 1954 article about his origins served to condemn the social system it formed a part of.[194] On an even more intimate level, his rejection of his biological family would make Roy proudly celebrate the fact that he did not have children. When friends welcomed additions to their families, Roy made sure his congratulations included reservations: 'We hope the mother and the child are doing well, and the proud father is happy. I always wondered why one should be proud to be a father. I would feel differently!'[195] On the occasion of the birth of a daughter to Philip Spratt,[196] Roy wrote:

> The experience of fatherhood must be most impressive, but I would like to impress the world in other ways! You may have noted my view of life – I consider it to be a blemish on the majestic harmony of the physical universe. Legally, it has no place in the scheme of the world. And I do not want to encourage illegal activities all over the front.'[197]

Considering a cosmopolitan persona involves the signalling of a familiarity with difference, or even a love thereof, overt declarations of scepticism towards biological familiar relationships easily count as an extension of this. The pinnacle

---

[191] *Documents regarding Bihar project 1962–1980*, 1733–1029, Archive of the International Humanist and Ethical Union, Het Utrechts Archief, Utrecht, the Netherlands (hence HUA).
[192] V. M. Tarkunde, 'A Brave Woman', in *The World Her Village; Selected Writings and Letters of Ellen Roy*, ed. Sibnarayan Ray (Dehradun: Indian Renaissance Institute, 1979), 85.
[193] Manjapra, 'The Impossible Intimacies of M. N. Roy', 173.
[194] M. N. Roy, 'The Disintegration of a Priestly Family', *The Radical Humanist*, 7 February 1954, 73.
[195] Letter from M. N. Roy to Guy Wint, 12 October 1949, Guy Wint Correspondence, Catalogue 70: M. N. Roy Papers Section 1, NMML.
[196] Spratt considered his marriage to an Indian woman as an essential part of his particular kind of cosmopolitanism. In his autobiography, *Blowing Up India*, he would write about his problems ever fitting into the middle-class English milieu he hailed from: 'Perhaps the clearest evidence of my alienation is the fact that since the period of infantile sexuality I have never fallen in love with an Englishwoman. The only women I have fallen in love with are Jewish and Indian.' Philip Spratt, *Blowing Up India: Reminiscences and Reflections of a Former Comintern Emissary* (Calcutta: Prachi Prakashan, 1955), 5–6.
[197] Letter from M. N. Roy to Philip Spratt, 28 April 1945, Philip Spratt Correspondence Section 2, Catalogue 70: M. N. Roy Papers Section 1, NMML.

of celebrating chosen bonds over received ones was in not just the rejection of parenthood for oneself, but doubting its wisdom in general.

Conclusion

In the way that the architects of the Mexican night club called M. N. Roy emphasized the eclecticism of their design, drawing on elements such as '... puuc art, maya arch, pyramids ...' as well as the history of the Mexican communist party and that of the anti-colonial Indian movement,[198] displaying the range of one's affiliations and richness of connections one had was a way in which cosmopolitans like Roy did not merely live a mobile life, but turned it into an aspect of their persona. In doing so, showing that they were making some selection was more important than the exact selection they did make. This was part and parcel of a lifestyle that in some way was a goal unto itself, and it they became part of a habitus and a persona they would come with advantages – advantages discussed in the following chapters. What could be put on display was not the undivided privilege of state pomp and power, but a more subtle version where danger and deprivation were an inherent aspect both of a politics that took on powerful empires and of a knowing familiarity with the finer aspects of different cultures, as well as the ability to distinguish between their various merits. Even here, the night club's architects' decision to maintain the crumbling original facade of M. N. Roy's house and to match it with a glossy new interior is apt.[199] While dangers and deprivations were real, they could also be made into a central aspect of a life that was not only cosmopolitan, but cosmopolitan in a distinguished sense, its privileges tempered by danger and struggle. When highly precarious episodes were committed to paper, one function of danger was to even heighten the value of affiliative bonds. This resulted in the existence of exclusive clubs of distinguished cosmopolitans, rather than merely mobile people.

A memorial volume that was published on Ellen after her death makes clear the role of both difficulty and ease of movement, danger and privileges, that played a role in the nature of Roy and Ellen's relationship and its institutionalization in writing. It tells the story of Ellen's escape from Nazi Germany to France, where her US passport put her in need of constant visa renewal, and she did not have

---

[198] Frearson, 'M. N. Roy'.
[199] Ibid.

a stable address to which Roy could send his monthly letter from prison. So instead, they used the address of Ellen's future sister-in-law, who was studying at the Sorbonne and lived with a '… university-approved, very proper, very bourgeois family'. The properness and bourgeoisness of the host family served as a contrast to underline Ellen's dissident status, especially compared to her sister-in-law who '… never satisfied their curiosity as to why she, a young American student, should regularly receive, once a month, an officially stamped censored letter from the Central Jail, Bareilly, India.'[200] The letters bring together the extreme hardships of being a refugee from Nazism and an inmate in an Indian colonial prison, both with life-threatening dimensions. They also show the value of networking in exile, with distant connections having immediate practical value, and the way in which contrast could serve to underline the importance of affiliative bonds created. Suffering became noble, and could be vanquished by stressing the adventure and humour of such episodes, and the ways they set Ellen apart from her direct environment.

The realm that distinguished cosmopolitans separated themselves from was that of the immobile, but also that of various groups whose values and practices were largely in line with the existing order. The movement they embraced was also a temporal one, where received notions were no longer suitable for the world they lived in and new ideas were required. This could be the case for simpler things such as food and drink, as well as important relational practices such as language and as the next chapter will show, names and clothing. This chapter has delved into the shared way of life that gave coherence to these groups of cosmopolitans, and the way they were united against what they perceived to be the established practices of the global bourgeoisie and religion. The most fundamental aspect of this way of life was its approach to relationships and reproduction. To various extents, choice of partners was an individual one, having nothing to do with family and being subject to changes. Reproduction was an individual choice independent of family expectations of continuity too, one to be taken independent from the enjoyment of sex. All of these practices meant that those included, even as receptive audiences, were minorities in the various places where they were. And also for those minorities, borders between what was in – and excluded were porous. There was for example some space for fascist ideas among a largely leftist set, as well as plenty of animosities, rifts and even violence among those sharing spaces and practices.

---

[200] Robert Gottschalk, 'My Sister Ellen: Some Recollections', in *The World Her Village; Selected Writings and Letters of Ellen Roy*, ed. Sibnarayan Ray (Dehradun: Indian Renaissance Institute, 1979), 51–2.

Nostalgia was a key element in recollections and in the (re-)construction of spaces, bonds and practices. There was, after all, a great deal of instability in terms of the spaces that gave rise to distinguished cosmopolitan practices at a time of world wars and revolution, so their constitution was highly temporary. The First World War had pushed Germans and German allies out of the countries who joined the war on the Allied side, such as the United States in 1917. The Russian Revolution exercised a magnetic force on leftist forces far and wide, but the Civil War, a stricter political line from 1928 and the Purges of 1937–8 pushed many people out again, or ended their lives. Communists and Jews tried to get out of Germany when the Nazis came to power there, and out of Europe when the Second World War broke out. So when Roy was incarcerated, he wrote to Ellen to ask: 'How are all the friends? The wandering Jews of the twentieth century!'[201] And when Betram Wolfe to Roy in 1949, not having seen him since 1929, it was to say that Roy had featured in the reminiscences of Wolfe and Louise Geissler. '… [A]s did hundreds of other acquaintances some of whom have risen to the puppet rulership of "People's Democracies" and others who have perished or been scattered to the four ends of the world.'[202] For a set of loose-knit groups for whom their central characteristic was that they moved in a combination of privilege and precarity, the temporary nature of the circles they constituted was keenly felt. Nostalgia bestowed a degree of coherence onto their lives and memories as they would be cultivated up to many decades later.

---

[201] Roy, *Letters from Jail*, 63.
[202] Letter from Bertram Wolfe to M. N. Roy, 5 April 1949, IC/FOR/9 W-13, Bertram Wolfe Correspondence, M. N. Roy Papers Section 1, NMML.

2

Foreign bodies – The making of a cosmopolitan persona

Among its offer of memorabilia and souvenirs, the Dr Sun Yat-sen museum in Hong Kong sells a key ring that represents Sun Yat-sen (1886–1925), the Chinese Republic's first provisional president as well as a paragon of anti-imperialist heroism in the circles Roy moved in during the late 1910s. The keyring comes with three different outfits that magnetically attach to Sun's metal silhouette. One can choose to dress him in either the *changshan* or long robe he wore as a medical student in 1880s Hong Kong; the New York-made three-piece European-style suit he often wore abroad, during the long stretches of his life where his revolutionary activities had turned him into an exile; or the eponymous Zhongshan suit he popularized when he briefly served as the first president of China's provisional government after the 1911 revolution.[1] As he adjusted to different environments and hid from certain authorities, Sun reflected on the power of clothes to change the way in which he was perceived; in 1895 Honolulu, for example, a European costume and a haircut meant people took him for Japanese.[2] The requirements for Sun to remain clandestine when abroad, or to adjust to different cultural environments, as well as the way in which he wrote about his itinerant life all contributed to his image as a chameleonic, cosmopolitan figure, captured in the key ring.

Even though not all of the characters in these pages were famous enough to warrant their own museums with gift shops, some of the practices that contributed

---

[1] It was this last outfit that would later morph into the well-known Mao jacket. François Hourmant, 'La Longue Marche De La Veste Mao', *Vingtième Siècle. Revue D'histoire* 121, no. 1 (2014): 116–17.
[2] About his 1895 escape to Hawaii after the failed First Guangzhou uprising, Sun wrote: 'I changed my Chinese attire for a European costume à la Japanese. I removed my queue, allowed my hair to grow naturally and cultivated my moustache.' When he met Japanese people there, they '… addressed me in the Japanese language, taking me for a countryman.' Zhongshan Sun, *Kidnapped in London: Being the Story of My Capture by, Detention at, and Release from the Chinese Legation, London* (Bristol: J. W. Arrowsmith, 1897), 28–9.

to Sun Yat-sen's iconic image were shared by them. Even lesser luminaries of international anti-imperialism and alternative politics became somewhat iconic through these practices, in the sense that they became recognizably cosmopolitan figures. Becoming iconic involves '... the transformation of the human into a meaningful symbol,' in an interaction between the surface of the body and deeper meanings attached to it. The process of becoming iconic involves many people and practices beyond the human who is being transformed, but nevertheless starts from the individual body. More than that, the specific looks of the individual play a role in the process.[3] One historian who called Roy an 'icon,' at least among radicals in Mexico City, noted that '... in the midst of many narratives about ideological struggles, betrayals, and conspiracies, one could always find references to Roy's beauty.'[4] Not all anti-imperialists were equally good-looking,[5] but even then, distant longings and projections could render a body desirable. This calls attention to the more general importance of surfaces and first impressions in cosmopolitan connections, the unfamiliar was encountered as an immediate bodily presence, and closely scrutinized. A recognizable cosmopolitan could become the centre of gravity of a cosmopolitan circle.

This chapter is concerned with the moving bodies individuals who became recognizably cosmopolitan figures through social and performative practices that at their most basic level negotiated persecution and clandestinity, cultural difference and racial discrimination. In an added layer, they cultivated these requirements into markers of cosmopolitanism in their own right. Tim Harper has pointed out that clandestinity did not only serve to hide the true identities of Asian revolutionaries, but contributed to creating their identities as revolutionaries to begin with.[6] This occasionally involved blending into environments that might see them as undesirable aliens,[7] or becoming something that has been called an 'acceptable foreigner.'[8] Beyond recognizability and acceptability, cosmopolitan affiliative practices could make outsiders highly

---

[3] Jeremy Prestholdt, *Icons of Dissent: The Global Resonance of Che, Marley, Tupac and Bin Laden* (London: Hurst & Company, 2019), 5–6;10;14.

[4] Tenorio-Trillo, *I Speak of the City*, 278.

[5] Virendranath Chattopadhyaya has even been labelled as 'downright homely.' Price, *The Lives of Agnes Smedley*, 88.

[6] They '... obsessively tried to forge connections to advance their struggles; the police obsessively looked to uncover connections in order to prove the existence of wider conspiracies and plots. Each helped fashion the other and this drove forward events.' Harper, *Underground Asia*, xxix.

[7] Shompa Lahiri has described this as 'racial passing,' aided by the relative ignorance of colonial racial classification schemes among metropolitan populations. Shompa Lahiri, 'Performing Identity: Colonial Migrants, Passing and Mimicry between the Wars', *Cultural Geographies* 10, no. 4 (2003): 411–13.

[8] Carrasco, 'From British Colonial Subject to Mexican "Naturalizado"', 180.

desirable – if in clearly circumscribed ways. The ways in which the moving body became known ranged from the clandestine to the chameleon and the convert. The practices involved in doing so included the use of pseudonyms and lasting name changes, as well as disguise and dressing practices. Finally, they included writing practices that reflected on these themes, as well as linking individuals to the wider world. In such writing, a great deal of attention was spent on the way things looked and the role of bodies in first impressions of encounters with the unfamiliar.

Making an impression

The way in which Roy made an impression on a wide range of interlocutors and audiences across various continents drew on the interplay between his body and actions, and audiences' ideas and expectation of Indians – or in India, expectations of returning revolutionaries who had seen much of the world. They ranged from him possessing an air of mystery and distinction to him becoming well-known and desirable. During the late 1910s, when Roy was pursuing contacts with representatives of Imperial Germany in California, the attaché of the German consulate in San Francisco, Wilhelm von Brincken (1881–1946) left a written impression of Roy. In his recollections, Roy appeared as both mysterious and distinguished:

> One of those who came here from the Orient in connection with the matter was a very high caste Brahmin whose real name I did not learn but whom we knew as 'Mr. Martin.' He was a tall, well-dressed and well-groomed man, very dignified and of obvious refinement and good education.[9]

Roy's height was striking to contemporary observers, and was immediately connected to a sense of him being upper caste and upper class. Like many revolutionaries hailing from Bengal's underground movement, Roy was from an upper-caste, Brahmin family.[10] His father was a Sanskrit teacher and the head priest of a Bengal village.[11] With time, his caste and class background would become something for Roy to intellectually contend with,[12] but as an otherwise

---

[9] Quoted in Roy, 'Introduction', in *The Path to Durable Peace*, 5–6.
[10] Durba Ghosh, *Gentlemanly Terrorists: Political Violence and the Colonial State in India, 1919–1947* (Cambridge: Cambridge University Press, 2017), 1–2.
[11] Leonard A. Gordon, 'Portrait of a Bengal Revolutionary', *The Journal of Asian Studies* 27, no. 2 (1968): 197–216.
[12] See Chapter 5.

unknown stranger, it helped him to make a distinctive impression on a German aristocrat and spy – who would become a middling Hollywood actor.[13] There was a sense of recognition or even similarity mixed in with the impression of strangeness in Von Brincken's lines, of a distinguished individual spotting another, even if they were from different places. This interplay between distance and closeness, and the implications it had for the worldly impression Von Brincken could himself make through his recollections of Roy, featured widely in such descriptions. In a life lived between places, often dealing with people as of yet unknown, the quality to quickly make an impression, however superficial, was exceedingly important, and Roy's body played a key role in the impressions that he made.

Aesthetics were a constitutive part of the radical lifestyle Roy became a part of in Mexico City, and would be present in more of the places he frequented through the presence of artists like Magda Nachman Acharya, or filmmakers and actors like Von Brincken and the Wadias. Among radicals, aesthetics and lifestyle were political. Radicals disregarded religious and moral prescriptions they associated with older generations, and saw cultural transformations as an inherent part of political ones. This meant they were remarkably concerned with lifestyle and aesthetics alongside issues of social and economic justice – ranging from jazz music and modern dance to experiments with different forms of dress, drink and sex.[14] Politics and aesthetics could merge to forge push-and-pull factors shaping itinerant lives; when the Japanese socialist Sen Katayama went to New York in 1916, it was to help organize the Socialist Party of America, but also because his daughter Yasuko wanted to 'check out the New York scene' in order to pursue her career in choreography.[15] Politics and aesthetics would also merge in the way that Roy's kind of cosmopolitanism would become distinct from that of other revolutionaries.

An important element in being perceived as iconic was the impression that one was singular. In the way Roy was remembered by other cosmopolitans, or in which he recounted his own life, his unusualness was emphasized. His published recollections are full of famous foreign figures but largely left out the presence of other Indians Roy had worked with in Soviet Russia, such as Mohamed Barakatullah and Mahendra Pratap, who had met Lenin back in 1919, as well

---

[13] Elliot Einzig Porter, 'The Two Vons: The World War I Secret Government Investigation of Erich Von Stroheim', *Film History: An International Journal* 22, no. 3 (2010): 332.
[14] Christopher Lasch, *The New Radicalism in America, 1889–1963: The Intellectual as a Social Type* (New York: Vintage Books, 1965), xiv–xv.
[15] Spenser, *Stumbling Its Way through Mexico*, 85–6.

as Roy's direct colleagues Abani Mukherji (1891–1937), and M. P. T. Acharya. Indians were a small minority in cities like Mexico City, Berlin and Moscow, but Roy further emphasized his singularity there, and the impression he made on others often occluded the presence of his peers. In his memoirs, the US radical Bertram Wolfe recalled how Roy had stood out to him while he was travelling to Russia by ship in 1920 – after having made the acquaintance of all other Indians in Mexico City.

> I walked over to the tall, handsome Indian, at least three inches taller than my six feet, and well built. A Brahman, I thought, no one else would be so well fed in India that he could grow to be so tall – Roy, too, was a Brahman, maybe it *was* M. N. Roy. 'I beg your pardon, sir, do you speak Spanish?'
> He stared at me in astonishment. Then, after a pause, 'Yes, I do.'
> 'Then I know who you are.'
> 'How could that be?'
> I come from Mexico City. There were five Hindus there in 1919. I know Gupta, Sen, Khankhoji, and Basra. You must be the fifth.[16]

By recalling Roy as he did in his memoirs, Wolfe positioned himself as a clever and knowing subject, not merely familiar with all of the Indians in a foreign city, but astute enough to deduce what the distinguishing features of a Brahmin might be. His astuteness was so that he even professed to having astonished Roy, who was travelling hoping not to be noticed. Apart from positing Wolfe as a discerning cosmopolitan, his writings contributed to the making of Roy as an icon, whose existence was less pertinent to the actual Indians living in Mexico City in 1919 than to the projections Wolfe made onto the canvas of the highly unusual man he had known.

In another description, Russian revolutionary Victor Serge portrayed Roy and his first wife Evelyn among a long list of delegates to the Second Congress of the Comintern in a scene where all of their appearances merited description; Christian Rakovsky (1873–1941) was bearded and dressed in a crumpled uniform but spoke perfect French, Vasil Kolariov (1977–1950) was large, heavy and important, David Wijnkoop (1976–1941) looked aggressive with his protruding jaw, but Roy and Evelyn were the pièce de resistance of the scene: 'From India, by way of Mexico, we had the Manabendra Nath Roy: very tall, very handsome, very dark, with very wavy hair, he was accompanied by a statuesque Anglo-Saxon woman who appeared to be naked beneath her very

---

[16] Wolfe, *A Life in Two Centuries*, 318.

flimsy dress. We did not know he had been under suspicion in Mexico ...'[17] Hinting at future rumours and mistrust, Serge's sensual intensifiers suggest the orientalist excitement the appearance of Roy and Evelyn at times caused. Whereas Evelyn could have been seen as a sign of Roy's Europeanization, more often she underlined his very exoticness by contrast, tinged with eroticism. The slightly breathless quality of descriptions of encounters with Roy and Evelyn certainly have to do with Roy's looks,[18] but their repeated nature make it clear that Roy was not merely good-looking, but that his appearance satisfied a desire for difference that existed more generally in cosmopolitan circles.

During Roy's time abroad, considerable resources were devoted to creating visual evidence of his presence there. In Mexico City, he was enough of a remarkable figure for a German society lady there to paint his portrait.[19] But a particular effort was made by the Communist International, as capturing images of foreign delegates was part of the propaganda efforts it made towards establishing its global credentials.[20] During his time with the Comintern, not only was he photographed wearing a Red army uniform,[21] he was also the subject of a more intimate portrait in which he pensively looks beyond the frame of the picture, one hand supporting his chin. Even in the old, grainy image, he looks strikingly handsome with his hair curly and neat, wearing a white shirt with an open collar. The photograph must have been carefully taken and developed between 1920 and 1928. While the pose suggests reflection, there seems to have been a romantic element to it as well. This impression is heightened by the fact that the picture was kept for many years by Roy's first wife, Evelyn Trent. When Roy died in 1954, his second wife Ellen asked Evelyn for images of her time with Roy. Trent-Jones responded: 'I feel sure I have some, but not many, as one did not carry photographs around in those days or have them taken and I have moved so many times in my life, so things get lost or destroyed.'[22] The practical exigencies of mobility and clandestinity would co-determine what pictures remained and what image was built, but so did the affectionate memories of and letter-writing between two women who had never met and were on different continents – yet who had had the same husband. When Trent-Jones sent the

[17] Victor Serge, *Mémoires d'un revolutionnaire, 1905–1945* (Montréal: Lux Éditeur, 2010), 143.
[18] Although the English translation of Serge's memoirs have it that his face was pockmarked. Serge, *Memoirs of a Revolutionary*, 106.
[19] Tenorio, *I Speak of the City*, 278.
[20] Sergei Morozov, Anry Vartanov, Grigory Shudakov, Olga Suslova, Lilya Ukhtomskaya, eds., *Soviet Photography: An Age of Realism* (New York: Greenwich House, 1984), 9.
[21] See below.
[22] Letter from Evelyn Trent-Jones to Ellen Roy, 27 June 1954, Evelyn Jones Correspondence, Catalogue 71: M. N. Roy Papers Section II, NMML.

The Making of a Cosmopolitan Persona 67

Figure 2.1 Delegates to the Second Congress of the Comintern at the Uritsky Palace in Petrograd. Niday Picture Library / Alamy Stock Photo.

picture, Ellen Roy responded: 'To have sent me these photos! I cannot thank you; [...] The Moscow photo is haunting.'[23] One thing the picture shows is how a particular body could be presented as beautiful in a way that was political, as it did not merely reflect the looks of the individual but also showed the politics of its presence in revolutionary Russia. What Ellen perhaps found haunting was seeing the man she had shared her life with, once their life together was over, captured at a time when it had not yet begun.

More than the cherished portrait, the above image of delegates to the 1920 Second World Congress of the Comintern would come to shape Roy's legacy.[24] It shows the steps of the Uritsky Palace in Petrograd, with a group of leading Cominternians, including Vladimir Lenin, Grigory Zinoviev (1883–1938) and Maria Ilyinichna Ulyanova (1878–1937). M. N. Roy stands at the centre on the

---

[23] Letter from Ellen Roy to Evelyn Trent-Jones, 21 June 1954, Evelyn Jones Correspondence, Catalogue 71: M. N. Roy Papers Section II, NMML.

[24] In 2007, the picture was adapted for the poster of a documentary film called *Le Brahmane du Komintern*. Théodor Bergmann, Ludmila Karlova, Roy Medvedev, Ignacio Saldivar, Daniela Spenser, Paco Ignacio Taibo II. *Le Brahmane du Komintern*. Directed by Vladimir Léon. Paris: Institut National de l'Audiovisuel, 2007.

steps, and barely visible over his shoulder is Evelyn. The image shows how M. N. Roy stood out among European and North American communists through the colour of his skin as well as his imposing height, yet fitting in quite seamlessly through the way he was dressed and the seeming ease of his pose. It also shows him centrally and confidently, ready to hold the attention of the communist world, and offering it something in return that is otherwise not in the picture: not just an image, but a perspective from India. He was not present as merely a body, but as a speaker and intellectual, and his opinions would often be at odds with his audiences' expectations and desires.

For audiences in India, Roy became a recognizable figure – beyond small groups of leftists – once he had returned there in 1930, emerged from prison in 1936 and tried his hand at All-India politics. His past exploits abroad were a key part of his image, as a Kolkata-based newspaper emphasized '... he succeeded not only in overcoming [his trials and tribulations] but also in establishing his name and fame in alien countries and himself as a political force of considerable intellectual and spiritual significance.'[25] An invitation a Muslim student group in West Bengal sent to Roy in 1939 contrasted the provincial nature of their own environment with Roy's experiences: 'Your kind visit to this poor district in the foot of the Himlayas [sic], neglected and exploited so long, will be conducive toward its progress. [...] You will be simply astonished how the people of this district appreciate your sacrifice and your cosmopolitanism.'[26] Roy's itinerant past was a powerful projection screen, whether it was for describing supposedly masculine ideals of adventure or for a notion of cosmopolitanism that was intimately linked with ideas of modernity and progress, assumed to be originating outside of India.

A cosmopolitan persona could be good or bad, but it certainly was worth mentioning. The *Hindustan Times* went with a cosmic angle when it editorialized:

> We [...] have a constellation of stars in India – Pandit Jawaharlal, Rajaji, Sardar Vallabhai, B. Rajendra Prasad[27] and a faint star in the horizon coming into view – Mr. M. N. Roy. Who will become the one sun of the constellation, for two suns may turn out to be too many for us? [...] The only 'foreign' body for this priesthood is Mr. Roy – but it is a small one at present.[28]

---

[25] *Hindustan Standard*, 23 January 1938, Press Clippings section (vi) 1937–44 Editorials, Catalogue 70: M. N. Roy Papers Section I, Nehru Memorial Library and Museum, Delhi, India (hence NMML).
[26] Letter from District Muslim Students' League to M. N. Roy, 17 May 1939, Papers relating to Muslim Radicals 1939–40, Subject Files 10, Catalogue 71: M. N. Roy Papers Section II, NMML.
[27] Well-known politicians: Nehru, C. Rajagopalachari (1878–1972), Vallabhbhai Patel (1875–1950) and Rajendra Prasad (1884–1963).
[28] '... IF GANDHI LIVES', *The Hindustan Times*, Press Clippings (iii, iv, v, vi, ii) Catalogue 70: M. N. Roy Papers Section I, NMML.

In this overt comparison of the respective importance of political figures, Roy only features as a minor entity. And yet, it is the foreignness of his body that earns him a place in the lineup to begin with. What made Roy potentially desirable to audiences in India was often different from what had made him so abroad; for one, orientalist or theosophical longings were hardly an ingredient. Yet, the way in which he had been a cosmopolitan abroad and that had allowed him to make his way through various spaces also meant that he became recognizable as an elite cosmopolitan figure in India, not only through the fact of the road he had travelled, but through the associations others had with his past and the practices through which he would come to cultivate this image in his way of life, politics and writings.

Changing names

If cosmopolitans reached a degree of an iconic status, it would be attached to their name – a name which in many cases was not the one their parents had given them. The use of aliases and pseudonyms was among the most obvious ways in which to change one's affiliations and the associations others attached to one's person. A popular article about the Indonesian Tan Malaka cites the many names he used throughout his highly itinerant life that took him across Asia and Europe, and links them not only to the need for him to escape police detection as a wanted revolutionary and communist, but also to his Pan-Asian beliefs. Tan Malaka was, for example, delighted that he only needed a different name to be taken for Filipino, or to pass for Chinese in the eyes of the British police in Hong Kong.[29] Tan Malaka himself reflected on some of his pseudonyms in his writings, and seems to occasionally have used them as puns at colonial authorities, with names that approximated the word 'alias' or one underlining his status as a refugee from the authorities: 'Howard Law'.[30] Malaka's Comintern

---

[29] Born as Ibrahim, he received the title of Datuk Tan Malaka in his youth, and variously lived as Hassan, Cheung Kun Tat, Howard Law, Elias Fuentes, Eliseo Rivera, Ossorio, Tan Ho Seng, Hasan Gozali, Ramli Hussein, Iljas Hussein and Oong Song Lee. Oliver Crawford, 'The Many Names of Tan Malaka', Afro-Asian Visions (blog), Medium, 21 May 2019, Accessed 10 June 2020, https://medium.com/afro-asian-visions/the-many-names-of-tan-malaka-163a6f2e0bc8#:~:text=In%20his%20autobiography%2C%20titled%20From,Hussein%20and%20Oong%20Song%20Lee.

[30] 'Two of his names, Elias Fuentes and Iljas Hussein, are puns on the word 'alias'. […] Hasan Gozali, the name he used to travel to Singapore in 1926, is an allusion to the mediaeval Islamic philosopher Al-Ghazali.' Like Al-Ghazali, whose books had been taken by robbers, Tan Malaka too was forced to work from memory, as he wrote several books while in prison. *Ibid.*

colleague Ho Chi Minh would become world famous under a name that was among dozens of pseudonyms he had used.[31] Subversiveness and a need for clandestinity could become part of an image or identity that became publicly known, as a badge of adventurousness and cosmopolitanism. As such, it was in the possession of several names that belonging to their group could be signalled.

Roy's journey around the world could be rendered into the different aliases he used along the way. By the time he left India in 1915, he was known to British intelligence under his birth name, Narendranath Bhattacharya. During the ten following months, moving from India to the Dutch East Indies, the Philippines, China and Japan, he used the names 'Hari Sing, Mr. White, D. Garcia, Dr Mahmood, and Mr. Banerjee.'[32] Contemporary observers remembered him as having assumed the name of Charles Allen Martin,[33] or 'Father Martin' for his dealings in California.[34] On his way from Mexico to Europe in 1920, he used a Mexican passport with the name Roberto Allen y Villagarcía – the partly English name intended to help explain his poor Spanish.[35] While working from Paris in 1924, Roy used the name 'Richard,'[36] and some of his letters were signed as 'Buddy'; all these different names could be confusing, as the repeated questions of the US oppositional communist and close friend of Roy's Jay Lovestone showed when he was communicating with Roy's associates in India in 1934: 'I am not sure we are positive as to who is "Buddy."'[37] What could provide a point of recognition could also shroud someone in mystery.

Name changes could form a point of recognition between different actors, even if they hailed from different spaces and pursued different political projects. Of his meeting with Roy in Mexico City, US radical Charles Phillips would later remember this similarity between the two men: 'In early spring 1919 […] I met a tall, slim, handsome Hindu Brahmin of twenty-nine known as Manabendra Nath Roy. Another pseudonym. (Mine, at the time, was Frank Seaman.)' Phillips saw this as the marker of professional revolutionaries, who were '… destined

---

[31] Peter Neville, *Ho Chi Minh* (Boca Raton, FL: Routledge, 2018), 1.
[32] Lahiri, *Indian Mobilities in the West*, 71.
[33] Lala Lajpat Rai, *Autobiographical Writings* (New Delhi: Delhi University Publishers, 1965), 216.
[34] Quoted in Samaren Roy, 'Introduction', in *The Way to Durable Peace*, ed. M. N. Roy (Calcutta: Minerva, 1986), 5–6.
[35] Tenorio, *I Speak of the City*, 275.
[36] Lahiri, *Indian Mobilities in the West*, 71.
[37] Letter from Jay Lovestone to Comrade, 15 August 1934, Jay Lovestone Correspondence, Catalogue 70: M. N. Roy Papers Section 1, NMML.

to live several very different lives under a variety of names.'[38] The ideological itineraries of Roy and Phillips up until their meeting had been vastly different; Roy's being in the revolutionary branch of Bengal's Swadeshi movement, and Phillips' in the radical socialism of early-twentieth-century New York City. A sense of recognition between them was nevertheless possible in a milieu of anglophone expatriates in Mexico City, where ideas of radical change were embraced by various young intellectuals. For them, going by various names was the rule rather than the exception.

In the case of the US radicals, Roy associated with in Mexico, aliases were common, especially as they entered the fold of the Communist International, but had to be more permanent if they wanted to build up a life in anti-communist times in the United States. Charles Phillips would variously be known as Frank Seaman, Jesus Ramirez, Manuel Gomez, comrade Tanner or mister Gordon, and spent his later years as a financial analyst on Wall Street under the name of Charles Shipman. Louis C. Fraina, founding member of the American Communist Party in 1919, later became a professor of economics under the name Lewis Corey.[39] The names Agnes Smedley used during the years she travelled across the United States, Europe and Asia as a reporter, advocate for Indian independence as well as birth control, and later a communist spy, were particularly wide ranging, among them 'Ayahoo, Violet Ali Khan Hussain, Mary Rogers, Alice Bird, and Mrs. Petroikos.'[40] For Smedley, an alias could reflect her chosen affiliations with cultures other than the one she grew up in. Her first pseudonym, Ayahoo, for example, was one Smedley assumed to underline her partly Navajo heritage in a rejection of the racial hierarchy she was raised with in the American West of the early 1900s.[41] A chosen name could go a long way to establishing such an affiliative identity.

Established grounds for name changes among Roy's circles were to escape antisemitism in the United States upon migrating there,[42] as well as the practice of women changing their names after marriage. Yet, as a distinguished cosmopolitan practice they were imbued with added implications for either going unnoticed or signalling affiliations. For Roy's first wife Evelyn, née Trent, her married names would often serve the purpose of pseudonyms. During the

---

[38] Shipman, *It Had to Be Revolution*, 75; xii.
[39] Spenser, *Stumbling Its Way through Mexico*, 64.
[40] Fuechtner, 'Agnes Smedley between Berlin, Bombay', 401.
[41] Price, *The Lives of Agnes Smedley*, 37.
[42] Shipman, *It Had to Be Revolution*, 6.

years she worked alongside Roy, Evelyn often published under the name 'Evelyn Roy' in the *Labour Monthly*, a journal associated with the Communist Party of Great Britain. When she wrote the journal she and Roy published from Berlin and Paris for a largely Indian readership, she used the pen name Santi or Shanti Devi.[43] In this way, she associated herself with the cause of Indian independence, even though she had never been to India.[44] Back in the United States during the McCarthy years, she kept her past hidden from public view and lived under her second husband's name as Evelyn Jones, declining to be publicly associated with her first husband and their communist past.[45] What could be indicated by a name could also be hidden again. Using married or unmarried names in order to hide was something the wife of Mikhail Borodin (himself occasionally known as 'Chambers'), Fanya Borodin (born Orluk), attempted. In 1927, she was taken hostage in China as the wife of a high-ranking Soviet representative. According to Rayna Prohme, she was in danger of being '… put to death with telling effect,' by a militarist who had made a habit of abducting and abusing women.[46] Asked for her identity, Fanya gave her last name as Grossberg but when confronted with the truth and at risk of being detained for her lie, she insisted it was her maiden name, the continued use of which was common Soviet practice.[47] Fanya was captured but not killed, and her attempt to navigate different naming conventions to her own advantage shows some of the possibilities and constraints under which itinerant women could change how and as what they were recognized.

From other figures' biographies, it becomes clear that the use of different aliases was common enough to serve as a point of recognition, but could have different implications. Har Dayal's multifaceted career was reflected in the different aliases he used, for example the pseudonym 'x.y.z.' with which he signed publications in Calcutta's *Modern Review*, the Turkish passport he received in 1914 in the name of Ismail Hakki Hassan, or a 1915 letter to the renowned US anarchist Alexander Berkman signed Israel Aaronson. During the end of the First World War, Har Dayal resided in several German spa towns

---

[43] See for example M. N. Roy, Abani Mukherji, Santi Devi, 'An Indian Communist Manifesto', *Glasgow Socialist*, 24 June 1920. Marxists Internet Archive (2011) https://www.marxists.org/archive/roy-evelyn/articles/1920/manifesto.htm.

[44] Letter from Evelyn Trent to Henk Sneevliet, 13 March, [1926], Roys Correspondence Inventory 362, Archive Henk Sneevliet, International Institute for Social History, Amsterdam, the Netherlands (hence IISH).

[45] Biographical File, Correspondence P. C. Joshi, Muzaffar Ahmad, Box 1, Collection Number 71023: Evelyn Jones Papers, Hoover Institution Library and Archives, Palo Alto, California, USA (hence Hoover).

[46] Hirson, Knodel, *Reporting the Chinese Revolution*, 96; 73.

[47] Jacobs, *Borodin*, 238.

to bolster up his failing health, using the name of Professor Mizra Osman.[48] The name Aaronson may have signalled his affinity with the leading figures of US anarchism, Berkman and Emma Goldman, both of whom were Jewish immigrants from the Russian Empire,[49] whereas the use of Muslim-sounding names in Germany could have something to do with the fact that agents from the German Foreign Office who worked with anti-British Indians during the First World War had intellectually been prepared to do so by orientalist studies that mainly concerned themselves with Muslims.[50] Har Dayal's names represented a step he made towards those he found himself in cooperation with or a means to blend in with different environments. Less known revolutionaries also adopted monikers that related to their travels and knowledge of the world. M. P. T. Acharya, for example, used the pseudonym Marco Polo, for an article he wrote for the Bombay journal *Freedom: The Anarchist Weekly* in 1951, signalling his transcontinental past.[51] Mahendra Pratap also adjusted his name to suggest his wide perspective. In 1920, he published a religious text in Germany, *The Book of the Religion of Love*. The extended moniker he used as his pen name signalled his religiously inflected pan-Asianism; Pratap presented himself as 'the chief Lover, Mahendra Pratap (Raja), Servant of Mankind,' on the title page, and signed the text as 'Mahendra Pratap, Singh, Moses, Peter, Mohammed Peer, etc.'[52] Pratap's signalled affiliations were as wide as his name was long, the 'etc.' suggesting an expansiveness that could not be contained.

Beyond shifting aliases as a distinguishing feature, a change of name could be embraced as a more stable shift in identity. Or in other words, what could be a mark of a clandestine or chameleon could become the marker of a convert. Converts were not uncommon among cosmopolitan circles. Apart from the Hindu monk from Austria Swami Agehananda, Roy's circles in India included the Austrian Baron Rudolf Omar von Ehrenfels (1901–80) who was an anthropologist as well as a convert to Islam.[53] Further afield, the life course of Mohamed Barakatullah was co-determined by two Muslim converts: in 1895, he

---

[48] The different aliases are detailed in Brown, *Har Dayal*, 119–20; 183; 208; 214.
[49] Kenyon Zimmer, *Immigrants against the State: Yiddish and Italian Anarchism in America* (Urbana: University of Illinois Press, 2015), 1–13.
[50] Kris Manjapra, 'The Illusions of Encounter: Muslim Minds and Hindu Revolutionaries in First World War Germany and after,' *Journal of Global History* 1, no. 3 (2006): 370–1.
[51] Ole Birk Laursen, 'M. P. T. Acharya: A Revolutionary, an Agitator, a Writer', in *We Are Anarchists: Essays on Anarchism, Pacifism, and the Indian Independence Movement, 1923-1953*, ed. M. P. T. Acharya (Edinburgh, Scotland: AK Press, 2019), 34;254–7.
[52] Mahendra Pratap, *The Book of the Religion of Love* (Marburg: Pratap, 1920), 1;89.
[53] Letter from Philip Spratt to M. N. Roy, 27 July 1948, Philip Spratt Correspondence, Catalogue 70: M. N. Roy papers 1, NMML.

was invited by the well-known British Abdullah Quilliam (1856–1932) to work at the Muslim Institute in Liverpool. And when he left for New York in 1899, it was because of the US Muhammad Alexander Russell Webb (1846–1916).[54] Spiritual mobility could go hand in hand with a geographical kind, or the two could provide for mutual support and recognition.

The alias that ended up becoming the name he is still known under, Manabendra Nath Roy, was one he assumed in California in 1916. One of Roy's biographers has conjectured that his assumed name signalled a move away from caste belonging as his original name had been a caste name, signalling the bearer's belonging to a Hindu, Brahmin family.[55] That Roy's sense of caste and class belonging had undergone changes both among revolutionary circles in Bengal and abroad is likely.[56] There was also the matter of convenience; for most non-Bengalis his new name would be easier to pronounce and remember than Roy's birth name. But by 1952, Roy wrote about his adopted name as the mark of a conversion to irreligiosity. In a letter to Swami Agehananda, discussing philosophical idealism, Roy signed with: 'M. stands for Materialist. – M. N. Roy.'[57] Few personal characteristics signal a given belonging, or filiation, as do inherited names. Lastingly changing a name to suit one's own purposes signalled a move away from all that came before. And in the environment of humanists, converts and philosophically inclined intellectuals surrounding him, Roy's name assumed extra meaning once again as a marker of him belonging to a group of people who did not belong either.

Swami Agehananda Bharati was a central example. He was born in Vienna in 1902 as Leopold Fischer. In his youth, he began learning Hindi and Sanskrit, and during the Second World War he volunteered to join Hitler's 'Free India Legion.' At the end of the war, he had been a captive of the British army and hoped to be taken for an Indian – and to be deported to India. To his dismay, he was found out as a non-Indian and sent back to Austria, from where he travelled to India on his own accord, and joined the Ramakrishna order, which would eventually give him his new name. In India, Agehananda became a religious figure as well as an academic, teaching at Benares and Delhi.[58] In the late 1940s, he joined Roy's humanist movement, and in 1956 he moved to the

---

[54] Khan, 'Universal Islam', 58; 59.
[55] Roy, *M. N. Roy*, 14.
[56] Suchetana Chattopadhyay, 'War, Migration and Alienation in Colonial Calcutta: The Remaking of Muzaffar Ahmad', *History Workshop Journal*, no. 64 (Autumn, 2007): 228.
[57] Letter from M. N. Roy to Swami Agehananda, Dehradun, 28 March 1952, Agehananda Bharati Correspondence, Catalogue 71: M. N. Roy Papers Section 2, NMML.
[58] Bharati, *The Ochre Robe*, 25–143; 175;206.

United States, where he would teach anthropology at several universities.⁵⁹ In his self-presentation, Agehananda's name assumed fundamental importance, as shown in his account of receiving it from his teacher when he became a monk:

> Victory to you, HOMELESS BLISS, Victory, Master Agehānanda Bhāratī, be thou the light to the three worlds' – he spoke loudly and distinctly. This then, was the name he had chosen for me – and he must have known why. Bliss through homelessness, bliss that is homelessness, bliss when there is no home – the Sanskrit compound of the privative prefix a + *geha* + *ānanda* covers all of these meanings.⁶⁰

Agehananda had had some experience of trying to appear to belong to a different group than he had been born into, and ended up spending many years studying for his conversion as well as travelling India on foot. So even though he did not hail from the anti-colonial underground and belonged to a religious group that was in many ways anathema to Roy, the shared practices of re-calibrating belonging and always remaining weary of too much of it brought them together.

Changing clothes

Clothing featured prominently among Roy's cosmopolitan circles, both as a practice involved in negotiating perceptions of difference, and as a common topic for cosmopolitan reflection. In her description of Mexico, for example, Evelyn Roy used clothing in order to characterize the way in which the upper classes there affiliated themselves with Europe: '[The aristocrat] invariably makes himself more European than the Europeans in education, manners and habiliments.'⁶¹ The interests of this performatively European aristocrat, Evelyn wrote, coincided with those of imperialist Europeans and North Americans, and therefore the Mexican aristocrat formed a danger to the achievements of the revolution. Real Mexicans, in contrast, affiliated themselves with many things which were encaptured in their dress:

---

⁵⁹ Alfonso Narvaez, 'Prof. A. Bharati, 68, A Monk Who Served on Syracuse Faculty', *The New York Times*, 16 May 1991, https://www.nytimes.com/1991/05/16/obituaries/prof-a-bharati-68-a-monk-who-served-on-syracuse-faculty.html.
⁶⁰ Bharati, *The Ochre Robe*, 154.
⁶¹ Evelyn Trent-Roy, 'Mexico and Her People Chapter I', *El Heraldo de México*, 22 September 1919; Evelyn Trent-Roy, 'Mexico and Her People Chapter III', *El Heraldo de México*, 6 October 1919.

Men and women turned beast of burden jostle brilliant equipages; lace mantillas and broad sombreros vie with millinery from Paris and London; [...] The Mexican of post-revolutionary days has few prejudices; he may take on new creeds and fashions, but this is no reason in his mind for abandoning the old.[62]

Paying attention to clothing came naturally to people who operated in environments where they were perceived as different, and where a set of clothes could alter perceptions of class, national belonging and sometimes those of race.[63] Covering the body, it plays a large role in connecting possibilities for manipulation by the individual to public perception and social implications.[64] When changing clothes, people change the way they are seen – even if these changes cannot be controlled precisely. If the change is sustained enough, it will affect the way they see themselves and behave in turn. There is a link between clothing and identity, as it can on the one hand display an individual as belonging to a group, and on the other a distinction – but in this display it at the same time creates the notion that there is indeed such a thing as this group, or the possibility for distinction from this group.[65] On an international stage, clothing assumes even more importance for the clear associations with certain places attached to various forms of dress.[66]

There were important colonial and anti-colonial legacies to the use of South Asian and European styles of clothing among the Indian anti-colonial underground. Under the colonial gaze, different clothing types could function as a classificatory system for various kinds of 'natives,' and the use of European clothing by Indians could function as acts of resistance.[67] In addition, Indian

---

[62] Evelyn Trent-Roy, 'Mexico and Her People Chapter II', *El Heraldo de México*, 29 September 1919.
[63] Lahiri, 'Performing Identity', 414.
[64] Hildi Hendrickson, *Clothing and Difference: Embodied Identities in Colonial and Post-colonial Africa* (Durham: Duke University Press, 1996), 2.
[65] Margrit Pernau, *Bürger Mit Turban: Muslime in Delhi Im 19. Jahrhundert* (Göttingen: Vandenhoeck & Ruprecht, 2008), 349.
[66] Bayly, *The Birth of the Modern World, 1780–1914*, 2.
[67] Bernard S. Cohn, *Colonialism and Its Forms of Knowledge: The British in India* (Princeton, NJ: Princeton University Press, 1996), 106–62; Regardless of his own fondness for European suiting, Nirad Chaudhuri (1897–1999) wrote a personal memoir mocking upper-class Bengalis as well as Englishmen in European dress in early-twentieth-century Bengal. Of the first group, he recorded that '... there were no set of people better posted about the appropriate times and occasions for the different kinds of English clothes, and a wrong tie or hat was likely to give rise to more trouble among them than in the best English society.' Of the second: 'There was no costume which was more unsuited to the Indian climate than theirs. It was not simply that they themselves were uncomfortable in the clothes: if these latter could be supposed to have consciousness they would have been even more miserable. In the Indian climate and weather English clothes lost their firmness of structure, the colour simply faded away, the hang became limp and awry, and there was a general transformation towards the shabby which nothing could arrest.' Nirad Chaudhuri, *Culture in the Vanity Bag* (Bombay: Jaico Publishing House, 1976), 59–60; 72–3.

nationalist politicians' wearing of European fashions might underline their claim to parity with the colonizer, which did not exist in practice.[68] Women were largely excluded from this, as their dress was often seen as related to the private realm only instead of the public one of politics.[69] In addition to overt clothing practices, there were its capacities to conceal, which were adopted by those Bengali revolutionaries who adopted more violent methods, such as Roy. Secretive groups of revolutionaries who favoured direct action to remove the British from Bengal consisted of a largely upper-caste membership, which meant that they created a new image in the eyes of the police, as '… the robbers were unusually well dressed – often in jackets, ties, and hats – for criminal activity.'[70] Under the colonial classificatory terms used for the people living in British India, this was a surprising visual, since European styles were associated with the upper classes. Competing aesthetics of civility and competing needs for hiding versus communicating made the sartorial matrix all the more complicated.

Beyond the visual nature of clothing practices, the early-twentieth-century Swadeshi movement in Bengal sought to stop the economic exploitation of British India by boycotting foreign goods – particularly textiles. Apart from a focus on trade, this also included efforts to change people's tastes away from European styles. The alternative it put forward, however, was exclusive and costly, largely limited to a Hindu elite.[71] Concerning Swadeshi aesthetics, the poet Rabindranath Tagore (1861–1941) was a key influence. He came from a wealthy family in which European dress was common for males, a practice he began to resist out of an overall commitment to devising alternatives to colonial aesthetic and intellectual practices, drawing inspiration from Asia.[72] Tagore's biography is rife with instances of the poet and his nephews irritating their peers by, for example, attending a party in dhoti[73] and sandals – not even wearing socks – consciously flouting accepted standards of decency in dress.[74] In a collection of

---

[68] Mina Roces, Louise Edwards, 'Trans-national Flows and the Politics of Dress in Asia and the Americas', in *The Politics of Dress in Asia and the Americas*, ed. Mina Roces, Louise Edwards (Brighton: Sussex Academic Press, 2007), 7.
[69] Partha Chatterjee, *The Nation and Its Fragments : Colonial and Postcolonial Histories* (Princeton: Princeton University Press, 1993), 120.
[70] Ghosh, *Gentlemanly Terrorists*, 6.
[71] Sumit Sarkar, *The Swadeshi Movement in Bengal 1903–1908* (Ranikhet: Permanent Black, 2010), 78–86.
[72] Stephen N. Hay, *Asian Ideas of East and West: Tagore and His Critics in Japan, China, and India* (Cambridge, MA: Harvard University Press, 1970), 4; Cemil Aydin, *The Politics of Anti-Westernism in Asia: Visions of World Order in Pan-Islamic and Pan-Asian Thought* (New York, NY: Columbia University Press, 2007), 113.
[73] Draped and knotted garment covering the lower body.
[74] Krishna Dutta, Andrew Robinson, *Rabindranath Tagore: The Myriad Minded Man.* (New York: St. Martin's Press, 1996), 123.

letters written to his niece Indira in the 1890s, his concern with the relationship between dress and subjugation is an important theme:

> If we begin to rate the applause of Englishmen too highly we shall come to reject much that is good in us, and adopt much that is bad from them. We shall grow ashamed to go without socks, for instance, and cease to feel shame at the sight of their ball dresses. [...] Our *achkans*[75] will be cast aside as unsatisfactory apparel, but we shall replace them on our heads with hats that are hideous. In short, consciously or unconsciously, we shall have altered our lives and trivialized them, according to whether we are clapped or not.[76]

Iconic as Tagore would become,[77] from the 1920s onwards it was Gandhi who would increasingly define what looked Indian on an international stage. As the Mahatma, he burnt a powerful image of Indian dress onto retinas all over the world. With the Non-Cooperation Movement (1920–2), Gandhi's vision of properly Indian clothing was to have a central role in nationalist politics, when the revival of Indian textile production was once again a political strategy, encouraging all Indians to take part in its production and consumption. At the same time, homespun cotton or *khadi* was meant to be a leveller, all castes and classes wearing the same cloth rather than distinguishing themselves.[78] Almost from the start of Gandhi's khadi campaign Roy opposed its efficacy, as well as its messaging, describing it as one of bourgeois nationalism's 'impotent tactics' in his first book *India in Transition* (1920).[79] But the image was a strong one and Gandhi himself was its most powerful bearer. In his autobiographical writings he reflected at length on developing the iconic image of the man who attended the Round Table Conferences (1930–2) in a loin cloth, a shawl and sandals – a long way from the lawyer in a top hat and spats who had first travelled to London in 1888.[80] The Mahatma style had come after a deal of experimentation with various forms of Indian dress. What he created was not obviously tied to specific regions, but was developed in order to communicate an abstracted, highly symbolically charged, ascetic version of Indianness that attempted to

---

[75] A robe-like coat.
[76] Quoted in Dutta and Robinson, *Rabindranath Tagore*, 141–2.
[77] See Chapter 3.
[78] Lisa Trivedi, *Clothing Gandhi's Nation: Homespun and Modern India* (Bloomington & Indianapolis: Indiana University Press, 2007), 1–37.
[79] M. N. Roy, Abani Mukherji, *India in Transition* (Geneve: Edition de la Librairie J. B. Target, 1922), 272–4.
[80] Susan Bean, 'Gandhi and Khadi, Fabric of Independence', in *Cloth and Human Experience*, ed. Annette B. Weiner, Jane Schneider (Washington: Smithsonian Institute Press, 1989), 356.

The Making of a Cosmopolitan Persona 79

encapsulate all the people of the subcontinent.[81] In the process, Gandhi's saint-like image became more compelling within and outside of India than that of any politician before him.

Gandhi would come to stand out in London seeming quite so uncovered, but there are much earlier examples of forms of dress unsuited to certain environments acquiring a marked political significance.[82] Har Dayal had moved to Britain on an Oxford scholarship, and when he abandoned it in 1907, he began wearing a dhoti and kurta, recognizably Indian garments as political statements rejecting British civilization, notwithstanding friends' warning he would catch a cold. Yet, the meaning of Har Dayal's sartorial statement was different depending on who saw it; Ramsay MacDonald (1866-37), who would become Britain's first Prime Minister from its Labour Party, wrote that Har Dayal's clothing must have a religious implication. The cousin of Har Dayal's wife Sundar, science writer Gobind Behari Lal (1889-1982), however, later wrote that Har Dayal was not a religious man, but was only interested in the cultural aspects of his religion.[83] Even though clothing is a central way to alter the visual impression a body makes, the way its messages are received greatly depends on viewers' expectations and assumptions.

Beyond national independence and resistance, clothing offered an avenue to experiment with ways of displaying social and political affiliations. In early-twentieth-century New York's East Village, clothing was an inevitable part of what has been called 'lifestyle radicalism' and entailed a break with clothing that had been seen as looking good until then, especially when it came to femininity.[84] The radical Agnes Smedley also wedded sartorial experiments with her persona with political statements. She experimented with clothes signalling various belongings, for example using rural 'cowgirl' dress to stand out among the urban intellectuals in New York, but also later, by wearing a Red Army uniform in

---

[81] Emma Tarlo, *Clothing Matters: Dress and Identity in India* (Hurst & Company: London, 1996), 64-77.
[82] In a mirror image, writer Nirad Chaudhuri reflected at length on the unsuitability of English dress for Indian climates, as well as its wearers' persistence to nevertheless put it on: 'There was no costume which was more unsuited to the Indian climate than theirs. It was not simply that they themselves were uncomfortable in the clothes: if these latter could be supposed to have consciousness they would have been even more miserable. In the Indian climate and weather English clothes lost their firmness of structure, the colour simply faded away, the hang became limp and awry, and there was a general transformation towards the shabby which nothing could arrest.' Chaudhuri, *Culture in the Vanity Bag*, 72-3.
[83] Brown, *Har Dayal*, 36-41.
[84] Price, *Lives of Agnes Smedley*, 58.

China – as a woman.[85] For Smedley, standing out through her dress was a part of her radical politics, rejecting the standards of respectability of her native country through the medium of what she put on and what she did with her body. Apart from that, living among ever-changing circles, in changing places, required the construction of changing forms of self-projection to adequately meet them. Apart from cowboy hats and uniforms, Smedley had also used South Asian dress as a part of her political repertoire. In 1917, she moved to New York, to conduct energetic campaigns protesting the deportations of Indians and agitating for Indian independence as the head of an organization called Friends of Freedom for India. Smedley's work included putting on displays of solidarity, for example at the St Patrick's Day parade of 1920. To the supporters of the FFI, she wrote:

> All the Hindus in the city, practically, will wear native costume and turbans and march; then at least as many American women dressed in Indian costumes will march. We have the Indian republic flag and banners demanding independence. Watch for the movies and you will see us big as life. […] I will be there all dressed up with nowhere to go, hair blackened and all.[86]

Smedley's parade aimed to make the Indian people appear in the streets of New York, using bodies, items of clothing and flags. Since there was a dearth of Indian women in the United States of the early twentieth century, US women substituted them, clad in saris, their hair dyed. Clothing allowed Smedley and her colleagues to make a part of the Indian population virtually present in the streets of New York, asking for attention to her cause.[87] This meant that she herself assumed a mobility, across spatial and racial divides, that was available to her, but not to the women she sought to represent. Smedley often met with the accusation that she took on a role that was not properly hers within the movement, purporting to be more of an Indian nationalist than the Indian nationalists.[88] Clothing could play a role in visually crossing boundaries between what was assumed to belong to one's own culture or to another. The ability to do

---

[85] Janice MacKinnon, Steve MacKinnon, 'Introduction', in *Portraits of Chinese Women in Revolution*, ed. Agnes Smedley (New York: Feminist Press, 1976), vvxi.
[86] Letter from Agnes Smedley to Friends of Freedom for India, 1 March 1920, Correspondence, Agnes Smedley Microfilm, NMML.
[87] Minh-Ha Pham has theorized about the role of clothing as an orientalist technology that can achieve '… the virtualization of racialized environments and bodies.' Minh-Ha T. Pham, 'Paul Poiret's Magical Techno-oriented Fashions (1911): Race, Clothing, and Virtuality in the Machine Age', *Configurations* 21, no. 1 (2013): 7.
[88] Kumari Jayawardena, *The White Woman's Other Burden: Western Women and South Asia during British Colonial Rule* (New York: Routledge, 1995), 237; Barooah, *Chatto*, 172.

so was unevenly distributed between genders, races and classes, and met with uneven levels of resistance.

The preoccupation with Indian dress found among US radical circles would be a subject of criticism of Roy's, as well as of Dhan Gopal Mukerji's. In his autobiography, Mukerji described his student days at Berkeley, where he struggled to make ends meet. Then, one day, he was told about a landlady who would rent him a room, free of charge: '… she asked me to put on my Hindu robe and sit in the parlour one hour a day in exchange for which she offered to give me my meals. I was astounded at this kindness.'[89] It seems that clothing played a role in Mukerji's ability to transfer the symbolic capital of his exoticism into economic capital, or at least free room and board. At the same time, the sarcastic praise of his landlady's largesse encapsulates a resistance to the requirements he had to fulfil in order to be Indian in the right way, from her point of view. It is as though without his turban, he was not Indian enough to meet her spiritual desires and deserve her largesse.

Smedley's wearing of a Red Army uniform in China was part of a much wider Comintern practice that allowed delegates to don it as a special honour. Doing so had strong implications of seriousness during a time Soviet Russia was at war. Roy had done so, and in his memoirs set himself apart from lower echelon delegates who had looked silly in their uniforms, not possessing the serious demeanour, and mere masculinity required to make them look right:

> The honoured delegates were proud of their distinction and went about in their ill-fitting military uniforms. In the summer, high boots were replaced by puttees. The novice could not tie them neatly, particularly when the legs were thin. They kept slipping down to the ankles or trailed behind on the ground when the inexperienced walker walked. The sight, verging on clownishness, naturally caused a good deal of fun among other delegates.[90]

In Roy's description, other delegates' lack of experience and insufficiently masculine bodies made for a frivolous picture where gravity would have been required. This contrast played a role more generally in reflections on dress, which could all too easily signal excessive frivolity. At the 1920 Comintern congress, for example, chairman Grigory Zinoviev warned that some men

---

[89] Dhan Gopal Mukerji, *Caste and Outcast* (Stanford: Stanford University Press, 2002), 283; 285.
[90] In uniform, only the upper echelons looked good. Lev Trotsky '… looked every inch a soldier, by birth, as it were,' and for Josef Stalin it was even more beneficial: 'In the long Red Army soldier's coat and with the star-marked peaked cap on, he looked taller than his five feet six inches.' Roy, *Memoirs*, 536; 363; 388.

had taken to communism as a 'fashion.'[91] This implied a lack of commitment and seriousness, matters that played a large role in the self-presentation of Roy and other communists.

Charles Phillips, for example, would come to write about his lack of 'seriousness' when experimenting with clothing while in New York's East Village:

> In those days some prominent rebels wore black flowing windsor ties to proclaim their bohemian individuality. [...] It had become a fashion, a badge. In effect a convention of unconventionality. [...] I wore one for a while (at least a short while) until I realized that a person concerned with the remaking of society should not risk compromising the issue with something so frivolous as eccentricity in dress.[92]

What may have been a way to fit into a radical environment during his youth became a way for Phillips to distinguish himself in terms of seriousness by the time he committed his memories to paper. When it comes to his narration of his journey to Russia from Mexico, Phillips' story of reaching Moscow did not only signal the life-threatening danger and daring of the enterprise, but also the trope of leaving everything behind. When illegally crossing the border at Narva in Estonia, Phillips decided to jump onto a train with Cyrillic writing on it – but only after having handed his suitcase to an inspector, in order not to raise suspicion of his escaping. It was thus without material possessions that he arrived, save for the clothes on his back, into which the 'silk credential' accrediting him as a delegate to the Comintern congress was sewn.[93] To immerse himself completely in the new ideology, in other words, to convert, Phillips had to fully cast off the old, which clearly communicated his full commitment to the cause.

In the milieu that formed around Roy in India in the 1940s and 1950s, clothing would remain a topic for reflection and method of communication. Incidentally, Agehananda would name his autobiography *The Ochre Robe*, taking his swami dress as a metaphor for his conversion. Clothing would also be an ingredient in Agehananda's anthropological reflections, as it was for another intellectual linked to Roy's humanist journals of the late 1940s and 1950s: Baron Rudolf Omar von Ehrenfels. As an anthropologist, he had promised Roy's journal *The Humanist Way* an article on 'Khaddar [khadi] Clothes and Social Change' in 1948.[94]

---

[91] Vatlin, *Das Jahr 1920*, 113.
[92] Shipman, *It Had to Be Revolution*, 19.
[93] Ibid., 99–100.
[94] Letter from Philip Spratt to M. N. Roy, 27 July 1948, Philip Spratt Correspondence, Catalogue 70: M. N. Roy papers 1, NMML.

Apart from an object for reflection, khadi was by then also an inevitable ingredient of political life. During the 1930s, Roy had made fun of his forced spinning activities in prison,[95] but during the brief time both him and his second wife Ellen worked for the Congress, both wore khadi. To those who knew his political ideas, this was worthy of comment. In J. B. H. Wadia's collections of Roy, clothing had become an essential feature of the man he had known. Recalling 'one fine morning' in 1938:

> ... we had to rub our eyes to believe the spectacle. We saw Roy coming down the staircase, immaculately dressed in a long flowing dhoti in Bengali style, a kurta and shawl and a cap [...] his sartorial makeup was most unusual. We had always seen him in a bush coat and trousers or sometimes in a suit.
>
> Hilla[96] joked at the transformation saying: 'Why Roy, you are metamorphosed. You have become a hundred per cent Indian all of a sudden.'[97]

In Wadia's recollection, Roy was emphatically non-Indian, without necessarily being labelled with another geographical belonging. Instead, his dress formed a part of a persona that signalled neutrality – or even something universal.

In his writing, Roy underlined that he embraced an aesthetic of practicality and comfort, things that ostensibly transcended cultural specificity. His own seriousness and the frivolity of others were often communicated with reference to their clothing. He paid detailed attention to what people had worn and often had his judgement ready, ranging from fellow Indian revolutionaries looking unkempt or downright odd,[98] to Mexican socialists aping a bourgeois clothing style – but poorly,[99] US radicals in Mexico City who looked ridiculous in their

---

[95] 'Meanwhile, I am learning to ply the divine spinning wheel, with which Gandhi proposes to save the world. It is an irony of fate that I should have to do this! The Mahatma has finally scored a point on me. If he only knew it!' Roy, *Letters from Jail*, 14.

[96] Hilla Wadia (?–1986).

[97] J.B.H. Wadia, *M N Roy, the Man - an Incomplete Royana* (Bombay: Popular Prakashan, 1983).

[98] Chandra Kanta Chakravarty, the leader of the Berlin India committee in New York, was described as a '... wizened figure in a soiled dressing gown, oil dripping from his unkempt hair,' leading the 'oily revolution' Roy, *Memoirs*, 35–6; To describe Chempakaraman Pillai, Roy dwelled on his claims to connections in high places, '... with men like Hindenburg and Ludendorff, whom he mentioned with their Christian names,' and focused on his appearance and occupation: 'Dressed up in a black frock-coat and striped trousers, his waving black hair oiled to shine, he looked the most attractive display in his curio shop.' Roy, *Memoirs*, 292.

[99] According to Roy, these intellectuals '... fiercely preached anarchism, but punctiliously wore celluloid collars, often soiled, as the badge of respectability. On Sunday mornings, they would compromise their anti-clericalism to accompany piously catholic wives to the Church. On that occasion, they never failed to put on frayed striped trousers, shabby cutaway morning coats and aged top hats. White spats worn on black shoes and yellow gloves, carried in hand, completed the conventional armour of the disguised revolutionary knight-errants. [...] The hallmarks of bourgeois respectability also penetrated the proletarian ranks. Executive members of the Socialist Party attended the committee meetings, not to mention formal social gatherings, in conventional Sunday clothes.' *Ibid.*, 164.

bad copies of Indian dress,[100] and leading figures in the Comintern wearing luxurious materials – and wearing them well.[101] These evaluations based themselves on minute distinctions, and showed Roy as a knowing observer. They were also accompanied with Roy's own style as an emphatic counterpoint: '... for years I was known to friends throughout Europe for my uniform grey flannels and brown coat.'[102] The symbolic charge he gave his sartorial preference was one of comfort and sensibility. These aesthetics were linked to his broader self-conception as a humanist, or a rational man of science, and eschewed intentional signallings of geographical belonging or particularity, even though the visuals deployed to do so were European. This visual claim of impartiality contained responses to the different meanings with which the practice of clothing had been imbued across the different milieus in which Roy had lived. Together, they also elevated Roy above them, free from particular associations, with a clear view of others' fashion mishaps.

Characters

Distinguished cosmopolitans wrote about their own lives and experiences for a range of purposes, but shared the notion that there would be readers for the stories they produced. The ego documents Roy and others produced constructed both an image of the author and an image of the world in relation to one another, intimately linking the two figures. Ego documents that showed an itinerant present or past cultivated a cosmopolitan public persona in a performative act.[103] Roy's memoirs are performative in this sense, and follow

---

[100] Of a social call at Linn Gale's, Roy described the garments of his partner in order to mock their interests in theosophy: '... Magdalena [...] had bundled herself clumsily in a loose garment, presumably to be taken for a *sari*. She had painted her feet red and went without shoes and wore a garland of white flowers on the head. It looked all very dramatic.' Ibid., 185.

[101] Of his first meeting with Borodin, Roy remembered the 'gorgeous silk dressing down' he wore, as well as his dislike of the 'long-haired males' among the US radicals. Ibid., 183–4; Of Grigory Zinoviev, he remarked: 'He was dressed in baggy trousers and a soft white shirt, its collar held together with a black silk string instead of a necktie.' Ibid., 347. Of Lev Karakhan: 'Perhaps because of his extraordinary good looks, he tended to be rather meticulous about his clothes, and was scornful of the fashionable affectation of dressing shabbily as the token of revolutionary fervour. His jealous detractors called him a bourgeois. No epithet could be more damaging in those days of demonstrative proletarian purity.' Ibid., 317.

[102] Ibid., 135.

[103] The '... autobiographical is intrinsically interpretative and performative.' Anshu Malhotra, Siobhan Lambert-Hurley, 'Introduction: Gender, Performance, and Autobiography in South Asia', in *Speaking of the Self: Gender, Performance, and Autobiography in South Asia*, ed. Anshu Malhotra, Siobhan Lambert-Hurley (Durham: Duke University Press, 2015), 14.

the model of 'Sanskritic usage' where '... [t]he actor's self is twice-created, or twice born.'[104] Roy literally labelled Mexico the land of his 'rebirth' as a cosmopolitan.[105] He also specified that it was not a rebirth as someone attached to Mexico, but rather as someone attached to nowhere: 'The fundamental change in the outlook on life enabled me to overcome the emotional attachment to the land of my rebirth. The new ideal of freedom was not to be attained within national or geographical boundaries.'[106] Cosmopolitan writing constituted a shared practice, contributing to the author's image as one claimed an intimate operational knowledge of the workings of difference. It also contributed to the making of other cosmopolitan characters, since other itinerant revolutionaries and intellectuals were almost unfailingly a part of these narratives. Even appearing in works of fiction was a practice cosmopolitans shared.

Counsel

Some cosmopolitan writing offered specific advice about specific places to readers less current with them. In 1901, Katayama published a guide for Japanese students who wanted to travel to the United States, drawing on his own experience studying at various colleges and universities and working to pay his way through school. Katayama's book was one of the most popular titles in a flourishing genre of advice literature that told students how to get into good colleges, how to behave in the city and how to make their way in the United States.[107] It was a highly practical piece of work, in that it spoke of the nature of the house work, cooking and cleaning that Japanese students might have to engage in order to make a living in the United States, as well as the best way to deal with Americans, expenses and having enough time to study.[108] It was on the strength of his own experience that Katayama offered his advice, which made his writings very specific to the environment and audience it addressed.

In 1920, Har Dayal published a piece of travel writing that also claimed to offer guidance on specific parts of the world. *Forty-Four Months in Germany and Turkey* was published ostensibly '... for the benefit of the people of India

---

[104] Kathryn Hansen, *Stages of Life; Indian Theatre Autobiographies* (New York: Anthem Press, 2011).
[105] Roy, *Memoirs*, 23.
[106] *Ibid.*, 217.
[107] Peter Duus, Kenji Hasegawa, eds., *Rediscovering America: Japanese Perspectives on the American Century* (Berkeley, CA: University of California Press, 2011), 46.
[108] *Ibid.*, 52–4.

and Egypt.'[109] The text concerned Har Dayal's experiences cooperating with agents of Imperial Germany during the First World War and amounted to a warning not to follow his example: 'During that one year I learned that the triumph of Germany would be a great calamity for Asia and the whole world.' It was on the strength of his direct experience with Germans that he offered this advice: '… no words can measure the depths of infamy to which the Germans can sink. They must be shunned as utterly unsociable and immoral bipeds.' To Muslims seeking Pan-Islamic alliances, in Turkey, he assured: 'There is nothing but dirt, and dead dogs, and scheming rascals in Stamboul.'[110] An important motivation for writing the text seems to have been Har Dayal's need to get into the good books of the British again, so he could acquire a passport and travel home to India. Likely with that goal in mind, he portrayed those Britain had recently found itself at war with as utter brutes, and wrote an apologia of empire that made him a topic of derision among other revolutionaries.[111] His experiences were then translated into Hindi by the India Office and distributed free of charge in India.[112] Regardless of his efforts, though, Har Dayal never made it back to India.

In the United States, Dhan Gopal Mukerji offered his perspectives on the land of his birth to new audiences when established himself in New York's East Village as a writer.[113] As a student at Stanford University, Mukerji had started publishing short stories with some success, and in 1923 he published his autobiography, *Caste and Outcast*. The book details Mukerji's life in Bengal in the first part, and his years as a student in Japan and the United States in the second part. Its themes, the differences between India and the United States, would remain at the centre of Mukerji's work when he wrote books both for children, which would win him a prize, and for grown-ups. *Caste and Outcast* was both a critical and commercial success, celebrated in the United States as the first book written about India by an Indian. But there were limits to what his US audience wanted to read about: '… Mukerji's observations about America […] were taken less seriously by the reviewers. Few commented on his thoughts about this country.'[114] Mukerji's US

---

[109] Har Dayal, *Forty-Four Months in Germany and Turkey; February 1915 to October 1918* (London: P. S. King & Son, 1920), 1.
[110] Dayal, *Forty-Four Months in Germany and Turkey*, 73; 1; 94; 49.
[111] Brown, *Har Dayal*, 223–6.
[112] Brown, *Har Dayal*, 221.
[113] Mukerji won the Newbery award, which celebrated writing for children in the United States, in 1928. Daniel J. Elam, 'Take Your Geography and Trace It: The Cosmopolitan Aesthetics of W. E. B. DuBois and Dhan Gopal Mukerji', *Interventions* 17, no. 4 (2015): 577.
[114] Chang, 'The Life and Death of Dhan Gopal Mukerji', 17.

audiences more readily took his cosmopolitanism as something that told them about India than about the United States.

Dramatis personae

Cosmopolitanism being a relational phenomenon, ego documents often contributed to creating others as cosmopolitan characters. In the memoirs of several of the US radicals Roy met in Mexico, Roy figured as a paragon of anti-imperial scheming, embarking on daringly improvised journeys, being at the same time fundamentally exotic as well as a close friend. In this way, the character Roy served a purpose of self-stylization, his globe-trotting character being created simultaneously. Carleton Beals' *Glass Houses* (1938) portrayed their author as an international left-wing journalist, always in the middle of the action, wherever in the world it happened. In this self-narrative, Beals used the character of Roy to craft his own worldly persona, using Roy's 'spectacular career' spanning clandestine travel around half the world, the international revolutionary intrigue of the Indo-German conspiracy, as well as the 1917 San Francisco trial that tried to put an end to it – and that included a courtroom murder. It also dwelled on an apocryphal story about Tsarist crown jewels Borodin was to have lost on his way to Mexico, and was now at great pains to retrieve. In his mobilization of Roy as a character, Beals made him at the same time exotic, writing that while in Mexico, '… he believed firmly in child marriages, the caste system and most of the traditional evils that thus far have prevented India from achieving nationhood, …' but also as a close confidant: 'He left a trunkful of effects, which I was to destroy. Roy then took me into his confidence about many things I have here related.'[115] It was through the simultaneous marking of Roy's difference and yet his trust in Beals and therefore their closeness that Beals established his own affiliation with difference.

Apart from Roy, a character who often appeared in cosmopolitan memoirs was Borodin. He too was a tall, impressive man, who was described as having a 'massive authority' as well as 'physical magnificence.'[116] His travels between Russia, the United States, Britain, Mexico and Spain added a mysterious tinge to his persona,[117] and his doctrinaire beliefs gave him an air of ruthlessness. An

---

[115] Beals, *Glass Houses*, 43; 52; 45.
[116] Quoted in Jacobs, *Stalin's Man in China*, 262.
[117] Jacobs, *Borodin*, 16; 69–2; 69–71; 85–6; 102–5.

iconic figure in her own right, Soong Mei-ling (1898–2003), sister-in-law of Sun Yat-sen, would commit her memories of the conversations with Borodin she had in Wuhan in 1926 to paper: '... his was the practiced mannerism of a man attuned over the years to talking, expounding, elucidating, guiding, evangelizing policies, strategy or tactics to various stations and posts around the world. [...] He was a man who gave the impression of great control and personal magnetism.'[118] These recollections were drawn up a long time after the communist cooperation with Sun's Kuomintang ended in disaster, so they may have been coloured by the animosity of subsequent events. Yet, they draw attention to the role of physicality and impressions in cosmopolitan encounters.

In letters written by Rayna Prohme, she felt her descriptions of Borodin ought to be preserved for posterity:

> Some day I must write you at long length about him – and when I do I want you to keep it for me. He has impressed me more than any person I have met in a long time, as a mind, a personality, a social force. [...] There are others I admire and respect, but B[orodin] is the only person I have felt who grasps the significance of forces, personalities, who sees the whole movement here in big historic terms. He has the power of throwing on his search light and making things stand out in bold relief, so the irrelevant disappears. Bill [her husband] thinks I am utterly dominated by him. I imagine I am.[119]

Writing about other cosmopolitans one encountered contributed to their iconic status, as in Prohme's descriptions that turned Borodin into a singularly great mind able to hold within it all the world's forces while clearly distinguishing which among them would make history. Her request that the recipient of the letter would keep its contents safe suggested that Borodin's greatness was something to be made in letters, and carried through time. At the same time, it betrayed an awareness of connections and a shared way of life being temporary, the realization of their end setting in before it had arrived.

Roy would do his own part in contributing to the public persona of some of the figures he had met along his way. In a collection later published as *Men I met* he evoked a chatty first-name basis with communist icons such as Lenin and Stalin, dwelling on the former's 'bald dome,' the latter's 'slightly pock-marked

---

[118] Chiang Mei-ling, *Conversations with Mikhail Borodin* (1970), 7; 9.
[119] Hirson, Knodel, *Reporting the Chinese Revolution*, 72–3.

face' and the diminutive height of both – at least compared to Roy himself.[120] Roy had a particular interest in Soong Ching-ling (1893–1981), Soong Mei-ling's sister and by then the widow of Sun Yat-sen, whom he described as '… the widow of the Father of the Nation, […] a sacred institution, not a human being of flesh and blood, even though the flesh may be young, throbbing with life, and the blood reaching fever heat under the pressure of suppressed emotions.' And there were other international celebrities Roy had gotten close and personal with. Before he had become the ruler of communist China, Roy had gotten to know Mao Tse-tung as '… a man who evidently knew what he wanted and was not to be deflected, either by reason or by authority.' Chou En-lai, it seemed, had also shown great promise already in the 1920s, as '… a dominating personality with the necessary physical appearance, tall and extremely handsome.'[121] Roy wrote as someone who had been on a par with these historic figures but also paid detailed attention to their appearances and bodies, suggesting that their close physical proximity was what qualified him as distinctly cosmopolitan.

Confinement

Many accounts of itinerant lives were written when their author was forced to stay put, as a place of pride among revolutionary autobiographies is assumed by the prison memoir. The genre's most famous authors include Gandhi, Nehru and Ho Chi Minh.[122] When it came to prison memoirs of mobile intellectuals, the contrast between their previous travels around the world and their confinement was often stressed.[123] Tan Malaka called his autobiography *Dari pendjara ke pendjara* or *From Jail to Jail*.[124] He had experienced imprisonment before the two-and-a-half-year confinement by Indonesia's republican authorities that allowed him to write his memoirs in the late 1940s. In 1922, Tan Malaka had been arrested by the Dutch East Indies' authorities after working for a trade union and the Communist Party of Indonesia (PKI); in 1927, by the United States administration of the Philippines; and in 1932, by the British

---

[120] Roy, *Memoirs*, 342; 534.
[121] The essays were later compiled in the volume *Men I Met*. Roy, *Men I Met*, 37;74;105;128.
[122] Majeed, *Autobiography, Travel and Postnational Identity*, 38; Helen Jarvis, 'Introduction', in *From Jail to Jail, Vol. I*, ed. Tan Malaka (Athens: Ohio University Center for International Studies, 1991), xxvi.
[123] Jarvis, 'Introduction', i.
[124] Ibid., xi–xiv.

government of Hong Kong.¹²⁵ In *From Jail to Jail*, Tan Malaka reflected on what it meant to change places when recounting his 1921 move to Semarang, Java after years spent in Deli, Sumatra and Bussum, the Netherlands.

> At first I was not aware that I was now in Java, in a physical situation as different from Deli as the earth from the sky. I did not notice that houses in Java were not like those in Deli or Bussum, and neither was the food. Nor was I aware that the climate in Semarang was different from that of the other places.¹²⁶

In his narrative, his focus on the revolutionary struggle against Dutch rule made Tan Malaka ignore all of the geographical and physical borders he had been crossing, showing the magnitude of his dedication – for who would not notice the differences between the food in Java, Deli and Bussum? It was his body itself that forced him to take notice, as every move between disparate regions caused Tan Malaka's tuberculosis of the lungs to flare up. 'Just as a glass of water plunged into boiling water will certainly break, so even a strong body will fall ill if suddenly put into a very different situation.'¹²⁷ Tan Malaka's account required the groundedness of the body to highlight the liberty of movement of his mind.

M. N. Roy too would publish his prison notes that reminisced about his itinerant past. During his six years behind bars, Roy filled nine A4-sized notebooks with dense handwriting, their contents divided into chapters and subchapters.¹²⁸ What was on these pages was clearly intended to be read one day. Roy's prison writings formed the bulk of the material printed by the publishing house Ellen and he set up after his release. Between 1940 and 1943, his Renaissance Publishers put out several volumes of prison writing. His *Letters from Jail* in particular evoked the contrast between Roy's confinement to various tiny cells, suffering the brutal heat and various diseases, and his glamorous past. His letters were rife with cosmopolitan longings for cold Berlin winters, reminiscences of a beheading in China, digressions on New York bohemians, the charm of Mexican and Dutch cursing and a homesickness for the 'Mecca of the snob,' Paris.¹²⁹ Such longings were felt under the dire circumstances of colonial imprisonment, when Roy was frequently ill and cut off from meaningful human contact. As he wrote

---

[125] Harry A. Poeze, *Tan Malaka: Strijder Voor Indonesië's Vrijheid: Levensloop Van 1897 Tot 1945* ('s-Gravenhage: Nijhoff, 1976), 160–6.
[126] Tan Malaka, *From Jail to Jail*, Vol I, 64.
[127] Ibid., 64.
[128] Nine A4-Sized Notebooks Filled with Dense Handwriting, Prison Notebooks, Catalogue 71: M. N. Roy Papers Section 2, NMML.
[129] Roy, *Letters from Jail*, 9–10; 78; 55.

to Ellen Gottschalk in his one permitted letter for May of 1934: 'A prisoner is a thing. He does not stay in one place or another. He is kept.'[130] There were more references to Roy's prison life, which he experienced as less-than-human, in his letters. Over the years, he would describe its 'inhuman atmosphere,' doubting his ability to physically withstand another year of it, and even contemplating suicide – while lamenting his inability to exercise even that freedom.[131] This sharp contrast between immobility and cosmopolitanism, and the refuge into the past it may have called forth as a mere survival strategy, did a great deal to contribute to Roy's public image.

In prison, art affected life. From friends abroad, Roy received books and magazines, though the amount he was allowed to receive was limited, and life became increasingly difficult for his friends in Europe as the 1930s progressed. Apart from works on science, philosophy and literature he had requested, Roy received 'some good detective stories [...] to satisfy my mean literary taste.'[132] Novels by S. S. Van Dine about a New York sleuth named Philo Vance, particularly *The Benson Murder Case* (1926) would become quite influential on Roy's language and his own writing.[133] He absorbed small turns of phrase from the fictional detective, referring to the Indian public he wanted to educate with his own views as 'these babes in the wood,'[134] and likely felt a modicum of identification with the singularly brilliant character. Like Roy, who would come to see himself, and came to be seen as, a Renaissance man, Vance was exceedingly knowledgeable about almost all subject matters, and described as '... a man so apparently diversified, and yet so fundamentally consistent.'[135] Particularly in terms of languages, Roy may have felt a pang of recognition for the main character when he declared: '"Culture [...] is polyglot; and the knowledge of many tongues is essential to an understanding of the world's intellectual and aesthetic achievements."'[136] Even the minutiae of dress were similar to how Roy came to describe himself: '... always fashionable – scrupulously correct to the

---

[130] The published version of the letters mentions that after these sentences, there were passages struck out by the prison censors. Roy, *Letters from Jail*, 88.
[131] *Ibid.*, 7–8; 135–6; 192.
[132] Roy, *Letters from Jail*, 150.
[133] *Ibid.*, 12; 17.
[134] *Ibid.*, 89.
[135] S. S. Van Dine, *The Benson Murder Case* (London: Hogarth Press, 1988), 19. The character's areas of expertise were described as including: '... Greek classics, biology, civics, and political economy, philosophy, anthropology, literature, theoretical and experimental psychology, and ancient and modern languages.' *Ibid.*, 21.
[136] *Ibid.*, 21.

smallest details – yet unobtrusive.'[137] Vance was built up as a truly individual character, far above all others:[138]

> An aristocrat by birth and instinct, he held himself severely aloof from the common world of men. In his manner there was an indefinable contempt for inferiority of all kinds. The great majority of those with whom he came in contact regarded him as a snob. [...]
>
> Being singularly free from the conventional sentimentalities and current superstitions, he could look beneath the surface of human acts into actuating impulses and motives. Moreover, he was resolute both in his avoidance of any attitude that savoured of credulousness and in his adherence to cold, logical exactness in his mental processes.[139]

Roy may have taken to the description of a man who was often seen as arrogant, but whose aloofness was instead explained with reference to his scientific disposition. In instances of self-making, fiction could provide a source of inspiration just as experience could.

Fact and fiction

Something that united the lives under scrutiny here is that, to many observers, they seemed stranger than fiction. Contemporary historians have needed the word 'quixotic' to describe both Mahendra Pratap[140] and Har Dayal, resorting to the title of a 1970 Grateful Dead song to accurately portray the strangeness of the latter's life.[141] Maia Ramnath has even written about Muhammed Barakatullah: '... if this unique figure had not existed, I might have been tempted to invent him.'[142] Beyond the cross-pollination between fact and fiction already discussed, authors of ego documents could use the strangeness of their experiences in order to portray themselves as having experiences their audience could never dream of having, or they could use it to push their worldliness into the realm of the otherworldly. In addition, they could become subjects of overtly fictitious literature – and draw on its imagery in their own self-making in turn.

---

[137] *Ibid.*, 20.
[138] '... I cannot remember ever having met a man with so undeveloped a gregarious instinct ...' *Ibid.*, 22.
[139] *Ibid.*, 19; 21.
[140] Carolien Stolte, 'Enough of the Great Napoleons!' Raja Mahendra Pratap's Pan-Asian Projects (1929–1939)', *Modern Asian Studies* 46, no. 2 (2012): 403–23.
[141] Zachariah, 'A Long, Strange Trip', 585.
[142] Ramnath, *Haj to Utopia*, 222.

Like Roy's Memoirs have been found wanting in their accuracy, other revolutionary autobiographies too have frustrated historians. Mahendra Pratap's reminiscences, for example, have been described as offering '... little insight into his thoughts. Pratap's autobiography is an account of his travels, detailing the trials and tribulations of life on the road, from the price of donkeys in Tibet to armed skirmishes on the steppes of Central Asia.'[143] Rather than seeing this as a lack, this aspect of Pratap's memoirs is here considered as exactly the point of them: they helped to create his own image as a man who could authoritatively write about the world. In this way, they form a logical extension of his other intellectual endeavours. There existed a meaningful link between Pratap's journal *World Federation (1929–39)* where he proposed designs for an ideal Pan-Asian future and the displaying of his itinerary. The latter served as a source of authority for his level of understanding of the world as a whole. In *My Life Story of Fiftyfive Years* (1947), published in India, Pratap used an account of his travels to bolster his identity as 'Mahendra Pratap (Raja), *Servant of Mankind*' and founder of *World Federation*, writing his books, '... sittig [sic] quiet at our Center World Federation Center for Japan, Kokubunyi Tokyo-Fu, Dai-Nippon.'[144] Even the title page made clear that Pratap's worldliness rested on his experience of various parts of the world.

Key is that Pratap's life story was full of experiences his readers were presumed to not have had, detailed in episodes titled, for example, 'Round the World in 1907,' 'India to Germany,' 'Back to Germany via Russia,' 'Japan to U.S.A.,' 'Our Tibetan Mission,' 'The Mongolian Adventures,' 'World Federation Movement in Philippines,' 'China Disappoints Me,' ending with 'As a Subject of No Land.'[145] In the final episode of his reminiscences, Pratap detailed a bureaucratic obstacle faced by British subjects in Japan, and his resolve to circumvent it using his connections: 'I knocked at five different doors of three different nationalities. [...] Now I have a document establishing the fact that I am not a subject of any country [...] Thank God!.'[146] What Pratap communicated in accounts of his life's journey is that when he wrote about the world and its organization, he was speaking from experience rather than from theory. As much is surmised by Stolte when she writes Pratap's vision of a future world order, in which he designed a new political make-up for the map of Asia. According to Stolte, it

---

[143] Stolte, 'Enough of the Great Napoleons', 406.
[144] (Raja) Mahendra Pratap, *My Life Story of Fiftyfive Years; December 1886 to December 1941* (Dehradun: World Federation, 1947), i–ii.
[145] *Ibid.*, 1–2.
[146] *Ibid.*, 357–8.

looked like 'more of a landscape of his own experiences than a serious plan.'[147] Painting a picture of his own experience, then, was exactly the way in which he established his credentials.

When Agnes Smedley published her fictionalized memoirs in 1929, they took the crossing of borders as their theme. This included the border between fact and fiction, as at one point in the text, the narrator mused: '… [e]ven now – sometimes I wonder what is real and what is phantasy; even now I think, sometimes, that perhaps these past years will fade and I shall know that I was only dreaming; for it is difficult to know what is lasting.'[148] Smedley's novel was emphatic in its blending of reality and fabulation, as well as in developing the idea of what it meant to change allegiance beyond everything one knew, but in the way in which she used her own past to craft an image of herself that exuded worldliness was not singular. Written as a novel, *Daughter of Earth* painted a picture of its protagonist Marie Rogers, an alias more often used by Smedley, as a character with allegiances extending far beyond those she was born into.[149] As the protagonist told a police officer in New York, who was investigating her ties to the Indian revolutionaries in that city: 'I have no religion – except to help people who work for freedom.'[150] Instead, the protagonist used kinship terms to define her relationships to the Indians in New York, signalling her elective affinities.[151] Overall, *Daughter of Earth* communicated that a sense of belonging was a matter of choice rather than being owed to those of the same race, country or religion.

At the conclusion of the novel, the cosmopolitanism of the main character was pushed beyond the physical earth when Smedley's character had a dream in which she visualized her own place in the world: 'I stood on the outer edge of the world. The earth lay back and below me. I was suspended in the air by my own weight. About me was the universe – deep blue, shot through with gray. Unchanging, ever-ending.'[152] Over the course of the novel, then, a perspective was developed that changed from being distant from one's country of birth, to

---

[147] Asia, or the 'Province of Buddha, was to have five districts: 'Golden Land' (Japan, Korea, Manchukuo, Tibet and China); 'Aryan' (Persia, Afghanistan and India up to Assam); 'Golden Aryan' (Burma, Siam, Anam, Cambodia, Malaya, the Philippines and Indonesia); 'Turan' (a proposed union of Turkish- and Russian-speaking peoples); and 'Arab' (including North Africa). [...]Shanghai was to be Sun-Ching ('Sun' because of Sun Yat-sen), and Moscow was to be rechristened 'Carl Marx'. Stolte, 'Enough of the Great Napoleons', 416.
[148] Agnes Smedley, *Daughter of Earth* (New York: Coward McCann Inc, 1929), 31.
[149] Price, *The Lives of Agnes Smedley*, 67.
[150] Smedley, *Daughter of Earth*, 263.
[151] Ibid., 267.
[152] Ibid., 335.

being on the outside of all notions of affiliation. The character possessing this perspective, Marie Rogers, was clearly a version of Smedley as they shared so many of their life's experiences, but through not making her a literal version of herself, Smedley opened the narrative to readers who might recognize themselves in it.

Even those who did not write memoirs or novels might make an appearance in them, as the life stories of cosmopolitans drew the attention of novelists in their own time. In a fictional portrayal of Har Dayal, the breadth of his intellectualism was deployed in order to broaden the horizon of a novel's romantic universe. Har Dayal inspired the character Dar Hyal in *The Little Lady of the Big House* (1915), a novel by the successful US writer Jack London.[153] The novel was set on a Californian ranch, where a series of philosophically inclined house guests made for a welcome contrast with the rural characters who otherwise populated the story and spoke a great deal of horse breeding. The guests included 'an epicurean anarchist,' an Australian 'making original researches in anthropology, or folk-lore-ology,' and a poet.[154] Dar Hyal was introduced as:

> A revolutionist, of sorts. He's dabbled in our universities, studied in France, Italy, Switzerland, is a political refugee from India, and he's hitched his wagon to two stars: one, a new synthetic system of philosophy; the other, rebellion against the tyranny of British rule in India. He advocates individual terrorism and direct mass action. That's why his paper, *Kadar*, or *Badar*, or something like that, was suppressed here in California, and why he narrowly escaped being deported; and that's why he's up here just now, devoting himself to formulating his philosophy.[155]

Jack London based various of his characters on real people, and Dar Hyal was no exception. The character was part of the scenery of the novel, providing a diverting background to an otherwise straightforward story of longing for the married mistress of the house by the visiting narrator. Including Dar Hyal in the story meant that considerations of the colour of her eyes and the figure she cut in a swimming costume could be alternated with references to the anarchist organization *International Workers of the World*, Herbert Spencer and the Hottentots.[156] The wider world, its politics and intellectual currents could, in this way, be introduced into an otherwise thoroughly provincial place. And this

---

[153] Roy, *M. N. Roy; A Political Biography*, 16.
[154] Jack London, *The Little Lady of the Big House* (New York: Grosset & Dunlap Publishers, 1916), 115; 6.
[155] *Ibid.*, 117.
[156] *Ibid.*, 257.

could happen in a neat and succinct way, through the force of one character who already counted as cosmopolitan and invoked associations with a large range of places, allowing for the exact details of the unknown, 'Kadar, or Badar, or something like that,' to remain fuzzy.

The British author Somerset Maugham had much more specific information to work with when he based a character in his spy novel series *Ashenden: Or a British Agent* (1927) on Virendranath Chattopadhyaya. Maugham had worked for the British Secret Intelligence Service during the First World War, and drew on his experience of shadowing the real Chatto for the story titled *Giulia Lazarri*. There, the Indian revolutionary Chandra Lal featured as 'the most dangerous conspirator in or out of India,'[157] who was certainly more dangerous than the real one, and in line with colonial fears, he was portrayed as a lascivious character with poor taste in women. Maugham's portrayal of Chattopadhyaya nevertheless positioned the protagonist, Ashenden, in a positive light, through his admiration of Chandra Lal's courage:

> ... his admiration for his adversary, [...] emanates from Ashenden's superior intellect, a product of his aristocratic upbringing. In contrast, Ashenden's supervisor, R., can only understand Chandra Lal through crude and explicitly racialist terms. Ashenden repeatedly attributes R.'s limited understanding to the latter's working-class background and his lack of cosmopolitanism.[158]

Through his identification with Ashenden, Maugham used Chattopadhyaya to portray himself as a person of cosmopolitan distinction, far superior to some of his more narrow-minded characters.

The most enduring fictional character based on a living revolutionary was inspired by Tan Malaka. During Tan Malaka's absence from Indonesia between 1922 and 1942, several spy novels based on the sparse information available about his doings had been published in Medan, Sumatra. The first among them was *Spionnage-dienst (Patjar Merah Indonesia)* (1938), which drew a newspaper article its author had written that had introduced Patjar Merah as a title for Tan Malaka. Soon, it was picked up by other newspapers, and Patjar Merah became widely understood to designate Tan Malaka.[159] The Patjar Merah books became a popular series of cheap novels.[160] Further instalments incorporated

---

[157] Bose, 'Transnational resistance and fictive truths', 508.
[158] *Ibid.*, 507.
[159] Their author was Matu Mona, the pen name of journalist Hasbullah Parinduri (1910–1987). Noriaki Oshikawa, 'Patjar Merah Indonesia and Tan Malaka: A Popular Novel and a Revolutionary Legend', in *Reading Southeast Asia*, ed. Takashi Shiraishi (Ithaca: Cornell University Press, 2018), 22; 34.
[160] *Ibid.*, 3.

Patjar Merah into many of the major news stories of the 1930s, such as '... the independence movements that dominated Asia at the time (in the Philippines, Thailand, French Indochina, and India); the Sino-Japanese war; the rise of fascism in Europe; the Spanish civil war; Stalin's purge of his opponents; and the war in Palestine.'[161] Tan Malaka had thus become a fictional celebrity in Indonesia, even while he was still abroad.

When Tan Malaka returned to Indonesia in 1942, as the Japanese occupation had ended Dutch rule, he read *Spionnage-dienst*.[162] It was thus after encountering himself as a character that Tan Malaka wrote his autobiography. There were telling similarities between the novels, in the account of his arrest and incarceration in the Philippines, in 1927, or his deportation from Hong Kong to China in 1933 – Helen Jarvis noting that Tan Malaka's own memoirs also read like adventure literature.[163] Novelists would continue to use Tan Malaka's name for a spy character who lived through highly adventurous accounts in places around the world – even after Tan Malaka himself died.[164] The image of Tan Malaka that had been created through the accounts of others in combination with those of Tan Malaka himself would thus outlive the historical actor, and remain mobile.

When Roy appeared in a novel, it was as a philosopher rather than an itinerant revolutionary. In a book by Mulk Raj Anand (1905–2004), one of the founders of the Progressive Writers' Association, Roy had been a source of inspiration for the character of Professor Varma in the novel *The Sword and the Sickle* (1942). The portrait was a critical one; full of theoretical knowledge of the world, Varma was a revolutionary who was '... too intellectual to be practical.'[165] As Anand would write in a 1983 newspaper article: '... I show Varma hoping to make revolution by writing about it. [...] I showed the failure of the Indian revolution at the stage: the failure of the intelligentsia; the failure of M. N. Roy and all the others.'[166] It is conceivable that Anand included his own failure among them, as his oeuvre evidenced a struggle of his own between the popular principles of the Progressive writers, who sought to create novels in a social realist style, addressing topics of social justice without religious qualms in all of India's vernaculars, and the fact that he wrote much of his work in English, which had a very limited readership within the subcontinent, and a

---

[161] Ibid., 29.
[162] Poeze, *Tan Malaka*, 486.
[163] Jarvis, 'Introduction', xxxix.
[164] Poeze, *Tan Malaka*, 482–90.
[165] Neena Arora, *The Novels of Mulk Raj Anand: A Study of His Hero* (New Delhi: Atlantic, 2005), 195.
[166] Quoted in S. A. Khan, *Mulk Raj Anand: The Novel of Commitment* (New Delhi: Atlantic, 2000), 55.

large one outside of it.[167] As was the case with Roy, Anand's socialist political project and linguistic and social focus were not obviously connected. Instead, he sought to address an audience more similar to himself, in Anand's case somewhere between British India and Britain, or even trying to create such an audience that would be receptive to his message. In a later interview, Anand described it as such: 'The English writing intelligentsia of India was ... a kind of bridge trying to span, symbolically, the two worlds of the Ganga and the Thames through the novel ... having to transcreate certain human beings into the as yet small third world of international men.'[168] In order to populate this small world, Anand had found a convincing character in the retired revolutionary Roy was by the time they met, even as the revolution he had tried to bring about never came.

Wanted: Life story

Whether it was in journalism or in fiction, cosmopolitan's life stories attracted attention. They could even be sold. Like many returned revolutionaries in India, M. P. T. Acharya tried to make some money by publishing his memoirs. In 1935, he published *Reminiscences of a Revolutionary* in Bombay's *The Mahratta*, detailing his wandering through India, Europe and North Africa.[169] Apart from that, he also wrote for the newspaper *Thought* about his dealings with communist luminaries such as Lenin, Angelica Balabanoff and Alexandra Kollontai.[170] It is from these memoirs that we know about the precarious life he lived abroad, meaning that even experiences of hardship could provide a minor compensation when they were later put into a story.

Among humanist circles in India, several members wrote memoirs, cultivating their transnational lives and the experiences and insights they had provided them with, often mentioning Roy as a cosmopolitan touchstone. The one-time British communist Philip Spratt (1902–71) published his memoir *Blowing Up India* in 1955. Its themes were the differences between Britain and India, and the flawed manner in which Spratt had tried to 'apply' Marxist laws to India as an emissary of the Communist Party of Great Britain, even though his knowledge

---

[167] Ben Conisbee Baer, 'Shit Writing: Mulk Raj Anand's Untouchable, the Image of Gandhi, and the Progressive Writers' Association', *Modernism/modernity (Baltimore, Md.)* 16, no. 3 (2009): 585–6.
[168] *Ibid.*, 581.
[169] Ole Birk Laursen, 'M. P. T. Acharya: A Revolutionary, an Agitator, a Writer', in *We Are Anarchists: Essays on Anarchism, Pacifism and the Indian Independence Movement, 1923–1953*, ed. Ole Birk Laursen (Edinburgh: AK Press, 2019), 20–1.
[170] Laursen, *We Are Anarchists*, 31.

of his new working environment was extremely limited. The memoir recounts Spratt's brief preparation for his mission in India: 'I hastily read up two or three books for the background, fixing firmly in my mind that Bombay is on the West coast and Madras on the east, not vice versa.'[171] Following accounts of his activities in India, including his arrest and trial at the Meerut Conspiracy Case (1929–33), Spratt emphasized the point of communists' lacking understanding of difference: 'In jail I had leisure for the first time to read about India, and found it a little disturbing. It was clear that the history of India had been very different from that of Europe.'[172] While his exposition served to establish Spratt's credentials to criticize doctrinaire communism, it also established his level of insight into the differences between India and Europe as being on a higher plane.

Part of the same humanist circles was Swami Agehananda Bharati, whose memoir *The Ochre Robe* (1961) explicitly stated why his life was worth reading about: '… great men have suggested that a man should write his autobiography at the age of about fifty. As it happens, I am only thirty-seven, but I propose to ignore their advice because I think I have already amassed sufficient material for an interesting autobiography.'[173] Arguably, it was Agehananda's crossing of linguistic, cultural and religious borders that had made his first thirty-seven years as interesting as another person's fifty. Agehananda believed his career had been unique enough to inspire his readers in their own lives, dedicating his book to people who '… feel that the tradition in which they were born, and which they once confidently accepted has failed them …'[174] His life story was written for readers who felt their filiative bonds were as constrictive as his had been. What Agehananda tried to show in his autobiography was that his perspective always remained unclouded by too high a degree of belonging, keeping everything in view at the same time. Reminiscing about his break from his own family, his conclusion was that he had not simply replaced it with a new matrix of belonging but had gone somewhere beyond that:

> I have been trying to be whatever I am, with no racial allegiance: a Hindu, yes, but not an Indian; a philosopher, but not a British nor an Austrian, neither a European nor an Indian philosopher; a humanist, but not a European humanist; a man mildly fond of comfort, but not dependent on American standards of plumbing. […] For without my hair, with the ochre robe, with *pān* in my mouth, with Hindi and Sanskrit on my lips and in my thoughts, I was becoming a

---

[171] Spratt, *Blowing Up India*, 29.
[172] *Ibid.*, 56.
[173] Bharati, *The Ochre Robe*, 9.
[174] *Ibid.*, 10.

Banarasi, and the idea of being sized up as a *pukka Banarasi bhayyā* is about as nauseating to me as that of being an *echter Wiener* – a typical Viennese.[175]

In Agehananda's profession of non-belonging, this was something that immediately and happily linked him to Roy: 'Instances of this criticism of a cultural environment into which the critic is born but which he never made are on the increase: M. N. Roy's cultural criticism was mainly of India, and my own initial criticism was of a German or a Continental set of thoughts and ideas.'[176] Agehananda cast both Roy and himself as intellectuals who marked their distance from the societies they had been born into.

When Roy considered writing his memoirs, it was explicitly because these might earn him some money, hopefully not just rupees, but pounds or dollars.[177] The fact that he seemed to be able to publish his memoirs abroad made him try to interest a literary agent for his other work. He attempted to have his book on European intellectual history, *Reason, Romanticism and Revolution* (1952 and 1955) published in the United States, offering his seemingly more desirable memoirs if the publisher would also take on these tomes.[178] Yet, Roy's life seemed more interesting to many than his other works. The US South Asianist Richard Park encouraged Roy to market his autobiography rather than '… heavy philosophical stuff.' Park was helpful enough to suggest writing '… a brief statement concerning the proposed scope for the Memoirs, in terms of dates, locations, and general subject matter …' Park could practically taste the book he would like for Roy to write for the US market, ending his suggestions with a few last points of advice: '3) Journal entries plus interpretation, a la Andre Gide; 4) M.N. Roy – Unique style! 5) Simple narrative, etc. etc.)'[179] The British journalist Guy Wint (1910–69) also tried to convince Roy to author of the appeal of his autobiography, and his imagination of their content was even more cinematic: 'It seems to me that you could paint an extraordinary

---

[175] *Ibid.*, 206.
[176] *Ibid.*, 275.
[177] Letter from Guy Wint to M. N. Roy about interest in London, Wint to Roy, 21 February 1954, Manchester, Guy Wint Correspondence, Catalogue 70: M. N. Roy Papers Section 1, NMML; Letter from M. N. Roy to Mavis McIntosh about interest in New York, 18 November 1951, McIntosh Correspondence, Catalogue 70: M. N. Roy Papers Section 1, NMML; Letter from Amarendranath Chattopadhaya to Ellen Roy on translation of memoirs into Bengali, 31 August 1950, Amarendranath Chattopadhaya Correspondence, Catalogue 70: M. N. Roy papers Section 1, NMML.
[178] Letter from M. N. Roy to Richard Park, 13 December 1951, Richard Park Correspondence 1, Catalogue 70: M. N. Roy Papers 1, NMML.
[179] Letter from Richard Park to M. N. and Ellen Roy, 24 January 1952, Richard Park Correspondence, Catalogue 70: M. N. Roy Papers Section 1, NMML.

panorama – India, Mexico, Russia, Germany, China; Pancho Villa, Lenin, Trotsky, Borodin, the Chinese etc …'[180] It was not only a wide ranges of places that would make Roy's memoirs appealing to readers, but also his experiences of famous people. Writing this would mean catering to that which many people found most desirable about him – his life's journey.

The way in which Roy ended up writing his memoirs did a great deal to determine what kind of an intellectual he became known as, especially concerning his links to the leading communists of his days. This is in part because his narrative only covered his first years abroad, leaving out his childhood, his involvement in Bengal's revolutionary underground, the years after he was expelled from the Comintern, as well as his life partners. This highly specific account of his life would be Roy's only book to be reviewed in the London *Times Literary Supplement*. There, Roy was introduced as '… one of the most colourful personalities in the Communist International […] His career, up to 1928, is like something out of a thriller of the politico-cosmopolitan variety,' and, according to the reviewer, included a '… series of James Bondish episodes.' Dwelling on the more personal aspects of the book, the review concluded that the reminiscences were '… carelessly written, badly arranged and historically unreliable – and as exciting as anyone could wish.'[181] The market-oriented notions of his friends and agent went a long way to shaping the kind of narrative that Roy wrote about his life abroad. They focused neatly on his experiences and itinerary, where these intersected with people and subjects they already felt were exciting and interesting. Such considerations were as limiting as Roy's own interests were expansive.[182]

Conclusion

Like the working class, distinguished cosmopolitans were made rather than born. Unlike the working class, their strength was not in numbers. Individuals like M. N. Roy and Virendranath Chatopadhyaya became iconic revolutionaries in their own right to subsequent itinerant Indians who sought to make their

---

[180] Letter from Guy Wint to M. N. Roy, 21 February 1954, Manchester, Guy Wint Correspondence, Catalogue 70: M. N. Roy Papers Section 1, NMML.
[181] Newspaper clipping of review titled 'The Reddest Indian: Review Memoirs (Bombay: Allied Publishers, London: Allen and Unwin)' in *The Times Literary Supplement*, 16 September 1965 M. N. Roy/ 61, M.N. Roy Papers, PCJ.
[182] See Chapter 4.

way across Europe.¹⁸³ Practices relating to their names changed according to the pressures of persecution as well as being linked to their own sense of their shifting identity, and finally this changing could become a marker in its own right. On top of that, the adopting of various styles of clothing and thereby assuming a chameleon-like identity integrated an unusual dynamism into their image. Naming and clothing practices that directly linked the body to identification, group belonging and distinction contributed to a cosmopolitan habitus and persona. Their iconic status was further shaped by writings by Roy and his peers in which they put forward their cosmopolitan experiences and insights, but also happened in writings about them and one another. In this writing, their exoticism, cosmopolitanism, experiences and adventure contributed to making their life's stories be the most coveted thing about them – something that could both get them an audience as well as circumscribing their further intellectual and political efforts. Particularly writing practices meant that cosmopolitan icons continued being created after the people they referred to were gone.

Similarly, Roy's transformation continued after his heydays with the Comintern. He became a different kind of icon among his humanist circles, and the body came to play a central role in his humanist writings, as the material base of human existence that guaranteed equality among different individuals.[184] Yet, the associations he and others attached to his body, in terms of his charisma and reputation, set him apart from others. With Philip Spratt, Roy joked about the 'magnetic glances' he could resort to in order to convince people to do what he wanted, suggesting his commanding physical presence.[185] His presence could be experienced as unusual, otherworldly, even by those close to him. After his death, Ellen Roy resorted to religious language in order to characterize the role he had come to play for his fellow humanists: 'He came to be known as somewhat like a "prophet," and not only in this country, but with many devoted admirers and followers in Britain and USA.'[186] The distance between him and others was not only a mental practice, but physical, Richard Park remarking on his distaste for physical touch, linking it to his Brahmin

---

[183] Lahiri, 'Performing Identity', 417.

[184] The ideal of the equality [...] can be attained, in an increasing degree of approximation, because human beings, as biological units, are endowed with equal potentialities of development in every respect. M. N. Roy, *Radical Humanism* (New Delhi: The Janta Press, 1952), 25.

[185] 'Well, I remember your weakness for magnetic glances. I am afraid there is no other alternative for me than to resort to that contrivance.' Letter from M. N. Roy to Philip Spratt, 28 July 1947, Philip Spratt Correspondence, Catalgue 71: M. N. Roy Papers II, NMML.

[186] Letter from Ellen Roy to Evelyn Trent-Jones, 3 May 1954, Evelyn Jones Correspondence, Catalogue 71: M. N. Roy Papers Section II, NMML.

background.[187] He implied it was the behaviour of '... an aristocrat, not in the social or economic orders, but in the orders of ideas.'[188] Such aloofness from the world at hand went hand in hand with Roy's reputation as having been connected to the greats. When Philip Spratt met a particularly well-connected character in 1950, he incredulously wrote to Roy that '... [h]e seems to have met everybody – I think he has met more people than you have.'[189] Roy's cosmopolitan past had become a fixed quantity, which involved distance from the mundane and closeness to the figures and ideas that gave the great world out there its texture.

Roy would come to count an individual's self-confidence or 'man's faith in himself' as the safeguard against superstition and erroneous political philosophies, and thereby as a most desirable yet elusive quality.[190] It was clear that Roy possessed this confidence in spades, as for example the poet Sudindranath Dutta wrote to him: '... I think your life must have been more full of circumstantial change than of anybody else I know or have heard of; and [...] you still hope and keep your faith; your confidence in yourself is never for a moment dimmed.'[191] And when Roy published a small volume with the title *If I Were Stalin* (1946), Spratt wrote: '... [it] sounds as though you are in quite robust form again.'[192] The volume did indeed place Roy on a par with Stalin, as it detailed tactics and policies Roy believed the dictator should have pursued, instead of the ones he chose.[193] What to Roy seemed like a naturally leading role for him to play could raise eyebrows with others. In the political realm, Roy's persona could occlude his other efforts. A Calcutta journalist published an article in the US journal *Asia and the Americas* in 1943, in which Roy's short-lived Radical Democratic Party was described as: '... India's One-Man Party. This is not so much a slur cast on its meager membership as a reference to the fact that the party belongs to Roy, not Roy to the party.'[194] While Roy's persona

---

[187] Park, 'Ellen Roy', 61.
[188] Letter from Richard Park to M. N. Roy and Ellen Roy, 10 August 1952, Richard Park Correspondence, Catalogue 71: M. N. Roy Papers Section 2, NMML.
[189] Philip Spratt on Felix Valyi. Letter from Philip Spratt to M. N. Roy, 8 July 1950, Philip Spratt Correspondence, Catalogue 70: M. N. Roy Papers 1, NMML.
[190] M. N. Roy, *Reason, Romanticism and Revolution: Volume Two* (Calcutta: Renaissance Publishers, 1955), 235.
[191] Letter from Sudindranath Datta to M. N. Roy, 12 January 1944, Sudindranath Datta Correspondence, Catalogue 70: M. N. Roy Papers Section 1, NMML.
[192] Letter from Philip Spratt to M. N. Roy, 12 August 1946, Philip Spratt Correspondence, Catalogue 71: M. N. Roy Papers Section 2, NMML.
[193] M. N. Roy, *If I Were Stalin* (Calcutta: Samaren Roy, 1988).
[194] Paresh Nath, 'M. N. Roy: India's One-Man Party', *Asia and the Americas* 43, no. 3 (March 1943): 151.

was among his main assets, it could also occlude the political efforts of both himself and his associates. During the same period, Archibald Wavell, Viceroy of British India between 1943 and 1947, noted in his diary how he received a letter from Roy in 1944, '… practically demanding seats for himself and some of his party on the Executive Council, and a subsidy; my comment […] was that I was Viceroy and did not propose to be vice-Roy.'[195] For Wavell, Roy's confident manner provided an opportunity to tell a colonial subject to stay in his lane, while Roy felt at ease in a realm that was much more wide-ranging than that over which the Viceroy ruled.

In his own estimation, Roy was often above others, having amassed a breadth of experiences that was difficult for many to reproduce. This superiority could easily put a great measure of distance between him and others, making the finding of political allegiances more difficult. From magnetic glares to a prophet in various lands, the effects of Roy's persona were stronger than those of his philosophy, and even made it questionable to what extent it could be applied to people beyond himself. Being a Renaissance man, claiming a wide range of knowledge, was not an attitude that was available to a majority of people. In addition, the independence that Roy embraced in a personal, intellectual sense, and which long outlasted the commitment to national independence with which he had started his political life, placed him fundamentally apart from others.

---

[195] Archibald Percival Wavell, *The Viceroy's Journal* (London: Oxford University Press, 1973), 55.

3

We are the world – Bengali actors on world stages

Figure 3.1 Isaak Brodsky. Lenin's speech on the Second World Congress of the Comintern. 1924. State Historical Museum.

This painting, measuring 3.2 by 5.3 metres, made by the Russian artist Isaak Brodsky (1883–1939) and up to ten colleagues, depicts the Second World Congress of the Communist International, held in 1920 in Petrograd and Moscow. It took until 1924 until it could be put on display; portraying over 600 characters took time, and the politically volatile period between Lenin's stroke in 1923 and death in 1924 meant that some of the faces needed to be painted over before the picture was even finished.[1] The enormous canvas showed Lenin's

---

[1] Originally depicted in the Presidium seat, Paul Levi (1883–1930) of the Communist Party of Germany (KPD) was painted over when he was expelled from the party in 1921, his image replaced

opening speech in Petrograd's Tauride Palace, and contrasted the stateliness of the environment, speaking of a bygone world of aristocrats and inherited wealth, to the unwieldy mass of the revolutionary audience.[2] Both men and women were listening in rapt attention, although some were talking and gesticulating, with their appearances betraying a variety of nationalities.[3] This variety was an essential element in Lenin's address:

> Our comrade chairman has said that our congress merits the title of a world congress. I think he is right, particularly because we have here quite a number of representatives of the revolutionary movement in the colonial and backward countries. This is only a small beginning, but the important thing is that a beginning has been made. At this congress we see taking place a union between revolutionary proletarians of the capitalist, advanced countries, and the revolutionary masses of those countries where there is hardly any proletariat, that is, the oppressed masses of colonial, Eastern countries. It is upon ourselves that the consolidation of unity depends, and I am sure we shall achieve it.[4]

Lenin's theory of imperialism divided the world into two essentially different parts, with on one side the six capitalist Great Powers: Great Britain, Russia, France, Germany, the United States and Japan; and on the other the colonial or 'semi-colonial' countries, which located in Africa, Polynesia, Asia, Australia and America, as well as Eastern Europe and Ireland.[5] Painting a picture of the whole world in this way only required two kinds of paint. Because the membership of the Comintern would throughout its existence largely be made up of those from the Soviet Union, Europe and the United States, those who hailed from

---

by that of KPD-representative Clara Zetkin (1857–83), even though she had not been at the original conference. Levi or Zetkin were sat between Alfred Rosmer (1877–1964) of the Communist Party of France and Grigory Zinoviev (1883–1936), a leading Bolshewik. Rosmer's following of Trotsky meant he was expelled from the Comintern in 1924, and Zinoviev came head to head with Stalin after Lenin's death in 1924, eventually becoming one of the first victims of the Stalinist Purges in 1936. Unable to keep up with the political changes, the painting was put into storage in 1927. Wladislaw Hedeler, Jörn Schütrumpf, 'Der II. Weltkongress der Kommunistischen Internationale: Nachrichten über eine Petitesse', in *Vergessene Kommunisten: II. Kongress der Kommunistischen Internationale 1920; Porträts – gezeichnet von Isaak Brodski*, ed. Wladislaw Hedeler, Jörn Schütrumpf (Hannover: Offizin Verlag, 2020), 7–8.

[2] An eighteenth-century palace where the double-headed eagles of the tsarist coat of arms were hidden by red banners. Vatlin, *Das Jahr 1920*, 61.

[3] The 218 delegates present came from forty different countries on four different continents; 148 of them represented communist parties, and twenty were women. Vatlin, *Das Jahr 1920*, 54–5.

[4] Quoted in John Riddell, ed., *Workers of the World and Oppressed Peoples, Unite! Proceedings and Documents of the Second Congress, 1920: Vol. I* (New York: Pathfinder Press, 1991), 123.

[5] Semi-colonial countries, according to Lenin, were Persia, China and Turkey, which were nominally independent but in the process of becoming Great Power-dominated colonies. Vladimir Ilyich Lenin, *Imperialism; The Highest Stage of Capitalism* (Sydney: Resistance Books, 1999), 82–5.

elsewhere, like Roy and several others, were particularly important in Comintern claims of global appeal.[6] Vice versa, it was under this system, dividing the world in two fundamentally different kinds of places, that Roy would end up claiming to speak for colonial – and semi-colonial – countries in general.

Representative claims

The ability of individuals to credibly invoke the wider world on a political stage, supporting claims of universal validity, and the opportunities and limitations this stage provided them with in turn, form the subject of this chapter. It argues that feats of representation involved careful balancing acts between difference and sameness – difference from that which was already represented on the global stage they played their roles on, yet dissolving some of it into enough sameness to make the role recognizable to their audiences. The political practice of representation drew on aesthetic conventions to create platforms on which alternative political claims and universal designs could be put forward – but were still shaped by these conventions. After a brief theoretical exposition of the mechanics of representation, the chapter goes into several examples of Bengali intellectuals who engaged in representations of the world on various political stages in the late nineteenth and early twentieth centuries in an exploration of the mechanisms that allowed them to do so – and gave them a platform to expound their own ideas. This places the way in which M. N. Roy was able to draw on his cosmopolitan persona in order to represent the world into a historical perspective.

One of the most fundamental aspects of representation is that a representation is not quite the same as what it represents – otherwise the represented would '… simply be present.'[7] This puts a paradox at the core of representation: it characterizes something simultaneously being '… not present yet somehow present.'[8] Gayatri Spivak has distinguished between '… representation as "speaking for," as in politics, and representation as "re-presentation," as in art or philosophy,'

---

[6] Studer, *The Transnational World of the Cominternians*, 6.
[7] Quoted in Dario Castiglione, Johannes Pollak, 'The Logics of Democratic Presence in Representation', in *Creating Political Presence: The New Politics of Democratic Representation*, ed. Dario Castiglione, Johannes Pollak (Chicago and London: The University of Chicago Press, 2019), 17.
[8] Hanna Fenichel Pitkin, 'Representation and Democracy: Uneasy Alliance', *Scandinavian Political Studies* 27, no. 3 (2004): 336.

or in other words: '... the contrast between a proxy and a portrait.'[9] It is in the casual blending of these different types of representation, Spivak argues, that it seems straightforward to speak for the subaltern subject, who is in fact silenced in the process as their position with regard to power goes unacknowledged.[10] Focusing on the historical claims of colonial modernity, Prathama Banerjee has emphasized how the feat of representation also makes present people in the present who are assumed to be stuck in the past.[11] In the representative role under scrutiny in this chapter, the difference of a representative with regards to their audiences overshadowed their difference from the represented. When acknowledged, this latter difference became problematic, as claims more akin to those of the proxy were made on the basis of portrait-like legitimacy, rather than democratic mandates.

Representations of the world have been explored as instances of imperial propaganda and worldmaking in histories of colonial exhibitions and literature.[12] Yet, alternative visions of world order relied on similar representative techniques for their own instances of worldmaking, whether they were anti-imperial, supportive of an expanding Soviet Empire, or different sketches of a hopefully post-imperial but nevertheless global vision. In one example, Rebecca Karl has investigated the literal staging of anti-imperialist world views at a 1904 Beijing opera.[13] Less obviously performative, the twentieth century would see a wide

---

[9] Spivak finesses the distinction with reference to Marx' *The Eighteenth Brumaire of Louis Napoleon* and the difference between the German 'vertreten', or 'speaking for', and 'darstellen', or 'making present'. Gayatri Spivak, 'Can the Subaltern Speak?' in *Marxism and the Interpretation of Culture*, ed. Cary Nelson, Lawrence Grossberg (London: Macmillan, 1998), 70;71. On the metaphor of painting as representation, see F. R. Ankersmit, 'Representation as the Representation of Experience', *Metaphilosophy* 31, no. 1/2 (2000): 148–68.

[10] Ritu Birla, 'Postcolonial Studies: Now That's History', in *Can the Subaltern Speak? Reflections on the History of an Idea*, ed. Rosalind Morris (New York: Columbia University Press, 2010), 91; J. Maggio, '"Can the Subaltern Be Heard?": Political Theory, Translation, Representation, and Gayatri Chakravorty Spivak', *Alternatives: Global, Local, Political* 32, no. 4 (2016): 422.

[11] Prathama Banerjee, *Politics of Time: 'Primitives' and History-Writing in a Colonial Society* (Oxford; New Delhi: Oxford University Press, 2006), 6.

[12] Paul Greenhalgh, *Ephemeral Vistas: The Expositions Universelles, Great Exhibitions and World's Fairs, 1851–1939* (Manchester: Manchester University Press, 2017), 2. See also Alexander C. T. Geppert, *Fleeting Cities: Imperial Expositions in Fin-de-siècle Europe* (Basingstoke: Palgrave Macmillan, 2010); Timothy Mitchell, 'The World as Exhibition', *Comparative Studies in Society and History* 31, no. 2 (April 1989): 226; Timothy Mitchell, *Colonising Egypt* (Berkeley: University of California Press, 1991), 1–33; Sophie-Jung H. Kim, 'An International Event and Its Multiple Global Publics: The Parliament of the World's Religions (Chicago, 1893) and Vivekananda', in *Global Publics: Their Powers and Their Limits (1870–1990)*, ed. Valeska Huber, Jürgen Osterhammel (Oxford: Oxford University Press, 2020), 181–2; Sanjay Krishnan, *Reading the Global: Troubling Perspectives on Britain's Empire in Asia* (New York: Columbia University Press, 2007), 1–4.

[13] Rebecca E Karl, 'Creating Asia: China in the World at the Beginning of the Twentieth Century', *The American Historical Review* 103, no. 4 (1998): 1097; Rebecca E. Karl, 'Staging the World in Late-qing China: Globe, Nation, and Race in a 1904 Beijing Opera', *Identities* 6, no. 4 (2000): 555.

range of events staging the world, from the Assemblies of the League of Nations (1920–46) to the World Congresses the Comintern (1919–35), which posited a directly competing world view. In addition, various organizations organized events supporting regional visions of world order, for example, the Pan-Asiatic Association meeting in Nagasaki, in 1926, the Pan-Islamic conference in Mekka, 1926, the inaugural conference of the League Against Imperialism in Brussels, 1927, as well as a range of international Youth Congresses and Peace Conferences.[14]

During the 1930s and 1940s, fascist powers also staged internationalist events, notwithstanding ideologies of ultranationalism. From Italy, the Comitati d'Azione per l'Universalità di Roma (CAUR) projected various versions of fascist or 'Roman' universalism and planned on organizing the 1941 universal exposition in that city.[15] In the 1940s, fascist Japan's 'Greater East Asia Co-Prosperity Sphere' was embodied in a series of Greater East Asia Conferences, '… which were not dissimilar to Western forms of internationalist conferencing, although the organisers wanted these gatherings understood as a better, Eastern form of internationalism.'[16] Iconic of the emergence of the post-colonial world was the first Afro-Asian Conference held at Bandung in 1955, which has been described as an elaborate piece of theatre.[17] All these meetings put forward vastly different political projects, and world views, but all represented a gathering motion, where representatives were brought together to manifest a whole, in a pars pro toto that suggested the outlines of that world. Political meetings required vocal delegates rather than exhibited bodies, but aesthetic conventions continued to shape their performances, as well as the political claims they could

---

[14] Manjapra, 'Communist Internationalism and Transcolonial Recognition', 168. On Pan-islamic Internationalism, see Martin Kramer, *Islam Assembled: The Advent of the Muslim Congresses* (New York: Columbia University Press, 1986). On Pan-Islam and Pan-Asianism, see Aydin, *The Politics of Anti-Westernism in Asia*.

[15] In addition to the '"myth of Rome" as a millenarian spiritual force inextricably linked to the physical space of the city', geographic imaginaries sustaining the 'Fascist regime's drive for global primacy' were 'mediterraneità: a scheme seeking to unite the diverse cultures and histories of the Mediterranean basin – spreading across three continents – under the putative cultural hegemony of Italy. Another was the imperialist drive in northern and eastern Africa and the creation of the new Italian impero. A final trope was that of latinità, a linguistic and cultural metaphor fusing the Roman and Catholic heritage – one often used in contrast to Germanic and Anglo-Saxon cultures – with a transnational horizon that reached as far as South America.' Aristotle Kallis, 'From CAUR to EUR: Italian Fascism, the "myth of Rome" and the Pursuit of International Primacy', *Patterns of Prejudice* 50, nos. 4–5 (2016): 362.

[16] Madeleine Herren, 'Fascist Internationalism', in *Internationalisms: A Twentieth-Century History*, ed. Glenda Sluga, Patricia Clavin (Cambridge: Cambridge University Press, 2017), 200–1.

[17] Naoko Shimazu, 'Diplomacy As Theatre: Staging the Bandung Conference of 1955', *Modern Asian Studies* 48, no. 1 (2014): 225–52.

make. In Spivak's sense, the exhibition and the congress mixed in the same way as did the representative legitimacy of the portrait and the proxy. And precisely this blending is what gave conviction to their claims.

Icons of Indian difference

The world stages of the late nineteenth and early twentieth centuries were made worldly in large part because Bengali intellectuals appeared on them. Because Kolkata, then Calcutta, was until 1912 the capital of British India and as such its seat of trade and administration, it had a long-standing history of English education that would play a specific role in the formation of its elites. To members of wealthy upper-caste families, the field of literature was an avenue to achieve distinction and deploy their intellectual talents, as other spheres were closed to colonial subjects. For less wealthy upper-caste families, often with minor possessions in land, education was a crucial form of cultural capital, and an opportunity for employment in the colonial bureaucracy.[18] For those from outside of India, both within the British Empire and beyond, looking for intellectuals with a religious, racial, cultural difference, members of this Anglophone elite were much more easily connected to than elites from other colonized lands. As such, it is not surprising that many of the Indians who made an impression on foreign audiences in the nineteenth and twentieth centuries were upper-class Bengalis.[19] Especially for audiences in Europe and the United States, they could play the role of recognizable intellectuals with a difference.

The Indian representatives on various more or less explicitly global stages under scrutiny here are the monk Swami Vivekananda (born Narendranath Datta 1863–1902) who spoke at the 1893 World Parliament of Religions in Chicago. Second is Vivekananda's one-time classmate at Calcutta's General Assembly Institution during the late 1870s, the later professor of Philosophy Brajendranath Seal (1864–1938).[20] In 1911, he gave the keynote speech at the

---

[18] These different groups were both known as 'bhadralok' or respectable people. Tithi Bhattacharya, *Sentinels of Culture: Class, Education and the Colonial Intellectual* (New York: Oxford University Press, 2005), 39–63. See also, Tapan Raychaudhuri, *Europe Reconsidered: Perceptions of the West in Nineteenth-Century Bengal* (Delhi: Oxford University Press, 1988), ix.

[19] Srinivas Aravamudan, *Guru English: South Asian Religion in a Cosmopolitan Language* (Princeton: Princeton University Press, 2006), 29;30.

[20] According to Seal, Vivekananda and him were united through their interest in European philosophy and read Hegel, Comte, Spencer and Mill together. David Kopf, *The Brahmo Samaj and the Shaping of the Modern Indian Mind* (Princeton: Princeton University Press, 1979), 60.

First Universal Race Congress in London. Perhaps the most inevitable Bengali intellectual during the early twentieth century was the poet Rabindranath Tagore (1861–1941). His 1913 Nobel Prize in Literature meant he became a global phenomenon of sorts in his own right. Particularly in the case of Vivekananda and Tagore, their celebrity was something for other Bengali and Indian actors to navigate when abroad, as it involved a learned set of rules about people being different in particular ways. Even though Roy and other revolutionaries operated in clandestinity during most of their travels, these celebrities shaped the way people outside of India perceived them, and sometimes gave them a point of access to new environments. As such, these three intellectuals are relevant here not for their contributions to intellectual history, but explicitly as they were considered from outside, as they shaped what differences could be expected from Indian intellectuals abroad. Seal was not a celebrity, but his role in the Universal Race Congress shows how the dividing line of race could be used to make humanity legible as a whole.

As far as exhibitions can be made into political stages where their own power structures are thoroughly questioned, the performance of Swami Vivekananda at the 1893 World Parliament of Religions was in a class of its own. The Parliament was organized by the World Congress Auxiliary, which claimed 'higher and nobler' aims than the general Exposition. These lofty ideals required a crucial ingredient: people. Or, as the organizers put it: 'Not things but men! Not matter but mind!'[21] The organizers sought to invite living practitioners of various religions to freely discuss their differences and agreements, or as the chairman put it: '... the Committee at once perceived that the religious world, in its historic developments, and not any one section of that world, should be invited to make some representation.'[22] Under this display of diversity hid a universal claim, about Christianity as a universal religion. The conference included representatives from Christianity, Hinduism, Buddhism and Judaism, and aimed for them to take a common stance of 'religion against irreligion,' but did so with Christianity as the overarching religion, containing all others: 'Although a dazzling array of costumes and persons were on the grand stage at the Art Institute of Chicago, each day's session opened with a recitation of the Lord's Prayer, noted as the "universal prayer" in the published proceedings

---

[21] Kim, 'An International Event and Its Multiple Global Publics', 177; see her forthcoming book on the congress' gender aspects.
[22] Quoted in *Ibid.*, 183.

of the parliament.'[23] In short, the conference had been designed to enlist representatives from different religions, using their different appearances and knowledge, to bolster the argument of Christianity as a truly universal religion, encompassing those outside of it.[24] The paradoxical logic to be focused on is that in order to prove the universal appeal of a religion, and therefore the unity of the world it encompassed, what was required were spokespersons who possessed a difference, in appearance, experience and knowledge, of this presumed oneness. This gave them a particular kind of authority to demonstrate that what seemed different was in fact part of the same universal whole.

Vivekananda, however, considered himself a speaker on a world stage that did not require christianity as a unifying factor at all. Instead, he considered the 'scientific Hinduism' he had developed as a religion that was suitable for everyone in the world, during what he perceived as a secularizing age.[25] Sophie-Jung Kim has argued that Vivekananda's success with US and European audiences stemmed from his skill at combining his 'foreign appearance' with 'familiar ideas'; rather than focusing on scriptural technicalities, Vivekananda presented his audience with something they already knew. He presented Hinduism as a method of self-actualization and self-improvement, presumably familiar to his bourgeois audience.[26] The monk made a lasting impression at the conference, because of the resonance of both his message and his appearance; his ochre monastic robes and 'colorful turbans' were widely commented on.[27] After appearing in Chicago, Vivekananda became a public figure in the United States and Europe, part of a pantheon of intellectuals portrayed by the French author Romain Rolland (1866–1944). His writings and speeches on Hinduism and universal religion became so popular that he has been called the 'first Hindu missionary', evidenced in his attracting disciples and the establishment of the Ramakrishna-Vivekananda Mission.[28] Those mission centres would be one of the spaces giving Indians abroad a foothold in years to come.[29] Vivekananda's

---

[23] Scott R. Stroud, 'The Pluralistic Style and the Demands of Intercultural Rhetoric: Swami Vivekananda at the World's Parliament of Religions', *Advances in the History of Rhetoric* 21, no. 3 (2018): 250.
[24] The original agenda of the gathering was underscored in the 1895 publication *The World's First Parliament of Religions: Its Christian Spirit, Historic Greatness and Manifold Results*, which intended to dispel the notion that the Parliament had been high-jacked by speakers such as Vivekananda, who had used its platform for his own purposes. Kim, 'An International Event and its Multiple Global Publics', 200.
[25] Thomas J. Green, *Religion for a Secular Age* (London: Routledge, 2016), 10; 5.
[26] Kim, 'An International Event and Its Multiple Global Publics', 192–3.
[27] Raza, Roy, Zachariah, 'The Internationalism of the Moment', xv.
[28] Gwilym Beckerlegge, 'The Early Spread of Vedanta Societies: An Example of "Imported Localism"', *Numen* 51, no. 3 (2004): 298.
[29] See Chapter 1.

career provided many opportunities to test battling claims of universality, or as he told a New York audience in 1896: 'The Christians say universal brotherhood; but any one who is not a Christian must go to that place and be eternally barbecued.'[30] To an extent, putting forward alternative universal claims required the utilization of categories and presuppositions held by one's audience, in order to appeal to the range of diversity known to them instead of falling into the realm of the completely unintelligible. It was only through the mobilization of such circumscribed differences that their parameters could be changed.

A much lesser-known world stage was that of the Universal Races Conference held in London in 1911. Organizing the various people in the world according to their religion was one way of organizing the world, but the most notorious organizing principle for humanity of the late nineteenth and early twentieth centuries, as well as the intellectual backbone of slavery, colonialism and genocide, was race.[31] At their most theoretical, the divisions of this hierarchical and violent world view also provided a notion '... through which the globality of the imperial age could be envisioned.'[32] The whole of the earth's population could be made visible, because it consisted of a limited number of different constitutive parts. This meant that representing the whole was possible if the different parts – the different races – were represented by individuals. At the 1911 race conference, there were many noteworthy attendants, including Vivekananda's companion Sister Nivedita or Margaret Noble, British socialist, theosophist and later president of the Indian National Congress Annie Besant (1847–1933), the Black US sociologist, writer and civil rights activist W. E. B. Du Bois (1868–1963) and the not-yet Mahatma, Mohandas Gandhi. Even though the organizing principles of international gatherings differed, sometimes the same cosmopolitan individuals could contribute to their being perceived as international because of their presence.

The conference did not only aim to discuss race theories, but also to include attendees representing different races, in some ways turning the conference itself into a representation of the world. This involved gathering '... racial theorists and evolutionists as well as of sociologists, economists, historians, and political

---

[30] S. Vivekananda, *The Ideal of a Universal Religion: Address on Vedanta Philosophy Delivered at Hardman Hall, New York, Sunday, 12 January 1896* (New York: 1896), 6.
[31] Richard H. King, *Race, Culture, and the Intellectuals, 1940–1970* (Baltimore: The Johns Hopkins University Press, 2004), 1; Siep Stuurman, *The Invention of Humanity: Equality and Cultural Difference in World History* (Cambridge: Harvard University Press, 2017).
[32] Christian Geulen, 'The Common Grounds of Conflict', in *Competing Visions of World Order: Global Moments and Movements 1880s–1930s*, ed. Sebastian Conrad, Dominic Sachsenmaier (New York: Palgrave Macmillan, 2007), 70.

intellectuals from Europe, America, and especially from Africa, Australia, India, Japan, China, Southeast Asia, Russia, and Latin America.'[33] There was an ambiguity at play in this guest list between the status of the invitees as subjects and as objects, as scientists and racialized beings who featured in a panoramic view of the world represented as a range of races. This was explicit in the comments of the Austrian anthropologist Felix von Luschan (1854–1924), who '… described his trip to London rather as visiting an ethnographic revue than as participating in a scientific Congress.'[34] In his speech, von Luschan denied that there were inferior and superior races, for which he was applauded by W. E. B. Du Bois. Du Bois' overall impression of the 'great anthropologist,' however, was mixed at best, as Von Luschan celebrated '… racial separation, Social Darwinism, and militarism,' in the same speech.[35] Even though his race conception was somewhat fluid, it still formed the basis for the distinction between who could attend a conference as a scientist – and who as a specimen.

It was on this stage that philosophy professor Brajendranath Seal gave the keynote speech. Seal had published widely, on topics ranging from Romantic literature to a comparison of Christianity, Hinduism and Buddhism. In a book on Vaishnavism, a major denomination of Hinduism, he wrote that the important notions from Christianity had been preceded by Hinduism and Buddhism. Later, he published *The Positive Sciences of the Hindus* (1902) which claimed Indian pedigree for many scientific discoveries celebrated as Europe's finest achievements.[36] He also was a believer in what he called 'scientific positivism' and generally interested in problems of 'unity and diversity,' or of the many faces of human life combined with a belief in universal truths of science. In his own words: '… history is a confluence of many streams, bringing together conflicting cultures, conflicting national values and ideals, and those who can find peaceful solutions of these conflicts are the true heroes of latter-day Humanity.'[37] Before attending the 1911 race conference, Seal had been to the 1899 International Congress of Orientalists in Rome as well as other events. His international engagements built his reputation abroad to the extent that in 1902, he was considered for a professorship in philosophy at Cambridge.[38] On

---

[33] Geulen, 'The Common Grounds of Conflict', 82.
[34] Ibid., 83.
[35] John David Smith, 'W.E.B. Du Bois, Felix Von Luschan, and Racial Reform at the Fin De Siècle', *Amerikastudien / American Studies* 47, no. 1 (2002): 23–5.
[36] Hayden J. A. Bellenoit, 'Missionary Education, Religion and Knowledge in India, C.1880 1915', *Modern Asian Studies* 41, no. 2 (2007): 377; 383.
[37] Kopf, *The Brahmo Samaj*, 63.
[38] Ibid., 60.

the international scene, he had thus already established himself as a speaker with some authority on the differences constituting the world.

At the time of the Race Congress, Seal had critically engaged with the universalizing tenets in Hegel's work, finding that his philosophy of history held that '… "all other races and cultures have been a preparation for the Greco-Roman-Gothic type," which is now the "Epitome of Mankind, the representation of Universal Humanity, the heir of all the ages."'[39] Seal, instead, would come to believe that:

> … humanity is 'a circle of which the center is everywhere and the circumference nowhere.' To be sure, each culture is 'diversely embodied, reflected in specific modes and forms.' But 'in spite of multiformity and in spite of the diverse ethnic developments all very real, all very special, there has been a general history of human culture and progress, the unfolding of a single ideal, plan, or pattern, a universal movement.'[40]

Seal combined critique of one universal view, which he found underlying much academic endeavours, with an attachment to universal knowledge that nevertheless paid more respectful attention to its various constitutive parts.[41] At the race congress, his opening address titled 'Meaning of Race, Tribe, Nation,' tackled the matter of race as an opportunity to provide knowledge that was universal, in line with his own ideas on universality:

> A scientific study of the constituent elements and the composition of races and peoples will alone point the way to a settlement of interracial claims and conflicts on a sound progressive basis, the solution of many an administrative problem in the composite United States and the heterogeneous British Empire, and even the scope and methods of social legislation in every modern State.[42]

Understanding difference made it possible to overcome the problems generated by it, but Seal's brand of universalism problematized the question of who it was that was able to do such knowing. In this, he differed sharply from von Luschan, who would only recognize his white colleagues as being colleagues indeed. Seal's lecture ended with a set of proposals to found several

---

[39] Quoted in *Ibid.*, 62.
[40] Quoted in *Ibid.*, 62–3.
[41] Towards the end of his life, Seal published a philosophical epic titled the *Quest Eternal* (1936), thematizing his own, and man's universal quest for understanding. Kopf, *The Brahmo Samaj*, 64–6.
[42] Quoted in Projit Bihari Mukharji, 'The Bengali Pharaoh: Upper-Caste Aryanism, Pan-Egyptianism, and the Contested History of Biometric Nationalism in Twentieth-Century Bengal', *Comparative Studies in Society and History* 59, no. 2 (2017): 450.

institutions, such as a 'World Humanity's League' of which he specified: '(not an Aborigines Protection Society)'; as well as an 'International Journal of Comparative Civilisation.' Both institutions drew attention to Seal's own role, and his objection to white anthropologists doing the studying, while everyone else was being studied. To remedy this practice, he proposed:

> The endowment of Professorships of Oriental Civilisation and Culture in Western Universities and Academies, to be held by Orientals from the countries concerned; and *mutatis mutandis* in the East (in countries in which European civilisation does not already hold a dominant position). No scheme of national values, ideals, cultures, in one word, world-ideas, will in the present day be dealt with by foreigners, as other than curiosities of an Archaeological Museum (or an Entomological Laboratory).[43]

In Seal's view, acts of display could become platforms for intervention. The proper appreciation of a race, required to 'promote understanding' among the different ones, could only come from inside of it. His use of race as an organizing principle for humanity, while not devoid of a sense of hierarchy, thus came with the contention that racial scientists failed to appreciate the different races they came across, only able to consider them as relics from a bygone age or specimens of various physiognomies – as anthropologists were wont to do.[44] It would take many scientists from a variety of races, not only Europeans, to come to an understanding of humanity that could truly be called universal. In his speech, Seal did not mobilize a particularity against the dominant universalism of the day, and did not entirely disregard the power of this universalism either. Instead, he tweaked the conditions under which it could be considered valid, drawing attention to its flaws and blind spots, thereby creating it as an alternative kind of universalism that he saw as a far more encompassing one.

Much more so than Seal, the poet Rabindranath Tagore became renowned the world over after he won the Nobel Prize in Literature in 1913. His persona that audiences far and wide got to know had been carefully crafted over the course of many years, in several cosmopolitan environments and literary circles in India, Japan and the UK. As an artist, Tagore had explicitly connected his anti-colonial projects of education and politics in with his aesthetic efforts in

---

[43] Brajendranath Seal, 'Meaning of Race, Tribe and Nation', in *Papers on inter-racial problems, communicated to the first Universal Races Congress, held at the University of London, July 26–9, 1911* (London: P.S. King & Son, 1911), 1–13.

[44] A. Zimmerman, *Anthropology and Antihumanism in Imperial Germany* (Chicago: University of Chicago Press, 2001), 1–11.

art and literature – a connection that was mirrored in the crafting of his own image and style.⁴⁵ Tagore regularly made a stunning visual impression on his audiences. The Japanese writer Yasunari Kawabata (1899–1972), who won the 1968 Nobel Prize in Literature, recalled seeing Tagore's image as a boy:

> ... the features and appearance of this sage-like poet, with his long bushy hair, long moustache and beard, standing tall in loose-flowing Indian garments, and with deep, piercing eyes. His white hair flowed softly down both sides of his forehead; the tufts of hair under the temples also were like two beards and linking up with the hair on his cheeks, continued into his beard, so that he gave an impression, to the boy that I was then, of some ancient Oriental wizard.⁴⁶

There was a clear moment when Tagore's crafting of his own persona influenced the way in which his art was received abroad. The poet took an important decision when in 1911, William Rothenstein (1872–1945), a British artist and family friend of the Tagores, asked for more of Rabindranath's stories to be sent to London. Rothenstein had gotten to know these stories during a visit to Bengal and wanted to have them published in the UK. Instead, he received a selection of poems, which seemed 'highly mystical' compared to the work he was familiar with. The selection of writings sent to Britain '... was required to lift Tagore beyond the small circle of English people interested in India.'⁴⁷ It was this mysticism and its openness to interpretation that made Tagore's poetry an international hit.

This openness meant Tagore's work could be interpreted in various ways. In the preface to the collection of poems that won Tagore's Nobel Prize, *Gitanjali* (1911), the Irish poet and theosophist William Butler Yeats (1865–1939) wrote: '... we are not moved because of [India's] strangeness, but because we have met our own image.'⁴⁸ Even though in much of the West, Tagore represented a different civilization and its art, his poetry could be interpreted as not different at all. The dividing lines between being unlike Tagore, and like him, could easily be crossed. Together, Yeats and Tagore found they had many things in common, and corresponded on the '... mystical union of Celtic and Indian spiritualism [even though] no self-respecting philosopher of religion would

---

⁴⁵ On his clothing in particular, see Chapter 2.
⁴⁶ Quoted in Pankaj Mishra, *From the Ruins of Empire: The Revolt against the West and the Remaking of Asia* (London: Penguin, 2013), 227–8.
⁴⁷ Dutta, Robinson, *Rabindranath Tagore*, 160, 9.
⁴⁸ Quoted in Ana Jelnikar, 'W.B. Yeats's (Mis)Reading of Tagore: Interpreting an Alien Culture', *University Of Toronto Quarterly* 77, no. 4 (2008): 1014.

venture in that direction ...'⁴⁹ Beyond representing a specific difference, Tagore easily rose to a level where he offered insights that could be considered universal. In some ways, he could then make the world present by himself, merely aided by the audience that was already there. This is evidenced in recollections of the German philosopher Hans-Heorg Gadamer (1900–2002) would recall a 1921 visit of Tagore's to the University of Marburg, where he was received by the philosopher Paul Natorp (1854–1924) – much admired by Gadamer. Nevertheless, the impression Tagore made on Gadamer made his own esteemed professor disappear into the background:

> ... I remember a university celebration [at which] Rabindranath Tagore and Paul Natorp were sitting next to one another. What contrast! With such similarity! Two faces, turned inwards, of two venerable, grey-bearded men ..., both certainly people of a deep sensitivity and great charisma. And yet; how thin and feeble seemed Natorp, the great scholar and shrewd methodologist, next to the statuesque Tagore, his face and apparition, a lordly figure from a different world.⁵⁰

Tagore was characterized as exotic, but on top of that he called forth associations of grandeur that were both familiar and strange, encompassing both known and unknown aspects of the world. Tagore's image was thus emblematic of India, but could also be seized upon to summon the world much more broadly.

Tagore's image was powerful enough to reach Russia before the man himself did.⁵¹ If Lenin really told Roy he had expected a '... grey-bearded wise man from the East' when they first met, as Roy described in his *Memoirs*,⁵² it was likely the case because he had seen an image of Tagore. It was in an associative, but

---

⁴⁹ Srinivas Aravamudan, 'The Colonial Logic of Late Romanticism', *South Atlantic Quarterly* 102, no. 1 (2003): 185.
⁵⁰ '... ich erinnere mich der Universitätsfeier [bei der] Rabindranath Tagore und Paul Natorp nebeneinander saßen. Was für ein Kontrast! Bei welcher Ähnlichkeit! Zwei nach innen gewandte Gesichter, beide ehrwürdige alte Männer mit grauem Bart..., beides gewiss Menschen von einer tiefen Innerlichkeit und überzeugenden Ausstrahlung. Und doch, wie wirkte der große Gelehrte und scharfe Methodologe Natorp dünn und schmächtig neben der felsigen Größe von Tagores Antlitz und Erscheinung, einer Herrengestalt aus einer anderen Welt.' Dietmar Rothermund, 'Rabindranath Tagore und seine weltweite Friedensmission', in *Globale Lebensläufe*, ed. Bernd Hausberger (Vienna: Mandelbaum Verlag, 2006), 204.
⁵¹ Tagore visited the Soviet Union for two weeks in 1930, but already before, Russian translations of *Gitanjali* were popular among the literary public. Soviet minister of education Anatoly Lunacharsky (1875–1933) called him the 'Indian Tolstoy'. Choi Chatterjee, 'Imperial Subjects in the Soviet Union: M. N. Roy, Rabindranath Tagore, and Re-Thinking Freedom and Authoritarianism', *Journal of Contemporary History* 52, no. 4 (2017): 913–34.
⁵² Roy, *Memoirs*, 342.

also in a practical sense that Tagore's fame paved the way for several Bengali revolutionaries who left India. As tellingly as erroneously, M. N. Roy's US associate Carleton Beals would remember Roy as an 'Indian prince' named 'Rabindranath' in his 1938 account of their encounter.[53] And in 1915, on the other side of the world, Rash Behari Bose had managed to secure his passage to Japan by passing himself off as a member of the Tagore family.[54] The Tagore name provided revolutionaries with a degree of cultural capital and familiarity in an unfamiliar environment.

After having lived in cosmopolitan spaces where Tagore's image had determined a good deal of the expectations with which people approached other Indians, Roy took to exposing the mechanism that made him so fascinating. In a personal letter, he wrote 'Tagore's books are all translated, except for the best ones (!) written before he became famous and began to preach in a mystical prophetic language which none could really understand; nevertheless, precisely therefore, they adore it so fervently.'[55] The way in which Tagore had come to represent Indian difference in various parts of the world created both opportunities and constraints for those who came after him, and expectations Roy was met with and would come to resist, subvert and mock.

All the world stages

The world stages Roy and his cosmopolitan peers appeared on were a world away from liberal platforms such as the World's Fair, Race Congress, or the Nobel Prize committee, and could even be seen as their mirror image. In that sense, it is apt that the first stage among them was in fact a criminal trial, the so-called Indo-German conspiracy trial that was held in San Francisco from 1917 until 1918. The accused were a range of Indian revolutionaries and German diplomats, among them Taraknath Das and Wilhelm von Brincken, its audience a US public that had just entered the First World War. Roy was not among the accused, but his first publication was linked to the trial, and the trial determined to a great extent what associations were attached to Indian anti-colonial revolutionaries.

---

[53] Beals, *Ten Years of Free-Lancing*, 43.
[54] Mcquade, 'The New Asia of Rash Behari Bose', 646.
[55] Roy, *Letters from Jail*, 6.

Court proceedings provided material to the US press for months, which created a powerful image of a clandestine cooperation that became public knowledge. The reach of the secret networks of Germans and Indians, reaching from California to Calcutta via Honolulu, Manila, Tokyo, Shanghai and Bangkok, lent themselves to sensationalist headlines and vivid descriptions of a world revolution being plotted. The US attorney as well as national newspapers such as the *New York Times* and the *San Francisco Chronicle* created villains out of the mostly German and Indian defendants, enemies in the ongoing war or representatives of an officially lesser race, threatening to disturb Anglo-American dominance through scheming and deceit. The revolutionary Indian newspaper *Ghadar* was widely quoted from, particularly an article that argued a wartime alliance of Indians and Germans should establish self-government not only in India, but ought to drive out foreigners from Egypt, Persia, Malaya, Kandhar, Afghanistan, China, Turkey and Kabul.[56] Images invoking the wider world could underline the level of danger presented by an enemy as well as the legitimacy of one's own project.

Other stages Roy appeared on – or next to – were also oppositional to those of liberal imperialism; between 1920 and 1929, those of the Comintern, and in 1931, that of the Kanpur trial in which he was convicted for communist conspiracy, and which Roy and his followers turned into an international event. Roy's fame waned after his expulsion from the Comintern, but he continued to try to claim representative roles, for example as an oppositional communist or as an Indian humanist at the inaugural congress of the International Humanist and Ethical Union in Amsterdam in 1952. Many of the mechanics of representation in gatherings with universal claims proved highly enduring.

Bringing the world to Moscow

When the Communist International was founded at its First World Congress in 1919, one of its central aims was to make future congresses live up to their worldly name. To that end, it was decided to send emissaries to Germany, Great Britain, the United States and Mexico in order to found communist parties there and to bring their representatives back to Russia.[57] Comintern emissary Mikhail Borodin travelled to the United States in 1919, where the radical press informed him of developments in revolutionary Mexico and supplied him with names of the leftists there he would want to speak to, Roy among them.[58] In the

---

[56] Sohi, *Echoes of Mutiny*, 192–5.
[57] Alexander Vatlin, 'The Comintern', in *The Oxford Handbook of the History of Communism*, ed. Stephen A. Smith (Oxford: Oxford University Press, 2014), 188–9.
[58] Spenser, *Stumbling Its Way through Mexico*, 48.

minor power struggle for Borodin's ear that ensued in Mexico City, the powers of representation possessed by the various candidates for leadership were given great weight. There was, after all, almost no information the Comintern had on the current state of affairs in Mexico, or anywhere else in Latin America. In such a context, gossip and slander became powerful tools for personal and political struggles. Particularly in the competition for leadership within the Communist Party of Mexico between US radical Linn Gale and Roy, rumours were created or divulged quickly, and preoccupied communists in the United States, Europe and Soviet Russia.[59] For lack of hard facts that could be presented to support either case, the issue of representativeness became a crucial one by which to decide the legitimacy of a candidate, and it greatly relied on the power of suggestion.

The Mexican Chapter of the anarchist International Workers of the World, for example, sent a letter to the Executive Office of the Comintern in July of 1920, concerning:

> ... the recognition granted to Manabendra Nath Roy, who as we understand, is now in your city. Roy seeks to represent the previously mentioned communist group in this city, which in no way represents the class conscious workers .... We call on you to repudiate this intriguer and not to pay attention to his pretenses. He has been accused of being an agent provocateur. We do not know if this is true or not, but if it is not, he is at least an ambitious politician only seeking personal gain and with habits and partners who are totally inconsistent with the aspirations of the working class.[60]

The letter admitted to a great deal of uncertainty, but still held that Roy's representative claims could not be given credence. And yet, even before Roy had arrived in Moscow, his representative status was advertised as a particularly covetable one from the point of view of a newly formed communist organization with global aspirations, even if Mexico City's anarchists did not appreciate them. In June of 1920, Borodin wrote to the British communist Sylvia Pankhurst (1882–1960) about his protégé's qualities, characterizing Roy's competitor Linn Gale, as '... a journalist out of touch with the masses.' In contrast, Borodin boasted, Roy '... is Indian and has worked ten years among natives who possibly have more in common with the Mexican peons.'[61] Unconcerned with the idea that Roy could

---

[59] *Ibid.*, 51.
[60] Quoted in *Ibid.*, 58.
[61] Letter from Mikhail Borodin to Sylvia Pankhurst, quoted in *Ibid.*, 58–9.

not properly speak for Mexican workers, Borodin's assumptions betrayed the wish that proximity to colonial oppression entailed an understanding of oppression of all kinds. In that way, Roy could speak for just about anyone who had not yet been represented within the ranks of the Comintern. A Leninist dreamscape in which workers in British India had a great deal in common with the agricultural indigenous population of Mexico, and where both could be represented by a upper-caste revolutionary was a fundamental condition for the making of Roy as a communist of international repute.

The stage upon which the Comintern delegates met had Lenin's theory of imperialism as its condition of possibility. This theory enabled a dialogue between revolutionaries from colonized and colonizing countries, as both were now fighting the same enemy in the global bourgeoisie. Lenin had departed from his Marxist inheritance in the early 1910s by beginning to consider Asia as an active historical subject, as opposed to a mere object upon which the forces of history worked, particularly in *The Awakening of Asia* (1913), which promised: 'Hundreds of millions of the downtrodden and benighted have awakened from medieval stagnation to a new life and are rising to fight for elementary human rights and democracy.'[62] Differently put, Lenin had found communism millions of potential new allies overnight. In Lenin's introduction to the debate on the colonial and national questions, the new reservoir of potential communists he foresaw in the colonized countries was numerically impressive: 'The vast majority of the world's population, over a billion, perhaps even 1.25 billion people, belongs to the oppressed nations, which are either in a state of direct colonial dependence or are semi-colonies …'[63] It was thus as a spokesperson for a potential of 1.25 billion people that Roy spoke at the congress.

Famously, Roy made his appearance there in order to politely disagree with Lenin. The latter had argued that colonial nationalism was an expression of anti-imperialism and therefore anti-capitalism, and deemed it progressive. In non-colonized countries, however, nationalism was deemed reactionary.[64] The policy of allying communist parties in colonial countries with nationalist

---

[62] Seth, *Marxist Theory and Nationalist Politics*, 38–9. The possibility of revolution in Asia enjoyed a spike of importance in the early twenties, as hopes of revolution in Western Europe waned. At the start of the decade these had been high, with the Red Army reaching Warsaw in the summer of 1920, and the war-torn continent shaken by local communist uprisings. But with the defeats of communist uprisings in Germany in 1921 and 1923, most hopes of a proletarian regime in Marx' homeland began to disappear and the focus shifted elsewhere. Jean-François Fayet, '1919', in *The Oxford Handbook of the History of Communism*, ed. Stephen A. Smith (Oxford: Oxford University Press, 2014), 123.

[63] Riddell, *Workers of the World*, 212.

[64] Seth, *Marxist Theory and Nationalist Politics*, 46–50.

movements became known as the United Front policy, and was a guiding principle of the Comintern's work between 1920 and 1927.[65] By contrast, Roy insisted on the application of Marxist categories to India in a manner that had not been adjusted to its colonial conditions; in India too, the bourgeoisie was the enemy. Rather than siding with 'bourgeois-democratic' nationalist movements, the Communist International was to support truly revolutionary movements that had been initiated by the proletariat or by landless peasants. Roy would put forward this point of view throughout his time in the Comintern, and in a wider sense, the question of which groups to seek allegiances with in colonial countries remained a topic of debate for many years.[66] His authority on a situation with a difference, assumed to be prevalent in India and Mexico, allowed Roy to argue that this situation was in fact not different at all.[67]

The rarity of being a politically vocal Indian intellectual in Mexico City and Moscow, who had travelled a long way, spurred on by individual connections and high-stake allegiances, was what drove Roy's ability to represent hundreds of millions. In an equation, an individual's representative capacities would be proportionate to the unlikelihood of their presence, multiplied by the distance from the represented. In Charles Phillips' recollections of the congress, this even translated into the idea that Roy had been the only attendant from a colonized – or semi-colonized – country: 'He was the only "native colonial" and thus the only delegate able to speak with experience and intelligence from the standpoint of the struggle in the subject countries, and he made a tremendous impression on everybody, Lenin included.'[68] In reality, several attendants hailed from colonized countries, such as the Korean Pak Chin-sun (1897–1938) and Roy's partner Abani Mukherji, whereas others represented the semi-colonial world, such as the Chinese Liu Shauzhou (?–?) and the Armenian Avetis Sultan-Zade (1889–1938), who headed the Communist Party of Iran.[69] Yet, Roy

---

[65] Sobhanlal Datta Gupta, 'Communism and the Crisis of the Colonial System', in *The Cambridge History of Communism*, ed. Silvio Pons, Stephen A. Smith (Cambridge: Cambridge University Press, 2017), 218–21.

[66] Known as the debate between 'revolution from above' and 'revolution from below', this debate was inherent in the tension between Marx' condemnation of nationalism, with class as the only meaningful category; and policies of the Soviet state to encourage national identities (within strict boundaries) of peoples within and outside the Soviet Union, who had been oppressed by tsarist Russia or other empires. Adrienne Lynn Edgar, 'Nation-Making and National Conflict under Communism', in *The Oxford Handbook of the History of Communism*, ed. Stephen A. Smith (Oxford: Oxford University Press, 2014), 524–32; see also, Gupta, 'Communism and the Crisis of the Colonial System', 212–31.

[67] For this line of argument, see Chapter 5.

[68] Shipman, *It Had to Be Revolution*, 121.

[69] Riddell, *Workers of the World*, 51.

became known as one of the main voices from the colonial world, aided by his convincing cosmopolitan habitus and persona, including his arguments, great reservoir of intellectual self-confidence and eloquent English. While Roy had been invited as a delegate of the Mexican Communist Party, he did not attend as such, but spoke for India without representing a party there.[70] This meant that rather than representing the interests and concerns of an Indian party, Roy represented India *for* his audience in Petrograd and Moscow. The suitability of the congress representative had, after all, been decided upon by Comintern emissaries seeking them out in various countries, instead of by the wishes of their local parties or groups.

Universal aesthetics

In terms of daring global claims, few tournaments can beat a yearly baseball tournament that has been taking place among teams from the United States and Canada since 1913, and calls itself the World Series. Sports events are among the most pedestrian ways in which the world is represented using a limited number of people; in 1920 Moscow, two teams representing Russia and Anglo-America played a game of football that went into the annals of the World Congress – with Roy playing on the latter team.[71] At the 1920 World Congress, aesthetics and appearances were an inherent part of its organization. The congress included mass events such as demonstrations, a play depicting the history of socialism with 80,000 spectators and fireworks, lasting until four o'clock in the morning.[72] There were several audiences for the spectacles – both the war-weary populations of Petrograd and Moscow, and the visiting delegates themselves. Even before the congress, many delegates joined a twelve-day tour of several villages where they congregated with farmers and workers, unhindered by the inability of most of them to speak Russian; their very physical presence was enough to demonstrate the solidarity of foreign workers with their Russian counterparts.[73] In terms of foreign propaganda, the impressions of the delegates themselves were particularly important, who, in the words of the Polish-German Comintern official Karl Radek (1885–c. 1939), were to '… have an impression of

---

[70] Charles Phillips spoke as a PCM delegate.
[71] Vatlin, *Das Jahr 1920*, 60–70.
[72] Ibid., 53.
[73] Ibid., 53.

the state of the first living workers' revolution,' which they could take home to their various countries.[74]

As a souvenir to aid their memory, delegates were given a volume of drawings made by the painter Isaak Brodsky and his colleagues, with impressions of the events they had witnessed, as well as sketched portraits of many of the delegates.[75] The individuals portrayed in the memorial volume included some of the most powerful men in the Comintern hierarchy such as Lenin, Karl Radek, Grigory Zinoviev and Nikolai Bukharin, as well as leaders of national parties in Europe such as Angelica Balabanoff and Giacinto Serrati from the Italian Socialist Party; Clara Zetkin, Paul Levi and Ernst Meyer from the Communist Party of Germany; Béla Kun and Mátyás Rákosi of the Hungarian Communist Party; and Alfred Rosmer of the Communist Party of France. More surprisingly, the volume included three men whose names were not yet familiar in revolutionary propaganda: Pak Chin-sun, representing the Socialist Party of Korea, An Enhak (?–?), representing the Chinese Socialist Workers Party – both parties that had recently been founded in Russia – and Manabendra Nath Roy, representing the Communist Party of Mexico.[76] These drawings were to be spread around the world by international delegates, showing that they had been to a gathering at which the world had been present. Propaganda that aimed to capture the world had to work in various directions at the same time.

When it came to its universality, the Comintern lambasted its predecessor, the defunct Second (socialist) International, whose internationalism had, '... in reality recognized the existence only of people with white skin'.[77] This was not entirely true, as the Indian nationalist Bhikaji or Madame Cama and the Japanese socialist Sen Katayama had had their dealings with the Second International.[78] Katayama would even be honoured as an old-time socialist when he came to Moscow in 1921. In fact, there he was '... [p]araded before the public, popularized in the press,' which had more to do with him being Japanese than a socialist – or communist.[79] The Comintern's attempts to recruit a racially

---

[74] Ibid., 71.
[75] Hedeler, Schütrumpf, 'Der II. Weltkongress', 27–37.
[76] Ibid., 40–132.
[77] Riddell, Workers of the World, 38.
[78] On Cama, see Raza, Roy, Zachariah, 'The Internationalism of the Moment', xv.
[79] Katayama was not celebrated '... because they were all apprised about the particulars of his past life. It was enough that he had been one of the "grand old men" of the Second International, that he had thrown his weight behind the expanding Communist movement, and that he was, above all, Japanese, hence, Asian.' Hyman Kublin, Asian Revolutionary: The Life of Sen Katayama (Princeton, NJ: Princeton University Press, 1964), 288–90.

Figure 3.2 Manabendra Nath Roy by Isaak Brodsky, 1920.

diverse range of revolutionaries resulted in a highly specific picture of the whole world; delegates from Africa were largely absent from the Comintern throughout the interwar, and the continent was mainly represented by the Union of South Africa,[80] and partly by African American and Afro-Caribbean intellectuals.[81] Racial appearance also had consequences for delegates who were not from Asia, as is indicated by the recollections of Charles Phillips on how the whiteness of John Reed made him a more desirable US delegate than the Italian-born and Jewish Luis Fraina: 'Of all the American delegates to the congress, Fraina was the only one who impressed the Russians. Yet when it came to electing an American to the Executive Committee the choice was Reed. No doubt the desire to see a native-born and quintessentially American exemplar on the Executive Committee was a factor.'[82] A display of racial diversity was a constitutive element of the global claims of the Comintern, so in painting its picture, looks mattered.

In a 1922 article for his own journal, *The Vanguard*, Roy emphasized the universal membership of the Comintern, but specified that it lied not merely in the diverse racial makeup of those in attendance, but in the role they played:

> Almost all the Congresses of the Second International [...] were attended by Indian nationalists looking for sympathy. Seldom they were listened to. [...] Today the situation is altogether changed. The revolutionary leaders of the Western proletariat extend their comradely hand to the subject peoples. They are not doing it in a spirit of humanitarianism, nor are they content with expressing platonic sympathy. They want to have close union in an active struggle.[83]

Roy's writing spoke a great deal to the role he envisioned for himself, but in wider Comintern effort, aesthetics and propaganda were at least as important a part of the active struggle as were political arguments and analysis. Aesthetic requirements even shaped the theoretical debates that took place at the congress. A consequence thereof was that debates went on so long that many delegates left Soviet Russia even before the congress was over.[84] During the discussion

---

[80] Apollon Borisovič Davidson, *South Africa and the Communist International: Volume 1: Socialist Pilgrims to Bolshevik Footsoldiers, 1919–1930* (London: Frank Cass, 2003), 2–3.

[81] Minkah Makalani, 'Internationalizing the Third International: The African Blood Brotherhood, Asian Radicals, and Race, 1919–1922', *The Journal of African American History* 96, no. 2 (2011): 151–78. Bankole Awoonor Renner (1898–1970) from the Gold Coast was probably the first African student at the Communist University of the Toilers of the East, where he arrived in 1925. Holger Weiss, *Framing a Radical African Atlantic: African American Agency, West African Intellectuals, and the International Trade Union Committee of Negro Workers* (Leiden: Brill, 2014), 68.

[82] Shipman, *It Had to Be Revolution*, 123.

[83] 'A World Congress' by M. N. Roy, *The Vanguard*, Vol. I, No. 8, 1 September 1922, Collection 10: Communist International, PCJ.

[84] Vatlin, *Das Jahr 1920*, 101.

of the National and Colonial Questions, several delegates put forward motions to keep the discussion brief and abstract, complaining that too much time was being spent on individual places and problems – from those of Black people in Chicago to imperialism in Korea and the sovereignty of the Finnish Åland islands.[85] But what was more pressing than the need for brevity was the incentive to have delegates from different places speak about everything they knew. After all, the Comintern had troubled itself to find delegates from a great variety of places, and not letting them speak would defeat the purpose of having invited them to begin with. In the end, senior Comintern official Karl Radek decided to let everyone speak, which meant the discussion lasted until 2.30 in the morning, and then into a second day:

> … our debates cannot start from the consideration that one or another individual is acquainted with the matter. Rather, the political significance of the colonial question must be considered. We have a political interest in the workers reading the record of the proceedings and seeing that the representatives of the oppressed peoples spoke here and participated in our deliberations.[86]

In the end, the fact of the congress having happened, attracting delegates from oppressed countries, discussing the nature of this oppression was more important than the technical outcome of the discussions. Upon the closing of proceedings, the Comintern devoted itself to making sure that speeches and discussions were translated into various languages so that the leaders of international communism could be quoted in various journals.[87] The Comintern journal, *Communist International*, gave wide publicity to the congress as a feat in itself, for example in an article by Pak Chin-sun, who promised:

> … our western comrades (we may be sure) will meet with a hearty and brotherly reception on the part of the proletariat and working peasantry of Asia; the East was always opposed to foreign intervention only when it brought with it chains and slavery; but the intervention of the Socialist proletarian West will be a great and needed help to the working masses of Asia in their struggle against every kind of exploitation. The proletariat of the East is thirsting such 'intervention.'[88]

---

[85] Riddell, *Workers of the World*, 234.
[86] Ibid., 235.
[87] Ibid., 14; 55.
[88] 'The Revolutionary East and the Next Task of the Communist International by Pack Dinshoon' *Communist International*, nos. 11–12 June–July, 1920 – Collection 9: Communist International, PCJ.

Pak's article spoke broadly for Asia, which through him could make statements that would sound like music to the ears of European communists who might even see his portrait. As an operative, Pak was sent to Shanghai in 1920, but replaced in 1921 already.[89] To an extent, delegates having spoken outweighed the importance of what they had said, as was the promise of showing their words – and images – to audiences far and wide.

Right after the Second World Congress, the Comintern put together an even more ambitious display of differences in order to communicate its universal reach: the Congress of the Peoples of the East, held in Baku in 1920, with more than 2000 delegates from Asia in attendance.[90] In the historiography on the congress, its main significance is symbolic, counting as the extension of the Second Congress' focus on colonial countries to extend more literally into colonial and semi-colonial territory.[91] In inviting delegates displaying a multiplicity of dress, language, race and religion, the spread of communism was made visually manifest – the very difference of the participants displaying the universal applicability of a theory. As the Dutch communist Henk Sneevliet wrote in a report to the red newspaper *De Tribune*: 'The whole organized population of Baku passed in review for hours under the burning sun of the Orient. [...] workers, woman, [sic] youth and the schools, Persians and Turks, all the services of the Red Army, and congress delegates from all the nations.'[92] Through an enumeration of specific groups, a totality was implied.

Such a display came with an inherent tension. The problem was that what was on view in Baku was not the same thing as what many observers had come to think of as communism. The English science fiction writer H. G. Wells (1866–1946), for example, published a well-known account of his 1920 visit to Moscow, during which he saw footage of the Baku congress.[93] His account of the event the Comintern orchestrated was one of a gathering of difference: 'They sought out factory workers and slum dwellers in the tents of the steppes. They held a congress at Baku, at which they gathered together a quite wonderful accumulation of white, black, brown, and yellow people, Asiatic costumes

---

[89] Yoshihiro, *The Formation of the Chinese Communist Party*, 141.
[90] John Riddell, *To See the Dawn; Baku, 1920 – First Congress of the Peoples of the East* (New York, London, Montreal, Sydney: Pathfinder, 1993), 11.
[91] Stephen A. White, 'Communism and the East: The Baku Congress, 1920', *Slavic Review* 33, no. 3 (1974): 492.
[92] Quoted in Riddell, *To See The Dawn*, 24.
[93] Wells depicted his impression of the Comintern as an organization which tried to slot phenomena into boxes in which they did not fit. Grigory Zinoviev, who asked about the civil war in Ireland, came across '... like a man with a jigsaw puzzle trying to get the Irish situation into the class war formula.' H. G. Wells, *Russia in the Shadows* (New York: George H. Doran Company, 1921), 95–6.

and astonishing weapons.'⁹⁴ Wells' clashing of factory workers with tents, and slum dwellers with steppes, found their apotheosis in the description he gave of a dancer performing at the congress, dwelling at length on his attire of '… a fur-trimmed jacket, high boots, and a high cap,' as well as the dexterity of his dancing, involving a balancing act with several knives. Wells juxtaposed what he perceived as a piece of folklore with its questionable explanans in Marxist theory:

> I tried to find out whether he was a specimen Asiatic proletarian or just what he symbolised, but I could get no light on him. But there are yards and yards of film of him. I wish I could have resuscitated Karl Marx, just to watch that solemn stare over the beard, regarding him.⁹⁵

On the one hand, having adherents to communism come together in a display of variety and internal difference could show the spread of communism to new lands, ever more people being convinced of its truth. On the other hand, these differences could assume centre stage of their own, hindering the message of communism being the container holding everything together. At least in Wells' imagination, communists wore something else than fur-trimmed jackets, and performing martial dances was not one of their characteristic occupations.

An intellectual like Roy, who infused the difference he brought to the table with a style that rendered it universal, might have helped to make the spectacle more convincingly communist. His interpretation of communism in a colonial setting was not the same as Lenin's, but this was a clash that was recognizable as one occurring within communist doctrine. Unfortunately for the Comintern presidium, Roy was conspicuous in Baku only because of his absence. In his own telling of events, written long after they took place, he emphasized that it was his own '… precocious seriousness' and commitment to begin to do actual work that made him decide not to attend the Baku congress – against the explicit wishes of Grigory Zinoviev and the Karl Radek. In his memoirs, Roy situated himself on a different level from Baku's picturesquely oriental communists, writing that he considered the congress as:

> … a wanton waste of time, energy and material resources in frivolous agitation, and went to the extent of calling it 'Zinoviev's Circus.'
>
> Notwithstanding the temptation of being the star of the show, I refused to join the picturesque cavalcade to the gates of the mysterious Orient.⁹⁶

---

⁹⁴ *Ibid.*, 96–7.
⁹⁵ *Ibid.*, 98–9.
⁹⁶ Roy, *Memoirs*, 392.

In Roy's recollections, there was a clear tension between doing actual or 'serious' work and being recruited to star in a 'show'. But the shows and performances were a part of the serious work that the Comintern envisioned, as propaganda was one of its most important activities. Even seriousness could be an important stylistic feature of the show being put on.

Deciding which event was symbolic or frivolous, and which significant or serious, is of course most easily done with hindsight. When Roy founded the Communist Party of India, together with Evelyn Roy, Abani Mukherji, his Russian wife Rosa Fitingov and M. P. T. Acharya, they surely considered this a part of their active struggle, even if its importance has later been considered symbolic, considering a rival communist party was founded in 1925, which grew into the present-day Communist Party of India.[97] Symbolic importance potentially means other kinds of importance, and before a party is a real mass movement, it has the potential to become one.[98] Before then, even a name could make sure a group of people was nervously observed by British intelligence, and had a seat at the table within international organizations like the Comintern, able to join an organization that sought global representation.

Counter stages

Having been a representative among one international organization helped with joining another, as cosmopolitan capital did not simply disappear. M. P. T. Acharya, for example, was expelled from the Communist Party of India soon after he had helped found it, and left Russia to return to Berlin. There, he attended the founding congress of the syndicalist International Working Man's Association in 1922 – not to be confused with the International Workingmen's Association or First International that existed from 1864 until 1876.[99] Beyond the realm of international communism too, founding international organizations depended on the construction of component, often national, parts.

---

[97] Seth, *Marxist Theory and Nationalist Politics*, 77.
[98] This is not to say that Roy did not play an important role in the beginnings of Indian communism – his individual contacts included Muzaffar Ahmad (1889-1973) in Calcutta, S. A. Dange (1899-1991) in Bombay, Singaravelu Chettiar (1860-1946) in Madras, Ghulam Hussain (?-?) in Lahore and Shaukat Usmani (1901-78) in Bikaner, who would become important figures within the leftist movement. Just at this time, they were individual interested contacts in cities across India rather than leaders of an existing mass movement, who in no way functioned as Roy's 'lieutenants' across the subcontinent, but made their own plans. Seth, *Marxist Theory and Nationalist Politics*, 115.
[99] Laursen, 'Anarchism Pure and Simple', 247.

Roy's representative abilities also persisted after his expulsion from the Comintern in 1928. When out of the Comintern and staying in Berlin in 1930, Roy joined several groups of what were called 'right' communists from Sweden, Czechoslovakia, Alsace, the United States, Switzerland, Norway and Germany to set up an international network for the various groups opposing the Comintern's 'ultra-left' line, calling themselves the International Communist Opposition (ICO).[100] After Roy's leaving for India in the same year and his imprisonment there in 1931, members from Germany and the United States would keep in touch with Roy's associates outside of prison. Apart from supporting an international campaign to alleviate his prison conditions, they featured the trade union work of Roy's contacts in India '… in our national as well as international bulletins and publications.'[101] In its own small way, the ICO made an effort to appear like an organization with world-spanning appeal, relying on familiar techniques.

In reality, however, the ICO remained a small group, mostly kept afloat by its US and German members. Among themselves, they even complained that they were so dominant in what was meant to be an international organization that they appeared to themselves '… like ersatz Russians, doing everything alone.'[102] Unlike the Comintern, the oppositional communists did not manage to create the same longevity, or reach for their international organization, nor a similarly wide-ranging geographical spread of their doctrine. The rise of the Nazi movement exiled German members to France, and when the Second World War broke out they were further dispersed around the world and the ICO ceased to exist.[103] Even creating the mere appearance of global validity took something more akin to Soviet state power than what a dispersed group of intellectuals had to offer.

Many cosmopolitans were made part of political projects for the propaganda value that their mere presence promised. When Tan Malaka was exiled from the Dutch East Indies for belonging to its communist party (PKI), he travelled to the Netherlands, where he had also been a student, and was almost immediately recruited to stand in the 1922 general elections as a candidate for the communist party of the Netherlands (CPH). Tan Malaka's biographer has described how

---

[100] Robert Jackson Alexander, *The Right Opposition: The Lovestoneites and the International Communist Opposition of the 1930s* (Westport, CT: Greenwood Press, 1981), 278–9.
[101] Letter from Jay Lovestone to Comrades, 10 May 1934, Jay Lovestone Correspondence, Catalogue 70: M. N. Roy Papers Section 1, NMML.
[102] '… als eine Art Ersatzrussen alles alleine machen …' Letter from Heinrich Brandler to Jay Lovestone, 17 April 1931, Brandler Correspondence, Box 305, Collection 75091: Jay Lovestone Papers, Hoover.
[103] Theodor Bergmann, '*Gegen Den Strom*': *Die Geschichte Der Kommunistischen-Partei-Opposition* (Hamburg: VSA-Verlag, 1987), 231.

he published a range of articles in the communist press detailing the injustices perpetrated in the Dutch East Indies and the need for its independence. In addition, he was taken to provincial towns across the country as a 'show pony,' garnering a great deal of attention. These efforts were solely intended as propaganda, as Tan Malaka intended to travel on to Moscow, and had not yet reached the required age to serve as a parliamentarian.[104] The public relations' value of Malaka's participation was the sole reason to have him on the ticket.

Although their stakes went far beyond that of propaganda alone, criminal trials were among potential stages for anti-colonial revolutionaries and communists.[105] In 1933, Tan Malaka's one-time Comintern colleague Henk Sneevliet, whose work had taken him from the Dutch East Indies to Russia and China, had returned to the Netherlands and ran for the general elections fronting an anti-stalinist communist party. Because he had been arrested shortly before the elections, the entire campaign focused on his battle against bourgeois ideas of justice, urging voters to '… vote Sneevliet into parliament out of a prison cell.'[106] A party opposed to the bourgeois order could seize upon criminality as a piece of political advertising. In the 1929 and 1931 elections, the Communist Party of Great Britain listed Indian communist Shaukat Usmani (1901–78) as a candidate. Usmani had been a member of the Tashkent communist party and would be one of the one founded in India in 1925, but during the elections he was in prison after being indicted at the Kanpur, then Cawnpore, conspiracy trial of 1924, and the Meerut trial in 1929.[107] In several ways, national communist parties used individuals marginalized and criminalized by the system they sought to attack to gain publicity. This verged on creating world stages when the colonial dimensions of the system were under attack.

At the 1924 Kanpur trial, both Usmani and Roy had been indicted.[108] Roy did not stand trial because he was safely abroad, but commiserated with those who did in a letter that was intercepted by Criminal Intelligence.

---

[104] Poeze, *Tan Malaka*, 182–221.
[105] One of the most iconic among all Indian revolutionaries was Bhagat Singh (1907–1932), who was executed at the age of twenty-four and subsequently became the subject of songs, stories and pictures, many based on a highly recognizable photograph of the handsome young Singh wearing a fedora hat. See Kama Maclean, *A Revolutionary History of Interwar India: Violence, Image, Voice and Text* (Oxford: Oxford University Press, 2015), 53–79.
[106] Bart van Steen, 'Kiest Sneevliet Uit De Cel!' Henk Sneevliet, De RSP En De Verkiezingen Van 1933', *Helden Des Vaderlands. Heldenverering in Nederland Door De Eeuwen Heen* 22, no. December (2007): 79–80.
[107] John Callaghan, 'Colonies, Racism, the CPGB and the Comintern in the Inter-War Years', *Science & Society (New York, 1936)* 61, no. 4 (1997): 515–16.
[108] Abdul Gafoor Abdul Majeed Noorani, *Indian Political Trials* (New Delhi: Sterling, 1976), 244.

Poor fellows! If they could only have put up a better defence, four years in jail would have been worth while. We must have better Communists than this lot … […] With a better lot in the docks and less stupid heads at the Bar, the Cawnpore Case could have been made an epoch-making event in our political history … The Cawnpore Case had its good effects too. People have got used to hearing things which simply terrified them before.[109]

Roy clearly recognized the value of a widely publicized trial, and found the performance of the indicted sorely lacking. In 1931, he would have the opportunity to try and do better as he was back in India and could be physically arrested for communist conspiracy. Yet, by the time he was brought to trial it took place behind closed doors.[110] It is likely that the wide publicity generated by the Meerut conspiracy case put the authorities off the idea of providing yet another stage to communist intellectuals.[111] Not given the opportunity to make his case in front of an audience, Roy and his associates abroad sought to create an alternative stage for the political aspects of his case to become more widely known. Roy's by then ex-wife Evelyn Trent and his new partner Ellen Gottschalk were crucial in this process, working in the United States and Germany, respectively. On the German side, a campaign was held in the *Internationale Hilfsverein* in Germany.[112] In the United States, the International Committee for Political Prisoners played an instrumental role, gaining support from Jawaharlal Nehru and sending a petition to W. E. B. Du Bois and Albert Einstein (1879–1955), among others.[113] Roy had met Einstein in Berlin during the 1920s, and the physicist now suggested that a group of internationally known intellectuals protest Roy's sentence.[114] Evelyn contacted the ICCP with the plan, which would have created the suggestion of international

---

[109] *Ibid.*, 244.
[110] Manjapra, *M. N. Roy*, 100.
[111] The accused were allowed access to a wide range of proscribed communist literature in order to prepare their defence, partly because three of them were English. This preparation and the wide attention given to the trial resulted in a very public discussion of communist ideas. Ali Raza 'Separating the Wheat from the Chaff Meerut and the Creation of "Official" Communism in India', *Comparative Studies of South Asia, Africa and the Middle East* 33, no. 3 (2013): 323–4.
[112] 'IHV, Febr. '32' in Series II, India, *ZL-281 [Microfilm] International Committee for Political Prisoners Records, 1918–1942, Manuscripts and Archives Division, The New York Public Library, New York, USA (hence NYPL).
[113] Letter from Jawaharlal Nehru to Roger Baldwin about financial donation, 25 December 1931 *ZL-281 [Microfilm] International Committee for Political Prisoners Records, 1918–1942, Manuscripts and Archives Division, NYPL; 'Roy – Indian protest letter sent to the following names for signature' 16 October 1931, *ZL-281 [Microfilm] International Committee for Political Prisoners Records, 1918–1942, Manuscripts and Archives Division, NYPL; Letter from Evelyn Trent to Roger Baldwin, 27 January, 1932, *ZL-281 [Microfilm] International Committee for Political Prisoners Records, 1918–1942, Manuscripts and Archives Division, NYPL.
[114] Letter from A. Einstein to Evelyn Trent, 30 January 1932, *ZL-281 [Microfilm] International Committee for Political Prisoners Records, 1918–1942, Manuscripts and Archives Division, NYPL.

protest against Roy's incarceration through individual names from different countries. She wrote: 'Barbusse,[115] I believe, will take care of France; some signers could be found in Britain; what of America?'[116] Mobilizing different voices aimed at representing different countries suggested world opinion expressing universal disapproval at Roy's arrest and treatment.

As a part of the international campaign, a text Roy had prepared as his defence statement was published in New York. It inserted Roy's case into the history of left-wing intellectuals exposing miscarriages of justice through its title: *I Accuse!* Unlike the historic outcry of French author Émile Zola's, Roy's accusation concerned his own trial. Still, this was framed as being of much wider than individual relevance, amounting to '... not his personal defence but that of the right of the Indian people to self-determination and national freedom.'[117] In the introductory statement, these claims were emboldened through constant references to Roy's cosmopolitan past, his importance in the international workers' movement and his friends in high places. 'The demand for Roy's release was developing with momentum all over the world. The world famous scientist, Professor Albert Einstein, cabled to the Round Table Conference in London and demanded of the British government that Roy should be set free.'[118] If Roy was nevertheless jailed, it would be because in essence: '... imperialism had no regard for world opinion.'[119] Invoking the name of the scientist who had acquired world fame after winning the 1921 Nobel Prize in Physics was no coincidence; his name alone suggested an authority of even more than global dimensions.

Convincing the ICCP to work on Roy's case involved a careful balance between emphasizing the high-profile nature of his case as well as his helplessness. According to the president of the ICCP, the 1932 Civil Disobedience Movement – and the consequent banning of the Indian National Congress as an illegal organization – triggered such a wave of arrests that they could only be protested en masse.[120] Evelyn Trent disagreed,

---

[115] Henri Barbusse (1873–1935) was a member of the French Communist Party and an established writer.
[116] Letter from Evelyn Trent ro Roger Baldwin, 4 February 1932, *ZL-281 [Microfilm] International Committee for Political Prisoners Records, 1918–1942, Manuscripts and Archives Division, NYPL.
[117] Aswani Kumar Sharma, 'Introduction', in '*I accuse!*': *from the suppressed statement of Manabendra Nath Roy on trial for treason before Sessions Court, Cawnpore, India* (New York: Published for the Roy Defense Committee of India, 1932), 10.
[118] *Ibid.*, 8.
[119] *Ibid.*, 8.
[120] Letter from Roger Baldwin to Evelyn Trent, 6 January 1932, *ZL-281 [Microfilm] International Committee for Political Prisoners Records, 1918–1942, Manuscripts and Archives Division, NYPL. Emphasis mine.

and tried to make clear that Roy's case was much more high profile: '… the Indian papers I receive have devoted enormous and detailed space to the trial, something accorded no other except Gandhi himself. The government, too, has prosecuted him as an individual it deems worthy of singling out from the mass, and who merits unusual punishment.'[121] What needed to be clarified was why such a high-profile court case nevertheless needed the assistance of a small organization like the ICCP in New York. Here, Evelyn pointed to the class of those likely to support communism in India, and as such their lacking political influence:

> He finds himself almost alone, practically helpless, cut off from the Communist International, which might have provided funds for his defence, back in India after an absence of nearly fifteen years, and by the very nature of his case, forced to look for help to the poorest and most downtrodden, the majority of whom can give little for his defence, even if they know of his trial and what he represents to them, which is doubtful, beyond a small minority. Only his friends and well-wishers outside can help him, with moral and material bakcing [sic].[122]

There was a great responsibility for those outside of India able to contribute towards Roy's defence, neatly complementing Roy's previous years appearing on political stages as an emphatically cosmopolitan intellectual. He had made a leftwing movement more global, now it was up to its members to turn their attention to the other side of the world.

On a small stage, this occurred in December of 1932. That day, protesters gathered outside the British Consulate in New York, holding placards bearing texts such as 'FREE ROY,' or 'IMPERIALIST HANDS OFF INDIA.' The protest was reported in the *New York Post* under the title 'THE WORLD GETS SMALLER,' with a picture of the event. Its caption read: 'Protesting against the imprisonment of political prisoners in far-off India, here are members of the American Civil Liberties Union,[123] the League for Industrial Democracy and the Communist Party picketing the British Consulate in New York.'[124] In the report, the connection between a Manhattan protest and an Indian prison was given as a testimony of the world getting smaller, or indeed, more connected.

---

[121] Letter from Evelyn Trent to Roger Baldwin, 19 January 1932, *ZL-281 [Microfilm] International Committee for Political Prisoners Records, 1918–1942, Manuscripts and Archives Division, NYPL.
[122] *Ibid.*
[123] The ICCP was a part of this organization.
[124] Photograph and short article from *New York City Post*, 17 December 1932, *ZL-281 [Microfilm] International Committee for Political Prisoners Records, 1918–1942, Manuscripts and Archives Division, NYPL.

Roy, as a cosmopolitan intellectual, did not only have the power to bring new lands into the fold of an old ideology, but could represent the increasing connectedness of that world more generally. It was this faraway connection that counted as remarkable in the newspaper report, more so than the fact of Roy's arrest.

A humanist international

As a final episode in his representative career, Roy was to become a foundational figure at an international humanist congress without even attending. In 1952, several groups of mostly European humanists, concerned with the moral and spiritual bankruptcy they had witnessed around them during the Second World War, gathered in Amsterdam in order to found the International Ethical Humanist Union (IHEU).[125] Roy had been invited as a representative of the Indian Radical Humanist Movement he had established in 1948, but because he had had an accident on a walk in the Himalayas, he could not attend the congress. Yet, considering their mostly European attendees, the humanist organization was keen to give a platform to Indian humanism, even though Roy was not physically present. Committed to an international composition of delegates and audience, the IHEU turned Roy into an important virtual presence in the publication dedicated to their founding congress. The booklet included the text of his speech on 'Foundations for a New Social Philosophy,' and even added his voice to its 'Notes on the Discussion.'[126] The organization also listed Roy as one of its founding members,[127] and would continue to contact Roy's associates to seek connections to other humanists in India and Indonesia, trying to expand its networks.[128] The IHEU was keen to have a spokesperson representing Asian humanism, even in absentia.

The humanists congregating in Amsterdam in 1952 had several reasons to make Roy a virtually present representative, that both had to do with the geographical location of his humanist organization as well as what they hoped

---

[125] See for example Jaap van Praag, *Modern Humanisme: Een Renaissance?* (Amsterdam: Uitgeverij Contact, 1947), 7–18.
[126] *Proceedings of the First International Congress on Humanism and Ethical Culture* (Utrecht: Humanistisch Verbond, 1953), 94-9; 135-8. In: 1733-663, Archive of the International Humanist and Ethical Union, Documents regarding the organizing, and official publication of the Proceedings, 1951–1953, Het Utrechts Archief, Utrecht, the Netherlands (hence HUA).
[127] Ray, *In Freedom's Quest: Vol. 4, 2*, 359.
[128] Letters from Jaap van Praag to Ellen Roy, 15 September 1956 and 21 December 1956, 75-1065-2.04, Humanistisch verbond, Stukken betreffende contacten met humanisten in Amerika, België, Canada, Duitsland, India, Israël, Italië, Japan en Korea, 1954–1969, HUA.

Indian humanism could contribute to their organization. In his introductory address, the Dutch humanist Jaap van Praag (1911–1981) underlined the number of those in attendance: '... here and now more than two hundred people from all over the world have met to discuss their views on humanism ....' At the same time, he noted that the diversity involved was also a challenge: 'I suppose it will require much goodwill and patience to come to a close understanding between people of such different countries, languages, cultures and traditions as we are.' Having stressed the worldliness of the gathering by mentioning the differences of the groups coming together, van Praag naturally proceeded to its equally far-reaching importance, adding: '... as I may say perhaps without exaggerating – the eyes of the world are fixed on our proceedings.'[129] If the whole world was in attendance, the whole world would care about the congress. That was blatantly not the case, and yet it was a way to underline the importance of the conference's proceedings for those who were in fact there – or who were made virtually present.

In terms of the relationship between the envisioned internationalism and intellectual content of the IHEU's humanism, the presidential address by the chairman, British biologist and eugenicist Julian Huxley (1887–1975) was instructive.[130] Its theme was the construction of a humanist religion, which was an explicitly universalist project with scientific claims. Because the present was the first time in history, Huxley argued, when humanity possessed full knowledge of the cultures, religions and arts that had existed across the world and throughout history, now was the time to devise a religion for all.[131] As a biologist, Huxley sought the foundations for this belief system in science, particularly the principle of evolution, and his appeal to a unifying set of values for all of humanity was biological too; since humanity was '... the first dominant type to retain biological unity as a single species,' it would be no more than natural for it to achieve '... social and psychological unity as well ...' Sadly, until the present day, '... man has remained obstinately divided into separate and competitive inter-thinking groups, his common purpose obscured and hindered by their wars and ideological conflicts.'[132] Apart from a drive towards universality, Huxley's address also seemed to contain some hope for a contribution to a

---

[129] *Proceedings of the First International Congress on Humanism and Ethical Culture*, 9–10.
[130] Roy's journals regularly reprinted Huxley's articles, for example an article on 'Science in Russia' printed in *The Radical Humanist* of 4 February 1951, 53.
[131] *Proceedings of the First International Congress on Humanism and Ethical Culture*, 13; 14.
[132] *Ibid.*, 29.

humanist religion that could be expected particularly from South Asia, in the shape of '... communicable techniques for attaining satisfying kinds of mystical experience, such as are recorded for Yoga ...'[133] No such suggestion was to be expected from Roy, however, whose contribution to the congress was a text on the relevance of the work of Locke and Rousseau for the present moment.[134] Differences in content could be easily accepted by international organizations discussing their plans for internationalization, as long as the mere presence of international attendees was paramount.

Roy's connection to the IHEU would later be seized upon by historians emphasizing the global reach of postwar humanism; in a 2002 history published by the organisation itself, the founding of the organization is described as the result of '... two synchronous but fully distinct movements, one in the Low Countries and one in India.'[135] Beyond this institutional history, a 2017 edited volume on humanism, specifically claiming the 'universal' contributions made to its development, not only cited the efforts of anti-colonial revolutionaries in general as well as the work of Tagore and the Brahmo Samaj in order to prove its point, but also seamlessly transitioned to mentioning Roy as a '... co-founder of the Mexican Communist Party, and a Bengali revolutionary who collaborated with Lenin on the writing of his "Theses on the National Question," and his organization of radical humanists, as an example of humanism's universal history.[136] Listing several places and high-profile individuals connected to one individual still contributed towards the argument of universality.

Conclusion

Relying on defined, familiar elements in order to represent a totality meant picking up on those images and ideas that had travelled furthest, such as those of Vivekananda, Tagore and later Gandhi, even when the intellectual and political currents represented by these men were in marked contrast with many of the revolutionaries, communists and anarchists in Roy's circles. The relevant

---

[133] *Ibid.*, 20.
[134] *Ibid.*, 95.
[135] Hans van Deukeren, 'From Theory to Practice – A History of IHEU 1952-2002', in *International Humanist and Ethical Union 1952-2002: Past, Present and Future*, ed. Bert Gasenbeek, Babu Gogineni (Utrecht: De Tijdstroom, 2002), 8.
[136] Timothy Brennan, *For Humanism; Explorations in Theory and Politics*, ed. David Alderson, Robert Spencer (London: Pluto Press, 2017), 2; 4–5.

familiar images were determined by their travelling power rather than by the political or intellectual appropriateness of what they may have stood for. This meant that relying on such familiar images, as Roy and other revolutionaries did, involved both using and fighting them. Even though Roy was a much less iconic figure, he had something in common with the three Indian celebrities, as well as with philosophy professor Seal: being taken seriously as figures speaking for the world went hand in hand with their own beliefs they could speak and think about this world with some authority. Seal developed his own universalist humanism, Vivekananda, Tagore and Gandhi thought about the world in more obviously spiritual and religious idioms, and Roy came to feel highly at ease analysing and assessing global politics, science and philosophy. Chapters 4 and 5 will go into more detail on how this ease of world-wide thinking played out in Roy's life and oeuvre.

The interest of international organizations in representatives who did not only rely on but could also bend the lines of difference that allowed a limited amount of parts to represent the whole is clear, especially where they aimed to change the world in some way. This was the case for communists and anarchists as well as humanists, whose concepts otherwise differed quite meaningfully. The continuities in Roy's representative capacities show that something like – quite literally – an individual's international standing translated between ideological realms. There, beyond a central dividing principle, be it nation, religion or race, the matter of a representative's habitus was key. It required the combination of some apparent difference or distance from an audience with the ability to speak *to* this audience of the international organization itself, involving a degree of compatibility in terms of eloquence, charisma and thinking. In the case of Roy, the impression he made trumped the specific differences he was initially recruited for: presumed familiarity with the working classes of Mexico and India meant that he became an overall colonial expert. The relationship and tension between representation and political work are explored further in the next chapter, but have already proved to be a source of conflict in perceptions of pageantry versus 'serious work.' In the realm of representation, however, even seriousness was in and of itself an important ingredient in political communication.

Representing the whole by relying on its different parts required a careful balance between being recognizably different yet belonging to the whole that was being represented – a balance that frequently left the various audiences in this chapter unconvinced of the representation they witnessed. Representational abilities of individuals relied on the associations already present in the minds of their audiences that could link one person to a wider field, a region or a part of the world that he or she could stand in for, as it was otherwise mostly unfamiliar to the audience. Making 'the world' present in this way, relying on familiar associations, could give rise to a tension between changing that world at the same time – for example, according to the famous closing sentence from Marx' *Theses on Feuerbach* (1888) that was inscribed on the Marx family's tombstone: 'The philosophers have only interpreted the world in various ways; the point is to change it.' Walking the line between invoking the world through familiar signs and yet making that world one that broke with known versions of it required a skilled combination of elements of the familiar and the new, or of differences that were recognizable yet malleable. To an extent, representations were always an act of make-belief, even if their consequences could be quite real. Because of their ephemeral nature and appeal to associations and suggestions, such representations were inherently unstable, and could always be questioned. As such, it was mainly in environments where individuals were quite singular in their difference, and their version of it could not easily be called into question, that this version of representation thrived. It informed a kind of globality that relied not on increased connectivity by itself, but on the magnitude and shape of the distance that it could invoke.

4

Human resources – Opportunities for objective outsiders

While he was yet to become the centre of gravity of the California-based Ghadar movement, Har Dayal reflected on the intellectual advantages of involuntary movement in a 1910 article published in Paris: 'Exile has its privileges. It is the price paid for the right of preaching the truth as it appears to us. […] We may pay homage only to our conscience and defy all the governments of the world to make us deviate a hair's breadth from the path of Duty and Righteousness.'[1] His independent stance would lead Har Dayal to seek inspiration from and connections with Punjabi labourers, Bengali intellectuals, anarchists and feminists in the United States, with the German Foreign Office during the First World War and had him considering becoming a socialist when he realized the potential of the Russian revolutions for colonized peoples. He even sang the praises of the British Empire in a 1920 publication denouncing his former ties to Germany – likely a bid to allow for his return to India.[2] In the publication, Har Dayal told his Indian audience that

> … England has a moral and historical mission in Asia. The English people have built up an empire in Asia and Africa during the last two hundred years. They had previously prepared themselves for this task by establishing free institutions at home and developing a great and noble literature.[3]

Shocking as it was, news of Har Dayal's empire-supporting tract appeared in newspapers in San Francisco, London, Lala Lajpat Rai's *Young India*, *The New York Times*, and was roundly condemned by two papers in Allahabad.[4] Har Dayal's vast intellectual shifts accompanied a geographically unstable life, and

---

[1] Quoted from the *Bande Mataram* in Ramnath, *Haj to Utopia*, 13.
[2] See Chapter 2.
[3] Dayal, *Forty-Four Months in Germany and Turkey; February 1915 to October 1918*, 73;1,94,49,97.
[4] Brown, *Har Dayal*, 223–6.

made him a key example of a cosmopolitan who blended a persona that drew on mobility in space with one that took a flexibility of mind to be an equally covetable asset. This role of the independent outsider, able to claim a removed and therefore objective perspective was a possible avenue for distinguished cosmopolitans, apart from the role of representative. The flexibility that could allow a cosmopolitan to find various patrons could easily alienate others, and this chapter goes into the advantages and difficulties of adopting an intellectual persona to which instability was such a key ingredient.

Har Dayal was not the only Indian revolutionary with a chequered career, able to cite it as an asset yet also finding it could get him into trouble. Roy equally lived through a period of great disapproval when he publicly supported Britain during the Second World War, convinced that fascism was a global threat that had to be fought with any means available.[5] Before this time, ideological shifts had equally shaped his image; for example, his shifts from being an Indian anti-colonial revolutionary to communist internationalism at the end of the 1910s had been discussed by his contemporaries as lacking sincerity,[6] and his 1929 fall from grace within the Comintern was a cause for rumours that he was a British spy. For example, in a 1931 article in *Inprecor*, called 'Mr. Roy's Services to Counter-Revolution,' signed by The Young Worker's League of Madras,[7] or in a manuscript from Virendranath Chattopadhyaya titled 'The Adventurer Unmasked or The Career of M. N. Roy.'[8] In Roy's own reflections on his intellectually varied life, however, he turned the charge of intellectual instability into his strength. This involved using the term 'renegade' he had been slapped with at the time of his expulsion from the Comintern into his personal brand,[9] as well as positioning himself as a 'heretic,' building a persona of intellectual independence and open-mindedness.[10] His intellectual shifts were key to this self-image, as he wrote in the 1949 introduction to his 1937 history of the Russian Revolution: 'The test of objectivity is the readiness to change one's opinion when subsequent experience

---

[5] See Chapter 5.
[6] See for example Beals, *Glass Houses*, 52.
[7] 'Mr. Roy's Services to Counter-Revolution', *Inprecor*, 29 October 1931, Vol 11 No 55, 996, Virendranath Chattopadhyaya Papers, folder 39, PCJ.
[8] Manuscript Text for a Polemical Article 'The Adventurer Unmasked or The Career of M. N. Roy' Virendranath Chattopadhyaya Papers, folder 45, PCJ.
[9] Roy's adoption of renegade as a badge of honour did not go unnoticed; in his article, Chattopadhyaya wrote about Roy that: 'It is doing him to much favour to call him a 'renegade' for he never was a Communist.' *Ibid.*
[10] For example in M. N. Roy, *Heresies of the 20th Century* (Bombay: Renaissance Publishers, 1943) and in a biography written by Sibnarayan Ray, *The Twice Born Heretic: M. N. Roy and the Comintern* (Calcutta: KLM Private, 1986).

challenges its validity.'[11] Roy's insistence on his own intellectual independence meant that the fewer people agreed with him, the more he could see that as evidence of being right.

Ideological shifts are often problematized by historians, and potentially assessed for their authenticity or level of commitment, and the historiography on M. N. Roy is no exception.[12] Rather than considering ideological shifts as a problem, this chapter studies them as a shared cosmopolitan practice, engaged in by intellectuals who may have had particular political projects, but also needed to make a living abroad and to find different sources of support when circumstances changed. On top of that, flexibility could become a part of an intellectual's habitus and persona. A habitus shaped by changing places, peers and employers could then make subsequent shifts easier, and a persona could be made by re-interpreting the past in writing. Looking back on a lifetime of change, many cosmopolitan memoirs tried to find a sense of coherence in their variegated activities, making them a part of an overarching yet flexible persona, thereby turning this flexibility into something advantageous. In Roy's memoirs, for example, he would historicize his own enthusiasm for the Russian Revolution while he was in Mexico, among a community of 'left-wing socialists,' who lived 'in an atmosphere surcharged with great expectations.'

> It was a mutation in my political evolution: a sudden jump from die-hard nationalism to Communism. With the fanaticism of a new convert, reformism was an anathema. [...] Not only I experienced this psychological process, but many others subsequently underwent the same miraculous transformation, and consequently corrupted Communism. I also went a long way in that direction, but fortunately could discern the fatal pitfalls ahead before it was too late. I stopped to think and discovered the fallacies of the new faith.'[13]

Precisely because he had formerly embraced different ideologies quite so fervently, he was now immune to erroneous beliefs. Through re-interpretation, the strongly held beliefs that had turned out to be flawed could become a mark

---

[11] M. N. Roy, *The Russian Revolution* (Calcutta: Renaissance Publishers, 1949), viii.
[12] Roy's conversion from anti-colonial nationalism to communist internationalism is debated as either genuine or significant. In an interpretation that stresses the sincerity of his new-found internationalism, his participation in 1919 in the founding of the Communist Party of Mexico represents the cherry on top of this internationalist cake. A rival interpretation maintains that Roy always remained a nationalist, who, when German funds no longer came to him after 1918, switched his allegiance from Berlin to Moscow – as many anti-colonialists did at the time. For the first, see Alonso, 'M.N. Roy and the Mexican Revolution', 525. For the second see Goebel, 'Geopolitics, Transnational Solidarity or Diaspora Nationalism?', 492.
[13] Roy, *Memoirs*, 59.

of his present-day objectivity rather than merely being a testimony to youthful folly. Such re-interpretation was a part of a public persona that communicated its immunity from all-too-strong attachments. In the same way that distance from the past put it into its proper perspective, this would also be the case for issues that were distant in space. As such, an unattached perspective helped those who held it to reach objective judgements about anything far away enough, which could arguably contain most of the world. As much as flexibility could be cultivated as an intellectual asset, it never provided more than an unstable platform to stand on and could easily serve as an open flank for intellectual attacks.

Model outsiders

The figure of an objective outsider had historical purchase in two of the ideological realms Roy and his peers inhabited or possessed some links to, in the shape of the professional revolutionary and the development consultant. Brigitte Studer has emphasized that being a revolutionary truly was a professional identity, involving both a way of making a living and a way of life.[14] This chapter explicates what intellectual practices were a part of this profession. In the history of communism the professional revolutionary was an ideal type that had been thought up by Lenin in the tract *What Is to Be Done?* (1902). This text addressed a turn-of-the-century debate about the leadership of the intelligentsia over workers; in the 1890s, much of the Marxist intelligentsia – for example Lenin himself – had been arrested and exiled from Russia, and it turned out that workers' movements were managing without them. As such, the necessity of intellectuals' leadership came into question, and Lenin saw himself forced to prove the legitimacy of his own role. Lenin found the concept to do this in Beatrice and Sidney Webb's *Industrial Democracy* (1897), which his wife Nadezhda Krupskaya (1869–1939) and he had translated into Russian. The Webbs wrote that workers were too preoccupied with everyday struggles in order to acquire the necessary skill needed to lead a workers' movement in a complex society, and therefore had to rely on 'professionals'.[15] Professionalism here indicated a degree of removal from the struggle itself, which Lenin handily

---

[14] Studer, *Reisende der Weltrevolution*, 13.
[15] Robert Mayer, 'Lenin and the Concept of the Professional Revolutionary', *History of Political Thought* 14, no. 2 (1993): 250–3.

deployed to save his intelligentsia from their critics.¹⁶ Increased distance allowed him and his peers to see more of the situation at hand.

Crediting someone with a wider view was also possible by citing their geographical removal from the issue at hand. In a 1912 article on Sun Yat-sen, who had just acquired world fame after his role in and after the 1911 overthrow of the Qing dynasty, Lenin credited him with accidental insight into the situation in Russia:

> It is said that the onlooker sees most of the game. And Sun Yat-sen is a most interesting 'onlooker', for he appears to be wholly uninformed about Russia despite his European education. And now, quite independently of Russia, of Russian experience and Russian literature, this enlightened spokesman of militant and victorious Chinese democracy, which has won a republic, poses purely Russian questions.¹⁷

Sometimes, not knowing much about the situation at hand made it possible to see it all the more clearly, or so at least Lenin claimed. This conviction would pave the way for many itinerant intellectuals working for the Communist International in places they had so far been unfamiliar with.

Distance was an intellectual ideal with some longevity. In his 2007 autobiography, the French communist-turned-presidential adviser Régis Debray (1940) cited Roy and Henk Sneevliet as figures who had inspired his 1965 decision to travel to Latin America and join Ché Guevara's forces in Bolivia. His attachment to their example was characterized as adventurous on the one hand:

> I dreamed of being a *franc-tireur*¹⁸ of the shadows, ink and blood, machine gun in one hand and typewriter in the other. I saw myself as one of the *missi dominici*¹⁹ of the Centre, an envoy of Central HQ vaulting from maquis to maquis²⁰ and capital to capital. An 'Eye of Havana', along the same lines as the 'Eyes of Moscow' in Paris, Madrid and Berlin between the wars. [...] I thus identified with the pre-war 'professional revolutionary', an outmoded idealized type more in keeping

---

[16] Lenin celebrated the advantages of an outside point of view in many of his writings, for example in his well-known metaphor of the bricklayer. He contrasted the ignorance of the bricklayer when it came to the construction he was building with his very own hands to the perspective of the engineer, who was not getting his hands dirty, but who could plan an entire structure from an external – superior – vantage point. James C. Scott, *Seeing Like a State: How Certain Schemes to Improve the Human Condition Have Failed* (New Haven: Yale University Press, 1998), 151–2.

[17] Vladimir Lenin, 'Democracy and Narodism in China' (1912), in *Lenin Collected Works: Volume 18* (Moscow: Progress Publishers, 1975), 163–9, Lenin Internet Archive (2004) https://www.marxists.org/archive/lenin/works/1912/jul/15.htm.

[18] A historical French term used for partisan or guerrilla fighters.

[19] Latin: envoy of the ruler.

[20] French term for shrubbery, indicating hidden resistance during the Second World War.

with *Mitteleuropa*[21] than the Caribbean sea. That nomadic irregular, doomed to self-denial, switching between Underwood and 9mm automatic ... '[22]

Such romantic longings were not all that the communist figureheads meant to Debray. He specifically cited their perspective as covetable to him in the 1960s: 'Agents gain from being foreign to the countries where they operate: their gaze is more objective, their relationships more impartial.'[23] In the ideal image of the professional revolutionary, an image of the world as full of dangers and problems, to be navigated swiftly, was met with an image of the mind navigating it as cool, calm and collected, with these both poles mutually reinforcing one another. This combination and contrast neatly fit the emotional style of distinguished cosmopolitanism, which met an uneven and risky global terrain with superior individual ability to skilfully and swiftly find a way through.

Apart from professional revolutionaries, Roy would engage with professional outsiders in the shape of the development consultants that were meant to guide poor countries towards development after their independence. It was during his post-communist years in the 1930s and 1940s that Roy would edge closer to the realm of the development complex, particularly to the US government and US organizations that got involved in India in order to increase the people's standard of living – and dissuade them from seeking a better future with the help of communism.[24] Those working for organizations trying to bring about development, such as the Ford Foundation, were labelled technical experts or development consultants, and engaged in far-reaching cooperations with Nehru's government. Both in their-self-understanding and in the government's eyes, they were 'objective' and 'a-political,' which considerably aided their acceptance.[25] This perception of being non-political was important to the Indian government, eager as it was to avoid neo-colonial dependency, or the perception thereof, but was perhaps even more useful to the US government, which could rely on the Ford Foundation to work in areas where direct US government involvement would

---

[21] Central Europe.
[22] Régis Debray, *Praised Be Our Lords: A Political Education* (London and New York: Verso, 2007), 54.
[23] *Ibid.*
[24] Their policies would have lineages in both the League of Nations as well as colonial policies, making them quite anti-communist in history as well as the present. Marc Frey, Sönke Kunkel, Corinna R. Unger, 'Introduction: International Organizations, Global Development, and the Making of the Contemporary World', in *International Organizations and Development, 1945–1990*, ed. Marc Frey, Sönke Kunkel, Corinna R. Unger (London: Palgrave Macmillan UK, 2014), 4–6.
[25] Corinna R. Unger, 'Towards Global Equilibrium: American Foundations and Indian Modernization, 1950s to 1970s', *Journal of Global History* 6, no. 1 (2011): 131. For development as antithetical to politics more generally, see James Ferguson, *The Anti-politics Machine: 'Development,' Depoliticization, and Bureaucratic Power in Lesotho* (Cambridge: Cambridge University Press, 1990).

raise too much suspicion.²⁶ What they shared with professional revolutionaries was a claim of heightened insight into the conditions of the place they were working in, especially because they were considered to be outsiders.

Analytically, both groups have a lot in common with the professional category of management consultants, a profession finding its origins in the United States during the 1920s, presently characterized as the hallmark of global neoliberalism.²⁷ Lacking professional standards and codes, management consultants instead emphasized their legitimacy through a habitus that much relied on clothing, manners and language to underline its detached objectivity.²⁸ Beyond their habitus, consultants relied on abstract systems of thought in order to be able to capture widely different companies, in widely different places in ways that can be reminiscent of intellectual habits from the realm of communism. A beautiful example can be found in the memoirs of Albanian philosopher Lea Ypi, who juxtaposes a World Bank 'shock therapy' consultant she encountered during the 1990s with her Marxist school teacher named Nora:

> [The consultant's] capacity to draw parallels between the most disparate experiences, to identify commonalities between people in different parts of the world, to make you realize, for example, that a byrek in Albania tasted no different from a non-spicy samosa, or that a rubbish dump in Durrës looked just like a rubbish dump in Bogotá, sometimes reminded me of my teacher Nora. There was no overlap in the content of what they said, but there was a certain similarity in their attitude to generalization, in their ability to abstract from minute details, in the way they compared situations and used the comparison to explain a broader vision of the world, to reveal their knowledge of a whole system.²⁹

None of the cosmopolitans in these pages would have dreamt of institutionalizing some neoliberal project, and yet their ways of claiming legitimacy for sweeping insights possessed a similar shape as that of World Bank consultant. And as influential as management consultants are in the present, criticism of their practices and assumptions is at least as widespread, most poignantly so when these are said to add the mere sheen of objective approval to projects companies are about to embark on anyway.

---

²⁶ Unger, 'Towards Global Equilibrium', 132.
²⁷ Stephen Kern, *The Culture of Time and Space: 1880–1918* (Cambridge, MA: Harvard University Press, 2003), 115–16; Christopher Wright, Mattias Kipping, 'The Engineering Origins of the Consulting Industry and its Long Shadow', in *The Oxford Handbook of Management Consulting*, ed. Mattias Kipping, Timothy Clark (Oxford: Oxford University Press, 2012), 29–50.
²⁸ Christopher D. McKenna, *The World's Newest Profession: Management Consulting in the Twentieth Century* (Cambridge: Cambridge University Press, 2006), 200.
²⁹ Lea Ypi, *Free; Coming of Age at the End of History* (Dublin: Penguin, 2022), 238.

Roy and other cosmopolitans to an extent became specialists in offering outside points of view, and they could only do so because this point of view was, to certain parties, a desirable one. Looking at such 'employers' in succession shows how cosmopolitan intellectuals could make themselves desirable to a regime, and could create a particular role by doing so. Focusing on Roy's itinerary means that his intellectual offers, and those of his peers and competitors are contextualized as they were made in Mexico, Soviet Russia, British and independent India – all the while crucially relying on a cosmopolitan dimension that operated at a distance. Those living precarious and unstable lives often found themselves under circumstances were new opportunities and patrons had to be found and approached. Their writings were key to publicly claiming an objective perspective, offering it in the marketplace of ideas, and positioning themselves as possessing exactly such a point of view.

Open applications

When Roy and Evelyn arrived in Mexico City in 1917, it took time until they counted as important partners for the Foreign Office of Imperial Germany, and they received its funds.[30] After Germany had lost the war, money came from the Mexican government seeking to cultivate connections with anti-US radicals from abroad.[31] When Roy started publishing in Mexico City, it was during a time in Mexican politics that has been described as particularly open to foreign influences, ideas and people. After the dust of the Mexican Revolution (1910–c. 17) began to settle, '... everybody was looking for talent.'[32] The writings Roy and Evelyn published in Mexico City can be seen as elaborate business cards, offering their expertise in a way that could legitimize or strengthen their audience's political projects. It is noteworthy that Roy began his publishing in

---

[30] Price, *The Lives of Agnes Smedley*, 114. Ten years after their dealings, a German diplomat would complain to a colleague about Roy's inappropriate use of them to fund a comfortable lifestyle. Goebel, 'Geopolitics, Transnational Solidarity or Diaspora Nationalism?', 493.

[31] The government of Venustiano Carranza (1917–20) '... criticized U.S. and British imperialism, and which attempted to organize an alliance of Latin American states against the U.S. government's Pan-American imperialism,' and for that reason supported foreign partners in Mexico City such as US radicals criticizing their own government, or Roy, who battled the British Empire, and saw it as largely similar to US imperialism. He had been persecuted in both polities, after all. Dan La Botz, 'American "Slackers" in the Mexican Revolution: International Proletarian Politics in the Midst of a National Revolution', *The Americas* 62, no. 4 (2006): 577.

[32] Ibid., 584.

the English pages of *El Heraldo de México* and *Gale's Magazine*,[33] rather than in one of the several Indian-run anti-colonial newspapers that were published in North America, with *Ghadar* only being the best-known among them. In a sense, Roy's public career thus commenced with a persona as a cosmopolitan who was nevertheless different from his direct peers – by then mostly US socialists. When his first works were read, they offered a point of view from outside a group of outsiders.

Roy's first publication, *The Path to Durable Peace of the World*, published as *El Camino Para la Paz Duradera del Mundo* in 1919, was written as an open letter to US president Woodrow Wilson. During what Erez Manela has called the Wilsonian Moment of 1919, Winson's much-publicized words on the sovereignty of 'small nations' gave a global stage to anti-colonial intellectuals, using Wilson's language for their own purposes.[34] Because Roy's text was published for a Mexican audience, the US president really featured as a punching bag rather than an addressee:

> Your theory of granting liberty to small nationalities is really beautiful, when one refers to the people who are under control of the enemy; but, aren't we right to suspect the sincerity of this theory, when we find ourselves denied, and even reviled, by Your Excellency, the just complaints of the millions of beings in India, who as you already know very well, are dying of starvation under the yoke of your cousins and present allies?[35]

According to Erez Manela, the political bent of the piece was due to Roy's contact with anti-imperialist Mexican revolutionaries, who were deeply suspicious of their Northern neighbour, particularly since several US incursions on Mexican soil had occurred since the beginning of the Mexican Revolution in 1910.[36] But because Roy had started writing the text while still in the United States, it is more likely that it served to *seek* contact with the revolutionary government – and successfully so. Rather than a result of his contact with the Mexican regime, Roy's cynicism about Wilson's rhetoric served to show him as

---

[33] Both publications were sponsored by different parties within Mexico's government, Minister of the Interior, Manuel Aguirre Berlanga, sponsored the US socialist and war resister Linn Gale, who published *Gale's Magazine*, which combined opposition to US intervention, criticism of European imperialism and the First World War, advocating for anarchist and communist groups, as well as vegetarianism, birth control, spiritualism and the occult. General Salvador l. Alvarado hired the US socialist Charles Phillips to edit the English pages of *El Heraldo de México*, which the latter mostly filled with his own writing. La Botz, 'American "Slackers" in the Mexican Revolution', 576–8.

[34] Manela, *The Wilsonian Moment*, 223.

[35] M. N. Roy, *The Way to Durable Peace* (Calcutta: Minerva, 1986), 35.

[36] Manela, 'Imagining Woodrow Wilson in Asia', 1345–6.

an intellectual who was firmly on the side of Mexico, seeking admittance into its upper echelons. Roy, too, would for a time find patronage in these circles, receiving funds from the Carranza government like others in the milieu he was a part of, largely made up of US socialists.[37] Roy's remove from the Mexican situation made his welcome words all the more welcome, as they added the glow of objectivity to a shared line of thinking.

Among socialist, revolutionary and anti-imperialist circles the world over, the news of the Russian revolutions struck like a bomb. Quickly, the new Russia came to be seen as a potential partner in a range of struggles. Har Dayal, for example, found himself trapped in Vienna by the end of the First World War, as he tried to make his way to Sweden to disentangle himself from his wartime cooperation with Imperial Germany. Meeting a Ukrainian anti-imperialist in Austria had convinced him that the Indian revolutionaries present in Berlin ought to start a socialist publication, to tap into the political potential emerging in Russia. To a colleague in Berlin, he wrote:

> ... we shall make our voices heard much better than by shouting by ourselves about our grievances. Only the socialists are really interested in freedom. All other parties don't care about Asia and the Asiatics. [...] Give me one other friend and two 'socialists' from India who are quite sufficient to get a hearing as 'comrades.' Besides, I can write in the regular socialistic style, with quotations from Marx, etc., etc.[38]

Har Dayal was indeed well-positioned to write the right kinds of things, with the right kinds of quotations, having published the first biography of Marx in India, titled *Karl Marx, A Modern Rishi*,[39] in Calcutta's *Modern Review* 1912.[40] In this piece, he was quite sceptical of Marx' ideas, considering himself as '... one of those who do not attach much importance to these theories, and regard them as one-sided and defective ...' He surmised that '... [t]heir usefulness consists in supplying the justifiable aspirations of the labouring-classes with a nominal theoretical basis.'[41] Now that a Bolshevik polity struggled itself into existence, with state power and an army, the exact nature of Marx' ideas did not matter as much, as the hope of practical support for independence much outweighed theory.

---

[37] La Botz, 'American "Slackers" in the Mexican Revolution', 577.
[38] Quoted in Brown, *Har Dayal*, 215.
[39] An enlightened person.
[40] Sarkar, *The Swadeshi Movement*, 89.
[41] Har Dayal, 'Karl Marx, A Modern Rishi', *Modern Review*, Calcutta, March 1912, 23 in ML2A, Marx Legacy, PCJ.

Apart from Har Dayal in Vienna, other Indian revolutionaries in California, Kabul, Stockholm and Berlin equally sought contact with the new regime. From a San Francisco prison where he was awaiting the verdict in the 1917 Indo-German conspiracy trial, Taraknath Das instructed Sailendranath Ghose to write to a Bolshevist newspaper in New York, so they might publish an appeal to the Labour Party of Great Britain to support Indian freedom. Together with Agnes Smedley, Ghose also sent a letter to 'Workingmens' and Soldiers' Council of Russia c/o Leon Trotsky in Petrograd' that spoke of their plight and persecution, concluding: 'We beg the Russian people not to forget us in our sore distress. We beg to proclaim before the world if in this war for the defence of the right of the people, India should be given her freedom. Long live the Russian Revolution.'[42] It was clear to many that opportunities were opening up.

Professional revolutionaries

Opportunities for anti-colonial revolutionaries in the Comintern revolved around the organizations' efforts to connect with national independence movements and thereby drive out imperialist forces, ideally everywhere in the colonial empires of the European colonial powers and the United States. The task of fomenting revolution across Asia got more attention in Moscow as the likelihood of revolution in Europe decreased, and a range of experts from colonial countries in Asia was attracted and sent on various missions. Roy became a central expert on colonial matters within the CI, but he was far from the only one to join – and leave from – its ranks in the 1920s. Both emissaries' missions and the very organizational structure the Comintern adopted in order to orchestrate its activities in Asia betrayed the enormous complexity of the undertaking, which could never be fitted into a neat organogram, though not for lack of trying. Involved parties included the communist parties in respective metropolitan and colonial countries, as well as a series of bodies within the Comintern structure. From the Eastern Department (1919) and the Turkestan or Tashkent Bureau (1920), a Department of the Near East was created in 1921, and a Department of the Far East added to it in the same year. In 1922, the colonial question was felt to require unified attention and one Eastern Department was again organized, with sections focusing on the Near East, Middle East and Far East. In 1926, the

---

[42] Ramnath, *Haj to Utopia*, 130.

sections were re-organized to an Anglo-American and a Far Eastern division. Apart from these, there were Berlin-based Western European Secretariat (1919–25) and Western European Bureau (1927/8–33) which were involved in colonial work, and where many Asian revolutionaries spent time, as well as the short-lived International Colonial Bureau in Paris (1924–5), which Roy fronted until he was deported from France.[43] This plethora of departments and bodies call into question how much an abstract, schematic version of a chaotic reality can do to capture it.

Many of the revolutionaries within the various Asian departments shared the condition of exile from their home countries, meaning they could not operate there, but worked from third spaces between Moscow and their homes. They moved swiftly between different missions, assumed as they were to possess revolutionary expertise they could apply across contexts, and often it did not take long until they moved outside of the Comintern altogether. At the 1924 Fifth World Congress of the Comintern, the Eastern Commission contained not only the later world-famous Ho Chi Minh, but also the more middling figures of Tan Malaka, Sen Katayama and Roy. They would all work in various places in Asia and Europe, with only Ho Chi Minh finally being embraced as a national icon.[44] During his time with the Comintern, Tan Malaka went to Canton (now Guangzhou), editing an English-language newspaper there, and writing political tracts. He then worked in Manila, Singapore and Bangkok as a representative for Southeast Asia.[45] He remained in exile after leaving the communist fold in 1927, and would be faced with more arrests and escapes, taking him to Shanghai, India, Hong Kong and South China. He finally returned to Indonesia in 1942, when the Dutch had been driven out by the Japanese.[46] Even there, he would come to prove a troubling presence for its republican authorities, and would be imprisoned in 1946.[47] After his release from prison, he joined the entourage of a general who would come to be considered a guerilla by the republican army, and in the

---

[43] Gupta, 'Communism and the Crisis of the Colonial System', 219–20; Sabine Dullin, Brigitte Studer, 'Communism Transnational: The Rediscovered Equation of Internationalism in the Comintern Years', *Twentieth Century Communism* 14, no. 14 (2018): 74; Mustafa Haikal, 'Das internationale Kolonialbüro der Komintern in Paris', in *Jahrbuch für Historische Kommunismusforschung*, ed. H. Weber, D. Staritz, G. Braun (Berlin: Akademieverlag, 1993), 126–7; Kuck, 'Anti-colonialism in a Post-Imperial Environment', 142.
[44] William Duiker, 'In Search of Ho Chi Minh', in *A Companion to the Vietnam War*, ed. Marilyn B. Young, Robert Buzzanco (Oxford: Blackwell Publishing Company, 2006), 29; Neville, *Ho Chi Minh*, 28–30.
[45] Poeze, *Tan Malaka*, 250–60.
[46] *Ibid.*, 597.
[47] Rudolf Mrázek, 'Tan Malaka: A Political Personality's Structure of Experience', *Indonesia (Ithaca)* 14, no. 14 (1972): 47.

violent period of the Indonesian War of Independence, he was shot in 1949.[48] In some ways, Tan Malaka's outsiderhood never ended.

In 1920, Sen Katayama was taken on by the Comintern to apply his previously acquired expertise in socialist organizing in Japan as well as the United States. He would be a Comintern member until his death, when he was buried in the Kremlin wall mausoleum. After the 1920 Comintern Congress, Katayama was sent to Mexico to head the Pan-American Bureau in Mexico. This was a difficult task considering that the newly founded Mexican Communist Party had basically ceased to exist when most of its founding members, including Roy, Evelyn and Charles Phillips, had departed for Moscow. The only member who remained, the US-Mexican José Allen, had become an informant for US intelligence in the meanwhile. So even though Katayama was worried about being tracked by both Japanese and US intelligence, and therefore limited his contacts to an absolute minimum, the latter were aware of his every move as Allen was one of the few people he spoke to. Katayama's caution greatly limited his ability to work towards creating an alliance with local anarchists as he was meant to: 'I knew very little of Mexican comrades and their mental attitude, I might say, or national characteristics.'[49] Katayama's isolation only grew when the Mexican government, under US pressure, deported several groups of foreign activists – accidentally including Allen – but Katayama stayed in Mexico, even deeper into hiding, writing in July of 1921 he had hardly left his residence for two and a half months.[50] Unhappy with the results, the Comintern terminated the Pan American Bureau and in 1921 Katayama was welcomed in Moscow as an 'expert on Japanese and Asian revolutionary movements.'[51] It turned out that the extent to which his expertise could be generalized was limited.

Roy was more successful at widening his field of operation, and his writing of these years complemented this feat. While with the Comintern, Roy would extend his expertise from Mexico and India to the colonial world in general. In order to do so, he crafted an intellectual persona that was not bound to any one specific place; in fact, it was key that he remained at a distance from one of the key places he concerned himself with.

---

[48] Harry A. Poeze, *Verguisd en Vergeten: Tan Malaka, de linkse beweging en de Indonesische Revolutie, 1945–1949* (Leiden: KITLV Uitgeverij, 2007), 1465.
[49] Daniela Spenser, 'Emissaries of the Communist International in Mexico', *American Communist History* 6, no. 2 (2007): 157;160.
[50] Ibid., 161–2.
[51] Peter Duus, Kenji Hasegawa, 'Students and Immigrants', in *Rediscovering America, Perspectives on the American Century* (Berkeley: University of California Press, 2011).

It would be presumptuous to claim that my knowledge of India is perfect, but let me tell you that I have learned much more about our country, people and society in the last several years of my wanderings, than I ever did in those early days of romantic patriotism. It is indeed difficult to form a correct estimate of the present situation without intimate knowledge of the details, but it is also true that too much local colour often limits our vision and understanding.[52]

Ironically mirroring the belief of the liberal icon James Mill that he could be more objective in writing his *History of British India* (1817) by virtue of never having gone there,[53] Roy made a case for the intellectual benefits of distance in the manner of a detached scientist, who can see more clearly because of his more abstract view of the matter. He focused on styling himself as an objective outsider to India, who was less distracted by detailed matters than some of his rivals, who might have been politically active in India more recently than him. While it might seem difficult to do anything in India as an exiled revolutionary, he concluded that it really was an advantage in terms of his clear view.

Distance shored up Roy's intellectual authority, but could also undermine it. As the 1920s moved ahead, increasing contact between the Comintern and other Indian revolutionaries was what would make Roy's position increasingly difficult. At the Fifth Congress, held in 1924, Roy was charged with having exaggerated the extent of the revolutionary movement in India. Against his advice, it was decided that direct contact between the Comintern and mainstream nationalists in India was a necessity. Instrumental in this contact would become the Communist Party of Great Britain (CPGB), in which a new generation of India experts were waiting their turn, particularly the two brothers Clemens Dutt (1893–1975) and Rajani Palme-Dutt (1896–1974), who were from Cambridge, of Swedish-Bengali parentage. Particularly Rajani Palme-Dutt would become a leading voice on India within the Comintern, as well as one of Roy's nemeses. When the new line was discussed with Roy at a meeting in Amsterdam, it was revealed to him that the CPGB '... had been unable to find any "real revolutionaries" in India,' casting doubt on the efficacy of Roy's propaganda work.[54] The CPGB had begun to send emissaries to India from 1922, increasing its level of understanding of

---

[52] M. N. Roy, 'On Intellectuals', in *Political Letters* (Zurich: The Vanguard Bookshop, 1924), Marxists Internet Archive (2006), https://www.marxists.org/archive/roy/1922/11/10a.htm.

[53] Aravamudan, *Guru English*, 27.

[54] It was the Comintern's liaising with anti-colonial nationalists that would culminate in the 1927 founding of the League Against Imperialism, in which both Dutt brothers and Virendranath Chattopadhyaya played important roles. Roy thought such an organization would be 'futile,' and that only 'unreliable elements' would respond to the invitation. John Callaghan, *Rajani Palme Dutt: A Study in British Stalinism* (London: Lawrence and Wishart, 1993), 101–2.

what communism in South Asia, at that point, entailed.[55] Partly as a result of this increased contact, Roy's authority became more and more tenuous.

For all the effort that the Comintern had exerted to attract delegates and emissaries from a variety of places during the 1920s, many of these delegates would be promptly expelled from the organization, or even executed in the 1930s.[56] Roy's career within the Comintern ended in 1928, at the beginning of a period of so-called ultra-leftist tactics, or a policy banning cooperation with social democrats. Members of the Comintern who did not follow the party line were expelled as 'rightists', involving particularly members from the German and Swedish communist parties.[57] This meant that Roy's expulsion was a far from unique event; he was only one of many communists who would become branded as 'renegade' under the long years of Stalin's regime.[58] Yet, the way in which he fought his expulsion in a 1928 letter to his former comrades took issue with a particular reason for his demise; his absence from India since 1915 had been a reason for his colleagues to cast doubt on Roy's credentials, a line of argument that he immediately turned on its head:

> I am in exile in consequence of past revolutionary activities .... [...] If the representative character and usefulness of one were to be measured by the mechanical standard of bein ginside [sic] or outside the country, then, not a few of the leaders of the russian Revolution [sic], including Lenin himself, would have been ruled out as imposters![59]

Being far from his direct object had been a reason to take Roy on initially, as his wider view of the world was seen as an asset. But his was an unstable kind of authority, which was at its most convincing when the message it tried to bring across was a welcome one. It could easily be cast in a different light, and then possessing distance simply meant one was out of touch. Roy's defence diagnosed that this removed position was at the heart of the role that he had been cast for, which was a role that many of the early Bolsheviks had played themselves.

---

[55] Abdul Gafoor Abdul Majeed Noorani, *Indian Political Trials* (New Delhi: Sterling, 1976), 245–6.
[56] John Riddell has counted that of the delegates to the Second Congress, three-fifths of those hailing from outside of Russia were out of the Comintern by 1933. And from the seventy-six delegates who were still in the Soviet Union by the time of the Stalinist Purges in the late 1930s, fifty-two would be executed, or died in prison. Riddell, *Workers of the World*, 9. Among Roy's Indian peers, Virendranath Chattopadhyaya and Abani Mukherji died in the Purges.
[57] Kevin Mcdermott, 'Stalin and the Comintern during the "Third Period", 1928-33', *European History Quarterly* 25, no. 3 (1995): 409–17.
[58] Theodor Bergmann, *Ketzer Im Kommunismus: Alternativen Zum Stalinismus*. (Mainz: Decaton-Verlag, 1993), 7.
[59] Quoted in Purabi Roy, Sobhanlal Datta Gupta, Hari S. Vasudevan, eds., *Indo-Russian Relations: 1917-1947; Pt. 1: 1917–1928* (Calcutta: The Asiatic Society, 1999), 349.

The case of China

Before Roy's expulsion from the Comintern, China had become the main territory where the organization tried to put its theories of communists cooperating with anti-imperialist, nationalist forces into practice. A situation of internal warfare had ensued after the 1911 revolution in China, with the country split between an internationally recognized central government with its seat in Beijing, led by a range of rivalling generals or warlords and Sun Yat-sen's nationalist Kuomintang party with its stronghold in the South, mainly in Guangzhou. It was in this already complex situation, with several factions fighting one another, that the Comintern sought to encourage a proletarian revolution.[60] The alliance between the nationalists and the emerging Chinese communist movement was mainly directed against the Beijing-based central government. From the point of view of the young communist party, the nationalists were indispensable – especially since they had an army.[61]

Apart from Roy, leading revolutionaries sent to China were Grigory Voitinsky (1893–1953), Henk Sneevliet and Mikhail Borodin, none of whom had been to China before, and none of whom spoke a Chinese language.[62] Instead, both Voitinsky and Borodin had studied, worked and been politically active in the United States, and one reason for their deployment seems to have been the strength of their English.[63] Sneevliet had worked and organized a socialist party in the Netherlands and in the Dutch East Indies.[64] Working in new environments while trying to use their former experiences, the emissaries sought to reproduce some of their earlier work. After Voitinsky's arrival in Shanghai in 1920, propaganda activities commenced there that provided translations of articles from New York's radical press, for example the *New York Call* and *Soviet Russia*, to local left-leaning papers, most notable *Xin qingnian* or *New Youth* run by one of the later founding members of China's communist party, Chen Duxiu (1879–1942).[65]

---

[60] Jérémie Tamiatto, 'Des Révolutionnaires Entre Deux Mondes', *Monde(s)* 10, no. 2 (2016): 60–1.
[61] Bruce A. Elleman, 'Soviet Diplomacy and the First United Front in China', *Modern China* 21, no. 4 (1995): 452.
[62] Martin C. Wilbur, Julie Lien-ying How, *Missionaries of Revolution: Soviet Advisers and Nationalist China, 1920–1927* (Cambridge, MA: Harvard University Press, 1989), 9; Tony Saich, *The Origins of the First United Front in China: The Role of Sneevliet (alias Maring) Vol. I* (Leiden: E. J. Brill, 1991), 62; Tamiatto, 'Des Révolutionnaires Entre Deux Mondes', 63; 65.
[63] Yoshihiro, *Formation of the Chinese Communist Party*, 96.
[64] Max Perthus, *Henk Sneevliet, revolutionair-socialist in Europa en Azië* (Nijmegen: Socialistiese Uitgeverij Nijmegen, 1976).
[65] Chen Duxiu had been a leading member of the May 4th Movement, which was a student-led protest against the consequences of the Versailles Treaty for China; rather than gaining in self-determination, as US president Wilson had alluded to, Chinese territories lost by Germany were surrendered to Japan. Yoshihiro, *The Formation of the Chinese Communist Party*, 115–16.

Sneevliet would not reprint literature from Indonesia in China, but he was sent to China in 1921 with the explicit mission to reproduce the cooperation that had been achieved in Indonesia with the nationalist organization Sarekat Islam. What that meant in a Chinese context was for him to build a strong alliance with Sun Yat-sen's Kuo Min Tang.[66] Throughout the years Sneevliet travelled China to convince the new communist party members to join the KMT, the policy met with a great deal of resistance. For many Chinese communists, the policy of alliance was seen as contrary to their principles and many refused to join the 'bourgeois' KMT.[67] Founding CCP member and student radical Zhang Guotao (1897–1979) spoke at great length during the third-party congress held in Guangzhou in 1923, reminding Sneevliet that the KMT was no Sarekat Islam, and China no Java.[68] What was a welcome plan in Moscow did not necessarily go down well in Guangzhou.

Borodin replaced Sneevliet in China in 1923, and Roy joined him in 1927, as did his new partner, the German communist Louise Geissler. Their presence did not stop Chiang's Kai-shek's National Revolutionary Army from deciding that the CCP was becoming too influential and carrying out a massacre among communists and striking workers in Shanghai in April of 1927, killing thousands of people. Soon after, communist movements in Guangzhou and Wuhan too were violently repressed by nationalist forces.[69] The point here is not to overstate the Comintern emissaries' influence on events in China, where they were mostly powerless, but rather to outline the intellectual role they had within the organization – a role that was required yet often viewed sceptically. Some of this scepticism came from close quarters. Many years after she had left China and the realm of communism, Louise Geissler would remember the Comintern emissaries as rather clueless: 'When Roy was appointed to go to China, he himself, I guess, was surprised, as he wanted to go to India. As to your remark that he had no special knowledge of China: neither had Borodin before he went there, and neither had all the Russians …'[70] As a letter from a friend reassured Roy that Geissler thought 'fondly' of him, this was likely not part of a wholesale condemnation of some sort.[71] More likely, practices that had been part

---

[66] Tamiatto, 'Révolutionnaires Entre Deux Mondes', 66.
[67] Elleman, 'Soviet Diplomacy and the First United Front in China', 457; 462–3.
[68] Saich, *Origins of the First United Front*, 175–9.
[69] Elleman, 'Soviet Diplomacy and the First United Front in China', 473.
[70] Letter from Louise Geissler to Marshall Windmiller, 20 November 1956, Louise Geissler File, Box 1, Collection 2010C8: Windmiller Files, Hoover Institution.
[71] Letter from Bertram Wolfe to M. N. Roy, 12 April 1949, Betram Wolfe Correspondence, Collection 70: M. N. Roy papers Section 1, NMML.

and parcel of the Comintern approach lost their obvious quality when viewed from a different time and place.

The brutal suppression of Chinese communism had become world news and Roy's rivals readily held him responsible for it, particularly since it was not long after his return to Moscow that Roy was expelled from the Comintern. Many observers connected this with his actions in China.[72] In order to defend himself, Roy wrote a book called *Revolution and Counter-Revolution in China* after he had left Moscow for Berlin, which was translated into German and published in 1930. Before an English version could be published in India, Roy also published a slimmer volume called *My Experiences in China* there, in order to exonerate himself. His method for doing so was characteristic of the role he had grown accustomed to playing. He prefaced *Revolution and Counter-Revolution in China* with the following:

> Not being a treatise on Sinology, this book does not concern itself with an examination of the different theories set up regarding the history of China. Here the subject is approached positively. For the purpose of the book, it is immaterial whether Confucius lived six hundred years or eight hundred years before Christ; whether his teachings are codified in five books or nine books; whether he was the Prime Minister or the Minister of Finance of one of the innumerable Clan-States of ancient China. [...] The author has no desire to impose the reader with a show of vast learning.[73]

It was a lack of knowledge that Roy claimed made his judgement reliable. At the same time, this type of authority included practical experience – only, crucially, not a singular kind of practical experience with Chinese nationalists and communists, but revolutionary practical experience in several parts of the world that had been going through revolutions of the same nature as the one that had failed to materialize in China.

> The study [...] transcends the limits of one single country, and proceeds to ascertain the tactical and organisational principles of the revolutionary movements in the colonial countries generally in the light of the lessons learned in China. [...] As a matter of fact, I have been associated with the revolutionary movement in the entire colonial world, having for years played a leading role in the activities of the Communist International in that sphere. Even before the foundation of the Communist International, I had visited China, the Dutch

---

[72] A view already repudiated in John P. Haithcox, 'Nationalism and Communism in India: The Impact of the 1927 Comintern Failure in China', *The Journal of Asian Studies* 24, no. 3 (1965): 459–73.
[73] M. N. Roy, *Revolution and Counter-Revolution in China* (Calcutta: Renaissance Publishers, 1946), 2.

East Indies, the Philippines and Mexico, and took part in the revolutionary movements in those countries.[74]

Roy's own experiences were a source of legitimacy, given that they had been abstracted from several colonial and semi-colonial contexts. In order to argue that a distant view brought more clarity, disregarding the details occluding reality, a necessary conviction was that it was possible, through the 'layering' of experience of several places, to gain a more fundamental insight into all of them through a process of comparison and abstraction. Rather than gaining knowledge and learning the relevant languages of two distinct contexts, operating between them, Roy claimed to possess knowledge and experience that transcended context, as it was boiled down to the most fundamental of truths.

On top of this analytical perspective, distance could be framed as explicitly emotional, as Roy attempted to integrate his personal relationships as a legitimating element of his objective world view: 'Personal interest [...] has not been permitted to mar the objectivity of the study. [...] For example, Borodin is an old personal friend of mine, and I still cherish him as such; yet, he comes in for unsparing criticism.'[75] Both a lack of specific knowledge and the disregarding of personal ties were things Roy could frame as evidence of his objectivity, rather than marring his view.

Roy's projection of his image as a man whose understanding of revolutionary politics transcended specific contexts had mixed receptions, for example in Cold War-era US academia. *Revolution and Counter-Revolution in China* was reviewed in *Pacific Affairs* in 1949, by a horrified US historian of China: '... here is an Indian applying to China the categories which Russians have derived from a German who, like all of his generation, was under the shadow of the French Revolution,' a combination of perspectives which according to the reviewer could only be called 'europocentric,' and of little value in order to understand something about China itself.[76] In this review, the – geographical – layers going into the making of Roy's texts are given as evidence of their faultiness, rather than their opposite.

Some years later, Roy maintained the belief that practices from one context could be reproduced in another. While he was in prison during the early 1930s, a group of Indian students he had met in Berlin had joined the socialist wing of the

---

[74] *Ibid.*, 10.
[75] *Ibid.*
[76] John Fairbank, 'Revolution and Counter-Revolution in China (Book Review)', *Pacific Affairs* 22, no. 3 (1949): 278–82.

Congress party,⁷⁷ which had been founded by Jayaprakash Narayan (1902–79) in 1934.⁷⁸ Rather than becoming a CSP member himself, Roy instructed his followers to suddenly leave the party, intending to 'split' it into properly revolutionary and deplorably reformist elements. He based this policy on his experiences in China, where he felt that '… the nationalist Kuomintang, which he also regarded as "petty-bourgeois," had been the source of the most active cadre of the Chinese Communist party.'⁷⁹ His attack on the CSP had no such result, but only served to make Roy into a persona non grata with the congress socialists – who would go on to become quite influential in Nehru's government.⁸⁰ Considering different phenomena as expressions of the same underlying forces could mean Roy lost touch with the specific one at hand.

Who needs humanity

Until he returned to India, claims to an objective, outside point of view had been part and parcel of Roy's status as a foreigner who moved swiftly between various places. After he returned to India and was imprisoned there in 1931, his perambulations came to a grinding halt, but his development of an outsider's perspective continued. His outsiderhood had become political, as well as a fundamental part of his everyday experience in jail, but also caused him to take what he called a 'wider view' of human society, as he considered it from a distance. Roy's political isolation seemed complete, since he was imprisoned on account of engaging in 'communist conspiracy,' but was also excluded from international communist politics as well as the Communist Party of India after being expelled from the Comintern, with seemingly no one left on his side. In his prison writings, however, Roy turned his isolation into a sign of strength:

> My imprisonment [...] has ruined my health, but my spirit remains uncrushed. As a matter of fact, I am encouraged by this barbarous and vindictive treatment. It enhances my self-confidence, and affords me the feeling of satisfaction that,

---

[77] In his autobiography, Narayan would write that it was through Roy's works that he had come to Marxism, as a student in the United States in the 1920s. Pranav Jani, 'Bihar, California, and the US Midwest: the early radicalization of Jayaprakash Narayan', *Postcolonial Studies* 16, no. 2 (2013): 163.
[78] While in prison, jail wardens supporting the nationalist cause helped Roy to smuggle letters out of prison, and he was able to keep in close contact with his followers. Haithcox, *Communism and Nationalism in India*, 199–200.
[79] Ibid., 231.
[80] Ibid., 230–2.

though not recognised publicly, my contributions to the cause of freedom have not been altogether negligible.[81]

Beyond his exclusion from the communist realm, Roy also developed his prison perspective as one that was on the outside of human society altogether. Most emphatically, he did so in a prison text written from the point of view of one of the few creatures he met while behind bars: a prison cat. In Roy's words, the cat shared her scientific and philosophical considerations:

> The physical Universe, with myriads of stars of which our sun is a very ordinary one, and thousands of millions of star-galaxies, is not a gigantic stage for man to strut about. The phenomenon of life, particularly in the form of human egocentrism, is not the cream of the cosmic scheme. It is rather a blemish in the magnificent harmony of things. I am a part of this blemish, just as much as is Rabindranath Tagore or Edgar Wallace. Indeed, the credit belongs equally to every bit of crawling protoplasm.[82]

Beyond the immediate relief of an escape into the imagination, the stylistic device of the cat's point of view allowed Roy to describe humanity with a degree of scientific distance, as a species, and not a particularly valuable one. Choosing an animal's perspective places the observer at true alterity from humanity.[83] In addition, the cat's was an outsiderhood that came with the specific claim of intimate observation: 'Having had the opportunity of observing man in his unguarded moments, and in conditions of jail life which force the beast in man to show its teeth, I claim my judgement to be objective.'[84] Here, the outside perspective was not a widely all-encompassing one, but one that could get close to the subject at hand, unnoticed, so alien that its intimate closeness was no affront. Such invisibility, too, could support a claim of objective insight.

However unusual as a technique in anti-colonial prison writing, the advantages of the cat's point of view were legion. Beyond claims of an objective perspective, the cat's voice allowed Roy to criticize specific aspects of the society he read about in newspapers while doing so with a degree of distance. He wrote

---

[81] 'I shall keep on hunting lies. It is too late for popularity; and fortunately, I do not possess sufficient intellectual mediocrity to qualify for the dubious distinction.' Roy, *Fragments of a Prisoner's Diary: Volume II*, 100–1.

[82] Roy, *Fragments of a Prisoner's Diary: Volume I*, 11.

[83] On an animal perspective as an alternative to a human one, Peter Steeves has written that '... if there is alterity to be had in the animal, then it is radical alterity indeed.' Peter H. Steeves, 'Introduction', in *Animal Others: On Ethics, Ontology, and Animal Life*, ed. Peter H. Steeves (Albany: State University of New York Press, 1999), 9.

[84] Roy, *Fragments of a Prisoner's Diary: Volume I*, 9.

down some scathing judgements of Hindu beliefs, but integrated them into the cat's overall lack of enthusiasm about human religion. All of those took on their true irrationality when considered from the cat's point of view. So when Roy damningly wrote about the holiness of cows, vegetarianism, astrology, the doctrine of dharma, he made them specific examples of humanity's talent for keeping itself in the chains of faith, whatever that faith was called:[85]

> Hinduism is the ideology of social slavery. Every religion is an instrument for keeping the masses in spiritual darkness, so that they may be more amenable to the rule of the upper classes; so that they obey authority willingly and unquestioningly; so that they accept the inequities of life as ordained by divine justice ...[86]

From outside, different practices could be flung onto the same heap. This extended beyond religions, as the cat opined that all versions of nationalism too counted as similarly erroneous human beliefs. In the text, Roy equated religious beliefs with nationalist ones, both Indian and European, as equally exemplary of human folly.[87] Choosing a narrator from an entirely different part of the animal kingdom provided Roy with the ultimate outside point of view, not just to a particular part of the world, but all the people in it. Roy's way of writing about his objective point of view was highly individual and idiosyncratic. This highlights that highly impersonal claims, verging on the universal, rest on deeply personal practices and modes of thought.

Among former communists in the United States, Roy's one-time peers and potential sources for ideas and support, his continued dedication to the objective, outside point of view caused friction, particularly at the time of Stalin's Great Purge (1936–8).[88] One of Roy and Ellen's fellow ex-communists in the

---

[85] 'Cow-worship is not an expression of pantheism; it is the outcome of a utilitarian philosophy.' 'Repudiation of the cult of vegetarianism is a condition for the physical improvement and intellectual awakening of the Indian masses. Let this insignificant member of a carnivorous species tell you: Eat more meat; that is a high-road to the salvation of your precious souls.' 'I have heard any number of grown-up people expatiating upon the common cant that *dharma* is the essence of life. But ask them what is *dharma*; hardly one in a thousand has any definite notion about what the so freely, and so frequently used term stands for.' 'The pseudo-scientific Western astrology pretends to be free of any belief in the super-natural. It maintains that the stars exert physico-chemical (or electric, if you wish to be ultra-modern) influence upon the human beings inhabiting the earth. This notion is silly enough; but the doctrine of Hindu astrology is simply amusing.' *Ibid.*, 22; 27; 29; 86.
[86] *Ibid.*, 67.
[87] 'Nationalism is a typically human virtue or vice. I am free from it. Animals, and human beings deprived of human comforts and culture, as the majority of them are in India, are naturally indifferent to the empty ideals of nationalism.' *Ibid.*, 59.
[88] Including the show trials of old guard Bolsheviks such as Grigory Zinoviev, the Purges would claim the lives of three-quarters of a million of Soviet citizens '... in the name of cleansing the Communist Party and the Soviet Union of various vaguely "counterrevolutionary" elements.' J. Arch Getty and

United States shared his opinion of the regime he had previously enthusiastically supported in a 1938 letter that described events in Russia as 'horrible,' and Stalin as '... Gangster No. 1 – Public Enemy No. 1 of the world labor movement to-day. Ghengis Kahn [sic] was a polite drooping water lily compared to him. I do not believe in the execution of comrades over differences of opinion ...'[89] Roy begged to differ, not because he had more information than his friend, but instead citing his own remove from the situation as giving him a more objective point of view, akin to Stalin's own:

> I am fully aware that many heart-rending things are happening. I find it very difficult to explain some of the things. But what would happen if we are compelled to attack the Georgian's policy as 'positively counter-revolutionary'? I am afraid, being in the midst of things, you sometimes cannot look at them from a proper perspective. I can more easily. And therefore I am in a position to see how all these apparently counter-revolutionary behaviours may be compelled by circumstances and even determined by the desire to proceed cautiously according to a far-sighted plan.[90]

The style of remaining aloof from emotions clearly had emotional consequences of its own, driving a wedge between old friends. Correspondence would for a long time fall silent after this exchange, but Stalin remained a source of inspiration for Roy. Some years after this exchange, a close colleague and friend would also take issue with the emotional aspects of Roy's removed point of view. In a 1948 letter, Roy's Spratt took issue with the distance that Roy seemed to be keeping from the larger political questions of the day. Spratt often sent Roy articles or books exposing the murderous reality of the Soviet regime, and also took up the issue of the situation in Kashmir – at independence, it had become a part of India, even though its majority Muslim population meant that Pakistan also laid claim to it.[91] The Radical Humanists had been discussing the issue by

---

Oleg V. Naumov's book about the Purges opens with the execution of Alexander Yulevich Tivel, describing him as '... [a] journalist and editor, [...] midlevel bureaucrat, a minor figure whose records in no way stand out in the archives of the era.' It is highly likely that this is the same Tivel who later featured in Roy's memoirs as a highly unusual polyglot from a Jewish family in Baku, who, out of interest in the liberation of India, supported Roy's work in Tashkent as a translator. J. Arch Getty, Oleg V. Naumov, *The Road to Terror: Stalin and the Self-Destruction of the Bolsheviks, 1932–1939* (New Haven: Yale University Press, 1999), 1–5; Roy, *Memoirs*, 530.

[89] Letter from Jay Lovestone to M. N. and Ellen Roy, New York, 12 January 1938, Jay Lovestone Correspondence, Catalogue 70: M. N. Roy Papers Section 1, NMML.
[90] Letter of M. N. Roy to Jay Lovestone, Bombay, 19 October 1937, Jay Lovestone Correspondence, Catalogue 70: M. N. Roy Papers Section 1, NMML.
[91] Yasmin Khan, *The Great Partition: The Making of India and Pakistan* (New Haven: Yale University Press, 2008), 182–3.

calling for a plebiscite, allowing the population to decide. When a war raged in Kashmir in 1948, Spratt wrote to Roy: 'Anyway I have a feeling that we may have been guided to an undue extent by abstract political considerations where more human considerations would have led us to take a very different view.'[92] Spratt's objections suggest that it is not merely the resolution that changes when a subject is considered from a zoomed out perspective, but that it becomes essentially different. Rather than capturing more, then, the removed point of view captures a reality that is a different one from those unconcerned with a wider view.

In the post-communist intellectual milieu that Roy became a part of during the 1940s and 1950s, and in which he developed his humanist ideas, the subject of the human was often phrased as a question. A well-known impulse to this line of inquiry was given by the Hungarian-British author Arthur Koestler (1905–1983), who was a member of the German Communist Party until 1938, when the Stalinist Purges hit in full force. Ellen and Roy knew him from their time in the party, and in 1947 they corresponded, wondering which of their former comrades were still 'in,' and which were 'out.'[93] Koestler's books criticizing doctrinaire communism, notably *Darkness at Noon* (1940) and a collection of essays called *The God That Failed: Six Studies in Communism* (1950) were highly influential as testaments of a former communist on the deeply flawed project of the Soviet Union.[94] Koestler's work was discussed in Roy's humanist journals,[95] and he considered *Darkness at Noon*, a harrowing account of the Purges, 'the novel par excellence of its time.'[96] The novel's central theme concerned the tension between a philosophy of abstractions guiding politics, and the non-abstract human being supposed to put them into practice. Set against the backdrop of a fictionalized show trial, it had its protagonist, an aged

---

[92] Letter from Philip Spratt to M. N. Roy, 26 April 1948, Philip Spratt Correspondence, Catalogue 70: M. N. Roy Papers, Section 1, NMML.

[93] Letter from Arthur Koestler to Ellen Roy, 5 June 1947, Koestler Correspondence, Catalogue 70: M. N. Roy Papers Section 1, NMML.

[94] Dan Stone, 'The Uses and Abuses of "secular Religion": Jules Monnerot's Path from Communism to Fascism', *History of European Ideas* 37, no. 4 (2011): 470.

[95] His switch hade made Koestler far from universally popular. When Ellen Roy reviewed *The God That Failed* in 1950, this prompted her friend and fellow former communist Ruth Fischer (1895–1961) to remark that 'I would have treated Mr. Koestler's idiocies with less humanitarianism and told him more bluntly that he has never understood Communism and that therefore his discoveries are not worth a tinker's damn.' Letter from Ruth Fischer to M. N. and Ellen Roy, 4 December 1950, Ruth Fischer Correspondence, Catalogue 70: M. N. Roy Papers Section 1, NMML.

[96] 'When Koestler was in Bombay he had visited Roy at [Wadia's] Casa. I faintly remember both reminiscing over their contact abroad; and Koestler who had come to be with Roy and Ellen for a short while, only in view of his brief halt in Bombay, had stayed with us for dinner and drinks and left at midnight rather reluctantly.' Wadia, *M N Roy, the Man*, 24.

Bolshevik now accused of being a counterrevolutionary, muse on fundamental questions while in his cell:

> The sole object of revolution was the abolition of senseless suffering. But it had turned out that the removal of this [...] kind of suffering was only possible at the price of a temporary enormous increase in the sum total of the [suffering of individuals]. So the question now ran: Was such an operation justified? Obviously it was, if one spoke in the abstract of 'mankind'; but, applied to 'man' in the singular, [...] the real human being of bone and flesh and blood and skin, the principle led to absurdity.[97]

Because it exposed the absurdity of the revolutionary project, the I that the protagonist had discovered was '... a suspect quality. The Party did not recognize its existence. The definition of the individual was: a multitude of one million divided by one million.'[98] The only kind of individual that could be recognized by the system Koestler described was a faceless being, only definable by its mathematically constituting a minute fraction of a mass. In developing his humanist ideas, Roy attached great value to the individual, and individual freedom, as the starting point of any philosophy that was amenable to a fulfilling life. At the same time, he remained committed to a wider view, and the individualism he embraced had to be of an abstract nature, so it could become a highly generalizable phenomenon. This combination was a difficult proposition, that on one hand required a personality like Roy's, with a great deal of faith in his own capacities. Yet on the other, it involved the assumption that all individuals shared this ability equally.

In his final years, Roy sought to synthesize these contradictory demands in his own theory of everything, in the two volumes of *Reason, Romanticism and Revolution* (1952 and 1955). These books contain a dizzying romp through the history of European history and philosophy. Roy took his readers from prehistory to Greek antiquity, the Italian Renaissance, the Enlightenment, the French Revolution, German Romanticism, Liberalism and Utilitarianism, Hegel and Marx, and finally the Twins of Irrationalism: communism and Nazism, with the final chapter on New Humanism showing readers The Way Out. An astounding range of thinkers featured in the pages of *Reason, Romanticism and Revolution*, and a clear agenda grouped them all around a central problem. This was the combination of Roy's belief in the freedom of the individual, creatively

---

[97] Arthur Koestler, *Darkness at Noon* (New York: Random House, 1941), 255.
[98] *Ibid.*, 257.

shaping his or her own destiny, with the possibility of scientific knowledge, requiring a determined, predictable universe. The two perspectives on humanity came together in Roy's view of the historical occurrence of revolutions:

> The passionate belief in the creativeness and freedom of man is the essence of the romantic view of life. The idea of revolution, therefore, is a romantic idea; at the same time, it is rational because revolutions take place of necessity. Revolution, thus, may appear to be a self-contradictory concept. Can reason and romanticism be fitted into the self-same evolutionary process? That is the fundamental problem of the philosophy of history.[99]

In many ways, rather than the fundamental problem of the philosophy of history, this problem was Roy's own, as he had seen several universal thought systems falling apart and being duly criticized, but was not prepared to give up on their possibility. In the book, the builders of universal systems found their avatars in the thought of Hegel and Marx, and that of the free individual in the work of the French historian Jules Michelet (1798–1874).[100] Michelet was mostly known for his influential *History of the French Revolution* (1847) and his attempt to write a *Universal History*. In Roy's tome, he became a profoundly humanist thinker with whom '… literature became a means for dramatising history; he wrote history not as a mere chronicle of events, but as a vivid account of man's struggle for freedom through the ages.'[101] In Roy's theory of everything, the essential building block was that of the individual, without attention to whom human freedom would be an empty signifier. Yet, it had to be an account of the individual that was not so quixotic that nothing larger could be constructed on its foundation. Rather than in physics or psychology, Roy found this building block in a work of history:

> Michelet gave a larger, almost a metaphysical connotation to Humanism, thereby raising it far above the level of the subjectivist individualism [...] He conceived humanity not as a conglomeration of individual human beings, not as a 'concrete universal,' but as an abstraction from empirical facts, and held that humanity was greater than the great men of history. [...] He used the term 'tout le monde' to express the abstract conception of humanity, which appears in his writings as a person; but he did not idealise the abstraction. It was a democratic concept. The conception of humanity personified in abstraction is the maker of history.[102]

---

[99] M. N. Roy, *Reason, Romanticism and Revolution: Volume One* (Calcutta: Renaissance Publishers, 1952), 14.
[100] Roy, *Reason, Romanticism and Revolution: Volume One*, 1.
[101] Roy, *Reason, Romanticism and Revolution: Volume Two*, 22.
[102] *Ibid.*, 23.

A 'concrete universal' was a Hegelian answer to the problem of '... how to unite many distinct entities without denying their difference,' in that it is a universal that '... only exists through two distinct entities, or that their difference only exists through it.'[103] In Roy's conception, Michelet's tout le monde provided a superior alternative that was in some ways closer to the 'abstract universal' Hegel had thought of as inferior, where '... universals denominate or identify particulars, but they do not fully express what they are – and are thus also different from or abstract against them.'[104] It was this abstraction, however, that enabled humanity to play an active role in history like a unified personage, in a way that a loose collection of individuals could not. In other words, a generalization from particulars was what rendered an abstract conception of 'humanity' as something that was truly human, and free. Rather than conceiving of abstraction as inherently antithetical to freedom, Roy let go of a Hegelian and Marxist framework in order to make it the very possibility for individual freedom.

Reason, Romanticism and Revolution was his work that Roy was most keen to market abroad. As he wrote to his agent 'It is a humanist interpretation of the cultural, intellectual and political history of Europe; byt [sic] the approach is applicable to the study of the history of the world, and the theoretical conclusions can be generalised.'[105] The wide view it contained meant Roy saw it as not merely have something to say about one place but about the world. Apart from the content encapsulating the whole world, provided it was properly generalized, Roy was also convinced that the book had the potential to capture the attention of the whole world: 'Until now, all my works have been published in India; but this new one being a treatment of problems which are agitating the minds of all thinking and sensitive people throughout the world, I would like to have a larger market for it.'[106]

Only a large market would be able to do justice to the magnitude of the intellectual field Roy was working on, which contained all of world politics. Apart from *Reason, Romanticism and Revolution*, Roy also offered a selection of books

---

[103] Charlotte Baumann, 'Adorno, Hegel and the Concrete Universal', *Philosophy & Social Criticism* 37, no. 1 (2011): 78.
[104] 'Or you could say: universals unite many particulars, but only by reducing them to their common denominator, rather than expressing their manifold and differentiated relations. The unity does not arise organically from its own parts or members, but is something, at least partly, imposed on them.' Ibid., 74.
[105] Ibid.
[106] Ibid.

he could supply the agent with at a moment's notice: '1. Common Philosophical Parentage of Fascism and Communism; 2. The Crisis of Our Time; 3. A New Concept and Pattern of Democracy; 4. Asian Nationalism – a Cultural Conflict.' It was as an expert in world politics that Roy tried to place himself in the US book market, although he was very well aware that it would be more likely that he was expected to publish articles about Indian matters.[107] Indeed, the agent only commissioned a book named *Alternatives to Communism*, as it fit the profile of someone with first-hand knowledge of the Communist International, now criticizing his previous experience. Probably with the expectations of her target audience in mind, however, she suggested an alternative title for the book: *Immortal India*.[108] That hardly seems obvious for a collection of lectures on subjects such as radicalism, materialism, marxism and humanism, that were held together by the effort to find a philosophy appropriate to the contemporary moment, and improving upon the past.[109] Roy wanted to offer his humanist interpretation of the world to the United States, but what was asked of him was a mystical version of India. Even among humanists, audiences failed to see the value in Roy's humanist publications. When the Radical Humanists sought to pay their contribution to the International Humanist and Ethical Union by sending a selection of Roy's books to be sold in the Netherlands, the secretary requested that they send '… so-called gift parcels containing e.g. articles of real Indian industrial art or art needlework' instead.[110] While Roy's books presented a focus on the European Renaissance and the development of the individual, their prospective Dutch buyers put a higher price on recognizably Indian artefacts.

Minor opportunities

As Roy had tried to find new partners when he needed them during his time abroad, he once again had to do so when he was in India and left prison in 1936. His attempts would still involve mobilizing his cosmopolitan reputation

---

[107] 'I can supply articles on Indian philosophy and culture, if they will be easier to place. But they will not be the usual conventional stuff, but critical.' Letter from M. N. Roy to Mavis McIntosh, 19 June 1951, Mavis McIntosh Correspondence, Catalogue 70: M. N. Roy Papers Section 1, NMML.
[108] Letter from M. N. Roy to Richard Park, 21 May 1953, Richard Park Correspondence Section 2, M. N. Roy Papers Section 1, NMML.
[109] M. N. Roy, Philip Spratt, *Beyond Communism* (Kolkata: Renaissance Publishers, 2011).
[110] Letter from Jan Bijleveld to Ellen Roy, 2 January 1961, 75–1065–2.04, Humanistisch Verbond, Stukken betreffende contacten met humanisten in Amerika, België, Canada, Duitsland, India, Israël, Italië, Japan en Korea, 1954–1969, HUA.

and the perspective it endowed him with, though in various new ways. Both Ellen and Roy were politically active within the Congress party for a time, but were expelled for carrying out an anti-fascist demonstration in 1940.[111] They then started the Radical Democratic Party as well as a trade union named the International Federation of Labour of their own, both organizations that sought to rally the Indian population to the Allied war effort – an unpopular platform during a time when other politicians were engaged in the Quit India Movement, which aimed for the removal of the British from India without delay. As India was forced to fight on the side of the British Empire, it was a much resented war to which Congress leaders would declare their opposition in 1942, leading to mass arrests.[112]

Even to friends and sympathizers, Roy seemed to have manoeuvred himself into a difficult position; by the end of 1940, Roy's friend Amarendranath Chatterji (1880–1957), a fellow Bengali one-time revolutionary, wrote to Roy with encouragement as well as doubts about the seemingly awkward position Roy had gotten himself into.

> You have the intellectual acumen to adapt yourself to a changed situation and the experience of a veteran politician, & therefore you have my heart with you; but what shall you do with the flabby heart of an ageing man. [...] Your idiology [*sic*] is really tempting and all the youths of India will accept your idiology some day sooner or later. But your present step is not so clear to us and to many. Everybody has been asking along with me: is Roy a superchemist, he will dissolve all indissolubles into one Chemical mixture to prepare potent remedy against all our present evils.'[113]

Chatterji's letter suggested not only his image of Roy as adaptable to difficult situations and flexible when circumstances changed, but the figure of the chemist hinted at both his persona of a man of science and rationality, and the impossibility of the situation he found himself in: only a super chemist might be able to solve its inherent contradictions.

In 1942, Roy entered into a cooperation that crossed what for many would be a red line, when the IFL began receiving a monthly grant from the Labour

---

[111] Manjapra, M. N. Roy, 128–9.
[112] Some of Roy's closest associates at the time, such as Maniben Kara (1905–79) and V. B. Karnik (?–?) were active in the trade union movement, where they split from the All-India Trade Union Congress in order to form the IFL. Dipti Kumar Roy, *Trade Union Movement in India: Role of M. N. Roy* (Calcutta: Minerva Associates, 1990), 1–28.
[113] Letter from Amarendranath Chattopadhyaya, to M. N. Roy, 9 December 1940, Amarendranath Chattopadhyaya Correspondence, Catalogue 70: M. N. Roy Papers Section 1, NMML.

Department of the Government of India. It was paid to produce pro-war propaganda among workers in Bengal, Bombay, Bihar, Madras, Uttar Pradesh and Delhi. The same year, doubts arose in the Labour Department regarding the efficacy of the grant, as it was reported that the influence of the Roy group with workers was quite small.[114] Still in 1944, however, the department was weary of alienating Roy, thinking he might come in useful at some point, and kept his organization on their payroll.[115] Then, by the end of the year, news of the IFL's grant was published in the *Bombay Chronicle*, and condemnations in the nationalist press ensued.[116] While the IFL's receiving funds from the colonial government tarnished Roy's reputation in British India, the RDP sought to find new partners internationally.

One of the parties approached was the British Labour Party, by which the RDP sought to be recognized as a sister party. In its letters, the RDP suggested it had something potentially interesting to offer to war-plagued Britain. They offered the population of India as a promising feature in the context of destruction wrought by the war. In a text called *Indian Labour and Post-War Reconstruction* (1943), they presented the size of the population of India as a potential asset for the reconstruction of the entire world, declaring that the 'Indian Federation of Labour is very keenly alive to this great opportunity.'[117] The text conceded that '… wars always cause impoverishment,' but optimistically added: '… the evil is not unmixed,' as '… improved and new means of production […] can compensate for the loss in human life suffered during the war.'[118] In addition, a loss in human life also allowed the IFL to portray India's seemingly large population in a positive light. '… by virtue of being vast reservoirs of labour, the so-called Eastern countries are destined to make a great contribution to the post-war reconstruction of the world.'[119] Whereas Roy's writing on population generally lamented that there were simply too many people in India,[120] when it came to approaching a new potential partner, a vast reservoir of human beings could be portrayed in a positive light, optimistically offering solace to a country in need of assistance.

---

[114] 'Policy towards M.N. Roy, his activities connected with the Labour and Pro-war Propaganda, and his paper Independent India' Digitized Public Records/Home Political-I 1942, File 7; 9, National Archives of India, Delhi, India (hence NAI).
[115] *Ibid.*, File 10.
[116] *Ibid.*, File 19.
[117] Roy, *Indian Labour*, 17.
[118] *Ibid.*, 2.
[119] *Ibid.*, 36.
[120] See Chapter 1.

Letters written to the BLP had to admit an obvious fact: the Radical Democratic Party was not a political party of great significance in Indian politics.[121] Undiscouraged, the radical democrats asserted that it was an 'international outlook' which nevertheless gave the party credit as a political player, as it was so sorely lacking with other political parties, but an obvious requirement in a connected world. Here too, perspective was crucial. The RDP argued that factors more commonly used as indicators of political relevance, such as electoral success, were in fact highly damaging: 'A party's character cannot be assessed by such adventitious circumstances as its influencial [sic] following, or the votes that it gathers at a particular election.'[122] In fact, Roy and his fellow party members would time and again decry the 1937 provincial elections, since the franchise had been based on property qualifications, excluding the vast majority of the population. But even if suffrage was to be universal, their messaging to British Labour betrayed a deep suspicion of the votes that might then be cast, as the radical democrats emphasized the role of communalist politics in the upcoming elections of 1946, holding up the spectre of fascism making its mark in India as it had been tearing apart Europe.[123]

> The older nationalist parties may at the moment appear to have large followings but that is due chiefly to the circumstance of the ignorance of the people whose sentiments can be easily exploited on national and racial prejudices. If on the strength of such following, they are accepted as the representatives of the Indian people, India will have a government that will put a premium on popular ignorance and foment racial and national hatred.[124]

With their strategies including optimistic promises and dark predictions, the RDP also made an attempt that was positively daring when they tried to influence the process by which independent India would come by its constitution, suggesting their own Draft Constitution of India as a blueprint. In an accompanying letter, they urged British Labourites to '... consider it for your upcoming meeting with [viceroy] Wavell.'[125] With British India's independence just around the corner, the RDP had prepared a Draft Constitution of Free India, and attempted to get it passed on to the British Parliament. 'If the latter sponsors

---

[121] British Labour considered the Radical Democrats to be a 'small group with no wide influence or following,' concluding there was no reason not to 'encourage' them. The Radical Democratic Party – International Department, LP/ID/IND/2/40, PHM.
[122] Statement by Karnik about RDP, 2.9.44, LP/ID/IND/2/6i-v, PHM.
[123] For Roy on Indian fascism, see Chapter 3.
[124] Statement by Karnik about RDP, 2.9.44, LP/ID/IND/2/6i-v, PHM.
[125] Letter from Tarkunde to Phillips LP/ID/IND/2/37i, People's History Museum, Manchester.

such a constitutional draft and submits it to a referendum in India, there is no doubt that the vast majority of the people belonging to all the principal communities in the country will enthusiastically support and sanction it.'[126] The undemocratic implications of this attempt were clear to those around Roy. As a friend and collaborator would remind him in 1946: 'If the British Labour Party had listened to your argument and put you in power, would yours not be a dictatorship – a historically necessary dictatorship?'[127] Even to his friends, a seemingly a-political offer of expertise – in writing a sensible constitution, unmarred by communalist politics – looked clearly undemocratic.

Something circumscribing the RDP's international efforts was that Indian politics were hardly as mysterious to British Labour as they had been to the Comintern during the 1920s. When news of government funding for the IFL broke in the Indian press, S. A. Dange (1899–1991), president of the rival trade union AITUC, sent word of the scandal to the British Labour Party.[128] Dange wired a report of the controversy, which read that '... [t]he last three weeks have seen the complete disintegration of M. N. Roy's Indian Federation of Labour (the I. F. L.) ....' It detailed a debate in the Central Assembly that cast doubt on Roy's use of the government funds, and noted that '... Roy admitted the Government was subsidising Roy's Delhi Daily newspaper, The Vanguard, buying 1,500 copies in bulk every day.' Added in handwriting at the bottom of the page was the comment: 'The total number of copies printed is about 2000 only.' Apart from this detail, the report said that the leaders of the Railwaymen's and Seamen's Unions, '... on whose credit Roy was trading,' had quit the IFL, and that '... only a rump is left behind composed solely of Roy and his followers.'[129] In his accompanying letter, Dange cautioned the BLP to stop seeing the IFL as a 'bona fide union.'[130] The contact between British Labour and the RDP ends with this message, suggesting that outsiders' politics worked best when distances were in place and connections were thin.

The perspective from a distance that had represented such an asset also contained a great deal of blind spots. During their time involved in labour organizing, it is remarkable that the Roys never allied themselves with one of

---

[126] 'The Indian Problem – A democratic approach' LP/ID/IND/2/40, PHM.
[127] Letter from Sushil Dey to M. N. Roy, Manali, 24 June 1946, Sushil Dey Correspondence, Collection 70: M. N. Roy papers Section 1, NMML.
[128] 'Report from India received by cable, 18 December 1944', LP/ID/IND/2/15i, PHM.
[129] 'Report from India received by cable, 10 December 1944', LP/ID/IND/2/15ii, PHM.
[130] Letter from S. A. Dange to General Secretary of the Labour Party, 19 December 1944, LP/ID/IND/2/15i, PHM.

the great iconoclasts of the time: Bhimrao Ambedkar (1891–1956). Ambedkar's and Roy's superficial similarities included their professed cosmopolitanism, or as Ambedkar wrote to Gandhi in 1931: 'I have no homeland.' Yet, these cosmopolitanisms were of very different kinds: Ambedkar called his unfinished autobiography *Waiting for a Visa*, but it included meditations on 'the exclusionary and even racial foundations of modern citizenship,' which were not at the root of Roy's attacks on similar institutions.[131] Beyond cosmopolitanism, both men opposed Hindu nationalism, and possessed an aversion to the politics and writings of Gandhi. They also had several points of contact, for example when Roy had only just returned to the subcontinent and was hiding from the police, he met with Ambedkar. Ambedkar was not impressed with his visitor, and concluded that he '... had not thought over the problem of the Untouchables.'[132] Considering social issues from a general perspective, seeking their underlying reality and presuming that to be stable across the world meant that it became near impossible for Roy to see and seek to change issues that were specific to the caste system as they were attacked by Ambedkar. This difference in their preoccupations continued throughout the period that they were both active in the world of organized labour, often finding themselves on the same side in labour conflicts, and being colleagues at the Ministry of Labour during the Second World War when Ambedkar was the Labour member on the Viceroy's Executive Council.[133] While a shared opposition to Hindu-inspired politics, and rejection of much of what their homeland symbolized could have united them, Roy's perspective was too wide to find affinity with Ambedkar.

Ford and Rockefeller

At the beginning of the Cold War era, Roy's past as an international communist proved to be a commodity to US organizations, where considerable resources were invested in the study of communism in Asia, in order to stem its growth. In the early fifties, a review of 'communist propaganda' in India from the US Central Intelligence Agency grouped the Radical Humanists among 'Leftist

---

[131] Aishwary Kumar, *Radical Equality: Ambedkar, Gandhi, and the Risk of Democracy* (Palo Alto: Stanford University Press, 2015), 15.
[132] Dhananjay Keer, *Dr. Ambedkar: Life and Mission* (Bombay: Popular Prakashan, 1962), 162.
[133] *Ibid.*, 347; Christophe Jaffrelot, *Dr. Ambedkar and Untouchability: Analysing and Fighting Caste* (New York: Columbia University Press, 2005), 5.

Parties opposed to cooperation with the [Communist Party of India]' and concluded: 'Alert to the imperialist objectives of the Soviet Union and to its tactics of working through local communist groups, Roy advocates close Indian friendship with the United States.'[134] The connection that materialized between Roy and the US establishment came in the shape of the US South Asianist and development expert Richard Park (1920–80), whose ties to both the Rockefeller and the Ford Foundations meant that the US-sponsored view of development became one of the Roys' house guests.[135] Over the next few years, Park would try to acquire funding for a lecture tour of Roy and Ellen through the United States, as well as support for their Renaissance Institute and assist in getting Roy's work published in the US.

The Roys struck up a close friendship with Park that had to do with a shared tendency to consider world affairs from a general perspective. Park found himself as an outsider in India, always darting in and out, constantly on the go. With the Roys, he found a place where his foreignness was at home, writing to them about the troubles he had with an assignment, because of his lack of linguistic and contextual knowledge. 'My work on the elections goes along slowly but steadily. […] It is a bit difficult for me, an outsider, to press this study through to completion.' Park's role was to add a layer of 'social analysis' to election reports coming in from various parts of India, most of which he rated as 'incredibly bad' since they did not contain any analysis but amounted to '… the writing down of assorted "facts," all of the latter not being verified.'[136] The problems posed by the outsiderhood of the development expert, adding technical expertise to local – suspect – knowledge, were an inherent part of the role.[137] It is significant that they could count on the sympathetic reading of Roy and Ellen, even though they were critical of the brand of US soft power represented by Park.

The like-mindedness between Roy and Park was not total; when they discussed the so-called Etawah Plan, a collection of villages in Uttar Pradesh planned by the US planner and architect Albert Mayer (1897–1981) engineered

---

[134] 'Stage IV – Operating Action', CIA-RDP61S00750A000700120006-4, Crest, General CIA Records, accessed 25 June 2020, 20–1, https://www.cia.gov/library/readingroom/document/cia-rdp61s00750a000700120006-4.

[135] According to Inderjeet Parmar, these two foundations – alongside Carnegie – played a key role in US foreign policy during the Cold War and after. Inderjeet Parmar, *Foundations of the American Century: The Ford, Carnegie, and Rockefeller Foundations in the Rise of American Power* (New York: Columbia University Press, 2012), 1–30.

[136] Letter from Richard Park to Ellen and M. N. Roy, 5 August 1952, Richard Park Correspondence Section 1, Catalogue 70: M. N. Roy Papers Section 1, NMML.

[137] Markus Daechsel, *Islamabad and the Politics of International Development in Pakistan* (Cambridge: Cambridge University Press, 2015), 70.

to enhance the 'inner democratization' of their residents,[138] they disagreed on fundamentals. Park spoke glowingly of the model villages,[139] whereas Roy thought that the project he considered as an instance of 'pragmatic social engineering' failed to take into account 'the more fundamental aspects of India's social and economic problems.'[140] Yet, this did not mean Roy assumed such problems to be specific to India. Instead, his thinking about matters of development and human freedom went far beyond those offered by the physical environment.[141] What he considered as the contribution to India's development that he could offer was rather in the realm of education and the mind. The right kind of instruction could change people's minds much more than could their homes: '... scientific knowledge as well as the lesson of history, that man can make or mar his destiny, will change his outlook, awaken in him the consciousness of his creative power and help the unfolding of his untold potentialities.'[142] With a lot riding on the idea of education and its ability to change the nature of individuals and with that, the world, philosophical discussion called 'study camps' assumed a role of central importance at the Roys' Renaissance Institute. Ellen provided the following description of its activities to an acquaintance from communist days, Margarete Buber-Neumann (1901–89).[143]

> Here we hold periodical study camps attended by the younger leaders of public life, teachers and professors and members of the other free intellectual professions; also smaller circles for study and research work. We find that ideas spread more rapidly by thus educating the educators first than going straight to the masses.[144]

---

[138] Robert C. Emmett, *Guide to the Albert Mayer Papers on India* (Committee on Southern Asian Studies and Southern Asia Reference Center: The University of Chicago, 1977), 5.
[139] Letter from Richard Park to Ellen and M. N. Roy, 11 March 1952, Richard Park Correspondence Section 1, Catalogue 70: M. N. Roy Papers Section 1, NMML.
[140] Letter from M. N. Roy to Richard Park, 15 March 1952, Richard Park Correspondence Section 1, Catalogue 70: M. N. Roy Papers Section 1, NMML.
[141] It would likely have puzzled Roy that in the 1960s and '70s, his Radical Humanist Movement cooperated with the International Humanist and Ethical Union on a development project in Bihar. Following a famine in the state of Bihar, there existed an institutional cooperation to create a development programme to increase food production as well as the local income from other livelihoods. 'Stukken betreffende het ontwikkelingsplan van de IHEU voor de bevolking van de provincie Bihar in India, 1962–1975' in 75–1059–2.04, Humanistisch verbond, Archief van de international humanist and ethical union (IHEU), HUA.
[142] Roy, *Radical Humanism*, 26–7.
[143] Having lived through a chequered international career of her own, Buber-Neumann became famous for having been imprisoned by both Stalin's and Hitler's regimes, first as a communist fallen from grace, and then when she was extradited to Nazi Germany. Her sister, Babette Gross, had been the partner of Willi Muenzenberg, one of the initiators of the League Against Imperialism. Letter from Margarete Buber-Neumann to Ellen Roy, 30 July 1953, Buber-Neumann Correspondence, Catalogue 70: M. N. Roy Papers Section 1, NMML.
[144] Letter from Ellen Roy to Margarete Buber-Neumann, 5 March 1953, Buber-Neumann Correspondence, Catalogue 70: M. N. Roy Papers Section 1, NMML.

Rather than focusing on the physical environment, the radical humanist project focused on the creation of a new elite, assumed more likely to assume the required wider perspective to gain a proper view of things. Explaining the importance of this project to Park, Roy wrote that his aim was '... training up a sufficiently large number of young people capable of, and anxious to, lay down the foundation of a democratic social order.'[145] Considering the involvement of the foundations in development projects in India, Roy thought himself a likely partner in instituting the mindset necessary to their success. His vision for doing so involved expanding the Renaissance Institute:

> ... for years I have been dreaming of developing the Indian Renaissance Institute into a non-official University, where higher education will be imparted with out any control from any side. Mr. Gilpatrick [of Rockefeller] having seen all our Universities from close quarters, he must appreciate the supreme necessity of such an educational institution as I propose to build up. If the plan materialises, we would like to have some Americans to join the institute, either as permanent members of the staff, or as visiting professors. You shall, of course, top my list, assuming that you will consider the idea.[146]

The expertise Roy credited himself and other radical humanists with was thus not of the variety that planned towns or approaches to agriculture, but one that was able to create new human beings by means of education, and would then form a new enlightened elite, with no attachments to a single nation, but as cosmopolitan as Roy. In his eyes, the need for them being funded from abroad was obvious, as their aims transcended that of a single nation and extended to the planet at large. At the same time, this meant he could offer an opportunity to Park in turn. Before any of these plans could materialize, Roy died, in 1954. Instead of funding their educational work, the Ford Foundation ended up supplying Ellen Roy with a grant to preserve Roy's personal archive.[147] So while the US foundations did not become a long-term new employer for Roy, they played a role in preserving his writings after he was gone.

---

[145] Letter from M. N. Roy to Richard Park, 2 May 1953, Richard Park Correspondence Section 2, Catalogue 70: M. N. Roy Papers Section 1, NMML.
[146] *Ibid.*
[147] Letter from Ellen Roy to Evelyn Jones-Trent, 29 June 1956, Evelyn Jones Correspondence, Catalogue 71: M. N. Roy Papers Section 2, NMML; J.B.H. Wadia, *M N Roy, the Man - an Incomplete Royana* (Bombay: Popular Prakashan, 1983).

Conclusion

Teasing out what could make a distinguished cosmopolitan into an important political ally has much to do with that which they were presumed to see. Being observed from far away has a pleasant quality, as it suggests the importance or interest on what is being observed and noticed. Distance can have an ennobling quality. Outsiders' accounts of the eccentricities of one's own culture can be highly entertaining and satisfying to read, their mundane nature suddenly special to a fresh pair of eyes. But if this gaze becomes so transient that no details can be noticed, it can omit the specificity of what it is looking at. A gaze that filtered out the essentials was necessary in order to compose an image of the world that had some coherence, especially when the intended field of operation was global. Agents able and willing to consider the world from this point of view benefited from a cosmopolitan persona to be taken seriously, the bearing of someone familiar with many parts of the world supporting their authority to say what those shared. They were not merely seen as outsiders, but as professional outsiders, whose authority did not extend to one kind of difference, but to difference in general.

In Roy's life, this habitus served him well to an extent, as it made him an influential political figure within the Comintern for a time, but in other contexts, such as All-India politics in the 1940s, it had the effect of limiting the connections he was able to make. But as a habitus and an ingrained perspective, it was not something to be easily changed, and characterized even his personal relationships. The objectivity with which he characterized his view, considering the fact that he criticized his personal friend Borodin, or that Stalin's Purges left him unfazed, extended to other areas of life. Once he wrote his memoirs, as engaging as many audiences found them, Ellen Roy described them as follows in a letter to Evelyn Trent-Jones: 'His memoirs, as you would imagine, are written in a thoroughly impersonal style, dealing only with what he factually did and his impressions of men and events.'[148] The distinguished cosmopolitanism informed by distance to what was close at hand could end up creating distance not only on an intellectual, but on an emotional level too. Yet, it was precisely this distance that made it desirable. Being disconnected, and unattached to the status quo,

---

[148] Letter from Ellen Roy to Evelyn Trent-Jones, 19 March 1954, Evelyn Jones Correspondence, Catalogue 71: M. N. Roy Papers Section II, NMML.

made some cosmopolitans into appropriate staff for international organizations seeking to change the world.

A politically and geographically unstable life, marked by a firm degree of precariousness both required and produced an attitude of resilience and optimism regarding new opportunities to work and live under ever-changing circumstances. It was an embracing of optimistic flexibility that allowed Roy and his political colleagues to, for example, suggest that the death of millions of people in the Second World War was not an 'unmixed' evil, as it would provide new opportunities for Indian Labour. But there was a fine line between opportunities and the stench of opportunism, a term deployed with particular vitriol within the Comintern.[149] The border between the desired kind of outsiderhood and that which was despicable was easily crossed, mostly by changing politics within the organization rather than any direct actions of the individual concerned. But, if one survived long enough, like Roy did, this exclusion could be taken as a part of an objective outsider persona once again; the fact that he was a 'renegade' even among communists became a key touchstone of the way he presented himself. When one is outcast even by outlaws, one must be truly independent of mind. Such self-presentations and reinterpretations of their own lives were key ways in which cosmopolitan outsiders retrospectively gave coherence to their lives. In this sense, ego documents had an extra use, as they did not only present a particular picture to their readers, but reshaped and re-interpreted a diffuse past that could invite charges of disloyalty into a coherent narrative that could claim some level of stability and therefore reliability.

---

[149] See for example Ville Laamanen, 'From Communist Cadre to Outsider: Ideals, Opportunism, and Coping with Change in Moscow and Stockholm, 1929–1948', *Scandinavian Journal of History* 45, no. 3 (2020): 334–59.

.5

A flat earth – Assertions of equivalence

Years before Thomas Friedman wrote that the world was flat, M. N. Roy tried to convince audiences across several continents that there existed no meaningful differences between Asia, North America and Europe. He found stable elements across various places and ideological spheres that he could reveal to his various audiences, for example between ancient India and contemporary Mexico, as well as between the class connotations and psychological makeup of Europeans and Indians. Even after a lifetime of travelling, imprisonment, world wars, fighting for India's independence and then having severe reservations about its manner of coming about, Roy managed to find stable elements that looked different to the untrained eye. After his intellectual and practical activities had taken him around the world, in 1931 Roy landed in a colonial prison in British India for six years. He voraciously read history, psychology and science, and claiming equivalences between different things was a way to quickly gain insight into a range of themes. He wrote, for example, that the Sankhya system of philosophy contained '... the Cartesian *Cogito, ergo sum* – literally. There are points of similarity with Epicuros also; and what is most remarkable, some elements of Lockean Sensationalism';[1] and when his friend, the German communist and orientalist August Thalheimer (1884–1948) inquired about Indian philosophy, Roy wrote that he needed to be set straight: 'I don't quite see what he means by "the special form of Indian logic." In my view, there has been much imagination in this respect on the part of the Sanskritists and Orientalists of Europe.'[2] Where other people inquired about differences, from Roy's point of view things looked the same. This view allowed for a swiftness of intellectual freedom of movement, even when Roy was stuck in prison.

---

[1] He swiftly continued on with physics and psychology, adding that: '... Einstein's new paper seems to back up some of my ideas;' and that '... Freud, Adler and Jung can be combined into a system which does not suffer from such extravagant formulas as Father = Horse'. Roy, *Letters from Jail*, 16; 28; 196; 121.
[2] *Ibid.*, 25.

In this chapter, this intellectual habit of claiming equivalences between different contexts is investigated as a special case of the cosmopolitan practice of translation. Rather than scrutinizing the way in which the equivalents created through translation shifted meanings in various languages, it focuses on the social functions of the practice of translation, and its relationship to its audiences. Like cosmopolitanism, translation operates between assumptions about and respectful encounters with difference, against the background of a universality of meaning or value.[3] According to Lydia Liu, translation is not a process involving the search for neatly fitting and mutually operational equivalences across two languages, but involves the creation of such equivalences by translators, quite possibly affecting the subsequent meaning in the target language.[4] The various levels of power and prestige of different languages play a key role in this process.[5]

The equivalences Roy sought to create were not between different natural languages, but the creation of equivalences within the same language can function as a translation too.[6] The fact that Roy mostly operated in European languages, as discussed in Chapter 1, shows that his approach to difference and the fundamental question after the need for translation was shaped by the power differentials of his time and environments. While he as such considered translation to certain languages unnecessary, he tried to create equivalences of meaning between different contexts throughout his career, and these were contexts his audiences assumed to differ in meaningful ways. Even though assumptions of difference played a huge role in crafting the role Roy had been able to play on an international stage, as he was tasked with bringing unfamiliar parts of the world into an ideological realm, in his own interpretation such differences were nothing but illusory. These assertions of equivalence were supported by a persona that was cosmopolitan in a distinguished sense, because it claimed to be above difference. A careful consideration of the assertions of equivalence Roy deployed widens the field of possibility for what translations look like and what they achieve, as well as finding a new kind of coherence in Roy's variegated life.

---

[3] Lydia H. Liu, 'The Question of Meaning-Value in the Political Economy of the Sign', in *Tokens of Exchange; The Problem of Translation in Global Circulations*, ed. Lydia H. Liu, Stanley Fish, Fredric Jameson (Durham: Duke University Press, 1999), 1–19.
[4] Lydia H. Liu, *Translingual Practice : Literature, National Culture, and Translated Modernity – China, 1900–1937* (Stanford: Stanford University Press, 1995), 16.
[5] Einar Wigen, *State of Translation: Turkey in Interlingual Relations* (Ann Arbor: University of Michigan Press, 2018), 11.
[6] Liu, 'Question of Meaning-Value', 28.

Comparative advantages

Roy's predilection for seeing equivalences was an intellectual practice that built upon modes of thought from several of the domains he could draw upon. According to Kris Manjapra, Roy engaged in a practice named 'Brahmo exegesis,' which had allowed the Bengali philosopher Rammohun Roy (1774–1833) to argue about the equivalence of the religious texts of Hinduism, Christianity and Islam, finding common principles at their core.[7] In addition, Marxist historical dialectics provided '… the conviction that the same laws apply in the same way to external nature, human affairs, and thought,' laying a solid foundation for cross-cultural and cross-discipline borrowings.[8] Later on, the developmentalist framework Roy engaged with during his humanist phase possessed its own ways of seeing all places, particularly 'underdeveloped' ones, as interchangeable.[9] Under vastly different ideological flags, understanding different places in similar terms was both possible and useful when operating across different contexts.

More directly, comparisons were an important ingredient within anti-imperialist writings among Roy's circles. In the affiliative practices engaged in by anti-colonial actors seeking allegiances with others, emphasizing commonalities over differences made good practical sense.[10] Manu Goswami has advanced the notion of 'insurgent comparison,' where intellectuals drew on anti-imperialist universalisms to claim equivalences where colonial hierarchies denied them.[11] Defining where the lines of difference and sameness lied could be an anti-imperial practice in its own right,[12] especially since the logic of European empires meant that the perspective from nowhere required for such

---

[7] Manjapra, *M. N. Roy*, 13. Manjapra's approach has been criticized as too reductive to explain Roy's full intellectual life, but nevertheless draws attention to the existence of various universalisms to be drawn on. Most recently see Christopher Balcom, 'From Communist Internationalism to a "New Humanism": On M.N. Roy's Confrontation with Fascism', *South Asia: Journal of South Asian Studies* 46, no. 2 (2023): 353–69.

[8] Paul Thomas, *Marxism & Scientific Socialism; From Engels to Althusser* (London: Routledge, 2008), 87.

[9] Daechsel, *Islamabad and the Politics of International Development in Pakistan*, 83–4.

[10] Karl, 'Staging the World in Late-qing China', 555; Manjapra, *M. N. Roy*, 7.

[11] Manu Goswami cites the works of Rabindranath Tagore, Boy Kumar Sarkar, José Carlos Mariátegui, W. E. B. Du Bois and C. L. R. James as containing 'insurgent comparisons', or the 'linking of political and intellectual currents conventionally considered separate […] in an imperial age overrun by coercive differentiations'. Manu Goswami, 'Imaginary Futures and Colonial Internationalisms', *The American Historical Review* 117, no. 5 (2012): 1484.

[12] See for example Clemens Six, 'Challenging the Grammar of Difference: Benoy Kumar Sarkar, Global Mobility and Anti-Imperialism Around the First World War', *European Review of History = Revue européenne d'histoire* 25, nos. 3–4 (2018): 431–49.

comparisons was largely reserved for white men.[13] In his approach, Roy went a step further than to affiliatively compare different places. Instead, he diagnosed equivalences between them. This set him apart within the intellectual circles that drew on similar intellectual backgrounds and practices. At times, this served to get him an audience with useful contacts, or even their support, but it could also come with a great deal of criticism from other intellectuals to whom differences between, for example, the economic superstructure in Europe and India, or Indian nationalism and European fascism were glaring, obvious and needed addressing.

An example of Goswami's 'insurgent comparison' that was used by Ghadarites in the United States during the 1910s was one between India's independence and that of the United States in the eighteenth century. One of the Indian revolutionaries accused at the San Francisco 'Hindu Conspiracy Trial' in 1917 was Chandra Chakravarty (?–?). In his defence statement, he cast himself as a freedom fighter in an appeal to the democratic traditions of the country where he was being tried. Chakravarty compared himself and his fellow revolutionaries to the colonial subjects who had revolted against the British Empire in the American Revolution, winning the United States their independence: '… we in India are endeavoring to do just as America did in 1776. While Washington was struggling at home, Benjamin Franklin was seeking aid in France. While my countrymen are struggling at home I sought aid in Berlin.'[14] Chakravarty's use of this tactic in front of a US audience attempted to cast himself in a positive role in the eyes of his audience, referring to their own history to find there an example of a rightfully revolutionary nation, seeking allegiances against a shared enemy: the British Empire.

Such comparisons had been among the repertoire of Ghadarites in years before, as they attempted to forge connections between Indian revolutionaries and other parties who found themselves in opposition to the British Empire, such as Irish Republicans. In 1916, Ghadar leader Ram Chandra (1886–1918) published a pamphlet called *India Against Britain* that used the name of Ireland's nationalist party, as well as the name of the eighteenth-century rebel

---

[13] Vanessa Ogle has made this point in connection to the practice of comparison, where different parts of the world were compared in various ways, but the point from which the comparison occurred, and as such assumed to exist on a different plane outside of the sites of comparison, would be that of an empire's metropole. Vanessa Ogle, *The Global Transformation of Time: 1870–1950* (Cambridge: Harvard University Press, 2015), 5–6.

[14] Quoted in Sohi, *Echoes of Mutiny*, 190.

leader Robert Emmett, for the work of Ghadar: 'The truth in this statement is that India has her Sinn Feiners ... [...] Whether the Irish Sinn Feiners command any influence in Ireland today is not for us to say. But we do insist that the Hindu Sinn Feiners today are as influential as the Irish were in the days of Robert Emmett.'[15] Such comparisons dressed one group in the historical attributes of another, in an act of intellectual diplomacy geared to bring them closer together.

Roy's first publication, *The Path to Durable Peace of the World* (1919), did exactly what Chakravarty had done, casting Indian revolutionaries as the equivalents of the United States' founding fathers, as both had rebelled against the British Empire at different points in time.[16] In later years, he would use a similar method to write a text for his own legal defence, where actors were cast in a role presumed to make them highly uncomfortable. When he published a text containing his legal defence at the time of his trial in 1931, he recruited well-respected British philosophers and legal scholars to make his case.

> In refuting the absurd charge, I have purposely not called in the evidence of foreign and frankly revolutionary authorities. I have relied exclusively upon liberal English thinkers and respectable constitutional lawyers to establish my case. I justify what I have held and done on the unchallengeable authority of Locke, Hume, Bentham, Bagehot, Dicey and even Blackstone. You can not punish me unless you prescribe the writings of these political philosophers and constitutional lawyers as seditious, revolutionary and treasonable.[17]

In co-opting this venerable yet stuffy list of Enlightenment and Victorian thinkers to argue for the legitimacy of his resistance to British rule, Roy pointed to the limits of liberal thought.[18] Liberty in Britain was clearly one thing, while in British India it was quite another. In his text, Roy created a stage on which familiar figures suddenly played parts that did not suit them, and gave their hallowed thoughts new meaning – a meaning that pointed out the double standards at work throughout a respected tradition.

---

[15] Quoted in Matthew Plowman, 'Irish Republicans and the Indo-German Conspiracy of World War I', *New Hibernia Review* 7, no. 3 (2003): 86.
[16] See Chapter 4.
[17] Roy, '*I accuse!*', 29.
[18] Particularly A. V. Dicey, the author of anti-Irish independence tract *England's Case against Home Rule* (1887), and Walter Bagehot, author of the racist tract *Physics and Politics* (1872), were daring choices.

Mixed races

Moving beyond comparisons, Roy would use the intellectual practice of establishing equivalences throughout his career. Apart from his anti-Wilsonian pamphlet *The Path to Durable Peace*, Roy would publish a very different book while in Mexico, called *La India; Su Pasado, Su Presente, y Su Porvenir* (1918). This book often goes unmentioned in accounts of Roy's life,[19] is swiftly dealt with as 'an encyclopaedia entry of sorts,'[20] or a publication 'denouncing British colonialism in India.'[21] The book did indeed provide Mexican readers with detailed information about India's past, including the recent history of its nationalist movement, listing events that are likely not well-known in Mexico, such as the 'Guerra de Libertad' of 1857, explaining the impact of the 1905 partition of Bengal, celebrating the successes of the ensuing economic boycott, giving details of the Alipore bomb case and the repression represented by the Press Act and the Arms Act. About the moderate wing of the nationalist movement the text is brief: thirty years of its efforts had resulted in '... nada absolutamente.'[22] But apart from providing readers with up-to-date information about anti-British activities in India, the book delved into the themes of race and religion, subjects Roy would later ignore or dismiss. While the text thus seems aberrant in connection to Roy's later writings, as a text advertising his expertise to the politician and intellectual José Vasconcelos its relevance becomes quite clear. It also points to the benefits of Roy's ability to authoritatively create equivalences between familiar and unfamiliar places.

Vasconcelos was central in the little cosmos in Mexico City that Roy and Evelyn inhabited. He was an intellectual and politician active in the field of education, who moved between the United States, where he practised law and wrote his books, and Mexico.[23] He is mainly remembered as the author of *La raza cósmica: Misión de la raza iberoamericana* (1925), which made a passionate argument for racial mixing being 'providential, progressive, and beneficial for Mexico and Spanish America.'[24] Before, he had already published books

---

[19] It is, for example, not discussed in the authoritative biography by Kris Manjapra, *M. N. Roy; Marxism and Colonial Cosmopolitanism* (2007).
[20] Alonso, 'M.N. Roy and the Mexican Revolution', 524.
[21] Goebel, 'Geopolitics, Transnational Solidarity or Diaspora Nationalism', 488.
[22] M. N. Roy, *La India, su Pasado, su Presente y su Porvenir* (Mexico City, n. P., 1918), 173–4.
[23] Vasconcelos would become rector of the National Autonomous University of Mexico between 1920 and 1921, and Secretary of Public Education between 1921 and 1924. Ilan Stavans, *José Vasconcelos: The Prophet of Race* (New Brunswick: Rutgers University Press, 2011), 115–17.
[24] Marilyn Grace Miller, *Rise and Fall of the Cosmic Race: The Cult of Mestizaje in Latin America* (Austin: University of Texas Press, 2004), 27–30.

about a range of subjects, for example, the philosophies of Pythagoras and Plotinus, in 1916 and 1918, respectively.[25] In 1919, Vasconcelos was working on a book called *Estudios Indostánicos* (1920), in which he engaged with the ideas of Rammohun Roy, Swami Vivekananda and Rabindranath Tagore. His eclectic intellectual interests would come to be mocked by the painter and intellectual Diego Rivera (1886–1957), who wrote to a friend in 1926 that Vasconcelos was waging a war against all things Western and instead proposed an '"agitación socio-cristo-anarco-burgo-nacio – hispa-boli-rodo-confu-budi-pita-gore-pepe-vasconceliana."'[26] For the Roys, however, Vasconcelos' eclectic interests meant that they had something very relevant to offer to him.

Roy provided Vasconcelos with an Indian ingredient for a universal racial theory with his book *La India*. India, in the way Roy described it, was characterized by a large array of climatic zones and peoples. The latter had been achieved through the mixing of conquering races – notably Greeks and Muslims – with the original population, something which had never affected the 'true being of India.'[27] Particularly the mixing of Dravidians and Aryans had given India its particular genius: 'From the virility of the Aryans and the mental energy of the Dravidians originated the great family of Indo-Aryans, who gave birth to the universal philosophy of Vedanta.'[28] The version of Hinduism propagated by Swami Vivekananda, Vedanta, already had its adherents in Mexico City by the time Roy was there, and thus formed a discourse he could tap into.[29]

He did so in a way that was quite specific to his audience. While the idea of Aryanism was a part of orientalist knowledge, claiming a common descent for Indians and Europeans, it generally excluded South Indians or Dravidians and Muslims, although there were variations. Different nationalist thinkers used the Aryan idea in different ways, either specifying that Northern Europeans were quite barbarous Aryans, or that Dravidians, and sometimes Indian Muslims too, were equal heirs of the glorious Aryan past.[30] Roy's version, where the non-Aryans contributed the more noble elements to a

[25] Laura J. Torres-Rodríguez, 'Orientalizing Mexico: Estudios Indostánicos and the Place of India in José Vasconcelos's La Raza Cósmica', *Revista Hispánica Moderna* 68, no. 1 (2015): 85.
[26] As a translation, Tenorio-Trillo suggests '… something like "a socio-Catholic-anarchist-bourgeois – national-Hispanic-Rodó-like-Confucian-Buddhist-Pythagoras-like-José-Vasconcelian agitation."' Tenorio, *I Speak of the City*, 251–2.
[27] 'Ser de la India'. *Ibid.*, vii.
[28] 'La virilidad física de los Arios y la energía mental de los Dravidios dan origen a la gran familia de los Indo-ariános, con quienes nace la filosofía universal de Vedanta'. *Ibid.*, xiii.
[29] Torres-Rodríguez, 'Orientalizing Mexico', 85.
[30] Tony Ballantyne, *Orientalism and Race: Aryanism in the British Empire* (New York: Palgrave, 2002), 18–55; 169–87.

shared, highly developed civilization, was quite unique.[31] In tracing the origins of Vedanta to the combination of Aryan and Dravidian ingredients, Roy made the case that all Aryans, both Asian and European, were excessively aggressive people, and it had only been because of their mixing with Dravidians that India had known this superior philosophy since 'approximately ten centuries before Jesus Christ.'[32] Because Aryans outside of India had not mixed with other races, they had lost none of their aggressiveness and had been unable to gain the same level of insight into the nature of reality.[33] The mixed-race sages of ancient India, however, had been able to reach this insight, on behalf of all of humanity.

> In fact, discovering Unity among apparent diversity has been the object of all human efforts since the beginning of History, consciously or unconsciously. So, in order to develop Vedanta's philosophy, Indo-Aryan saints did something for us, not only for their homeland, but for all generations. Therefore, Vedanta is not a spiritual property of India, it is the inheritance of all human beings. India has only had the privilege of being the instrument to present this universal light to those who seek it.[34]

By connecting the esteemed philosophy of Vedanta to a history of India as the home of racial mixing, Roy gave his narrative a distinctly Latin American twist. The notion of *mestizaje*, or the idea that the mixing of races was a positively distinguishing feature of Latin American societies, had been put forward by several thinkers there. In the revolutionary years between 1910 and 1917, the ideal of a mestizo Mexican identity also served to distinguish the present from pre-revolutionary times, when Mexico was seen to have been ruled in the interest of Europeans.[35] Mestizaje, then, had been in the air for some time by the time Roy wrote about it, and made it a part of the fashionable 'being of India.'

Roy was not the only one lending his voice to mestizaje. The notion of racial mixing was taken up by Evelyn in her writing too, although it was situated in

---

[31] Generally, the non-Aryan was seen as the 'primitive within'. Banerjee, *Politics of Time*, 8–9.
[32] Roy, *La India*, xvi.
[33] *Ibid.*, iii.
[34] 'De hecho, descubrir la Unidad entre la diversidad aparente ha sido el objeta de todos los esfuerzos humanos desde el principio de la Historia, consciente o inconscientemente. De modo que, por desenvolver la filosofía de Vedanta, los sa bios indo-aria nos hicieron algo, no para su patria solamente, sino por todas las generaciones. Por lo tanto, Vedanta no es una propiedad espiritual de la India, es la herencia, de todos los seres humanos. Lá India solamente ha tenido el privilegio de ser el instrumento para presentar esta luz universal a los que la buscan'. *Ibid.*, xvi.
[35] Stavans, *José Vasconcelos*, 5.

contemporary Mexico rather than ancient India, and addressed her own role as a foreigner, involved in a mixed marriage. In *Mexico and her People* (1919), she wrote that the 'real Mexican' was middle-class and mestizo, 'of swarthy skin and hazel eyes,' separated from both the Indian peasants and the aristocracy who, if they had any mixed blood, would be sure to hide it. '[The aristocrat] invariably makes himself more European than the Europeans in education, manners and habiliments.'[36] Purity was nothing less than un-Mexican. Significantly, she signed her articles as Evelyn Trent-Roy, which among the readership of *El Heraldo de México*, where her writing appeared in serialized form, clearly associated her with one of the few Indians in town.[37] Together, Evelyn and Roy could underline their arguments by their very presence in Mexico City: 'A young U.S. woman (Trent) and a handsome Indian (Roy), both radicals, appeared as a sort of avant-garde canvas of what new notions of beauty and social solidarity ought to be. It was *mestizaje* at its best.'[38] Beyond their texts, the Roys delivered what Vasconceles wanted to read and see.

Roy's racially mixed India would return in Vasconcelos' *Estudios indostánicos*, and survive into *La raza cósmica* in several ways. Like in Roy's book, *Estudios indostánicos* held that the spiritual genius of India was shaped by the mixing of its original inhabitants, the Dravidians, with their Aryan conquerors. Where the Dravidians supplied elements more valued by Vasconcelos, such as 'ideas about the immortality of the soul, transmigration and the omnipresence of Brahma,' the Aryans brought rather technical additions to the table, notably Sanskrit and the caste system – which did not pose a problem to the practice of racial mixing in this text either.[39] For Vasconcelos, the mixing itself was what became the positive force in history, in a way that could be abstracted from an Indian context. He rather focused on the climates conducive to mixing – which he held to be temperate ones like those that could be found in Mexico – as well as the skin colour of mixed populations: in this book as well as later works, Vasconcelos' 'cosmic' race was meant to be brown-skinned.

> ... the aryan invaders with white skin mixed with the subtle and mysterious race of the dravidians, with dark skin, and so they both lived together in this

---

[36] Evelyn Trent-Roy, 'Mexico and her People Chapter I', *El Heraldo de México*, 22 September 1919; Evelyn Trent-Roy, 'Mexico and her People Chapter III', *El Heraldo de México*, 6 October 1919.
[37] For her later publications, published in Europe, Evelyn would use Santi Devi as a pen name, fully associating herself with India, instead of signalling her mixed marriage. See Chapter 1.
[38] Tenorio, *I Speak of the City*, 277.
[39] '... las ideas sobre la inmortalidad del alma, la trasmigración y la omnipresencia de Brahma'. Quoted in Torres-Rodríguez, 'Orientalizing Mexico', 82.

new warm medium ... What would certain schools think of the thesis that only mestizo races are capable of great creations?⁴⁰

It was the mixing of these white and dark-skinned peoples that gave rise to great creations, but also, crucially, turned it into the opposite of the British Anglo-Saxon space. This anti-British and anti-North-American motivation for a celebration of mestizaje is equally there in Vasconcelos' later work, in which he wrote that

> North Americans, who did not have '... in their blood the contradictory instincts of a mixture of dissimilar races ...,' had committed the sin of destroying other races, while the Spaniards and American born Creoles had assimilated them, thus providing '... new rites and hopes for a mission without precedent in history.'⁴¹

His celebration of racial mixing did not mean Vasconcelos did not adhere to any sense of hierarchy between races at all – his ideas have been described as insisting on a 'whitening' of Latin American populations, and excluding the continent's Black population.⁴² Significant here, however, is that according to Laura Torres-Rodríguez, it was in India that Vasconcelos found his '... racial model in keeping with his plan of a "brown" utopia for Latin America.'⁴³ Seeing the similarities between the accounts of racial mixing in Roy's book from 1918 and Vasconcelos' from 1920, it seems inevitable that this racial model was one Vasconcelos could borrow from Roy. It was by authoritatively representing a faraway civilization and yet linking it to Mexico's presence through his body, marriage and arguments, that Roy made himself relevant in Mexico City. Paradoxically, this authority involved his – desirable – difference from his direct environment and at the same time allowed him to collapse that difference.

Communist categories

Translating Marxist ideas for spaces its theories were not developed for (like Russia and other parts of Asia) was a mainstay of international communist theorizing, making it a fruitful area of investigation for present-day global

---

⁴⁰ '... los arios invasores de piel blanca, se mezclaron con la raza misteriosa y sutil de los dravidios, de piel obscura, y así que ambos vivieron juntos en el nuevo medio cálido ....? Qué opinarían ciertas escuelas, de la tesis de que sólo las razas mestizas son capaces de las grandes creaciones?' Quoted in Ibid., 81–2.
⁴¹ Quoted in Miller, *Rise and Fall of the Cosmic Race*, 30.
⁴² Ibid., 44.
⁴³ Torres-Rodríguez, 'Orientalizing Mexico', 82.

intellectual historians.[44] According to Ali Raza, the perception that communism was 'foreign' to India has determined much of its historiography. His recent work has painted a rich picture of the ways in which a myriad of activists translated communist ideas into popular songs and leaflets for audiences beyond educated elites.[45] It is as an Indian intellectual engaging with Marxist ideas and communist organizing that Roy has mainly been historicized, particularly for his disagreement with Lenin. Against Lenin's approach, Roy was of the opinion that strategies for political cooperation should be the same in colonized countries as they should be in colonizing ones, as there were no essential differences between economic developments in the two.[46]

When it came to other Indian revolutionaries joining the communist fold, the differences between Marx' theories and Indian realities were obvious to many, especially where the fundamental categories of class and religion was concerned. In 1919, the Pan-Islamist revolutionary Mohamed Barakatullah wrote *Bolshevism and the Islamic Body Politick* (1919), a book announced to its readers that it '... sought to justify a fusion of these two antipathetic creeds.'[47] The text was written for audiences in India and Central Asia, and distributed by the Comintern in several languages. In it, Barakatullah traced the lineage of Marxist ideas to be in common with the Abrahamic religions, in the shape of '... key principles for equality and the development of individual potential based in public, collective property.' Apart from finding shared values, Barakatullah also located reasons for the two antipathetic creeds to come together in the present, citing the Bolsheviks' 1917 message to 'Muslims of the East' that promised self-determination to the Muslims within the former Tsarist empire, as well as Turkish integrity. A reason external to Russia was also easily found, in a shared arch enemy: the British empire.[48] Barakatullah's text tried to address itself to Muslims living in South and Central Asia, operating with the assumption that Islam and communism were vastly different – and that it was Barakatullah's task to bridge the gap between the two.

Roy also had direct critics doubting his approach. In 1920, a group of Indian revolutionaries in Berlin, led by Virendranath Chattopadhyaya, travelled to Moscow to present a text that criticized Roy directly, arguing that divisions

---

[44] See for example Oliver Crawford, 'Translating and Transliterating Marxism in Indonesia', *Modern Asian Studies* 55, no. 3 (2021): 697–733.
[45] Raza refers to this as a translation from the 'language of orthodoxy' into the 'language of everydayness'. Raza, *Revolutionary Pasts*, 6–12.
[46] Seth, *Marxist Theory and Nationalist Politics*, 46–50.
[47] Quoted in Ramnath, *Haj to Utopia*, 227.
[48] Ibid., 228.

between castes and religions were much more meaningful in structuring Indian society than class. In a footnote, the authors added that errant reasoning was the result of '… vague enthusiasm and unscientific generalisation …' to be explained by '… the geographical distance and political isolation of India from the centres of world revolutionary congress and conferences, and the consequent lack of first-hand knowledge to neutralise the extravagances of *a priori* theorising.'[49] But it was geographical distance precisely that rendered Roy's take so influential.

Roy's central publication arguing for the equivalence of India and Europe, *India in Transition* (1922) was co-authored with Abani Mukherji and argued that India was no longer feudal but capitalist, just like Europe. According to Sudipta Kaviraj '… [i]t is characteristic that this, the most fundamental belief in the book, the one in most need of a demonstration, is simply asserted.'[50] In a similar appraisal of Roy, Sanjay Seth has called attention to '… his reductionism, his schematicism and his characteristic juggling of concepts in pursuit of neat and superficially persuasive analyses and solutions; […] his corresponding willingness to "flatten" and "fit" complex social phenomena into ready-made categories.'[51] Rather than constituting some kind of an intellectual flaw, assertions and a concomitant flattening were at the heart of Roy's approach and set him apart from his rivals.

Instead of seeing a gap between a theory and the context it was now applied to, *India in Transition* categorically stated that the theory was relevant, in its unaltered state. The book, as many of Roy's other texts, involved the claim that what was generally thought of a certain context – British India – was in fact no longer true. The assertion contained in *India in Transition*, of the capitalist system already holding India in its grip, extended to the assertion that older – feudal – caste divisions had already been rendered meaningless by changes in relations of production, even if to the casual observer they still looked important:

> … a little enquiry under the surface discloses the fact that the very foundation of the caste system has been undermined. The craft divisions on which the castes were built to all practical purposes have ceased to exist with the ruin of the craft industry. […] … in spite of their destruction as factors of social-economics, the caste-divisions continued to exist; but they were but the memory of something dead and gone ….[52]

---

[49] Virendranath Chattopadhyaya, G. A. K. Luhani and Pandurang Khankhoje, 'Thesis on India and the World Revolution', quoted in Barooah, *Chatto*, 163.
[50] Kaviraj, 'The Heteronomous Radicalism of M.N. Roy', 232.
[51] Seth, *Marxist Theory and Nationalist Politics*, 99, 102.
[52] Roy, Mukherji, *India in Transition*, 109.

A Flat Earth – Assertions of Equivalence 193

The familiarly orientalist picture of India as a colourful swirl of different religions, castes, tribes, races, Roy assured his readers, was out of date.[53] Those who studied the proper subject of historical development, the relations of production, knew better. They possessed a heightened insight into reality because of their specialized, exclusive, knowledge. The strength of the argument was that even if things looked very different from the way Roy and Mukherji claimed them to be, this was because superficial phenomena had not yet caught up with deeper developments.

Insisting on the equivalence of situations in India and Europe gave Roy's Marxist works a certain cachet with some Indian readers,[54] but crucially, their audience was also a different one; instead of bringing Marxist ideas to audiences not yet familiar with them, *India in Transition* addressed those already familiar with Marxist ideas, but not yet the context he applied them to. And yet, Roy did not go into a lot of detail to make the Indian context more familiar to such readers because it simply adhered to Marx' theories. For many European Marxists of the era, this claim will not have seemed so far-fetched, as they saw their theories as inherently universal.[55] This meant Roy could claim to translate India from something unfamiliar into something familiar without having to go into any specific details. Yet, this claim still required someone with knowledge and experience of India – Roy – to argue there was no need to emphasize its specificity, but painted a picture of fundamental similarity on the basis of his general experience of circumstances of oppression, that could be found in the colonized as well as the colonizing world.

Because *India in Translation* offered India to Marxism rather than adapting Marxism to India, the text could easily be found to be equally interesting for non-Indian readers. In the same year as its English edition, a German translation was published that offered India as a massive piece of the puzzle that was global capitalism.

> This book had originally been written for Indians. But the study of the forces that are at present developing in India will also be of use to non-Indians who wish to be educated about conditions in India, which are extraordinarily meaningful for

---

[53] A classic example stems from Rudyard Kipling's novel *Kim* (1901), in which the protagonist travels along India's Grand Trunk Road, upon which he meets individuals who can all be classified as belonging to one of the many circumscribed groups making up India's population. Rudyard Kipling, *Kim* (London: Macmillan, 1915), 102–4.
[54] By incorporating '… India in a universal arc of history …' Raza, *Revolutionary Pasts*, 12.
[55] Hélène Carrère d'Encausse, Stuart R. Schram, *Marxism and Asia: An Introduction with Readings* (London: Lane, 1969), viii.

our world movement. Since the power of international capital is rooted in the entire globe, only a worldwide revolution can put an end to the current order and can bring about the triumph of the western European proletariat.[56]

Inside the book, its German readers would find a picture that was much more familiar than they had perhaps anticipated.

An earlier text Roy, Evelyn, and Abani Mukherji wrote and published before they even reached Moscow connects their line of argument to the role they envisioned for themselves in the international communist movement.[57] In their joint article, the three sought to create a role for themselves that relied on their abilities to counsel or instruct the nascent Indian communist movement – an argument which involved making clear that there was such a movement to begin with. Writing for the *Glasgow Socialist* about a series of strikes that had swept India in protest against the 1919 Rowlatt Act, the authors claimed that these had been misinterpreted abroad: 'Though the nationalists used it as a weapon against political oppression, it was really the spontaneous rebellion of the proletariat against unbearable economic exploitation.'[58] The article outlined an authorial position of heightened insight, even though Roy and Mukherji had left India years before, and Evelyn had never been there. Yet, for a European audience, they could interpret civil unrest for what it really was, or even for what it really ought to be. In this way, the article ascribed an active and knowledgeable role to its authors, managing the tendency of the movement to truly become what it already was potentially. The vast mass of people who were natural allies for the communist movement, the strikers in British India, were in need of something to tip them over to the right side of history: instruction. Roy and his associates were ideally placed to provide just that. In their text, they offered a hitherto unknown, large and active communist movement to European socialists, with the clear potential to join its struggle.

At the Second World Congress of the Comintern in 1910, where the National and Colonial Questions were debated, differences between countries proved troubling for many of the communists present. When delegates discussed the different theses advanced by Lenin and Roy, a key question was about the

---

[56] M.N. Roy, *Indien* (Hamburg: Verlag der Kommunistischen Internationale, 1922), xii.
[57] Abani Mukherji (1891–1937) also hailed from the Bengal underground but had spent the past years in Japan, China, and the Dutch East Indies, only to meet the Roys in Europe, on their way to Moscow. Tim Harper, 'Singapore, 1915, and the Birth of the Asian Underground', *Modern Asian Studies* 47, no. 6 (2013): 1803–4.
[58] Roy, Mukherji, Devi, 'An Indian Communist Manifesto'.

difference between oppressed and oppressing nations, or as the former were referred to, backward countries, which were meant to merit a different approach. This quickly brought up the question of which countries could properly be considered backward, and which could not. If the only important distinction ran between the imperial capitalists and the rest, as Lenin's theory would have it, then who was the rest?

Giacinto Serrati (1874–1926) of the Italian Socialist Party worried Italy might be counted among the backwards countries, and noted: 'The theses' insufficient clarity threatens to provide the pseudorevolutionary chauvinism of western Europe with a weapon against truly communist internationalist action.'[59] The lack of explicitness in defining which countries were backward enough for the 'national revolutionary' elements there to receive Comintern support was a cause for grave concern. Serrati feared the proposal would be interpreted as his sanctioning of support to Italian fascists – which would have scandalized his comrades back home. Against Serrati's reservations, David Wijnkoop (1876–1941) of the Communist Party of the Netherlands submitted that Italy was clearly not a backward country, for obvious if hard-to-define reasons, so Serrati had nothing to worry about. Wijnkoop believed that it was in fact desirable to keep things vague, since any too specific a formulation would not be applicable in sufficiently many different situations: '... we weighed whether it would not be useful to define more precisely what is meant by a backward country. We decided against this. [...] ... we would immediately have other problems, such as with Bulgaria or Greece.'[60]

Taking a similar stance, the Dutch communist Henk Sneevliet urged his comrades 'not to be doctrinaire' about differences, which he thought to be not all that significant. He gave an example from his own area of expertise, the Dutch East Indies. As a communist, he had worked with a nationalist organization called Sarekat Islam, which according to him possessed a 'class character,' notwithstanding its religious name. This meant that whether to work with nationalist organizations or not, as the distinction between oppressing and oppressive countries implied, was not such a categorical matter. According to Sneevliet: 'A significant number in this mass organization are not consciously socialist, but they are revolutionary in the sense that Comrade Roy pointed out for India.'[61] Sneevliet also used the language of potential to argue that even

---

[59] *Ibid.*, 244.
[60] *Ibid.*, 264.
[61] Riddell, *Workers of the World*, 258.

those who did not seem to be obvious candidates for communist revolutionaries nevertheless might be, as Roy had. As such, both thought distinctions between colonizer and colonized countries were not all that significant, and their colleagues would not have to worry so much about a definition of backwardness. For every carefully tailored definition, a new real-world situation would pose new problems, and the only way to fit most of the world into a formula was to not look at the details too closely. It was the promise of such smooth applicability that Roy's kinds of translations held.

Struggling with class

It was one thing to grapple with Marxist concepts, but another to be dealing with those who were theoretically already communist in person. Roy, Evelyn and Mukherji encountered a group of people they had argued were potential revolutionaries in Tashkent in 1920. This was the site of the recently founded Turkestan Bureau of the Comintern, where they were sent in order to train Indian exiles into communist cadres. This mission was linked to the *Khilafat* movement, which was a migration of Indian Muslims who came to the defence of the Ottoman sultan after the First World War, protecting this Muslim polity against the forces of British Imperialism. After the war had ended, religious animosity against the British Empire persisted and some Northern Indian Muslims moved to Afghanistan, where they hoped to join local forces resisting British rule, as well as finding the possibility of bettering their livelihoods. Having found circumstances inhospitable, many moved back to India – but some moved on to reach the territory of Soviet Russia. The Comintern hoped to forge a revolutionary army out of these migrants known as *muhajirin*, and to take British India with their help.[62]

For Roy, this meant a concrete engagement with members of a group he had argued were in fact the revolutionary proletariat, presumably spurred on by their objective economic conditions rather than conservative motives such as religion or nationalism. Confronted with the reality of dealing with 'about 200' migrants, Roy wrote to a contact in the United States that he was having great difficulties with the '… terrible lot. [illegible] majority of them was either religious fanatic

---

[62] Ansari, *Emergence of Socialist Thought among North Indian Muslims*, 26.

or dirty adventurers without any idealism.' That said, that was no reason for him to adjust his views, but only to insist on his own role in revolutionizing the potentially revolutionary proletariat. 'At last the more hopeful element among them has been picked out and put to military and political training, but very few of them is desirable material.'[63] It was the human material which needed revising rather than the theory.

In their efforts, the Roys and Mukherji found themselves in an uneasy cooperation with the Inquilabiun-i-Hind or the Indian Revolutionary Association (IRA) of the one-time member of the diplomatic service in Kabul turned revolutionary Abdur Rab (?–?) and the future anarchist M. P. T. Acharya. Letters of both groups penned to functionaries in Moscow showed how their disagreement played out in practice. In 1921, Abdur Rab wrote to Georgy Chicherin, the Soviet Commissar for Foreign Affairs, to take issue with the manner in which Roy talked of an Indian proletariat as a logical ally for the communist international. 'These so-called communists deceive the Komintern by talking in communist terminology, [...] as if the Indian proletarist [sic] were class-conscious and would rise up one fine day as the champion of the social revolution.' Rab elucidated that the figure Roy had put on the number of Indian proletarians, 9 million, first of all sank into insignificance as compared to the country's total population, but also, that its qualities were completely different from the way in which Roy had portrayed them. First of all, most of them were seasonal labourers rather than class-conscious proletarians, deriving their identities from religion and caste rather than from supposedly belonging to the same class. This meant that to rely on the proletariat to act in unison, as a unified class with a common interest would be to rely on a figment of the imagination. Rab rather advocated focusing on India's 'puriah'[64] class, a group of which he estimated there to be 53 million, and which already had an awareness of itself as a group.[65] In a sense, Rab proposed 'puriah' as a translation for the

---

[63] Letter from M.N. Roy to 'Lord Byron' 5.2.1920 [false date] quoted in Roy, Gupta, Vasudevan (eds.), *Indo-Russian Relations* 12.
[64] While it had once referred to a specific caste in what was then the Madras Presidency, since about 1890, 'pariah' had been a commonly used term to refer to all castes who would later be referred to as Dalits or Untouchables, thought of as groups of 'morally inferior outsiders'. Rupa Viswanath, *The Pariah Problem: Caste, Religion, and the Social in Modern India* (New York: Columbia University Press, 2014), 3;21.
[65] Letter from Abdur Rabb Barq to Comrade Chicherin, Moscow, 29 July 1921, quoted in Roy, Gupta, Vasudevan, *Indo-Russian Relations*, 75–6.

proletariat, and criticized Roy's insistence on the use of purely Marxist categories for a space in which they had no referents in reality.

> The danger lies [...] in not taking into consideration the special conditions and particular situation. Lack of adaptability to circumstances, and development of fanatism are most injurious to institutions, especially in the beginning. In order to popularise [sic] and make these institutions attractive for outside world, it is necessary to be plastic in constitution and elastic in tactics.[66]

The difference in opinion was never resolved, and both Rab and Acharya were expelled from the communist party they founded with Roy the same year. In Roy's letters arguing why Rab and Acharya had to go, he said it was because of their 'pan-Islamic' tendencies that the two were the wrong partners for revolutionary work.[67] As with Roy's problems with the real khilafatists he encountered in Tashkent, cultural difference only emerged as a problem, rather than a basic aspect of reality that needed to be taken into consideration.

As it had in Mexico, Roy's approach to difference and equivalence carved out a viable role for himself. But in an intellectual field shaped by Marxism and Leninism, Roy's habitus brought up a problem in terms of this world view's most fundamental category: class. As was the case for many other upper-caste Indian communists, there were always enough critics to doubt Roy's affinities with the Indian working class.[68] This merited a translating effort. Roy's approach was not to go into the finer distinctions between caste and class. In an editorial published in March of 1923 in *The Vanguard*, he argued against a position surmising that that Bengali *bhadralok* (translated by a contemporary historian as an '... ethic, or a sentiment,' and a preoccupation with culture, education and the written word)[69] revolutionaries could not be communists, as they were essentially Bengal's bourgeoisie and the class struggle had to be waged against them – not by them. Explaining why those *bhadralok* nationalists or revolutionaries were

---

[66] Ibid., 77–8.
[67] Ibid., 61–3.
[68] In an article on one of Kerala's leading communists, E.M.S. Nambudiripad (1909–98), Dilip Menon has argued that Nambudiripad's publications from the 1950s were a way in order to balance his own Brahmin identity with communism's egalitarian project. Nambudiripad's way to do so was by turning to history, and finding a positive role for the Brahmins of Kerala in its economic development, making sure it progressed through the stages of history, even if in the present their influence was much maligned. Dilip Menon, 'Being a Brahmin the Marxist Way; E.M.S. Nambudiripad and the Pasts of Kerala', in *Research in Progress Papers 'History and Society'* (New Delhi: Centre for Contemporary Studies, Nehru Memorial Museum and Library, 1998), 27–8.
[69] Bhattacharya, *Sentinels of Culture*, 39–63.

in fact on the right side of history, he delved into the meaning of the words bourgeoisie and *bhadralok*.

> The term '*bhadralok*' literally means a cultured person – something like the English 'gentleman.' Certainly it has an indirect economic basis, inasmuch as culture has been so far available only to people enjoying certain economic privileges. The Indian term, however, is not so clearly economic as is 'bourgeoisie.'[70]

So far, so similar. But while Roy admitted this similarity, he argued what appeared to be the same was in fact different, and what appeared different was the same. What mattered was that the property-owning class denoted by the word bourgeoisie also existed in India and had a similar role in its economy. Using a category like *bhadralok* merely obfuscated this reality: 'It is perhaps thought that the Indian upper classes do not care for material things; their superiority is cultural, they are intellectual aristocrats. This is precisely the doctrine whose hypocrisy we mean to expose.'[71] The meaning of *bhadralok* as those people distinguished by education and culture, and its use as the translation for the word bourgeoisie meant, or so Roy argued, that many in Bengal would falsely identify themselves as bourgeois, in its properly economic sense. To these intellectuals, attached to their *bhadralok* identity, Roy addressed a little in-text monologue: 'Do not be so proud of your "*bhadralok*" descent, look at your real position closely with a realist's eye and you will see that you do not belong to the bourgeoisie, the present-day "*bhadralok*" that counts.'[72] Roy had access to a deeper reality than his fellow *bhadralok*'s cultural attachments, supplied by Marxist science, which allowed the seeming reality of the Bengali term to evaporate:

> You are de-classed: economically you have no place in the ranks of the bourgeoisie – you belong to the exploited working class; it is only the prejudice of birth, of tradition that does not allow you to have this realistic view of your position; materially you are an exploited worker pure and simple; spiritually you are bound hand and foot by the subtle propaganda of the upper classes, who are very much interested in keeping alive your prejudice against the 'illiterate mob,' so that the union of intellectual worker and manual worker will be delayed as much as possible.[73]

---

[70] M. N. Roy, 'Bourgeois Nationalism', *Vanguard* 3, no. 1 (15 August 1923), Marxists Internet Archive (2006), https://www.marxists.org/archive/roy/1923/08/15a.htm.
[71] *Ibid.*
[72] *Ibid.*
[73] *Ibid.*

Roy was essentially talking about himself, carving out a legitimate space for himself as a 'de-classed' intellectual, properly belonging with the proletariat. To do so, he lifted the veil of surface appearances, and peered into the economic heart of history to show that the present was already sufficiently different from the past in order for his own caste background, and caste more generally, to no longer be relevant to the subsequent development of history. Destabilizing what differences were real and eliminating those inconvenient to him made the foundations of his own position more solid.

A 1924 volume of letters added an extra dimension to Roy's translation by arguing that factors of religion had no real bearing on the development of history – only economics did. Ignoring his practical experience with Pan-Islam and khilafatists, he wrote:

> A landlord is first of all a landlord, and a Hindu or Mussulman or anything else after that. He does not take any less rent from a tenant who is his co-religionist than from one who is not. The same holds true of employers of labour. Have you ever seen a Muslim or Hindu or Parsi employer paying a higher scale of wages to his brothers in the faith? These are general laws of economics that hold good everywhere.[74]

Against charges that he did not pay attention to the specific situation he had to work with, Roy could defend himself by citing the forces of production as the only decisive forces in human history – everything else being a mere distraction. People still interested in these distractions, such as religion, could be dismissed as behind the times. In such a way, those Roy dismissed as 'pan-Islamists' were not a sign that religion clearly did play a role in spreading communism to India – or there would not be pan-Islamists to take into account in doing so – and their arguments did not require a more thorough dealing with.

In a text published by Evelyn, the scientific status of a Marxist view of contemporary India was juxtaposed with the popular works that had recently been penned by the French author Romain Rolland. Rolland had recently made a name for himself as a bit of a connoisseur when it came to India by writing biographies of Swami Vivekananda and Gandhi, as well as publishing a translation of some of the latter's writings. In 1923, Evelyn published an article in the British *Labour Monthly* to disavow European intellectuals such as Rolland of their attachment to Gandhi. According to Evelyn, a tendency to see Gandhi

---

[74] M. N. Roy, 'On Economic Determinism', in *Political Letters* (The Vanguard Bookshop: Zurich, 1924) Marxists Internet Archive (2006). https://www.marxists.org/archive/roy/1922/11/10a.htm.

as the saviour of humanity said much more about the European's state of mind than about the state of India.

> M. Rolland and the whole school of Spiritual Imperialists, who hold that the world is to be redeemed by soul-force, self-sacrifice, and suffering, are endeavouring to use Mr. Gandhi as a proof of their own thesis that Europe has brought about its own annihilation by the use of violence, of which Bolshevism is the final and concentrated form making for ultimate destruction of all that remains of European culture and civilisation.[75]

When Rolland wrote about India, Evelyn concluded, he was really talking about Europe – a continent that had just self-destructed in war. He had, however, drawn the wrong equivalence and misjudged the recent uprising in India for a spiritual affair, whereas in fact it was '… a very material one for land and bread. It is for this that the peasants of the Punjab, the United Provinces, Bengal, Madras, and the whole of India have shed their blood …'[76] The unity of the world was not in spiritual ideas but in the materiality of people's bodies. It took people like Evelyn and Roy, able to coolly appreciate the material circumstances of the Indian masses, to gain a real insight into their life world. To such people, then, the praise Europe's intellectuals bestowed upon non-violence, soul-force and other Gandhist notions then assumed their true character:

> For the scientific Marxist, who conceives the world to be built upon economic forces, subject to material laws, such a conception has all the grotesque mediævalism of the gargoyle, and we conceive of the minds of these sentimental idealists as full of such gargoyles – unreal, grinning, and out of tune with the age in which we live.[77]

Difference was history, the present economic. Like Evelyn, Roy singled out Rolland as having provided an influential and wrong account of contemporary India for European readers. In a 1925 article, he addressed Rolland's characterization of the population of India in order to expose his misguidedness. Rolland had painted the 300 million souls making up contemporary British India as a hodgepodge of languages and religions, races, languages, '… almost all of them highly emotive, reacting violently to minor excitements,' suggesting the danger

---

[75] Evelyn Roy, 'Mahatma Gandhi; Revolutionary or Counter-Revolutionary? A Reply to Romain Rolland and Henri Barbusse', *Labour Monthly* V, no.3 (September 1923), Marxists Internet Archive (2006). https://www.marxists.org/archive/roy-evelyn/articles/1923/gandhi_rev_counter.htm.
[76] Ibid.
[77] Ibid.

of Gandhi's attempt to orchestrate a movement out of them. If the leadership of the 'frail Mahatma' failed, Rolland suggested, the Indian masses could escape all forms of control.[78] According to Roy, 'M. Romain Rolland spoke of having seen a mysterious tide from India which was going to submerge Europe.'[79] Against this backdrop of India as a boiling mass of violent if diverse energies, Roy could hold up an image of a proletariat that was essentially the same, whether it was in France, India or elsewhere:

> Instead of thinking so exclusively in the terms of Asia and Europe, he might try to think in the terms of wage-slaves and capital, of the proletariat and the bourgeoisie. He will then see that his imagined Asiatic Peril is neither distinctly Asiatic not is it a peril except to capitalists (in both Europe and Asia.) It is just the struggle of the working classes of the whole world to free themselves from their common bondage to the same enemy.[80]

Rather than reading Gandhi to understand the way India was heading, one needed to read Marx, Engels and Lenin, or so Roy seemed to reassure his communist readers; only their theories provided access to the true state of the world. Yet, it still required someone with experience of India – Roy – to tell them there was no need to emphasize its specificity, but painted a picture of fundamental similarity on the basis of his general experience of circumstances of oppression, that could be found in the colonized as well as the colonizing world.

Fascists here and there

It was during Roy's humanist phase that he made some of his boldest claims of equivalence, with which he tried to engage new audiences. Roy's engagement with humanist ideas and his thinking about fascism as a global force has drawn more attention in recent years,[81] but the extent to which it asserted the validity of theories of the German Jewish humanist-Marxist psycho-analyst Erich

---

[78] … un peuple de trois cent millions d'hommes, de races, de religions, de langues différentes, la plupart incultes, et presque tous ultra-émotifs, réagissant violemment aux moindres excitations … Romain Rolland, 'Introduction', in *La Jeune Inde*, ed. Mohandas K. Gandhi, tr. Hélène Hart (Paris: Stock, 1924), v.

[79] *The Masses of India by M. N. Roy*, Number 7, July 1925, Collection 303: Rare Journals, PCJ.

[80] *Ibid.*

[81] Disha Karnad Jani, 'The Concept of Fascism in Colonial India: M.N. Roy and The Problem of Freedom', *Global Histories* 3, no. 2 (Oct. 2017): 121–38; Balcom, 'From Communist Internationalism to a "New Humanism"'.

Fromm's (1900–1980) in an Indian context has not been explored. In 1945, with European fascism on the brink of defeat, Roy published several texts explaining how Hindu nationalism and European fascisms were all expressions of the same human problem: the fear of freedom. This idea stemmed from the work of Fromm, with whom Roy shared a social circle in 1920s Berlin, which included several members of the Frankfurt School.[82] Engaging with Fromm's ideas placed Roy into a wider international conversation, and ensured his work was noticed by other humanist intellectuals, as well as being positively cited by Fromm himself.[83] While the suitability of the concept of fascism for some branches of Hindu nationalist thought and practice has been made plausible by historians,[84] Roy's assertions about the Indian nationalist movement as fascist are far beyond the scope of how the -ism is usually interpreted for India.

Roy made such strong claims in order to draw attention to his political ideas at a time when his political influence was waning. He had been expelled from the Indian National Congress party in 1940 for wanting India to support Britain in the Second World War, and his subsequent political endeavours never gained him a mass following. Fromm's ideas allowed him to interpret his own marginalization positively, since the framing of nationalism as fascism placed him on the right side of history. In Roy's own words, he had come to see that nationalism in colonized countries '... invariably turned towards Fascism,'[85] meaning it was high time other Indians would give up their attachment to the nation, like he had done. Internationally, Roy's networks had dwindled because he had become too oppositional for the doctrinaire communists of the day, and those alternative communists he was in contact with had '... perished or been scattered to the four ends of the world.'[86] New opportunities and audiences would be most welcome.

---

[82] Manjapra, *M. N. Roy*, 70; Ray, *In Freedom's Quest: Vol. 4*, 2, 326.
[83] Fromm cited Roy's *Reason, Romanticism, and Revolution* in his 1955 book *The Sane Society* as 'a thorough and brilliant analysis' of what he conceptualized as the problem of 'rootedness'. Innaiah Narisetti, 'Introduction', in *M. N. Roy; Radical Humanist; Selected Writings*, ed. Innaiah Narisetti (Amherst: Prometheus Books, 2004), 2.
[84] On psychology and practice, see Benjamin Zachariah, 'Rethinking (the Absence of) Fascism in India, c. 1922–1945', in *Cosmopolitan Thought Zones: South Asia and the Global Circulation of Ideas*, ed. Sugata Bose, Kris Manjapra (New York: Palgrave Macmillan, 2010), 182–98; for an intellectual history, See Christophe Jaffrelot, ed., *Hindu Nationalism; A Reader* (Ranikhet: Permanent Black, 2007).
[85] M. N. Roy, *The Problem of Freedom* (Kolkata: Renaissance Publishers Ltd., 2000), 85.
[86] Letter from Bertram Wolfe to M. N. Roy, 5 April 1949, IC/FOR/9 W-13, Bertram Wolfe Correspondence, M. N. Roy Papers Section 1, Nehru Memorial Museum and Library (NMML), New Delhi.

In 1941, Fromm had published *Escape from Freedom*, a work combining history and psychology in order to analyse the fascist Nazi regime then in the process of taking over Europe, and to assess what warnings it contained for all of humankind. Notwithstanding the criticism Fromm received from anthropologists for his universalist account of human development, and the unhistorical connections he drew between the rise of protestantism and Nazism in different centuries, the book became a bestseller.[87] It compellingly argued that authoritarian regimes such as those in Germany and Italy had acquired their popularity because they provided a refuge from individual freedom and responsibility in modern societies, where people no longer relied on received structures and belief systems, but had to make their own sense of life.

> It is the thesis of this book that modern man, freed from the bonds of pre-individualistic society, which simultaneously gave him security and limited him, has not gained freedom in the positive sense of the realization of his individual self; that is, the expression of his intellectual, emotional and sensuous potentialities. Freedom, though it has brought him independence and rationality, has made him feel isolated and, thereby, anxious and powerless. This isolation is unbearable and the alternatives he is confronted with are either to escape from the burden of his freedom into new dependencies and submission, or to advance the full realization of positive freedom which is based upon the uniqueness and individuality of man.[88]

Fromm's argument was partly engineered to caution against the effects of modernity wherever it struck, seeing what he called 'automaton conformity' as a refuge from individual freedom and a potential danger for inhabitants of the United States as well as Europe, but the meat of his subject matter was provided by Germany. As such, the historical explanations he provided were taken from there, and he argued that there existed a direct link between the authoritarianism engendered by protestant doctrines of predestination, which, Fromm argued, asked the individual to completely give up their sense of individual choice. The step to fascism was only small, in Fromm's account, as under that system individuals gave up their free choice as unquestioningly, to follow a strong leader.[89] These elements provided Roy with the building blocks to construct a theory about Indian nationalism as fascism, which asserted assertions of equivalence not only across space, but explicitly across time as well.

---

[87] Lawrence J. Friedman, *The Lives of Erich Fromm: Love's Prophet* (New York: Columbia University Press, 2013), 65; 104–6; 118.
[88] Erich Fromm, *Escape from Freedom* (New York: Ishi Press, 1991), x.
[89] Friedman, *The Lives of Erich Fromm*, 105–6.

Roy first wrote about these ideas in *The Problem of Freedom* (1945) and *Jawaharlal Nehru* (1945), but they remained a part of his work in years to come. In *The Problem of Freedom*, Roy set out to diagnose the Indian masses with the thoroughly modern condition of a 'fear of freedom,' while at the same time maintaining his habitual castigations for their backwardness. One opening for doing so had been provided by Fromm's direct link between the authoritarianism of Reformation thought, demanding absolute submission to god, and that of the contemporary Nazi movement, demanding obedience to the leader. Roy then diagnosed a similarity between Reformation-era Europe and contemporary India:

> When it is realized that Luther and Calvin, though revolting against the Catholic Church, laid the psychological foundation of a political authoritarianism, one should not be shocked by the discovery that Gandhi played the same reactionary role in India. And his role has been all the more reactionary because it was played in the setting of social conditions and cultural environments much more backward than those of Europe in the seventeenth century.[90]

In Fromm's account as well as in Roy's interpretation, progress and regress went hand in hand; the revolt against the Catholic Church was a revolt against unfreedom, but this revolt already carried the germs for new kinds of bondage within itself. This ambiguity gave Roy space to map his own evaluation of Indian nationalism onto Fromm's work, even if it meant a less neat logical progression from increased freedom to a fear of freedom and flight to authoritarianism. India's present, Roy argued, was like Europe's past in all the bad ways – just worse – while the fear of freedom Fromm had described as a particularly modern phenomenon could also be found there. As with resistance against the Catholic Church, the revolt against the British entailed the casting off of chains, but also came with dangers of new kinds of subjugation – to Gandhian religiosity, in the main. And this Gandhian religiosity, Roy held, would be even more repressive than the authoritarian tendencies in protestantism. While in Fromm's work, the fear of freedom was an essential attribute of modern, individualistic people who resented the responsibility their emancipation had come with, in Roy's text it was an essential aspect of an unchanging Hinduism that guided the majority in the past as much as in the present: '... the central theme of that culture was submission of man – either to the will of God or to his own karma.'[91]

---

[90] Roy, *The Problem of Freedom*, 12.
[91] *Ibid.*, 14.

While Fromm's fear of freedom was inherent in progress, with Roy it belonged in a world of stasis.

Yet, this is not where Roy's use of Fromm's theory ended. He wanted both its sixteenth- and twentieth-century aspects for India's present. Within a picture of stasis for the majority, Roy added a note of dynamism for the middle classes. As much influenced by Marxism as Fromm, a class dimension was a natural way for Roy to complicate the image of stasis. Fromm had identified the lower middle class as particularly prone to Nazism,[92] and Roy saw the urban middle class as the 'social basis' for an Indian form of fascism. It was among these classes that an unmooring from 'traditional' roles and patterns had occurred, when they moved to the emerging cities, enjoyed new forms of education and manned the colonial government machinery. These changes entailed a 'slight advance toward the concept of individual freedom.' When their employment prospects dimmed at the beginning of the twentieth century, 'the old tie was gone but there was no future,' and the only way to escape from new-found freedom was into older cultural certainties.[93] In Roy's hands, neither conceptions of tradition, nor conceptions of modernity could serve as a bulwark for what Fromm had called the fear of freedom.

In his texts on Indian fascism, Roy included strikingly similar psychological portraits of both Gandhi and Nehru, as precisely the kind of figures from classes whose lives had been profoundly changed in recent years, and who would be suspect to the modern type of fear of freedom identified by Fromm. Interestingly enough, he identified Gandhi's 'uprootedness' with his having lived in Britain and South Africa, where he had become a 'lonesome individual, frightened by the specter of freedom, [who] found refuge in submission to an authority …'[94] For one thing, Roy cast Gandhi's appeal to religious values as a response to modernity rather than as tradition itself. For another, he implied that Gandhi had not been able to embrace the freedom of living an uprooted life – in the way that Roy himself had been.

In order to cast Nehru as a figure suffering from the fear of freedom, Roy had to take a different tack. After all, Nehru's leftist ideas and more secular style were closer to Roy's own, making him a more similar kind of cosmopolitan. To start with, Roy tried to discredit Nehru's international leftist credentials, starting with

---

[92] Friedman, *The Lives of Erich Fromm*, 113.
[93] Roy, *The Problem of Freedom*, 14.
[94] Ibid., 15.

his election as the President of the League against Imperialism in 1926, which indirectly involved him with the Communist International:

> That accident (it was an accident) won for Nehru the reputation of being a Communist, and as such held in high esteem in Moscow. During his pilgrimage to Moscow the next year, Nehru was jealously chaperoned by his father, who evidently did not relish the wayward son's doubtful reputation. The visit to Moscow was very short; it lasted only four or five days, spent mostly in sightseeing interspersed with a few minor political interviews.[95]

On the one hand, Nehru was described as rooted in a powerful family, his father Motilal Nehru having served twice as Congress President, his leftist credentials a sham and stay in Moscow mere tourism. Yet, there was something modern about Nehru, although it came with the same problem that Gandhi's modernity had come with; neither Nehru nor Gandhi was able – contrary to Roy – to bear the weight of their personal responsibility for their lives and beliefs. As such, the adopting of any ideology, including those closer to Roy's heart such as socialism or communism, could be adopted for the wrong reasons, compromising their nature.

> [Nehru's] apparent advance towards Socialism and Marxism was the typical groping of the lonesome individual of the twentieth century. That typical groping for a vaguely conceived new world, in the context of the disintegrating capitalist society and dissolving bourgeois culture, also becomes the modern man's search for God, who is eventually found in Fascism.[96]

The psycho-social language Roy adopted was part of a Frommian universe where individual psychological conditions were inherently related to societal developments. Roy, however, needed many different societal developments to exist at the same time in order to see the different psychological phenomena he wanted to diagnose people in India with – the masses, Gandhi and Nehru. Roy's diagnoses – be they of the disintegration of capitalist society, the typical groping of the lonesome individual of the twentieth century, or general backwardness, depended on the phenomenon they were meant to pathologize. In a way, these strands of thought only came together in their opposition to how Roy saw himself.

Particularly Japanese fascism allowed Roy to juxtapose his unflattering portrait of Nehru with a heroic one of himself. He described a visit he had made to Calcutta in 1942, when the Japanese-supported Indian Army of Subhas

---

[95] M. N. Roy, *Jawaharlal Nehru* (Delhi: Radical Democratic Party, 1945), 26.
[96] Ibid., 41.

Chandra Bose was threatening to invade India. Bose's supporters were openly welcoming the event, and Roy's own political party, '... alone called for resistance to the imminent invasion.'[97] Roy's account of his attempt to rally Calcuttans against fascism posited himself as a heroic actor in a global war:

> In the midst of that electric atmosphere, I addressed several open air meetings in Calcutta. The theme of my speech on each occasion was that the responsibility of defending India belongs to Indians, and that the responsibility could be discharged if the people felt it keenly enough. [...] I proved the self-respect of Indian manhood by asking: 'How long will India be a football for any international freebooter who takes it in his head to invade this country?' The challenge went home. Open air meetings addressed by me were attended by thousands. 'Bamboo warfare' against the imminent invasion, became the talk of the town. The mass exodus stopped. The premier city of India steadied its morale.[98]

In his writings on fascism, Roy asserted that the phenomena Fromm had described taking place at different points in time in Germany all had their validity in different ways in contemporary India. Roy's assertion of equivalence required a distinction between two co-existing stages of development in contemporary India, both of which encouraged fascist tendencies – even though Fromm's theory would have had it that those living in blissfully pre-individualistic, non-modern conditions should be immune to its appeal, as they had not recently acquired new freedoms to be feared. In a review of Roy's work on fascism, its author took issue with Roy's methods of reaching his conclusions. It read: 'Any assertions can be proved and disproved with mere juggling with words. The author's undoubted scholarship – that it may be misguided is beside the point – and grasp of contemporary political tendencies make him a dangerous enemy full of surprises.'[99] But even for audiences who were extremely unlikely to be swayed by his arguments, Roy's bold claims got him a degree of attention.

As such, the fascist equivalence was also part of the renewed efforts Roy and his colleagues from the Radical Democratic Party made to make new international connections. Framing Congress leadership as a fascist threat was a part of the strategy Roy and his colleagues used in order to approach the British Labour Party in the 1940s. This involved a request to be acknowledged as a sister party,

---

[97] Roy, *Jawaharlal Nehru*, 43.
[98] Ibid., 44.
[99] 'Gandhi Psychoanalysed: Problem of Freedom – By M.N. Roy', *Civil & Military Gazette Lahore*, 19 May 1946, 44 Editorials, Press Clippings, Catalogue 70: M. N. Roy Papers Section 1, NMML.

but also a suggestion for their own design for a constitution for independent India.¹⁰⁰ Such a daring proposition required strong arguments. These were provided by an article of Roy's in which Gandhi's Congress party came in for heavy-duty accusations of fascist politics. It drew an equivalence between viceroy Wavell's support for Gandhi and that of General von Hindenburg for Hitler, arguing Wavell would enable the same kind of disaster in India that had been unfolding in Europe. The common element between the two situations, the article argued, had been the lack of majority vote for both winning candidates, as there had been no universal franchise at the time of the 1937 provincial elections.¹⁰¹ Gandhi was not just a typical modern individual, fearful of his new freedoms; he was as dangerous as Hitler. To gain a foothold with a party to whom Roy and his associates were unknown, this was an attention-grabbing, if ultimately unsuccessful, move.

Totalitarianism everywhere

Roy's later international approaches were a part of discussions of the subject of totalitarianism. Even though fascism had quickly become an unwieldy category, the period after the Second World War saw the fast rise of this even wider category.¹⁰² For different thinkers, ideas about the nature of totalitarianism served different intellectual projects, from a Cold War-era critique of the Soviet Union to the US new left in the 1960s and 1970s, particularly buoyed by Frankfurt School intellectuals, using it to establish '... how the United States was, in its own way, "totalitarian."'¹⁰³ For Roy, totalitarianism served the purpose of presenting the intellectual, spiritual and moral backdrop against which his kind

---

¹⁰⁰ See Chapter 4.
¹⁰¹ 'Lord Wavell Playing the Hindenburg of India? – Subtle Plan to Perpetuate Exploitation of Indian People – Indian National Congress Playing with Distributed Cards' LP/ID/IND/2/23ii, PHM.
¹⁰² The 1950s saw the beginnings of a vast literature on totalitarianism, which analysed fascism and communism as expressions of the same destructive outcomes of the worst potentials of twentieth-century mass society. In the 1920s, 'totalitarian' had been used as a term to characterize Italian fascism, and in the late '40s and early '50s it became a term mostly used in connection to Nazi Germany. Starting from Hannah Arendt's *The Origins of Totalitarianism* (1951) and Carl Friedrich's and Zbigniew Brzezinski's *Totalitarian Dictatorship and Autocracy* (1956), it began to be used as a term denoting both right-wing and left-wing dictatorships, beginning to serve as cornerstone for comparisons mainly between Hitler's and Stalin's regimes. Michael Geyer, 'Introduction: After Totalitarianism – Stalinism and Nazism Compared', in *Beyond Totalitarianism; Stalinism and Nazism Compared*, ed. Michael Geyer, Sheila Fitzpatrick (Cambridge: Cambridge University Press, 2009), 3–4.
¹⁰³ Geyer, 'After Totalitarianism', 7.

of humanism was indispensable. As such, it was as universal as his humanism, and had no clearly delineated outline that confined itself to particularly existing regimes. This was visible in his examples, which were drawn from Nazi Germany as well as contemporary India, and included sporadic references to the Soviet Union and occasional excursions to the 'land of rugged individualism,' the contemporary United States:

> America is greater than the greatest of the Americans; the so-called American way of life means the obligation of all individual Americans to conform with the will of the fiction of a collective ego. The Nation-State, in practice, makes no greater concession to the concept of individual freedom than the Class-State of the Communists, and also of the Socialists.[104]

Examples of political systems that were antithetical to what Roy saw as the good life existed everywhere, and could not be outlined so precisely. While Hindu nationalism was what Roy spent most of his time combatting, he would write about it in terms that were not specific to it. Instead, he conceived of it as one version of a force that had, by the 1940s, become a global threat. By diagnosing equivalences for what was happening in India in texts describing events elsewhere, he made the latter look less familiar than they appeared on the surface. It also ensured that a phenomenon could not only be discussed with those preoccupied with the same things, but that it could provide food for discussion with others too. One last example of a set of such thinkers in this section are those using theories of 'secular religion' in post-Second World War France.

In the postwar efflorescence of humanist and anti-totalitarian thought, France emerged as a key site full of left-wing thinkers.[105] The ubiquitousness of humanists in all political camps of post-war France was mocked by Michel Foucault in his memoirs: 'One cannot imagine into what a moralistic pond of humanist sermons we were plunged in the post-war period. Everyone was a humanist. Camus, Sartre, Garaudy were all humanists. Stalin was a humanist too …'[106] Particularly since the publication of *Existentialism Is a Humanism* (1946), Jean-Paul Sartre (1905–80) was the biggest name among them, and Roy fruitlessly sought contact with Sartre – rather because of his reputation as a

---

[104] Roy, *Radical Humanism*, 20–1.
[105] Tony Judt, *Past Imperfect: French Intellectuals, 1944–1956* (New York and London: New York University Press, 2011), 1–12.
[106] Quoted in Denis Kambouchner, 'Lévi-Strauss and the question of humanism', in *The Cambridge Companion to Lévi-Strauss*, ed. Boris Wiseman (Cambridge: Cambridge University Press, 2009), 19.

leading intellectual than because he had become a convinced existentialist.[107] His work was an inevitability for a humanist publication, and the most theoretical of Roy's associates, later professor in literature Sibnarayan Ray, explicated his work as the ultimate iteration of individual freedom.[108] Another article in Roy's journal focused on the social milieu of Sartre's existentialism rather than on its content, describing how the philosopher frequented a cosmopolitan environment of his own:

> ... in the Café Flore, a squalid little place, with low ceilings and ignoble furniture, much frequented by literary ladies and young men with their hair dressed in the long rolling bob of which Parisian coiffeurs have the secret, and as often as not, with ancient copies of the 'Daily Worker' thrust into their pockets, and by German Jews, either humble and reverent or themselves frowning portentously over piles of grubby manuscript; and American women smoking pipes, and tramps trying to borrow and odd coin.[109]

Jokingly, the article mentioned Sartre had moved on to a new bar, where drinks were considerably more expensive, and wondered if, as a result, his writings would become 'exuberantly petit-bourgeois'.[110] Drinks, appearances, furnishings and a mix of nationalities had not ceased to be of interest to those in Roy's cosmopolitan circles.

From the field of anti-totalitarian thinking, Roy took the notion of 'secular religion,' a notion critical of communism as well as fascism, considering them as various expressions of the same underlying phenomenon, and as such highly suitable to a way of conceptualizing world affairs that was prone to seeing the underlying unity in various phenomena. Thinkers associated with theories of 'secular religion' who were published in *The Radical Humanist* and *The Marxian/Humanist Way* were the sociologists Raymond Aron (1905–83) and Jules Monnerot (1909–95). Aron would become known through his work *The Opium of Intellectuals* (1955), which addressed the question why communism held such interest for French intellectuals after the war – Aron being one of the very few immune to its allure – and relied on the notion of secular religion to do so.[111] Monnerot would have been largely forgotten if it had not been for his turn to

---

[107] Letter from M. N. Roy to André Brissaud, 16 May 1949, Brissaud Correspondence, Catalogue 70: M. N. Roy Papers Section 1, NMML.
[108] Sibnarayan Ray, 'Existentialism and Jean-Paul Sartre', *The Radical Humanist* 12 June 1949, 275.
[109] 'Jean Paul Sartre' *Independent India*, 8 June 1947, 343.
[110] *Ibid.*
[111] Daniel Gordon, Peter Baehr, 'In Search of Limits: Raymond Aron on 'Secular Religion' and Communism', *Journal of Classical Sociology* 11, no. 2 (2011): 143.

the extreme right wing political party *Front National* in 1989.[112] His *Sociology of Communism* (1949) had been a popular book when it was first published, which described communism as a religion, specifically the 'Islam of the twentieth century.'[113]

In Roy's journals, Aron and Monnerot criticized the preoccupation with communism of their confrères in 'French intellectuals and Stalinism,' and 'Socialism and Freedom,' respectively.[114] Both texts conceptualized communism as a non-transcendental religion. The religious nature of communism was found in mass festivals and events, instilling a religious type of emotionality in crowds of spectators and followers, turning them ecstatic. Another important element was the creation of a cult of the leader, the nature of which would verge on that of religious worship.[115] Apart from conceiving of misguided politics under the name of religion, secular religion theorists offered an account of the ways in which these systems compromised the freedom of the individuals in them. In an article by Monnerot's reprinted in *The Marxian Way* that was strongly reminiscent of Gustav Le Bon's *Psychology of Crowds* (1895), the collectivities of the twentieth century had profoundly changed the nature of the individuals inside of them: '… an assemblage of men not taken as men, but as an assemblage of individuals stripped of what in everyone of them is singular and individual.'[116] Monnerot saw all peddlers of secular religions united in their knowledge of mass and crowd psychology, linking not only Islam, communism and fascism in the power they could have over their followers, but also '… their American contemporaries who created the psychotechnique and applied to the art of publicity, knew how to operate with certain simple, empirical, but efficacious notions of collective psychology.'[117] A theory about communism and fascism could quickly turn into an image making the entire world highly suspect, but at its heart required a conception of the free individual to define what it was that was lost under both systems.

Roy's approach to these French thinkers was to emphasize commonalities, particularly in the diagnosis of a protracted crisis humanity was living through, and not to worry about differences. For the enthusiasm with which

---

[112] Stone, 'The Uses and Abuses of "secular Religion"', 474.
[113] *Ibid.*, 469.
[114] Raymond Aron, 'French Intellectuals and Stalinism', *The Radical Humanist* 24 May 1952, 243; 250; Jules Monnerot, 'Socialism and Freedom', *The Marxian Way* III, no. 1 (1947–8): 16.
[115] Peter Baehr, *Hannah Arendt, Totalitarianism, and the Social Sciences* (Stanford: Stanford University Press, 2010), 94–9.
[116] Monnerot, 'Socialism and Freedom', 16.
[117] *Ibid.*, 19.

Roy approached intellectuals abroad to discuss the shared crisis of humanity, approaching this crisis as a truly shared one required certain objections to go unmentioned. One of the French writers Roy corresponded and exchanged articles with was André Brissaud (1920-96), a historian, author and propagator of Christian humanism. In their correspondence, the men agreed that humanity found itself in a crisis which needed to be thought about from different sides, but sensed different solutions for this crisis. According to Brissaud, there was a role for religiously inspired values. The current crisis could be a source for hope, he wrote, because addressing it would involve a complete overhaul of human values:

> We have to face the reality of certain spiritual norms, without which human existence is not possible. We have to live them ourselves and to implant them deeply in every living individual, and make them the point of departure of a new social existence, if western civilisation is to grow into a universal civilisation, and if humanity is to avoid brute annihilation or degeneration.'[118]

These spiritual norms, for Brissaud, were inspired by religion. That was also likely a part of what Brissaud expected from Roy; considering he wrote that they might meet in Calcutta the next year, as he would be in the Himalayas to make a film called *The Meaning of the Divine*.[119] Roy used the term spiritual in his humanist texts, but would never look to religion in order to supply its content. Instead, he required people to be 'spiritually free,' which implied an independence from dogmatic systems of thought. In fact, contemporary humanists in South India who cite Roy as a source of inspiration may criticize his absolutist anti-dogmatism, as some of them choose to synthesize their humanism with an adherence to Marxist principles.[120] Within Roy's own circles, spirituality was suspect. The engineer Sushil Dey took Roy to task for its vagueness, questioning how useful it was as a guide for finding political leaders.[121] In his explanation, Roy confessed that was the case because such people did not yet exist: 'Prosaically, what I am mean is that a higher type of human beings are required to build the new social order. Their appearance is historically determined, inasmuch

---

[118] Letter from André Brissaud to M. N. Roy, 29 April 1949, Brissaud Correspondence, Catalogue 70: M. N. Roy Papers Section 1, NMML.
[119] *Ibid.*
[120] Stefan Binder, *Total Atheism; Making 'Mental Revolution' in South India* (Zutphen: Wöhrmann, 2017), 18.
[121] 'How will these spiritually free men for our government be found? 'By what standards will their spiritual freedom be gauged?' Letter from Sushil Dey to M. N. Roy, 24 June 1946, Sushil Dey Correspondence, M. N. Roy Papers Section 1, NMML.

as they will embody the totality of human values produced since the dawn of history …'[122] Self-consciously, Roy made sure to point out he did not mean the creation of 'Hitlerite supermen,' and noted that his thoughts sounded 'like poetry.'[123] Humanist thought came with a great deal of soul-searching, and while Brissaud and Roy exchanged cordial letters agreeing there was a crisis the entirety of humanity found itself in, the differences in solutions they envisioned were hidden by their similar language.

Conclusion

In an age when the perspective from an aeroplane, and the bird's eye view it provided, was the privilege of extremely few people, possessing the confident authority to claim to be able to see the key similarities across widely ranging contexts was a rare commodity.[124] For such a wide-ranging point of view, speed of movement was of the essence. For Roy, speed of intellectual movement was provided by the easy access to new contexts and concepts created by equivalences. A key ingredient to the perspective Roy offered was that it rendered phenomena that had seemed unfamiliar familiar, or vice versa. It transformed phenomena generally described in one way by rendering them in a different lexicon, and by that, made them belong to a wider reality that made the familiar look new. This achieved a translation of a concept or a context without going into the nitty-gritty of histories and further intellectual baggage. It was an ideal figure of thought for an intellectual who was not only mobile, but who adopted a cosmopolitan persona that made a habit of travelling light.

Constructing a coherent wider reality in this way required many things to go unmentioned, so that racial mixing could be said to exist in the same way in ancient India and the Latin America of the early twentieth century; the proletariat could be construed as a political force to be reckoned with in India in 1920 and fascism could be seen as a force looming in human psychologies the world over. What these translations had in common was that they were smooth. So smooth, in fact, that they lacked the 'grip,' theorized by Anna Lowenhaupt Tsing, giving global encounters their purchase. Yet, its applications

---

[122] Letter from M. N. Roy tot Sushil Dey, 5 July 1946, Sushil Dey Correspondence, M. N. Roy Papers Section 1, NMML.
[123] *Ibid.*
[124] See Peter Adey, *Aerial Life: Spaces, Mobilities, Affects* (Chichester: Wiley-Blackwell, 2010), 1–11.

ranged from a means to approach new audiences, tapping into the tantalizing promise of a new universalist discourse, the appeal of speed of intellectual movement over hair-splitting and aporias, to asserting interpretative freedom from classifications of difference with colonial legacies. It is a testimony to the requirements of international organizations that this practice was a part of what gave Roy a platform in several of them. The greater the desire to incorporate and address the whole world, the greater the need for quick figures of thought and thinkers who were fast on their feet.

As odd of an approach to global politics and history it seems to consistently argue that things are the same everywhere, intellectuals' questioning of the status of difference continues; in *Postcolonial Theory and the Specter of Capital* (2013), for example, Vivek Chibber has attempted to undermine the foundations of Subaltern Studies, or Postcolonial Theory more generally, by arguing that the development of capitalism did not take fundamentally different courses in Europe and in India, thereby destabilizing claims of irreducible differences between them.[125] Like Roy's, Chibber's work has not gone uncriticized.[126] To historians, there is a strangeness to Roy's equivalences as one area of influence from post-colonial studies has been to take differences seriously and to problematize and deconstruct universalizing tendencies and modes of thought. Historians are justly keen to learn from actors who engaged with the specific challenges of specific translations, offering creative interpretations of ideas and practices that acknowledged differences between places and show the fault lines where grand narratives broke down. But for Roy, providing easy, swift access to new contexts and concepts for a range of audiences was a key feature of his intellectual approach to the international terrain he was operating on. Doing so was even an important ingredient in achieving the social and intellectual standing that he did. The authoritativeness of this approach was far from uncontested or perennially successful, as we have seen. But it tells us that our ideas surrounding difference have a history of their own, and can be confounded by historical actors with widely divergent problems and interests. Their struggles with expectations of difference confront us with our own assumptions about what difference looks like and what it can and cannot do.

---

[125] Vivek Chibber, *Postcolonial Theory and the Specter of Capital* (London: Verso, 2013).
[126] Gayatri Chakravorty Spivak, 'Postcolonial Theory and the Specter of Capital', *Cambridge Review of International Affairs* 27, no. 1 (2014): 184–98.

The face of the global

Apart from human beings, the terrain of the earth itself can be said to have a face. The slope of a mountain is sometimes described as facing South, North, East or West; faces are directional. They include certain things within their gaze, whereas others remain out of sight. In addition to a point of view, faces have a certain appearance to their spectators that can give rise to a range of associations – for example, the Iztaccíhuatl mountain northwest of Mexico City, which M. N. Roy remembered being referred to as the 'sleeping woman.'[1] When it is not the surface of the earth that is under consideration but something labelled the 'global,' it tends to evoke something impersonal, large scale, lacking detail and familiarity. And yet, when the global was invoked in political arguments that ostensibly included all of humanity, there were decidedly personal elements present in these politics, which meant that audiences for whom the global was invoked could imagine it to have a certain kind of face.

M. N. Roy was an intellectual who was able to give a face to the global, as it was imagined in discourses and displays of various world-changing ideologies that he interacted with during his lifetime. These ranged from his efforts under the banners of anti-colonial nationalism and anti-imperialist internationalism, to the expansion of communism to the colonized world, to his resistance to fascism, which he imagined as a global threat, to his development of a humanist philosophy, fit for all of humanity. For many of his audiences, Roy's presence allowed them to imagine that it was indeed the whole world that was the working territory of the ideology or thought system under discussion, or could make the world into an accessible object. This was not merely an aesthetic ploy as Roy was an intellectual in his own right, so he concurrently constructed a vantage point for himself from which he claimed to authoritatively speak about the world in

---

[1] Roy, *Memoirs*, 54.

its entirety – with varying degrees of conviction. In a combination of global intellectual history and global microhistory, this book surmises that the global is most productively considered as a claim, not a scale of analysis. It has argued that this claim was given texture and credibility by individuals such as Roy and the practices they engaged in, meaning the global was always something highly specific, as were the ways in which it was given a stamp of universality.

As singular as M. N. Roy was, he shared these claim-making abilities and the purchase those had with several other cosmopolitan intellectuals of his day. Many of those with whom he shared spaces and practices have been explored in the book. To various extents, this varied cast of Indian revolutionaries, international communists and humanist intellectuals as well as anarchists, politicians, development consultants, actors and artists shared not just the fact that a large part of their authority stemmed from the cosmopolitan impressions they could make, but from the specific kind of cosmopolitanism this involved. This kind has been labelled as a distinguished kind, in order to set it apart from the range of mobilities millions of individuals engaged in during the first half of the twentieth century. Distinguished cosmopolitanism relied on the more or less self-conscious cultivation of a cosmopolitan image that was characterized by distinction and distance. This did not mean distinguished cosmopolitans floated above the surface of the earth, as their cosmopolitanism was made up of bodily and social practices with highly specific people in highly specific places. To a high extent, they interacted with other cosmopolitans, and drew their social capital from connections to one another, more so than by forging thick connections to the new places where they worked and lived. They remained quick on their feet and ready to move on. An air of distance to what their audiences knew was a key part of the attraction of distinguished cosmopolitanism, suggesting the exoticism of their bodies or grasp of alien ideas and experience of faraway realities. This distance, however, could not be felt to be too large; like with Newtonian gravity, this attraction decreased to function as cosmopolitans became more distant from their audiences.

Distinguished cosmopolitanism's distinction involved a way of life that kept certain cosmopolitans in and left others out, as well as ways of communicating this way of life, as a knowing encounter with variation and difference. This could reach from more or less mundane remarks about assessing the merits of food and drink from various places, preference for certain languages over others, and display of familiarity with a range of them, to making a living from writings about the array of places one had been to, and the internationally known figures with whom one had crossed paths. In these practices, there was an element of knowing discernment, where what was on display was not so much the specific choices made – in wine, dress or companions – but more so the knowing itself, or the ability to select skilfully from an eclectic palette of varied options. Such discernment communicated not merely movement, but an ease of movement that set these cosmopolitans apart from other mobile people, and in no way neatly corresponded to the difficulties of their actual experiences. Such difficulties and dangers, rather, could be synthesized into tales of the skilled navigation thereof, emphasizing the narrator's lightness of movement. It was a habitus and persona oozing ease of movement that underpinned a sense of authority on variety and difference, which could be a real political or social asset.

Bodies have been a key way to think about the global, from discourses on rivalling races – be they of the spiritual East or an Asian 'yellow peril' – to proletarian masses rising up against oppression by the billions, to questions of famine and war, or humanistic ideas about the Family of Man, captured in a travelling photography exhibition in the 1950s. Speaking about the global as a body or bodies was possible only because of the bodies of speakers themselves. This even was the case when it came to the seemingly unpopulated extraterrestrial space of theoretical physics; Albert Einstein was as iconic for invoking an abstract idea of global space as Tagore was for invoking a wide world of culture and civilization. Such speaking were marked by race, class caste and gender, moved through space, marked by naming practices and clothing, impressed their interlocutors, engaged in relationships and created themselves and others anew in writing – as well as surviving long enough to tell the tale, with others not being as lucky. Their attraction to audiences was in part determined by the degree of distance that their presence could invoke – not too little and not too much.

This meant there were decidedly personal elements to the way the global was communicated and imagined, linked to what for many audiences involved parts of the world beyond those they knew, or places quintessentially marked by difference. For audiences in the West in the first half of the twentieth century, faces that looked like they were speaking for the world often looked Indian, specifically Bengali. As much as this had as much to do with the history of the British Empire there, it was also due to the performances of several Indian intellectual celebrities that had captured the imagination of their audiences, notably Vivekananda and Tagore. In doing so, they spoke of their own conceptions of what the world as a whole could mean, developing a version of Indian spirituality for international consumption. It was against that background that travelling Indian revolutionaries abroad were seen to possess certain kinds of difference, which they could both use as a resource and a stepping stone towards familiar associations in unfamiliar places, but which they also had to contend with as these expectations of difference could be very limiting. With the authority of distinguished cosmopolitanism, such difference could be played with or even collapsed into non-existence. The authority to do so mainly functioned in spaces where shared messages were politically expedient or desirable. It relied on the invocation of distance and the power of suggestion. Markedly, Roy's main skill did not lie in connecting various life worlds, but in offering the impression of access to one or more parts of the world international organizations with global aspirations had an interest in, but did not (yet) possess a connection to. When connections increased, the power of impression waned.

While Bengali intellectuals were overrepresented in global representations in Europe and North America, there were other patterns discernible in practices that allowed individuals to do so with any degree of convincingness. One was the enumeration of the breadth of their international experience, rather than reference to specific places they knew. In the descriptions of distinguished cosmopolitans, lists of places play a large role, suggesting not specific kinds of knowledge but a more general familiarity with the different parts making up the whole world. Apart from that, the intimate acquaintance with internationally known figures from the realms of politics and the arts was a key touchstone in distinguished cosmopolitan characterizations. Closeness to Lenin, Sun Yat-sen, Soon Mei-ling, Pancho Villa or others could serve to underline the ease with which someone moved in high circles, especially when descriptions were laced with intimate details and humour. Blended with recollections of less well-known figures, they could contribute to heightening the cosmopolitan standing of those lesser figures themselves. With connections being a mainstay of the study of global history, the way in which connections could be mobilized to contribute to a cosmopolitan persona that came with potential political and social benefits attunes us to the critical scrutiny of what it is we look for when we look for connections.

Corporeality was an important aspect of orchestrated acts of internationalism, not just in the internationalism of post-colonial states, as Naoko Shimazu has argued, but in the more personally driven internationalism of the beginning of the twentieth century and the interwar period. Then, a repertoire of dress and other cultural references – for example to history – were also part and parcel of practices of a more informal diplomacy that could find a shared basis in opposition to a certain state's power. Such displays of internationalism have mostly been studied as the prerogative of Western European imperial powers, but were here considered from a wider angle, specifically for the Soviet Union and to a lesser degree for oppositional communism and post-Second World War humanism. The book has gestured towards other universalizing ideologies, such as anarchism and pan-Asianism, and their ways to gather the world in one place through acts of representation, but a specific look at the mechanisms at work in each was beyond the scope of this study.

Considering Roy as a representative, it can be said that uniqueness was an important factor in the representative claims he was able to make; the rarity of being a politically vocal Indian intellectual who had come to Moscow via Mexico City, spurred on by individual connections and high-stake allegiances, was what drove Roy's ability to represent hundreds of millions. In his post-communist period, his representative efforts were equally buoyed by the rarity of an oppositional communist and later humanist movement in India. More generally, acts of personal, non-democratically mandated representation were helped if the entity being represented possessed an air of distance. Conversely, as communication between different parts of the world increased, such suggestive practices of representation decreased in their level of convincingness. In terms of its structure, it can be said that representing the world required either strict agreement on the outline of this world and its internal divisions, or a high degree of patience to negotiate these on part of the representatives – both of which were hard to muster for large gatherings. Barring rigidly imposed definitions about the nature of the world, it was too complex and varied to be collectively represented with any degree of coherence. As was the case with intellectuals, such as Vivekananda, Tagore and Brajendranath Seal, being taken seriously when speaking for the world or large parts thereof went hand in hand with being taken seriously when speaking about the world. Staring in the vortex of the global did not leave one unchanged.

In Roy's direct circles, a global perspective engendered by a habituation to speaking for the world was linked to a shared preoccupation with thinking about humanity as population. This was an abstract conception of people as a large mass, characterized by scientific and economic considerations about food, war, space, birth, death and reproduction. This perspective at a distance was, however, directly linked to highly personal practices of sex and marriage. For humanist intellectuals among Roy's circles especially, the most intimate connection between the individual body and the global one existed in the practice of birth control. The figure of all human bodies on earth making up a growing entity as they were being born faster than they were dying was skewed towards thinking about the population of India – specifically, thinking about it as too big. For Roy, part of his distinguished cosmopolitan persona was not only not to have children, but also to write about opting out of being a link in a global family, to even questioning the value of human life more generally.

Ideology and argument also were an aspect of cosmopolitan practice in which distance had a part. On the level of the historiography surrounding Roy, there are several connections evidenced in his writings that had gone unnoticed before. First, there was the relevance Roy's book *La India* (1918) had for José Vasconcelos' *Estudios Indostánicos* (1920) and his ideas about *mestizaje* or racial mixing as an essential attribute of Latin American society. The second was the extent to which Roy adopted Erich Fromm's theories of fascism from *Escape from Freedom* (1941) and applied them to his writings about Hindu nationalism in the 1940s, particularly *The Problem of Freedom* (1945) and *Jawaharlal Nehru* (1945). These and other such cross-fertilizations featured as instances of 'assertions of equivalence,' a thinking figure much used by Roy that assumed a deeper underlying unity of the world, meaning that separate phenomena in different places were nothing but disparate expressions of the same, deeper, reality. The book proposes to treat such assertions as translations in their own right, of a sort that did not assume difference between contexts, to then bridge this difference with translation, but sameness. Such assertions can nevertheless be viewed as translations because like in the case of other translations, they gave audiences unfamiliar with one of the contexts involved access to a phenomenon that had hitherto seemed out of reach. Vice versa, it could make a part of the world that seemed familiar appear in a new light, captured by a theory designed for a quite different context. Even though such assertion might confound the expectations of global historians interested in translations that grapple with difference, to their contemporary audiences they nevertheless provided a transformation of the subject at hand.

Among other cosmopolitan intellectuals arguing about universalization, Roy's insistence on equivalences between spaces often set him apart, and gave his opponents and competitors a great deal of space for intellectual attacks in tracts that demonstrated how different parts of the world were different indeed. On the plus side, he offered his audiences far easier access to various parts of the world than intellectuals who insisted on their difference. Even compared to Lenin, Roy was a particularly generalizing voice, disagreeing with him on the necessity of a different approach to spread communism in colonial countries than was required in colonizing ones. On the one hand, this approach could cost Roy opportunities, as he was often asked to fulfil expectations foreign audiences had of Indian intellectuals and refused to do so, and on the other hand, it occasionally made him a highly successful translator, who was employed to bring in an unfamiliar part of the world, and in doing so made it appear suddenly familiar. In general, careful scrutiny of Roy's perhaps unusual and occasionally confounding approach helps to solidify a tendency in global intellectual history to move beyond the binary of universalism versus particularism, towards an approach that considers various competing universalisms instead, with actors shifting between and combining them. This also provides a frame for intellectual change more accurately capturing Roy's shift from revolutionary anti-colonialism and a preoccupation with India, to international communism and then humanism; rather than seeing it as a move from a particular, Indian, belief system to a universalizing, Marxist and then humanist one, it interprets the shift as being from one system claiming universal validity to another, if both with highly specific ways of doing so.

Assertions of equivalence were part of a wider perspective that Roy laid claim to, which was that of the impartial outsider, who could see more, and see more objectively, than insiders could. The advantages of such a perspective held currency within the realms of communism and humanism, either in the shape of the professional revolutionary or the development consultant. During a life of upheaval, this was quite a stable strategy that Roy used in order to offer his skills and ideas to a series of partners throughout his ideologically and geographically varied lifetime. He embraced an intellectual outsiderhood not only as an Indian nationalist among US socialists and a company of mostly European and North American communists, but during the years after he returned to India in 1930 and initially saw himself excluded from human society as a prisoner, and then increasingly became an outsider to both communist and mainstream nationalist politics. This also involved de-emphasizing his own particularity in both bodily and intellectual practices, for example in his insistence on the sensibleness and comfort of his dress, eschewing too clear a signalling of class, radicalism or cultural belonging, as well as his published work's silence on the matter of race as it personally affected him, for example in the shape of racial discrimination in the United States. Positioning himself as a universal, non-particular man lent itself to the making of universal claims, but in their citations and make-up, his claims looked overwhelmngly European.

The tension between the roles of the representative and the outside adviser, where the former relied more on defined differences, brought together to represent a whole, whereas the latter was more prone to collapse differences into an underlying unity, was a productive one. It allowed individuals to both work with expectations of what the known world looked like, transcending them and thereby making the world seem larger yet more accessible than it had seemed before. Shared assumptions about parts of the world that were familiar and parts that were unfamiliar allowed for the whole to be represented, and at the same time attempts to change the world involved changing such assumptions. This was exactly what representatives such as Roy tried to do, and his intellectual practice of asserting equivalences between different parts of the world and different fields of thought was geared towards changing what was familiar and what was not. It was even meant to do so quickly and easily, as an intellectual approach to a global field that suited one who moved with ostensible ease across large physical distances.

Since M. N. Roy's itinerary has been at the centre of this book, its conclusions mostly centre around leftist ideologies, although shared cosmopolitan practices and intellectuals adopting rightist ideologies such as Subhas Chandra Bose, Nicola Bombacci and Jules Monnerot have played a minor role. It would be worthwhile to consider the ways in which intellectuals in rightist circles signalled the universalization of an ideology to increasing parts of the world, according to which principles this world was divided into more and less relevant parts, and if and how they managed to credibly speak about it in its totality. While race was a relevant aspect of the way in which Roy could play his roles abroad, so was his own disregarding of its relevance in his own life; for intellectuals universalizing a rightist ideology, its emphases and silences would likely have been quite different. In general, different world views possessed their own ways of incorporating and effacing difference, containing their own emphases and silences, resulting in a different face of the global, looking in a different direction.

Distant feelings

As distinguished cosmopolitanism was characterized by relationships of in- and exclusion and shared social practices, emotions had a significant part in its constitution. Cosmopolitan practices had marked emotional qualities, whether they pertained to shared lifestyles, shared lives and feelings of attraction and revulsion. Even the intellectual practices that cosmopolitans used to navigate an ideology's supposedly global terrain of extension possessed emotional aspects. There were several, at times, contradictory and complementary complexes of feelings marking lived and remembered distinguished cosmopolitanism, as well as feelings that accompanied invocations of the global itself.

From the realm of clandestine mobility, persecution, wars, famine, deprivation and revolutions, feelings of danger and fear were as characteristic for the constitution of distinguished cosmopolitanism as it was to ennoble them in retrospective remembering, or to avoid communicating them altogether. A shared experience was crucially marked by selective remembering, often with humour, by those who had survived to tell the tale. In such tales, highlighting difficulties and dangers could have the function to emphasize the value of the affiliative bonds to new places and people that cosmopolitans had forged against the odds. Evelyn Trent's recalling of the hardships she and Roy faced when they were married against her family's wishes heightened the meaning their bond had had for her as a young woman who saw her own country with critical eyes and assumed distance from it through tying herself to someone from a faraway place. Recalling hardships also underlined the unusualness of cosmopolitan life courses, singling them out as distinct in their experiences. And of course, dangers that could be remembered on later occasions heightened narrators' heroic profiles. For Tan Malaka, writing about the physical hardship of largely involuntarily moving between vastly different places in the world under difficult circumstances underlined the fact that he had mostly ignored the effects doing so had on his body. Feelings relating to danger and deprivation could thereby enhance the cosmopolitan persona of the person feeling them through contrast, in their ability to be ignored, suppressed, disregarded and even laughed off. This was certainly not the case for all individuals in these pages at all times, as they did not always have the opportunity to make light of their experiences in retrospect. But when they did, the joyful side of the lives they had lived lent themselves to being made a personal aspect of a character who was exceptionally light on their feet, able to take the world in their stride.

Feelings of nostalgia and (impending) loss were key in the contemporary constitution of affiliative bonds in a shared way of life that was presumed not to be able to last, because of its political and geographic instability. They also played a large role in re-constituting affiliative groups after the fact, when their short-lived and exceptional conviviality could only be remembered as a distant reality. Love relationships ended, friends left countries because they fell out of political favour or had to become refugees. Nostalgia's links to the awareness of a situation being temporary contributed to it being given heightened importance, both in the moment and after the fact. Complementing nostalgia were nearly opposite emotions of optimism and resilience that were a part of cosmopolitan practices, and that were required to go on finding new opportunities under changing circumstances. Roy's humanist emphasis on man's 'faith in himself' was a secularist principle, as well as a way of feeling about life and one's own abilities. This, too, was key to cosmopolitans who had to take into account the idea that soon, they might be moving on from where they were, and played a role in elevating them above others who did not have the gumption to keep going.

Another emotional aspect of shared social practices of groups of distinguished cosmopolitans both during the times of their acquaintance and after was that of (sensory) pleasure. A shared delight in selecting from eclectic offers of food, drink, languages, clothing, companions, art and music involved enjoying variety and the finer things in life. It was also the pleasure characterizing their conviviality that made distinguished cosmopolitanism could be claimed as being superior to other kinds. Pleasure could even be linked to naming practices, for example in the case of Tan Malaka who treated his changing pseudonyms and aliases as a field for puns and allusions. It could also extend to love relationships, for example the pages written 'in gold,' Bakar Ali Mirza thanked Agnes Smedley for after they parted, or Louise Geissler who recalled having relished various love affairs in her younger years and being 'saturated in every respect' now that she was older. Nostalgia, in turn, could enhance this pleasure. At the same time, pleasure could be turned into a political principle, as it was in some feminist thought about birth control making sex independent from reproduction, as well as Roy's humanist work where pleasure was a sufficient (and even superior) reason for which to have sex. Tellingly, his key example was of a cat living in the prison where he was incarcerated, not relying on complex moral systems to determine its course of action, but following the joy and pleasure of its sensory experience.

A last complex of feelings around distinguished cosmopolitan practices relate to seriousness versus superficiality. For the intellectuals in Roy's circles, political work, be it for national independence, a global proletarian revolution, the battle against fascism or the intellectual and economic progress of a part of the world was a serious business. But in their role in the communication and propaganda relating to such goals, seriousness itself could have a propagandistic function. In his dress and recollections of his own social ineptitude, Roy emphasized his own serious and even awkward behaviour, or his lack of social graces. In the annals of the Comintern there are warnings against young people who flocked to communist ideals as a mere 'fashion,' implying a lack of commitment. Photographs of the era were composed, non-smiling, and rhetoric was stark and combative. At the same time, by the virtue of constantly being on the move, cosmopolitans frequently interacted with unknown individuals whom they judged based on superficial qualities: their appearance, dress, the sound of their voice and composure, combined with the assumptions about their class, caste and background these engendered. This meant that in their dealings, superficial matters played a non-negligible role, which translated in the way cosmopolitans later wrote about their lives, witnessed in the great attention to detail and appearances in many ego documents. These range from the reflections on seriousness as against frivolity in the dressing practices Charles Phillips engaged in – and then rejected – in New York's Bohemian Greenwich Village, to the absurd advantages of wearing a turban at the request of his Californian landlady recalled by Dhan Gopal Mukerji. Often in remembrances, such frivolities by contrast underlined the seriousness of the person doing the remembering, but its presence in cosmopolitan practices nevertheless showed through.

Feelings tied to the global itself as it has received its shape and texture in this book can be described as feelings characterized by a sense of distance. They were nevertheless intimately linked to individuals as they characterized a perspective that held the global in view and thereby ostensibly kept its observer apart from too direct an engagement with the world it held within its gaze. For cosmopolitans, being associated with the distant in an emotional as well as intellectual sense contributed to them being desirable, as connections seemed more valuable the more faraway places provided links to. Of course, holding a global perspective from nowhere is not humanly possible, and claims that one could adopt it nevertheless constituted a set of practices in their own right. Their abstract nature was accompanied by emotional qualities. For example, when Roy and Ellen set up a news service in India in the 1930s, their feeling of India being far away from 'everywhere' betrayed that it were specific places they found important that they felt distant from, rather than the intellectual distance they claimed in a general sense. Their image of the global, as such, clearly had a centre.

Feelings of distance could be construed as the absence of feeling, as in Roy's emphasis on ignoring his personal ties to Borodin when judging the latter's work in China, or Ellen Roy's disappointment at the – habitual – abstractness of her late husband's memoirs. Neutrality was also the reason why Roy considered his dress sense superior to that of cosmopolitans adopting styles with geographic signifiers that seemed more obvious to him, such as saris or Russian peasant blouses. Putting emphasis on not standing out was a paradoxical way to reach distinction through claims of belonging that were global rather than referring to certain places all the while relying on highly specific ingredients. The personal feeling required to operate on such abstract levels, and one which many cosmopolitans often doubted or even despaired of, was what Roy would elevate into a principle of humanist philosophy as 'man's faith in himself'. It was tangible in his pride in the ability to stand alone politically and his adoption of the moniker renegade, expelled from various organizations, almost universally shunned.

Feelings of abstraction and neutrality related to the realms of science and physics, enabling the considering of people as population but also holding deep intrinsic appeal as realms of certitude, exactness and global validity, particularly against more obviously culturally inflected norms of religion. This negative emotional quality was present in Arthur Koestler's phrase characterizing the Soviet human individual as nothing more than 'a multitude of one million divided by one million,' but also in Roy's prison writings that characterized a living being as a 'bit of crawling protoplasm.' The technical, abstract language of natural science could give expression of a sense of life that doubted it being worthwhile. A positive example of the emotional quality of science can be found in Roy's attempt to mobilize the authority of his old acquaintance Albert Einstein in order to support the protest against his arrest. A man who understood the universe on such an intimate level had to be taken seriously on all other subjects too. This book has not approached the global as something large scale, but rather a claim relying on the support of specific individuals and social practices. Yet, on the level of feeling, distinguished cosmopolitan claims to be able to navigate the terrain of the global both required and engendered a sense of being larger than life.

Bibliography

Unpublished Sources

Nehru Memorial Library and Museum, New Delhi, Delhi, India.
    Catalogue 70: M. N. Roy Papers Section I.
    Catalogue 71: M. N. Roy Papers Section II.
    Agnes Smedley Microfilm.

P. C. Joshi Archives, Jawaharlal Nehru University, Delhi, India.
    M. N. Roy Papers.
    Virendranath Chattopadhyaya Papers.
    Marx Legacy.
    Rare Journals.
    Communist International.

National Archives, New Delhi, Delhi, India.
    'Policy towards M.N. Roy, his activities connected with the Labour and Pro-war Propaganda, and his paper Independent India', Digitized Public Records, Home Political-I 1942.

People's History Museum, Manchester, United Kingdom.
    Labour Party Archive, International Department, India.

Het Utrechts Archief, Utrecht, The Netherlands.
    Archive 75: Humanistisch Verbond.
    Archive 1733: International Humanist and Ethical Union.

International Institute for Social History, Amsterdam, The Netherlands.
    Henk Sneevliet Archive.

New York Public Library, New York, USA.
    ZL-281 [Microfilm] International Committee for Political Prisoners Records, 1918–1942, Manuscripts and Archives Division.

Hoover Institution and Library, Stanford, California, USA.
    Collection 77029: Bertram Wolfe Papers.
    Collection 71023: Evelyn Trent Papers.
    Collection 75091: Jay Lovestone Papers
    Collection 2010C8: Marshall Windmiller Papers.

Published Sources

Acharya, M. P. T. *Reminiscences of an Indian Revolutionary*. New Delhi: Amol Publications, 1991.

Adey, Peter. *Aerial Life: Spaces, Mobilities, Affects*. Chichester: Wiley-Blackwell, 2010.

Akerman, James R., ed. *The Imperial Map: Cartography and the Mastery of Empire*. London; Chicago: University of Chicago Press, 2009.

Alexander, Robert Jackson. *The Right Opposition: The Lovestoneites and the International Communist Opposition of the 1930s*. Westport, CT: Greenwood Press, 1981.

Alonso, Isabel Huacuja. 'M.N. Roy and the Mexican Revolution: How a Militant Indian Nationalist Became an International Communist'. *South Asia: Journal of South Asian Studies* 40, no. 3 (2017): 517–30.

Anderson, Benedict. *Under Three Flags: Anarchism and the Colonial Imagination*. London: Verso, 2005.

Andrade, Tonio. 'A Chinese Farmer, Two African Boys, and a Warlord: Toward a Global Microhistory'. *Journal of World History* 21, no. 4 (2010): 573–91.

Ankersmit, F. R. 'Representation as the Representation of Experience'. *Metaphilosophy* 31, no. 1/2 (2000): 148–68.

Ansari, Humayun. *The Emergence of Socialist Thought among North Indian Muslims (1917–1947)*. Karachi: Oxford University Press, 2015.

Appiah, Kwame. *Cosmopolitanism; Ethics in a World of Strangers*. London: Allen Lane, 2006.

Appiah, Kwame. *The Ethics of Identity*. Princeton: Princeton University Press, 2010.

Aravamudan, Srinivas. 'The Colonial Logic of Late Romanticism'. *South Atlantic Quarterly* 102, no. 1 (2003): 179–214.

Aravamudan, Srinivas. *Guru English: South Asian Religion in a Cosmopolitan Language*. Princeton, NJ: Princeton University Press, 2006.

Aron, Raymond. 'French Intellectuals and Stalinism'. *The Radical Humanist*, 24 May, 1952.

Arora, Neena. *The Novels of Mulk Raj Anand; A Study of His Hero*. New Delhi: Atlantic, 2005.

Aydin, Cemil. *The Politics of Anti-Westernism in Asia: Visions of World Order in Pan-Islamic and Pan-Asian Thought*. New York, NY: Columbia University Press, 2007.

Baehr, Peter. *Hannah Arendt, Totalitarianism, and the Social Sciences*. Stanford: Stanford University Press, 2010.

Baer, Ben Conisbee. 'Shit Writing: Mulk Raj Anand's Untouchable, the Image of Gandhi, and the Progressive Writers' Association'. *Modernism/Modernity* 16, no. 3 (2009): 575–95.

Bagchi, Amiya. 'Indian Economy and Society during World War One'. *Social Scientist* 42, no. 7/8 (2014): 5–27.

Balcom, Christopher. 'From Communist Internationalism to a "New Humanism": On M.N. Roy's Confrontation with Fascism'. *South Asia: Journal of South Asian Studies* 46, no. 2 (2023): 353–69.

Ballantyne, Tony. *Orientalism and Race: Aryanism in the British Empire*. New York: Palgrave, 2002.

Banerjee, B. N., G. D. Parikh, and V. M. Tarkunde. *People's Plan for Economic Development of India*. Delhi: Indian Federation of Labour, 1944.

Banerjee, Prathama. *Politics of Time: 'Primitives' and History-Writing in a Colonial Society*. Oxford; New Delhi: Oxford University Press, 2006.

Barooah, Nirode. *Chatto, the Life and Times of an Indian Anti-imperialist in Europe*. Oxford: Oxford University Press, 2004.

Bartelson, Jens. *Visions of World Community*. Cambridge: Cambridge University Press, 2009.

Bashford, Alison. *Global Population: History, Geopolitics, and Life on Earth*. New York, NY: Columbia University Press, 2014.

Baumann, Charlotte. 'Adorno, Hegel and the Concrete Universal'. *Philosophy & Social Criticism* 37, no. 1 (2011): 73–94.

Bayly, Christopher Alan. *The Birth of the Modern World, 1780–914: Global Connections and Comparisons*. Malden, MA: Blackwell Publishing, 2004.

Bayly, Christopher Alan. 'History and World History'. In *A Concise Companion to History*, edited by Ulinka Rublack, 11–28. Oxford: Oxford University Press, 2011.

Beals, Carleton. *Glass Houses: Ten Years of Free-Lancing*. Philadelphia: J. B. Lippincott, 1938.

Bean, Susan. 'Gandhi and Khadi, Fabric of Independence'. In *Cloth and Human Experience*, edited by Annette B. Weiner and Jane Schneider, 354–76. Washington and London: Smithsonian Institute Press, 1989.

Becker, Tobias. 'History and Nostalgia: Historicizing a Multifaceted Emotion'. In *Intimations of Nostalgia: Multidisciplinary Explorations of an Enduring Emotion*, edited by Michael Hviid Jacobsen, 52–69. Bristol: Bristol University Press, 2022.

Beckerlegge, Gwilym. 'The Early Spread of Vedanta Societies: An Example of "Imported Localism"'. *Numen* 51, no. 3 (2004): 296–320.

Bell, Duncan. 'Making and Taking Worlds'. In *Global Intellectual History*, edited by Samuel Moyn and Andrew Sartori, 254–79. New York: Columbia University Press, 2013.

Bellenoit, Hayden J. A. 'Missionary Education, Religion and Knowledge in India, C. 1880 1915'. *Modern Asian Studies* 41, no. 2 (2007): 369–94.

Berger, Mark T. *The Battle for Asia. From Decolonization to Globalization*. London: Taylor & Francis Group, 2003.

Bergmann, Theodor. *Gegen Den Strom: Die Geschichte Der Kommunistischen-Partei-Opposition*. Hamburg: VSA-Verlag, 1987.

Bergmann, Theodor, ed. *Ketzer Im Kommunismus: Alternativen Zum Stalinismus*. Mainz: Decaton-Verlag, 1993.

Bergmann, Théodor and Ludmila Karlova, Roy Medvedev, Ignacio Saldivar, Daniela Spenser, and Paco Ignacio Taibo II. *Le Brahmane du Komintern*. Directed by Vladimir Léon. Paris: Institut National de l'Audiovisuel, 2007.

Bhabha, Homi K. *The Location of Culture*. London: Routledge, 2006.
Bharati, Swami Agehananda. *The Ochre Robe*. London: George Allen & Unwin, 1961.
Bhattacharjee, G. P. *M. N. Roy: From Marxism to Humanism*. Kolkata: Minerva Associates, 2014.
Bhattacharya, Tithi. *Sentinels of Culture: Class, Education and the Colonial Intellectual*. New York: Oxford University Press, 2005.
Binder, Stefan. *Total Atheism; Making 'Mental Revolution' in South India*. Zutphen: Wöhrmann, 2017.
Birla, Ritu. 'Postcolonial Studies: Now That's History'. In *Can the Subaltern Speak? Reflections on the History of an Idea*, edited by Rosalind Morris, 87–99. New York: Columbia University Press, 2010.
Bose, A. C. *Indian Revolutionaries Abroad*. Patna: Bharati Bhawan, 1971.
Bose, Neilesh. 'Taraknath Das: A Global Biography'. In *South Asian Migrations in Global History: Labor, Law, and Wayward Lives*, edited by Neilesh Bose, 168. New York: Bloomsbury Academic, 2021.
Bose, Purnima. 'Transnational Resistance and Fictive Truths: Virendranath Chattopadhyaya, Agnes Smedley and the Indian Nationalist Movement'. *South Asian History and Culture* 2, no. 4 (2011): 502–21.
Bose, Sarmila. 'Love in the Time of War: Subhas Chandra Bose's Journeys to Nazi Germany (1941) and towards the Soviet Union (1945)'. *Economic and Political Weekly* 40, no. 3 (2005): 249–56.
Bose, Subhas Chandra. *The Indian Struggle (1935–1942)*. Calcutta, Chuckervertty: Chatterjee & Co., 1952.
Bose, Sugata. *A Hundred Horizons: The Indian Ocean in the Age of Global Empire*. Cambridge, MA: Harvard University Press, 2006.
Bose, Sugata. *His Majesty's Opponent: Subhas Chandra Bose and India's Struggle against Empire*. Cambridge: Belknap Press, 2011.
Bourdieu, Pierre. 'The Forms of Capital'. In *Readings in Economic Sociology*, edited by Nicole Woolsey Biggart, 280–91. Oxford: Blackwell, 2008.
Britton, John. *Carleton Beals; A Radical Journalist in Latin America*. Albuquerque: University of New Mexico Press, 1987.
Brown, Emily C. *Har Dayal: Hindu Revolutionary and Rationalist*. New Delhi: Manohar, 1976.
Brückenhaus, Daniel. *Policing Transnational Protest: Liberal Imperialism and the Surveillance of Anticolonialists in Europe, 1905–1945*. New York: Oxford University Press, 2017.
Callaghan, John. 'Colonies, Racism, the CPGB and the Comintern in the Inter-War Years'. *Science & Society (New York, 1936)* 61, no. 4 (1997): 513–25.
Callaghan, John. *Rajani Palme Dutt: A Study in British Stalinism*. London: Lawrence and Wishart, 1993.
Carrère d'Encausse, Hélène, and Stuart R. Schram. *Marxism and Asia: An Introduction with Readings*. London: Lane, 1969.

Castiglione, Dario, and Johannes Pollak. 'The Logics of Democratic Presence in Representation'. In *Creating Political Presence: The New Politics of Democratic Representation*, edited by Dario Castiglione and Johannes Pollak, 16–36. Chicago and London: The University of Chicago Press, 2019.

Chandra, Bipan. 'Colonial India: British versus Indian Views of Development'. *Review – Fernand Braudel Center for the Study of Economies, Historical Systems, and Civilizations* 14, no. 1 (1991): 81–167.

Chandra, Siddharth, Goran Kuljanin, and Jennifer Wray. 'Mortality from the Influenza Pandemic of 1918-1919: The Case of India'. *Demography* 49, no. 3 (2012): 857–65.

Chang, Gordon. 'The Life and Death of Dhan Gopal Mukerji'. In *Mukerji, Dhan Gopal, Caste and Outcast*, Stanford: Stanford University Press, 2002.

Charle, Christophe. *Naissance Des 'intellectuels': 1880–1900*. Paris: Ed. De Minuit, 1990.

Chatterjee, Choi. 'Imperial Subjects in the Soviet Union: M.N. Roy, Rabindranath Tagore, and Re-thinking Freedom and Authoritarianism'. *Journal of Contemporary History* 52, no. 4 (2017): 913–34.

Chatterji, Joya. *Bengal Divided; Hindu Communalism and Partition, 1932–1947*. Cambridge: Cambridge University Press, 1994.

Chattopadhyay, Suchetana. 'War, Migration and Alienation in Colonial Calcutta: The Remaking of Muzaffar Ahmad'. *History Workshop Journal* no. 64 (Autumn, 2007): 212–39.

Chaudhuri, Nirad. *Culture in the Vanity Bag*. Bombay: Jaico Publishing House, 1976.

Chaudhuri, Nirad. *Autobiography of an Unknown Indian*. Mumbai: Jaico Publishing House, 2016.

Chernilo, Daniel. 'Cosmopolitanism and the Question of Universalism'. In *Routledge Handbook of Cosmopolitanism Studies*, edited by Gerard Delanty, 47–49. London: Routledge, 2012.

Chiang, Mei-ling. *Conversations with Mikhail Borodin*. 1970.

Chibber, Vivek. *Postcolonial Theory and the Specter of Capital*. London: Verso, 2013.

CIA. 'Stage IV – Operating Action', *CIA-RDP61S00750A000700120006-4*, Crest, General CIA Records. Accessed 25 June 2020, 20–1. https://www.cia.gov/library/readingroom/document/cia-rdp61s00750a000700120006-4.

Clarke, J.J. *Oriental Enlightenment*. London: Routledge, 1997.

Cohn, Bernard S. *Colonialism and Its Forms of Knowledge: The British in India*. Princeton, NJ: Princeton University Press, 1996.

Collini, Stefan. *Absent Minds: Intellectuals in Britain*. Oxford: Oxford University Press, 2006.

Connelly, Matthew. *Fatal Misconception: The Struggle to Control World Population*. Cambridge: Belknap Press of Harvard University Press, 2008.

Conrad, Sebastian. *What Is Global History?* Princeton: Princeton University Press, 2016.

Conrad, Sebastian, and Dominic Sachsenmaier. 'Introduction: Competing Visions of World Order; Global Moments and Movements, 1880s–1930s'. In *Competing Visions* of World Order; Global Moments and Movements, 1880s-1930s, edited by Sebastian Conrad and Dominic Sachsenmaier, 1–25. New York: Palgrave Macmillan, 2007.

Cossart, Brice. 'Global Lives: Writing Global History with a Biographical Approach'. *Entremons: UPF Journal of World History*, no. 5 (2013).

Crawford, Oliver. 'The Many Names of Tan Malaka'. *Afro-Asian Visions* (blog), Medium, 21 May 2019. Accessed 10 June 2020. https://medium.com/afro-asian-visions/the-many-names-of-tanmalaka163a6f2e0bc8#:~:text=In%20his%20autobiography%2C%20titled%20From,Hussein%20and%20Oong%20Song%20Lee.

Crawford, Oliver. 'Translating and Transliterating Marxism in Indonesia'. *Modern Asian Studies*, 20 July 2020, 1–37. doi:10.1017/S0026749X20000104.

Daechsel, Markus. *Islamabad and the Politics of International Development in Pakistan*. Cambridge: Cambridge University Press, 2015.

Davidson, Apollon Borisovič. *South Africa and the Communist International: Volume 1: Socialist Pilgrims to Bolshevik Footsoldiers, 1919–1930*. London: Frank Cass, 2003.

Davies, Tony. *Humanism*. London: Routledge, 1997.

Davis, Mike. *Late Victorian Holocausts: El Niño Famines and the Making of the Third World*. New York: Verso, 2001.

Dayal, Har. *Forty-Four Months in Germany and Turkey; February 1915 to October 1918*. London: P. S. King & Son, 1920.

Deacon, Desley. *Transnational Lives: Biographies of Global Modernity, 1700 – Present*. Basingstoke: Palgrave Macmillan, 2010.

Debray, Régis. *Praised Be Our Lords: A Political Education*. London and New York: Verso, 2007.

De Certeau, Michel. *The Practice of Everyday Life*. Los Angeles, Berkeley: University of California Press, 1988.

Deepak, B.R., and Tansen Sen. 'The Colonial Connections: Indian and Chinese Nationalists in Japan and China'. *China Report* 48, no. 1–2 (2012): 147–70.

Del Castillo, Paola. 'M. N. Roy'. *Time Out Mexico*. 19 March 2012. Accessed 15 May 2020. https://www.timeoutmexico.mx/ciudad-de-mexico/nocturna/m-n-roy.

De Vito, Christian G. 'History without Scale: The Micro-Spatial Perspective'. *Past & Present* 242, no. Supplement 14 (2019): 348–72.

Deukeren, Hans van. 'From theory to practice—a history of IHEU 1952–2002'. In *International Humanist and Ethical Union 1952–2002: Past, Present and Future*, edited by Bert Gasenbeek and Babu Gogineni. Utrecht: De Tijdstroom, 2002.

Devji, Faisal. 'Morality in the Shadow of Politics'. In *Political Thought in Action: The Bhagavad Gita and Modern India*, edited by Shruti Kapila, 107–26. Cambridge: Cambridge University Press, 2013.

Dietze, Antje, and Katja Naumann. 'Revisiting Transnational Actors from a Spatial Perspective'. *European Review of History: Revue Européenne D'histoire* 25, no. 3–4 (2018): 415–30.

Dixon, Joy. *Divine Feminine: Theosophy and Feminism in England*. Baltimore: Johns Hopkins University Press, 2001.

Domeier, Norman. *Weltöffentlichkeit und Diktatur: Die amerikanischen Auslandskorrespondenten im 'Dritten Reich'*. Göttingen: Wallstein Verlag, 2021.

Dose, Ralf. *Magnus Hirschfeld: The Origins of the Gay Liberation Movement*. New York: Monthly Review Press, 2014.

Duiker, William. 'In Search of Ho Chi Minh'. In *A Companion to the Vietnam War*, edited by Marilyn B. Young and Robert Buzzanco, 19–36. Oxford: Blackwell Publishing Company, 2006.

Dullin, Sabine, and Brigitte Studer. 'Communism Transnational: The Rediscovered Equation of Internationalism in the Comintern Years'. *Twentieth Century Communism* 14, no. 14 (2018): 66–95.

Dutta, Krishna, and Andrew Robinson. *Rabindranath Tagore: The Myriad Minded Man*. New York: St. Martin's Press, 1996.

Duus, Peter, and Kenji Hasegawa, eds. *Rediscovering America: Japanese Perspectives on the American Century*. Berkeley, CA: University of California Press, 2011.

Eckstein, Arthur M. 'Stalinism and Clandestine Agents: The Real Agnes Smedley'. *Journal of Cold War Studies* 9, no. 4 (2007): 106–14.

Edgar, Adrienne Lynn. 'Nation-Making and National Conflict under Communism'. In *The Oxford Handbook of the History of Communism*, edited by Stephen A. Smith, 522–40. Oxford: Oxford University Press, 2014.

Edmonds, Daniel. 'Shapurji Saklatvala, the Workers' Welfare League of India, and Transnational Anti-colonial Labour Organising in the Inter-war Period'. *Twentieth Century Communism* 18, no. 18 (2020): 14–38.

Elam, J. Daniel. 'Take Your Geography and Trace It: The Cosmopolitan Aesthetics of W. E. B. DuBois and Dhan Gopal Mukerji'. *Interventions* 17, no. 4 (2015): 568–84.

Elleman, Bruce A. 'Soviet Diplomacy and the First United Front in China'. *Modern China* 21, no. 4 (1995): 450–80.

Emmett, Robert C. *Guide to the Albert Mayer Papers on India*. Committee on Southern Asian Studies and Southern Asia Reference Center: The University of Chicago, 1977.

Escobar, Arturo. *Encountering Development: The Making and Unmaking of the Third World*. Princeton, NJ: Princeton University Press, 2011.

Fairbank, John. 'Revolution and Counter-Revolution in China (Book Review)'. *Pacific Affairs* 22, no. 3 (1949): 278–82.

Falola, Toyin. *Nationalism and African Intellectuals*. Rochester, NY: University of Rochester Press, 2001.

Fayet, Jean-François. '1919'. In *The Oxford Handbook of the History of Communism*, edited by Stephen A. Smith, 109–24. Oxford: Oxford University Press, 2014.

Ferguson, James. *The Anti-politics Machine: 'Development,' Depoliticization, and Bureaucratic Power in Lesotho*. Cambridge: Cambridge University Press, 1990.

Fischer-Tiné, Harald. 'Indian Nationalism and the "World Forces": Transnational and Diasporic Dimensions of the Indian Freedom Movement on the Eve of the First World War'. *Journal of Global History* 2, no. 3 (2007): 325–44.

Fischer-Tiné, Harald. *Shyamji Krishnavarma: Sanskrit, Sociology and Anti-Imperialism*. London: Pathfinders, 2015.

Fischer-Tiné, Harald. '"White Women Degrading Themselves to the Lowest Depths": European Networks of Prostitution and Colonial Anxieties in British India and Ceylon ca. 1880–1914'. *The Indian Economic & Social History Review* 40, no. 2 (June 2003): 163–90.

Fourcade, Marion. 'The Construction of a Global Profession: The Transnationalization of Economics'. *The American Journal of Sociology* 112, no. 1 (2006): 145–94.

Framke, Maria. 'Shopping Ideologies for Independent India? Taraknath Das's Engagement with Italian Fascism and German National Socialism'. *Itinerario* 40, no. 1 (2016): 55–81.

Fraser, Thomas G. 'Germany and Indian Revolution, 1914–18'. *Journal of Contemporary History* 12, no. 2 (2016): 255–72.

Frearson, Amy. 'M.N.ROY by Emmanuel Picault and Ludwig Godefroy'. *dezeen*. 15 July 2011. Accessed 15 May 2020. https://www.dezeen.com/2011/07/15/m-n-roy-by-emmanuel-picault-and-ludwig-godefroy/.

Frey, Marc, Sönke Kunkel, and Corinna R. Unger. 'Introduction: International Organizations, Global Development, and the Making of the Contemporary World'. In *International Organizations and Development, 1945–1990*, edited by Marc Frey, Sönke Kunkel and Corinna R. Unger, 1–22. London: Palgrave Macmillan UK, 2014.

Friedman, Lawrence J. *The Lives of Erich Fromm: Love's Prophet*. New York: Columbia University Press, 2013.

Fromm, Erich. *Escape from Freedom*. New York: Ishi Press, 1991a.

Fromm, Erich. *The Sane Society*. Oxon: Routledge, 1991b.

Frost, Mark R. 'Imperial Citizenship or Else: Liberal Ideals and the India Unmaking of Empire, 1890–1919'. *Journal of Imperial and Commonwealth History* 46, no. 5 (2018): 845–73.

Fuechtner, Veronika. 'Agnes Smedley between Berlin, Bombay, and Beijing: Sexology, Communism, and National Independence'. In *A Global History of Sexual Science, 1880–1960*, edited by Veronika Fuechtner, Ryan M. Jones, Douglas E. Haynes, 398–417. Oakland, California: University of California Press, 2017.

Gammerl, Benno. 'Emotional Styles – Concepts and Challenges'. *Rethinking History* 16, no. 2 (2012): 161–75.

Gamsa, Mark. 'Biography and (Global) Microhistory'. *New Global Studies* 11, no. 3 (2017): 231–41.

Gandhi, Leela. *Affective Communities Anticolonial Thought, Fin-De-Siècle Radicalism, and the Politics of Friendship*. Durham: Duke University Press, 2006.

Ganguly, S. M. *Leftism in India: M. N. Roy and Indian Politics: 1920–1948*. Calcutta: Minerva Publications, 1984.

Ganguly, S.M. *Manabendra Nath Roy: An Annotated Bibliography*. Calcutta, New Delhi: K P Bagchi & Company, 1987.

Geppert, Alexander C. T. *Fleeting Cities: Imperial Expositions in Fin-de-siècle Europe*. Basingstoke: Palgrave Macmillan, 2010.

Getty, J. Arch. and Oleg V. Naumov. *The Road to Terror: Stalin and the Self-Destruction of the Bolsheviks, 1932–1939*. New Haven: Yale University Press, 1999.

Geulen, Christian. 'The Common Grounds of Conflict'. In *Competing Visions of World Order: Global Moments and Movements 1880s–1930s*, edited by Sebastian Conrad and Dominic Sachsenmaier, 69–96. New York: Palgrave Macmillan, 2007.

Geyer, Michael. 'Introduction: After Totalitarianism – Stalinism and Nazism Compared'. In *Beyond Totalitarianism: Stalinism and Nazism Compared*, edited by Micheal Geyer and Sheila Fitzpatrick. Cambridge: Cambridge University Press, 2009.

Ghosh, Durba. 'Whither India? 1919 and the Aftermath of the First World War'. *The Journal of Asian Studies* 78, no. 2 (2019): 389–97.

Ghosh, Durba. *Gentlemanly Terrorists: Political Violence and the Colonial State in India, 1919–1947*. Cambridge: Cambridge University Press, 2017.

Ghosh, Durba. *Sex and the Family in Colonial India; The Making of Empire*. Cambridge: Cambridge University Press, 2006.

Gilcher-Holtey, Ingrid, ed. *Zwischen Den Fronten: Positionskämpfe Europäischer Intellektueller Im 20. Jahrhundert*. Berlin: Akademie-Verlag, 2006.

Goebel, Michael. 'Geopolitics, Transnational Solidarity or Diaspora Nationalism? The Global Career of M.N. Roy, 1915–1930'. *European Review of History: Revue Européenne D'histoire* 21, no. 4 (2014): 485–99.

Goebel, Michael. *Anti-imperial Metropolis: Interwar Paris and the Seeds of Third World Nationalism*. New York, NY: Cambridge University Press, 2015.

Gordon, Daniel, and Peter Baehr. 'In Search of Limits: Raymond Aron on "Secular Religion" and Communism'. *Journal of Classical Sociology* 11, no. 2 (2011): 139–54.

Gordon, Leonard A. 'Portrait of a Bengal Revolutionary'. *The Journal of Asian Studies* 27, no. 2 (1968): 197–216.

Gosling, David L. *Science and the Indian Tradition: When Einstein Met Tagore*. London: Routledge, 2007.

Goswami, Manu. 'Imaginary Futures and Colonial Internationalisms'. *The American Historical Review* 117, no. 5 (2012): 1461–85.

Goswami, Manu. *Producing India: From Colonial Economy to National Space*. Chicago: University of Chicago Press, 2004.

Gottmann, Felicia, ed. *Commercial Cosmopolitanism?: Cross-Cultural Objects, Spaces, and Institutions in the Early Modern World. Political Economies of Capitalism, 1600–1850*. London; New York: Routledge, 2021.

Green, Nile. 'Anti-Colonial Japanophilia and the Constraints of an Islamic Japanology: Information and Affect in the Indian Encounter with Japan'. *South Asian History and Culture* 4, no. 3 (2013): 291–313.

Green, Nile. 'The Waves of Heterotopia: Toward a Vernacular Intellectual History of the Indian Ocean'. *The American Historical Review* 123, no. 3 (2018): 846–74.

Green, Thomas J. *Religion for a Secular Age*. London: Routledge, 2016.

Greenblatt, Stephen. *Renaissance Self-Fashioning: From More to Shakespeare*. Chicago: University of Chicago Press, 1980.

Greenhalgh, Paul. *Ephemeral Vistas: The Expositions Universelles, Great Exhibitions and World's Fairs, 1851–1939*. Manchester: Manchester University Press, 2017.

Grover, D. C. *M. N. Roy – A Study of Revolution and Reason in Indian Politics*. Calcutta: The Minerva Associates, 1973.

Grover, Verinder. *M. N. Roy. Political Thinkers of Modern India*. New Delhi: Deep & Deep, 1990.

Gupta, Sobhanlal Datta. *Comintern and the Destiny of Communism in India 1919–1943; Dialectics of Real and Possible History*. Kolkata: Seribaan, 2006.

Gupta, Sobhanlal Datta. 'Communism and the Crisis of the Colonial System'. In *The Cambridge History of Communism*, edited by Silvio Pons and Stephen A. Smith, 212–31. Cambridge: Cambridge University Press, 2017.

Hahnemann, Andy. *Texturen des Globalen: Geopolitik und Populäre Literatur in der Zwischenkriegszeit, 1918–1939*. Heidelberg: Winter, 2010.

Haikal, Mustafa. 'Das internationale Kolonialbüro der Komintern in Paris'. In *Jahrbuch für Historische Kommunismusforschung*, edited by H. Weber, D. Staritz and G. Braun, 126–30. Berlin: Akademieverlag, 1993.

Haithcox, John Patrick. 'Nationalism and Communism in India: The Impact of the 1927 Comintern Failure in China'. *The Journal of Asian Studies* 24, no. 3 (1965): 459–73.

Haithcox, John Patrick. 'Left Wing Unity and the Indian Nationalist Movement: M. N. Roy and the Congress Socialist Party'. *Modern Asian Studies* 3, no. 1 (1969): 17–56.

Haithcox, John Patrick. *Communism and Nationalism in India: M.N. Roy and Comintern Policy 1920–1939*. Princeton: Princeton University Press, 1971.

Hansen, Kathryn. *Stages of Life Indian Theatre Autobiographies*. New York, NY: Anthem Press, 2011.

Harper, Timothy. 'Singapore, 1915, and the Birth of the Asian Underground'. *Modern Asian Studies* 47, no. 6 (2013): 1782–811.

Harper, Timothy. *Underground Asia: Global Revolutionaries and the Assault on Empire*. London: Allen Lane, 2020.

Hatcher, Brian A. 'Great Men Waking: Paradigms in the Historiography of the Bengal Renaissance'. In *Bengal: Rethinking History: Essays on Historiography*, edited by Sekhar Bandyopadhyay, 147–8. Delhi: Manohar, 2001.

Hay, Stephen N. *Asian Ideas of East and West: Tagore and His Critics in Japan, China, and India*. Cambridge, MA: Harvard University Press, 1970.

Hayes, Romain. *Subhas Chandra Bose in Nazi Germany: Politics, Intelligence and Propaganda; 1941–43*. London: Hurst, 2011.

Hedeler, Wladislaw, and Jörn Schütrumpf. 'Der II. Weltkongress der Kommunistischen Internationale; Nachrichten über eine Petitesse'. In *Vergessene Kommunisten; II. Kongress der Kommunistischen Internationale 1920; Porträts – gezeichnet von Isaak Brodski*. Edited by Wladislaw Hedeler and Jörn Schütrumpf. Hannover: Offizin Verlag, 2020.

Hendrickson, Hildi. *Clothing and Difference: Embodied Identities in Colonial and Post-Colonial Africa*. Durham: Duke University Press, 1996.

Herren, Madeleine. 'Fascist Internationalism'. In *Internationalisms: A Twentieth-Century History* edited by Glenda Sluga and Patricia Clavin, 191–212. Cambridge, UK: Cambridge University Press, 2017.

Hill, Christopher L. 'Conceptual Universalization in the Transnational Nineteenth Century'. In *Global Intellectual History*, edited by Samuel Moyn and Andrew Sartori, 134-58. New York, NY: Columbia University Press, 2016.

Hirson, Baruch, and Arthur Knodel. *Reporting the Chinese Revolution: The Letters of Rayna Prohme*. London: Pluto Press, 2007.

Hoover, Karl. 'The Hindu Conspiracy in California, 1913-1918'. *German Studies Review* 8, no. 2 (1985): 245-61.

Hotta, Eri. 'Rash Behari Bose and His Japanese Supporters: An Insight into Anti-Colonial Nationalism and Pan-Asianism'. *Interventions* 8, no. 1 (2006): 116-32.

Hourmant, François. 'La Longue Marche De La Veste Mao'. *Vingtième Siècle. Revue D'histoire* 121, no. 1 (2014): 113-31.

Hughes, Thomas L. 'The German Mission to Afghanistan, 1915-1916'. *German Studies Review* 25, no. 3 (2002): 447-76.

Hung, Jochen. '"Bad" Politics and "Good" Culture: New Approaches to the History of the Weimar Republic'. *Central European History* 49, no. 3/4 (2016): 441-53.

Huxley, Julian. 'Science in Russia'. *The Radical Humanist*, 4 February, (1951): 53.

Independent India. 'Jean Paul Sartre'. *Independent India*, 8 June (1947): 343.

Iyer, V. R. Krishna. *Indian Secularism: Proclamation versus Performance and a Viable Philosophy*. Dehradun: Indian Renaissance Institute, 1975.

Jackson, Shannon. *Professing Performance: Theatre in the Academy from Philology to Performativity*. New York: Cambridge University Press, 2004.

Jacobs, Dan N. *Borodin: Stalin's Man in China*. Cambridge: Harvard University Press, 1981.

Jaffrelot, Christophe. *Dr. Ambedkar and Untouchability: Analysing and Fighting Caste*. New York: Columbia University Press, 2005.

Jaffrelot, Christophe, ed. *Hindu Nationalism: A Reader*. Ranikhet: Permanent Black, 2007.

Jani, Disha Karnad. 'The Concept of Fascism in Colonial India: M.N. Roy and The Problem of Freedom'. *Global Histories* 3, no. 2 (October 2017): 121-38.

Jani, Pranav. 'Bihar, California, and the US Midwest: The Early Radicalization of Jayaprakash Narayan'. *Postcolonial Studies* 16, no. 2 (2013): 155-68.

Jarvis, Helen. 'Introduction'. In *Tan Malaka From Jail to Jail, Vol. I*. Athens: Ohio University Center for International Studies, 1991.

Jayawardena, Kumari. *The White Woman's Other Burden: Western Women and South Asia during British Colonial Rule*. New York: Routledge, 1995.

Jelnikar, Ana. 'W.B. Yeats's (Mis)Reading of Tagore: Interpreting an Alien Culture'. *University of Toronto Quarterly* 77, no. 4 (2008): 1005-24.

Johari, Jagdish Chandra. *M. N. Roy, the Great Radical Humanist: Political Biography and Socio-political Ideas*. New Delhi: Sterling Publishers, 1988.

Johnson, Will J. *A Dictionary of Hinduism: Almost 2,800 Entries*. Oxford: Oxford University Press, 2009.

Judge, Rajbir Singh. 'Dusky Countenances: Ambivalent Bodies and Desires in the Theosophical Society'. *Journal of the History of Sexuality* 27, no. 2 (2018): 264–93.

Judt, Tony. *Past Imperfect; French Intellectuals, 1944 – 1956*. New York and London: New York University Press, 2011.

Kallis, Aristotle. 'From CAUR to EUR: Italian Fascism, the "myth of Rome" and the Pursuit of International Primacy'. *Patterns of Prejudice* 50, no. 4–5 (2016): 359–77.

Kambouchner, Denis. 'Lévi-Strauss and the question of humanism'. In *The Cambridge Companion to Lévi-Strauss*, edited by Boris Wiseman, 19–38. Cambridge: Cambridge University Press, 2009.

Karl, Rebecca E. 'Creating Asia: China in the World at the Beginning of the Twentieth Century'. *The American Historical Review* 103, no. 4 (1998): 1096–118.

Karl, Rebecca E. 'Staging the World in Late-Qing China: Globe, Nation, and Race in a 1904 Beijing Opera'. *Identities* 6, no. 4 (2000): 551–606.

Karnik, Vasant. *Bhagwant M. N. Roy: A Political Biography*. Bombay: Nav Jagriti Samaj, 1978.

Kaviraj, Sudipta. 'The Heteronomous Radicalism of M.N. Roy'. In *Political Thought in Modern India*, edited by T. Pantham and K. L. Deutsch, 209–35. New Delhi, Beverly Hills, London: Sage Publications, 1986.

Keer, Dhananjay. *Dr. Ambedkar: Life and Mission*. Bombay: Popular Prakashan, 1962.

Ker, James Campbell. *Political Trouble in India 1907 – 1917*. Delhi: Oriental Publishers, 1973.

Kern, Stephen. *The Culture of Time and Space: 1880–1918*. Cambridge, MA: Harvard University Press, 2003.

Khan, Mohammed Ayub. 'Universal Islam: The Faith and Political Ideologies of Maulana Barakatullah "Bhopali"'. *Sikh Formations* 10, no. 1 (2014): 57–67.

Khan, S. A. *Mulk Raj Anand: The Novel of Commitment*. New Delhi: Atlantic, 2000.

Khan, Yasmin. *The Great Partition: The Making of India and Pakistan*. New Haven: Yale University Press, 2008.

Kim, Sophie-Jung H. 'An International Event and Its Multiple Global Publics: The Parliament of the World's Religions (Chicago, 1893) and Vivekananda'. In *Global Publics: Their Powers and Their Limits (1870–1990)*, edited by Valeska Huber and Jürgen Osterhammel, 177–202. Oxford: Oxford University Press, 2020.

King, Richard H. *Race, Culture, and the Intellectuals, 1940–1970*. London: The Johns Hopkins University Press, 2004.

Kipling, Rudyard. *Kim*. London: Macmillan, 1915.

Kipping, Matthias. 'Hollow from the Start? Image Professionalism in Management Consulting'. *Current Sociology* 59, no. 4 (2011): 530–50.

Knorr Cetina, Karin, Theodore R. Schatzki, and Eike Von Savigny, eds. *The Practice Turn in Contemporary Theory*. London: Routledge, 2000.

Koestler, Arthur. *Darkness at Noon*. New York: Random House, 1941.

Kopf, David. *The Brahmo Samaj and the Shaping of the Modern Indian Mind*. Princeton: Princeton University Press, 1979.

Kramer, Martin. *Islam Assembled: The Advent of the Muslim Congresses*. New York: Columbia University Press, 1986.

Krishnan, Sanjay. *Reading the Global: Troubling Perspectives on Britain's Empire in Asia*. New York: Columbia University Press, 2007.

Kublin, Hyman. *Asian Revolutionary: The Life of Sen Katayama*. Princeton, NJ: Princeton University Press, 1964.

Kuck, Nathanael. 'Anti-colonialism in a Post-Imperial Environment – The Case of Berlin, 1914–33'. *Journal of Contemporary History* 49, no. 1 (2014): 134–59.

Kumar, Aishwary. *Radical Equality: Ambedkar, Gandhi, and the Risk of Democracy*. Palo Alto: Stanford University Press, 2015.

La Botz, Dan. 'American "Slackers" in the Mexican Revolution: International Proletarian Politics in the Midst of a National Revolution'. *The Americas* 62, no. 4 (2006): 563–90.

Lackner, Michael. *New Terms for New Ideas: Western Knowledge and Lexical Change in Late Imperial China*. Leiden: Brill, 2001.

Lahiri, Shompa. *Indian Mobilities in the West: 1900–1947: Gender, Performance, Embodiment*. New York: Palgrave Studies in Cultural and Intellectual History, 2010.

Lahiri, Shompa. 'Performing Identity: Colonial Migrants, Passing and Mimicry Between the Wars'. *Cultural Geographies* 10, no. 4 (2003): 408–23.

Lake, Marilyn, and Henry Reynolds. *Drawing the Global Colour Line*. Critical Perspectives on Empire. Cambridge: Cambridge University Press, 2008.

Lasch, Christopher. *The New Radicalism in America, [1889–1963]: The Intellectual as a Social Type*. New York: Vintage Books, 1965.

Laursen, Ole Birk. 'M. P. T. Acharya: A Revolutionary, an Agitator, a Writer'. In *We Are Anarchists; Essays on Anarchism, Pacifism and the Indian Independence Movement, 1923–1953*, Acharya, M. P. T. Edinburgh: AK Press, 2019.

Laursen, Ole Birk. '"Anarchism, Pure and Simple": M. P. T. Acharya, Anti-colonialism and the International Anarchist Movement'. *Postcolonial Studies* 23, no. 2 (2020): 241–55.

Lenin, Vladimir Ilyich. *Imperialism; The Highest Stage of Capitalism*. Sydney: Resistance Books, 1999.

Lenin, Vladimir Ilyich. 'Democracy and Narodism in China'. (1912) In *Lenin Collected Works: Volume 18*. 163–9. Moscow: Progress Publishers, 1975. Lenin Internet Archive (2004). https://www.marxists.org/archive/lenin/works/1912/jul/15.htm.

Liu, Lydia H. *Translingual Practice: Literature, National Culture, and Translated Modernity – China, 1900–1937*. California: Stanford University Press, 1995.

Liu, Lydia H. 'The Question of Meaning-Value in the Political Economy of the Sign'. In *Tokens of Exchange: The Problem of Translation in Global Circulations*, edited by Lydia H. Liu, Stanley Fish, and Fredric Jameson, 1–19. Durham: Duke University Press, 1999.

Loeffler, James. *Rooted Cosmopolitans: Jews and Human Rights in the Twentieth Century*. New Haven: Yale University Press, 2018.

London, Jack. *The Little Lady of the Big House*. New York: Grosset & Dunlap Publishers, 1916.

Loxley, James. *Performativity*. London: Routledge, 2007.

MacKinnon, Janice, and Steve MacKinnon. 'Introduction'. In *Agnes Smedley. Portraits of Chinese Women in Revolution*, 1–2. New York: Feminist Press, 1976.

Maclean, Kama, and Daniel J. Elam. 'Reading Revolutionaries: Texts, Acts, and Afterlives of Political Action in Late Colonial South Asia'. *Postcolonial Studies* 16, no. 2 (2013): 113–23.

Maclean, Kama. *A Revolutionary History of Interwar India: Violence, Image, Voice and Text*. Oxford: Oxford University Press, 2015.

Maggio, J. "' Can the Subaltern Be Heard?": Political Theory, Translation, Representation, and Gayatri Chakravorty Spivak'. *Alternatives: Global, Local, Political* 32, no. 4 (2016): 419–43.

Majeed, Javed. *Autobiography, Travel and Postnational Identity; Gandhi, Nehru and Iqbal*. Palgrave Macmillan: Houndmills, 2007.

Makalani, Minkah. 'Internationalizing the Third International: The African Blood Brotherhood, Asian Radicals, and Race, 1919–1922'. *The Journal of African American History* 96, no. 2 (2011): 151–78.

Malhotra, Anshu, and Siobhan Lambert-Hurley. 'Introduction: Gender, Performance, and Autobiography in South Asia'. In *Speaking of the Self: Gender, Performance, and Autobiography in South Asia*, edited by Anshu Malhotra and Siobhan Lambert-Hurley, 1–30. Durham: Duke University Press, 2015.

Manela, Erez. 'Imagining Woodrow Wilson in Asia: Dreams of East-West Harmony and the Revolt against Empire in 1919'. *The American Historical Review* 111, no. 5 (2006): 1327–51.

Manela, Erez. *The Wilsonian Moment: Self-Determination and the International Origins of Anticolonial Nationalism*. Oxford: Oxford University Press, 2009.

Manjapra, Kris. 'The Illusions of Encounter: Muslim Minds and Hindu Revolutionaries in First World War Germany and after'. *Journal of Global History* 1, no. 3 (2006): 363–82.

Manjapra, Kris. 'Communist Internationalism and Transcolonial Recognition'. In *Cosmopolitan Thought Zones: South Asia and the Global Circulation of Ideas*, edited by Sugata Bose and Kris Manjapra, 159–77. New York: Palgrave Macmillan, 2010.

Manjapra, Kris. *M. N. Roy; Marxism and Colonial Cosmopolitanism*. Delhi: Routledge, 2010.

Manjapra, Kris. 'The Impossible Intimacies of M N Roy'. *Postcolonial Studies* 16, no. 2 (2013): 169–184.

Manjapra, Kris. *Age of Entanglement: German and Indian Intellectuals across Empire*. Cambridge, MA: Harvard University Press, 2014.

Mannheim, Karl. *Ideology and Utopia: An Introduction to the Sociology of Knowledge*. London: Routledge & Kegan Paul, 1968.

Marsh, Kate. '"The Only Safe Haven of Refuge in All the World": Paris, Indian "revolutionaries" and Imperial Rivalry, C. 1905–40'. *French Cultural Studies* 30, no. 3 (2019): 196–219.

Massey, Doreen. *For Space*. London: Sage, 2005.

Massey, Doreen. *Space, Place, and Gender*. Minneapolis: University of Minnesota Press, 1994.

Mawani, Renisa. 'From Migrants to Revolutionaries: The Komagata Maru's 1914 "Middle Passage"'. In *Viapolitics; Borders, Migration, and the Power of Locomotion*, edited by William Walters, Charles Heller and Lorenzo Pezzani, 60–1. Durham: Duke University Press, 2022.

Mayenburg, Ruth von. *Hotel Lux*. Frankfurt am Main: Ullstein, 1981.

Mayer, David. 'Leo Katz (1892–1954): viele Welten in einer Welt'. In *Globale Lebensläufe; Menschen als Akteure im weltgeschichtlichen Geschehen*, edited by Bernd Hausberger, 233–56. Wien: Mandelbaum Verlag, 2006.

Mayer, Robert. 'Lenin and the Concept of the Professional Revolutionary'. *History of Political Thought* 14, no. 2 (1993): 249–63.

McCarter, Jeremy. *Young Radicals; In the War for American Ideals*. New York: Random House, 2017.

McDermott, Andrew. 2017. 'Terrible Experience'. Review of *M. N. Roy*. Facebook. 16 December 2017. Accessed 15 May 2020. https://tinyurl.com/y878ojyt.

McDermott, Kevin. 'Stalin and the Comintern during the "Third Period", 1928–33'. *European History Quarterly* 25, no. 3 (1995): 409–29.

McDermott, Kevin. *The Comintern: A History of International Communism from Lenin to Stalin*. Basingstoke: Macmillan, 1996.

McKenna, Christopher D. *The World's Newest Profession: Management Consulting in the Twentieth Century*. Cambridge: Cambridge University Press, 2006.

McKeown, Adam. 'Global Migration, 1846–1940'. *Journal of World History* 15, no. 2 (2004): 155–89.

McKeown, Adam. *Melancholy Order: Asian Migration and the Globalization of Borders*. New York: Columbia University Press, 2008.

McMeekin, Sean. *The Red Millionaire a Political Biography of Willi Münzenberg, Moscow's Secret Propaganda Tsar in the West*. New Haven: Yale University Press, 2005.

McMurtry, John. *The Structure of Marx's World-View*. Princeton: Princeton University Press, 1978.

Mcquade, Joseph. 'The New Asia of Rash Behari Bose: India, Japan, and the Limits of the International, 1912–1945'. *Journal of World History* 27, no. 4 (2016): 641–67.

Menon, Dilip. 'Being a Brahmin the Marxist Way: E.M.S. Nambudiripad and the Pasts of Kerala'. In *Research in Progress Papers 'History and Society'*. New Delhi: Centre for Contemporary Studies, Nehru Memorial Museum and Library, 1998.

Mignolo, Walter D. 'The Many Faces of Cosmo-Polis: Border Thinking and Critical Cosmopolitanism'. *Public Culture* 12, no. 3 (2000): 721–48.

Miller, Lulu. *Why Fish Don't Exist: A Story of Loss, Love, and the Hidden Order of Life*. New York: Simon & Schuster, 2020.

Miller, Marilyn Grace. *Rise and Fall of the Cosmic Race: The Cult of Mestizaje in Latin America*. Austin: University of Texas Press 2004.

Minh-Ha T. Pham. 'Paul Poiret's Magical Techno-oriented Fashions (1911): Race, Clothing, and Virtuality in the Machine Age'. *Configurations* 21, no. 1 (2013): 1–26.

Mishra, Pankaj. *From the Ruins of Empire: The Revolt against the West and the Remaking of Asia*. London: Penguin, 2013.

Mitchell, Timothy. 'The World as Exhibition'. *Comparative Studies in Society and History* 31, no. 2 (April, 1989): 217–36.

Mitchell, Timothy. *Colonising Egypt*. Berkeley: University of California Press, 1991.

Mohanty, Sachidananda. *Cosmopolitan Modernity in Early 20th-Century India*. Boca Raton: Routledge India, 2018.

Monnerot, Jules. 'Socialism and Freedom'. *The Marxian Way* III, no. 1, (1947–8): 15–30.

Moraña, Mabel, and Bret Gustafson. *Rethinking Intellectuals in Latin America*. Madrid: Iberoamericana and Frankfurt am Main: Vervuert, 2010.

Morikawa, Takemitsu. *Japanische Intellektuelle Im Spannungsfeld Von Okzidentalismus Und Orientalismus*. Kassel: Kassel University Press, 2008.

Moyn, Samuel, and Andrew Sartori. 'Approaches to Global Intellectual History'. In *Global Intellectual History*, edited by Samuel Moyn and Andrew Sartori, 3–30. New York: Columbia University Press, 2013.

Mrázek, Rudolf. 'Tan Malaka: A Political Personality's Structure of Experience'. *Indonesia* 14, no. 14 (1972): 1–48.

Mukerji, Dhan Gopal. *A Son of Mother India Answers*. Noida, India: Rupa&Co, 1922.

Mukharji, Projit Bihari. 'The Bengali Pharaoh: Upper-Caste Aryanism, Pan-Egyptianism, and the Contested History of Biometric Nationalism in Twentieth-Century Bengal'. *Comparative Studies in Society and History* 59, no. 2 (2017): 446–76.

Müller, H. D. 'Der Malik-Verlag Als Vermittler Der Jungen Sowjetliteratur in Deutschland 1919–1933'. *Zeitschrift Für Slawistik* 7, no. 5 (1962): 720–5.

Nair, Rahul. 'The Construction of a "Population Problem" in Colonial India 1919–1947'. *The Journal of Imperial and Commonwealth History* 39, no. 2 (2011): 227–47.

Narisetti, Innaiah. 'Introduction'. In *M. N. Roy; Radical Humanist; Selected Writings*, edited by Innaiah Narisetti, 7–28. Amherst: Prometheus Books, 2004.

Narvaez, Alfonso. 'Prof. A. Bharati, 68, A Monk Who Served On Syracuse Faculty'. *The New York Times*. May 16, 1991.

Nath, Paresh. 'M. N. Roy: India's One-Man Party'. *Asia and the Americas* 43, no. 3 (March 1943): 151–3.

Neville, Peter. *Ho Chi Minh*. Boca Raton, FL: Routledge, 2018.

Noorani, Abdul Gafoor Abdul Majeed. *Indian Political Trials*. New Delhi: Sterling, 1976.

North, Robert Carver, and Xenia J. Eudin. *M. N. Roy's Mission to China: The Communist-kuomintang Split of 1927*. Berkeley: University of California Press, 1963.

Ogborn, Miles. *Global Lives: Britain and the World; 1550–1800*. Cambridge: Cambridge University Press, 2008.
Ogle, Vanessa. *The Global Transformation of Time: 1870–1950*. Cambridge: Harvard University Press, 2015.
Ohsawa, George. *Two Great Indians in Japan; Sri Rash Behari Bose and Netaji Subhas Chandra Bose*. Calcutta: Kusa Publications, 1954.
Oshikawa, Noriaki. 'Patjar Merah Indonesia and Tan Malaka: A Popular Novel and a Revolutionary Legend'. In *Reading Southeast Asia*, edited by Takashi Shiraishi, 9–39. Ithaca: Cornell University Press, 2018.
Osterhammel, Jürgen. *Unfabling the East: The Enlightenment's Encounter with Asia*. Princeton, NJ: Princeton University Press, 2018.
Overstreet, Gene D., and Marshall Windmiller. *Communism in India*. Berkeley: University of California Press, 1960.
Pant, Alok. *Indian Radicalism and M. N. Roy*. Delhi: Adhyayan Publishers, 2005.
Panter, Sarah, Johannes Paulmann, and Margit Szöllösi-Janze. 'Mobility and Biography: Methodological Challenges and Perspectives'. In *Mobility and Biography*. Berlin, Boston: De Gruyter Oldenbourg, 2015.
Parmar, Inderjeet. *Foundations of the American Century: The Ford, Carnegie, and Rockefeller Foundations in the Rise of American Power*. New York: Columbia University Press, 2012.
Patwardhan, Padmini. 'Gobind Behari Lal: The Gentle Indian Firebrand of American Science Journalism'. *American Journalism* 20, no. 1 (2003): 33–55.
Pernau, Margrit. *Bürger mit Turban: Muslime in Delhi Im 19. Jahrhundert*. Göttingen: Vandenhoeck & Ruprecht, 2008.
Pernau, Margrit. 'Studying Emotions in South Asia'. *South Asian History and Culture* 12, no. 2–3 (2021).
Pettaco, Arrigo. *Il comunista in camicia negra: Bombacci, tra Lenin e Mussolini*. Milano: Mondadori, 1996.
Pitkin, Hanna Fenichel. 'Representation and Democracy: Uneasy Alliance'. *Scandinavian Political Studies* 27, no. 3 (2004): 335–42.
Plowman, Matthew. 'Irish Republicans and the Indo-German Conspiracy of World War I'. *New Hibernia Review* 7, no. 3 (2003): 81–105.
Poeze, Harry A. *Tan Malaka: Strijder Voor Indonesië's Vrijheid: Levensloop Van 1897 tot 1945*. 's-Gravenhage: Nijhoff, 1976.
Poeze, Harry A. *Verguisd en Vergeten: Tan Malaka, de linkse beweging en de Indonesische Revolutie, 1945–1949*. Leiden: KITLV Uitgeverij, 2007.
Porter, Elliot Einzig. 'The Two Vons: The World War I Secret Government Investigation of Erich Von Stroheim'. *Film History: An International Journal* 22, no. 3 (2010): 329–46.
Praag, Jaap van. *Modern Humanisme: Een Renaissance?* Amsterdam: Uitgeverij Contact, 1947.

Pratap, Mahendra. *My Life Story of Fiftyfive Years, (December 1886 to December 1941)*. Dehradun: World Federation, 1947.

Pratap, Mahendra. *The Book of the Religion of Love*. Marburg: Pratap, 1920.

Price, Ruth. *The Lives of Agnes Smedley*. New York: Oxford University Press, 2005.

Rai, Lala Lajpat. *Autobiographical Writings*. New Delhi: Delhi University Publishers, 1965.

Ramnath, Maia. 'Two Revolutions: The Ghadar Movement and India's Radical Diaspora,1913–1918'. *Radical History Review* 2005, no. 92 (2005): 7–30.

Ramnath, Maia. *Haj to Utopia: How the Ghadar Movement Charted Global Radicalism and Attempted to Overthrow the British Empire*. Berkeley: University of California Press, 2011.

Ramnath, Maia. 'Meeting the Rebel Girl; Anticolonial Solidarity and Interracial Romance'. In *The Internationalist Moment; South Asia, Worlds, and World Views 1917 – 39*, edited by Ali Raza, Franziska Roy, and Benjamin Zachariah, 125–49. New Delhi: Sage Publications, 2015.

Ramusack, Barbara. 'Embattled Advocates: The Debate over Birth Control in India, 1920-40'. *Journal of Women's History* 1, no. 2 (1989): 34–64.

Ray, Sibnarayan. 'Existentialism and Jean-Paul Sartre'. *The Radical Humanist* 12 June, (1949): 275–7.

Ray, Sibnarayan. *The Twice Born Heretic: M. N. Roy and the Comintern*. Calcutta: KLM Private, 1986.

Ray, Sibnarayan. *Selected Works of M.N. Roy: Volume I – 1917–1922*. Oxford; Delhi: Oxford University Press, 1987.

Ray, Sibnarayan. *Selected Works of M.N. Roy: Volume II – 1923–1927*. Oxford; Delhi: Oxford University Press, 1988.

Ray, Sibnarayan. *Selected Works of M.N. Roy: Volume III – 1927–1932*. Oxford; Delhi: Oxford University Press, 1990.

Ray, Sibnarayan. *In Freedom's Quest: A Study of the Life and Works of M. N. Roy, Volume One (1887–1922)*. Calcutta: Minerva Associates Publications, 1998.

Ray, Sibnarayan. *In Freedom's Quest: A Study of the Life and Works of M. N. Roy, Volume Two: The Comintern Years (1922–1927)*. Calcutta: Minerva Associates Publications, 2002.

Ray, Sibnarayan. *In Freedom's Quest: A Study of the Life and Works of M. N. Roy, Volume Three: Against the Current (1928–1939)*. Calcutta: Minerva Associates Publications, 2005.

Ray, Sibnarayan. *In Freedom's Quest: A Study of the Life and Works of M. N. Roy, Volume Four, Part One: From Anti-Fascist War to Radical Humanism (1940–1946)*. Calcutta: Minerva Associates Publications, 2007a.

Ray, Sibnarayan. *In Freedom's Quest: A Study of the Life and Works of M. N. Roy, Volume Four, Part Two: From Anti-Fascist War to Radical Humanism (1947–1954)*. Calcutta: Minerva Associates Publications, 2007b.

Raychaudhuri, Tapan. *Europe Reconsidered: Perceptions of the West in Nineteenth-Century Bengal*. Delhi: Oxford University Press. 1988.

Raza, Ali. *Revolutionary Pasts: Communist Internationalism in Colonial India*. Cambridge: Cambridge University Press, 2020.

Raza, Ali, and Franziska Roy, Benjamin Zachariah, 'The Internationalism of the Moment: South Asia and the Contours of the Interwar World'. In *The Internationalist Moment: South Asia, Worlds and World Views, 1917 – 39*, edited by Ali Raza, Franziska Roy, and Benjamin Zachariah, xii–xxxvi. Los Angeles: Sage, 2015.

Raza, Ali. 'Separating the Wheat from the Chaff Meerut and the Creation of "Official" Communism in India'. *Comparative Studies of South Asia, Africa and the Middle East* 33, no. 3 (2013): 316–30.

Reckwitz, Andreas. 'Toward a Theory of Social Practices: A Development in Culturalist Theorizing'. *European Journal of Social Theory* 5, no. 2 (2002): 249.

Reichardt, Sven. *Faschistische Kampfbünde Gewalt Und Gemeinschaft Im Italienischen Squadrismus Und in Der Deutschen SA*. Köln: Böhlau Verlag, 2009.

Reichardt, Sven. *Authentizität Und Gemeinschaft*. Berlin: Suhrkamp Verlag, 2014.

Rhodes, Carolyn H. 'Frederick Winslow Taylor's System of Scientific Management in Zamyatin's We'. *The Journal of General Education (University Park, Pa.)* 28, no. 1 (1976): 31–42.

Riddell, John. ed. *Workers of the World and Oppressed Peoples, Unite! Proceedings and Documents of the Second Congress, 1920a: Vol I*. New York: Pathfinder Press, 1991.

Riddell, John. ed. *To See the Dawn; Baku, 1920b – First Congress of the Peoples of the East*. Pathfinder: New York, London, Montreal, Sydney, 1993.

Roces, Mina, and Louise Edwards. 'Trans-national Flows and the Politics of Dress in Asia and the Americas'. In *The Politics of Dress in Asia and the Americas*, edited by Mina Roces and Louise Edwards, 1–8. Brighton: Sussex Academic Press, 2007.

Rolland, Romain. 'Introduction'. In *Mohandas K. Gandhi. La Jeune Inde*, translated by Hélène Hart, v–xxi. Paris: Stock, 1924.

Roper, Lyndal, and Steve Smith. eds. 'Global History and Microhistory'. of *Past & Present* 242, no. Supplement 14 (2019).

Rothermund, Dietmar. 'Rabindranath Tagore und seine weltweite Friedensmission'. In *Globale Lebensläufe*, edited by Bernd Hausberger. Vienna: Mandelbaum Verlag, 2006. 196–216.

Roy, Dipti Kumar. *Leftist Politics in India: M. N. Roy and the Radical Democratic Party*. Calcutta: Minerva, 1989.

Roy, Dipti Kumar. *Trade Union Movement in India: Role of M. N. Roy*. Calcutta: Minerva Associates, 1990.

Roy, Evelyn. 'The Crisis in Indian Nationalism'. *Labour Monthly* II, no. 2. February 1922. https://www.marxists.org/archive/roy-evelyn/articles/1922/nationalism.htm.

Roy, Evelyn. 'Mahatma Gandhi; Revolutionary or Counter-Revolutionary? A Reply to Romain Rolland and Henri Barbusse'. *Labour Monthly* V, no. 3 September (1923). Marxists Internet Archive (2006). https://www.marxists.org/archive/roy-evelyn/articles/1923/gandhi_rev_counter.htm.

Roy, M. N. *The Historical Role of Islam: An Essay on Islamic Culture*. Bombay: Vora & Co, 1937.

Roy, M. N. *My Experiences in China*. Bombay: Renaissance Publishing Company, 1938.

Roy, M. N. *New Orientation*. Calcutta: Renaissance Publishers, 1946a.

Roy, M. N. *Fragments of a Prisoner's Diary Volume Two – The Ideal of Indian Womanhood*. Renaissance: Dehradun, 1941.

Roy, M. N. *Fragments of a Prisoner's Diary; Volume One: Crime and Karma: Cats and Women*. Renaissance Publishers: Calcutta, 1957.

Roy, M. N. *Memoirs*. Bombay, New Delhi, Calcutta, Madras: Allied Publishers, 1964.

Roy, M. N. '*I accuse!*': from the suppressed statement of Manabendra Nath Roy on trial for treason before Sessions Court, Cawnpore, India. New York: Published for the Roy Defense Committee of India, 1932.

Roy, M. N. *Abani Mukherji, Santi Devi*. 'An Indian Communist Manifesto'. *Glasgow Socialist*, 24 June 1920, Marxists Internet Archive (2011). https://www.marxists.org/archive/roy-evelyn/articles/1920/manifesto.htm.

Roy, M. N. *Science and Superstition*. Dehradun: The Renaissance Association Limited, 1940.

Roy, M. N. *Politics, Power, and Parties*. Delhi: Ajanta Publications, 1999.

Roy, M. N. *Indien*. Hamburg: Verlag der Kommunistischen Internationale, 1922.

Roy, M. N. *La India, su Pasado, su Presente y su Porvenir*. Mexico City, 1918.

Roy, M. N. *Letters from Jail*. Dehradun: Renaissance, 1943.

Roy, M. N. *Men I Met*. Delhi: Ajanta Publications, 1981.

Roy, M. N. *Revolution and Counter-Revolution in China*. Calcutta: Renaissance Publishers, 1946.

Roy, M. N. *The Problem of Freedom*. Kolkata: Renaissance Publishers Ltd. 2000.

Roy, M. N. *The Russian Revolution*. Calcutta: Renaissance Publishers, 1949.

Roy, M. N. *The Way to Durable Peace*. Calcutta: Minerva, 1986.

Roy, M. N. 'Bourgeois Nationalism'. *Vanguard* 3, no. 1 August 15, 1923, Marxists Internet Archive (2006). https://www.marxists.org/archive/roy/1923/08/15a.htm.

Roy, M. N. 'Hold High the Banner of Humanist Freedom! M. N. Roy's Message to the East Bengal Convention of the Radical Democratic Party'. *Independent India*. 17 August, 1947.

Roy, M. N. 'Hunger and Revolution in India'. *The Call*, 18 September 1919, Marxists Internet Archive (2007). https://www.marxists.org/archive/roy/1919/09/18.htm.

Roy, M.N. 'The Disintegration of a Priestly Family'. *The Radical Humanist* 7 February, (1954): 66–7.

Roy, M. N. *Reason, Romanticism and Revolution: Volume One*. Calcutta: Renaissance Publishers, 1952.

Roy, M. N. *Reason, Romanticism and Revolution: Volume Two*. Calcutta: Renaissance Publishers, 1955.

Roy, M. N. and Abani Mukherji. *India in Transition*. Geneve: Edition de la Librairie J. B. Target, 1922.

Roy, Purabi, and Sobhanlal Datta Gupta, Hari Vasudevan, eds. *Indo-Russian Relations: 1917–1947: Select Documents from the Archives of the Russian Federation, Part I 1917–1928*. Calcutta: The Asiatic Society, 1999.

Roy, Samaren. 'Introduction'. In *M. N. Roy. The Way to Durable Peace*, 1–3. Calcutta: Minerva, 1986.
Roy, Samaren. *M. N. Roy; A Political Biography*. Hyderabad: Orient Longman, 1997.
Saich, Tony. *The Origins of the First United Front in China: The Role of Sneevliet (alias Maring) Vol. I*. Leiden: E. J. Brill, 1991.
Salesa, Damon Ieremia. *Racial Crossings*. Oxford: Oxford University Press, 2011.
Sarkar, Sumit. *The Swadeshi Movement in Bengal 1903–1908*. Ranikhet: Permanent Black, 2010.
Sartori, Andrew. *Bengal in Global Concept History; Culturalism in the Age of Capital*. Chicago: University of Chicago Press, 2008.
Sartori, Andrew. 'Global Intellectual History and the History of Political Economy'. In *Global Intellectual History*, edited by Samuel Moyn and Andrew Sartori, 110–33. New York: Columbia University Press, 2016.
Saward, Michael. *The Representative Claim*. Oxford: Oxford University Press, 2010.
Saward, Michael. 'Liminal Representation'. In *Creating Political Presence: The New Politics of Democratic Representation*, edited by Dario Castiglione and Johannes Pollak, 276–97. Chicago: The University of Chicago Press, 2019.
Saxena, Kiran. *Modern Indian Political Thought; Gandhism and Roy's New Humanism*. Delhi: Chetena Publications, 1978.
Schaffer, Simon. 'Introduction'. In *Aesthetics of Universal Knowledge*, edited by Simon Schaffer, John Tresch, and Pasquale Gagliardi, 14. Cham: Palgrave Macmillan, 2017.
Schechter, Brandon M. *The Stuff of Soldiers*. Ithaca: Cornell University Press, 2019.
Scheer, Monique. 'Are Emotions A Kind of Practice (And Is That What Makes Them Have a History)? A Bourdieuvian Approach to Understanding Emotion'. *History and Theory: Studies in the Philosophy of History* 51, no. 2 (2012): 217.
Schulz, Eva-Maria. 'Das Leben Eines Menschen Wird Durch Seine Ernährung Bestimmt'. *Zeitschrift Für Junge Religionswissenschaft*, no. 1 (2006).
Scott, James C. *Seeing Like a State: How Certain Schemes to Improve the Human Condition Have Failed*. New Haven: Yale University Press, 1998.
Sdvižkov, Denis A. *Das Zeitalter Der Intelligenz: Zur Vergleichenden Geschichte Der Gebildeten in Europa Bis Zum Ersten Weltkrieg*. Göttingen: Vandenhoeck & Ruprecht, 2006.
Seal, Brajendranath. 'Meaning of Race, Tribe and Nation'. In *Papers on Inter-Racial Problems*, communicated to the first Universal Races Congress, held at the University of London, July 26–29, 1911, edited by G. Spiller, 1–2. London: P.S. King & Son, 1911.
Sen, Amartya. *Poverty and Famines: An Essay on Entitlement and Deprivation*. Oxford: Oxford University Press, 1983.
Serge, Victor *Memoirs of a Revolutionary*. London: Oxford University Press, 1963.
Seth, Sanjay. *Marxist Theory and Nationalist Politics: The Case of Colonial India*. London: Sage Publications, 1995.
Shimazu, Naoko. *Japan, Race and Equality: The Racial Equality Proposal of 1919*. London: Routledge, 1998.

Shimazu, Naoko. 'Diplomacy As Theatre: Staging the Bandung Conference of 1955'. *Modern Asian Studies* 48, no. 1 (2014): 225–52.

Shipman, Charles. *It Had to Be Revolution; Memoirs of an American Radical*. Ithaca: Cornell University Press, 1993.

Sigurdson, Richard F. 'Jacob Burckhardt: The Cultural Historian as Political Thinker'. *The Review of Politics* 52, no. 3 (1990): 417–40.

Singh, Bhola. *The Political Ideas of M. N. Roy and Jayaprakash Narayan: A Comparative Study*. New Delhi: Ashish Publishing House, 1985.

Sinha, Babli. 'Dissensus, Education and Lala Lajpat Rai's Encounter with W.E.B. DuBois'. *South Asian History and Culture* 6, no. 4 (2015): 462–76.

Sinha, Mrinalini. *Colonial Masculinity: The 'Manly Englishman' and the 'Effeminate Bengali' in the Late Nineteenth Century*. Manchester: Manchester University Press, 1995.

Sinha, Mrinalini. *Specters of Mother India; the Global Restructuring of an Empire*. Durham: Duke University Press, 2006.

Six, Clemens. 'Challenging the Grammar of Difference: Benoy Kumar Sarkar, Global Mobility and Anti-imperialism around the First World War'. *European Review of History = Revue Européene D'histoire* 25, no. 3–4 (2018): 431–49.

Slate, Nico. *Colored Cosmopolitanism: The Shared Struggle for Freedom in the United States and India*. Cambridge: Harvard University Press, 2012.

Sluga, Glenda, and Julia Horne. 'Cosmopolitanism: Its Pasts and Practices'. *Journal of World History* 21, no. 3 (2010): 369.

Smedley, Agnes. *Daughter of Earth*. New York: Howard McCann Inc., 1929.

Smedley, Agnes. *Battle Hymn of China*. New York: A. Knopf, 1943.

Smith, John David. 'W.E.B. Du Bois, Felix Von Luschan, and Racial Reform at the Fin De Siècle'. *Amerikastudien/American Studies* 47, no. 1 (2002): 23–38.

Sohi, Seema. *Echoes of Mutiny: Race, Surveillance, and Indian Anticolonialism in North America*. Oxford; New York: Oxford University Press, 2014.

Speich, Daniel. 'The Use of Global Abstractions: National Income Accounting in the Period of Imperial Decline'. *Journal of Global History* 6, no. 1 (2011): 7–28.

Spenser, Daniela. 'Emissaries of the Communist International in Mexico'. *American Communist History* 6, no. 2 (2007): 151–70.

Spenser, Daniela. *Stumbling Its Way through Mexico the Early Years of the Communist International*. Tuscaloosa: University of Alabama Press, 2011.

Spivak, Gayatri. 'Can the Subaltern Speak?' In *Marxism and the Interpretation of Culture*, edited by Cary Nelson and Lawrence Grossberg, 271–313. London: Macmillan, 1998.

Spratt, Philip. *Blowing Up India: Reminiscences and Reflections of a Former Comintern Emissary*. Calcutta: Prachi Prakashan, 1955.

Stavans, Ilan. *José Vasconcelos: The Prophet of Race*. New Brunswick, NJ: Rutgers University Press, 2011.

Steen, Bart Van. 'Kiest Sneevliet Uit De Cel!' Henk Sneevliet, De RSP En De Verkiezingen Van 1933'. *Helden Des Vaderlands. Heldenverering in Nederland Door De Eeuwen Heen* 22, no. 3 (December, 2007): 79–98.

Steeves, H. Peter. ed. *Animal Others: On Ethics, Ontology, and Animal Life*. Albany: State University of New York Press, 1999.
Stoler, Laura Ann. *Carnal Knowledge and Imperial Power: Race and the Intimate in Colonial Rule*. Berkeley: University of California Press, 2002.
Stoler, Laura Ann. 'Making Empire Respectable: the politics of race and sexual morality in 20th-century colonial cultures'. *American Ethnologist* 16 (1989): 634–60.
Stolte, Carolien. 'The Meerut Conspiracy Case in Comparative and International Perspective'. *Comparative Studies of South Asia, Africa and the Middle East* 33, no. 3 (2013): 310–5.
Stolte, Carolien. '"Enough of the Great Napoleons!" Raja Mahendra Pratap's Pan-Asian Projects (1929–1939)'. *Modern Asian Studies* 46, no. 2 (2012): 403–23.
Stolte, Carolien. '"The Asiatic Hour" New Perspectives on the Asian Relations Conference, New Delhi, 1947'. In *The Non-Aligned Movement and the Cold War: Delhi – Bandung – Belgrade*, edited by Nataša Mišković, Harald Fischer-Tiné, and Nada Boškovska. London and New York: Routledge, 2014.
Stolte, Carolien, and Fischer-Tiné, Harald. 'Imagining Asia in India: Nationalism and Internationalism (ca. 1905–1940)'. *Comparative Studies in Society and History* 54, no. 1 (2012): 65–92.
Stone, Dan. 'The Uses and Abuses of "Secular Religion": Jules Monnerot's Path from Communism to Fascism'. *History of European Ideas* 37, no. 4 (2011): 466–74.
Stroud, Scott R. 'The Pluralistic Style and the Demands of Intercultural Rhetoric: Swami Vivekananda at the World's Parliament of Religions'. *Advances in the History of Rhetoric* 21, no. 3 (2018): 247–70.
Studer, Brigitte. *The Transnational World of the Cominternians*. Hampshire: Palgrave Macmillan, 2015.
Studer, Brigitte. *Reisende der Weltrevolution: Eine Globalgeschichte der Kommunistischen Internationale*. Berlin: Suhrkamp, 2020.
Stuurman, Siep. *The Invention of Humanity: Equality and Difference in World History*. Cambridge: Harvard University Press, 2017.
Sun, Zhongshan. *Kidnapped in London: Being the Story of My Capture by, Detention at, and Release from the Chinese Legation, London*. Bristol: J. W. Arrowsmith, 1897.
Suny, Ronald Grigor. *Intellectuals and the Articulation of the Nation*. Ann Arbor: University of Michigan Press, 1999.
Talwar, Sada Nand. *Radical Humanism: Political Philosophy of M. N. Roy Revisited*. New Delhi: K. K. Publishers, 2006.
Tamiatto, Jérémie. 'Des Révolutionnaires Entre Deux Mondes'. *Monde(s)* 10, no. 2 (2016): 51–68.
Tarlo, Emma. *Clothing Matters; Dress and Identity in India*. London: Hurst & Company, 1996.
Tarrow, Sidney G. *Strangers at the Gates: Movements and States in Contentious Politics*. Cambridge: Cambridge University Press, 2012.
Tenorio-Trillo, Mauricio. *I Speak of the City: Mexico City at the Turn of the Twentieth Century*. Chicago: University of Chicago Press, 2013.

Thakur, Vineet. 'An Asian Drama: The Asian Relations Conference, 1947'. *International History Review* 41, no. 3 (2019): 673–95.

Thomas, Ludmila. *Georgi Tschitscherin: 'Ich Hatte Die Revolution Und Mozart'*. Berlin: Dietz, 2012.

Thomas, Paul. *Marxism & Scientific Socialism; From Engels to Althusser*. London: Routledge, 2008.

Thomas, Rosie. *Bombay before Bollywood; Film City Fantasies*. Albany: State University of New York Press, 2013.

Torres-Rodríguez, Laura J. 'Orientalizing Mexico: Estudios Indostánicos and the Place of India in José Vasconcelos's La Raza Cósmica'. *Revista Hispánica Moderna* 68, no. 1 (2015): 77–91.

Trent-Roy, Evelyn. 'Mexico and Her People Chapter I'. *El Heraldo de México*, 22 September, 1919a.

Trent-Roy, Evelyn. 'Mexico and Her People Chapter III'. *El Heraldo de México*, 6 October, 1919b.

Trent-Roy, Evelyn. 'Mexico and Her People Chapter II'. *El Heraldo de México*, 29 September, 1919c.

Trent-Roy, Evelyn. 'Mexico and Her People Chapter VII'. *El Heraldo de México*, November 3, 1919.

Trivedi, Lisa. *Clothing Gandhi's Nation: Homespun and Modern India*. Bloomington & Indianapolis: Indiana University Press, 2007.

Trivellato, Francesca. 'Is There a Future for Italian Microhistory in the Age of Global History?' 2011. https://escholarship.org/uc/item/0z94n9hq.

Tsing, Anna Lowenhaupt. *Friction: An Ethnography of Global Connection*. Princeton: Princeton University Press, 2011.

Unger, Corinna R. 'Towards Global Equilibrium: American Foundations and Indian Modernization, 1950s to 1970s'. *Journal of Global History* 6, no. 1 (2011): 121–42.

Van Dine, S. S. *The Benson Murder Case*. London: Hogarth Press, 1988.

Vatlin, Alexander. *Das Jahr 1920: Der Zweite Kongress der Kommunistischen Internationale*. Berlin: BasisDruck, 2019.

Vatlin, Alexander. 'The Comintern'. Translated by Stephen A. Smith. In *The Oxford Handbook of the History of Communism*, edited by Stephen A. Smith, 187–202. Oxford: Oxford University Press, 2014.

Vester, Michael. *Soziale Milieus Im Gesellschaftlichen Strukturwandel: Zwischen Integration Und Ausgrenzung*. Köln: Bund-Verlag, 1993.

Viswanath, Rupa. *The Pariah Problem: Caste, Religion, and the Social in Modern India*. New York: Columbia University Press, 2014.

Vivekananda, S. *The Ideal of a Universal Religion: Address on Vedanta Philosophy Delivered at Hardman Hall, New York, Sunday, January 12, 1896*. New York, 1896.

Wadia, J.B.H. *M N Roy, the Man: An Incomplete Royana*. Bombay: Popular Prakashan, 1983.

Washington, Peter. *Madame Blavatsky's Baboon: A History of the Mystics, Mediums and Misfits Who Brought Spiritualism to America*. New York: Schocken Books, 1995.

Watson, William. 'Social Mobility and Social Class in Industrial Communities'. In *Closed Systems and Open Minds*, edited by Max Gluckman, 147–51. Edinburgh: Oliver and Boyd, 1964.

Wavell, Archibald Percival Earl of. *The Viceroy's Journal*, edited by Penderel Moon. London: Oxford University Press, 1973.

Weiss, Holger. *Framing a Radical African Atlantic: African American Agency, West African Intellectuals, and the International Trade Union Committee of Negro Workers*. Leiden: Brill, 2014.

Wells, H.G. *Russia in the Shadows*. New York: George H. Doran Company, 1921.

Wenner, Dorothee. *Zorros blonde Schwester: Das Leben der indischen Kinolegende Fearless Nadia*. Berlin: Ullstein, 1999.

White, Stephen. 'Communism and the East: The Baku Congress, 1920'. *Slavic Review* 33, no. 3 (1974): 492–514.

Wickberg, Daniel. 'Intellectual History vs. the Social History of Intellectuals'. *Rethinking History* 5, no. 3 (2001): 383–95.

Wigen, Einar. *State of Translation: Turkey in Interlingual Relations*. Ann Arbor: University of Michigan Press, 2018.

Wilbur, C. Martin. and Julie Lien-ying How. *Missionaries of Revolution: Soviet Advisers and Nationalist China, 1920-1927*. Cambridge, MA: Harvard University Press, 1989.

Wolfe, Bertram. *Three Who Made a Revolution*. New York: Dell, 1964.

Wolfe, Bertram D. *A Life in Two Centuries: An Autobiography*. New York: Stein & Day, 1981.

Wright, Christopher, and Mattias Kipping. 'The Engineering Origins of the Consulting Industry and Its Long Shadow'. In *The Oxford Handbook of Management Consulting*, edited by Mattias Kipping, Timothy Clark, 29–50. Oxford: Oxford University Press, 2012.

Yahaya, Nurfadzilah. 'Class, White Women, and Elite Asian Men in British Courts during the Late Nineteenth Century'. *Journal of Women's History* 31, no. 2 (2019): 101–23.

Yoshihiro, Ishikawa. *The Formation of the Chinese Communist Party*. Translated by Joshua A. Fogel. New York, NY: Columbia University Press, 2012.

Young, Robert J. *Postcolonialism*. Chichester: John Wiley & Sons, Incorporated, 2016.

Ypi, Lea. *Free: Coming of Age at the End of History*. London: Allen Lane, 2021.

Zachariah, Benjamin. 'A Long, Strange Trip: The Lives in Exile of Har Dayal'. *South Asian History and Culture* 4, no. 4 (2013): 574–92.

Zachariah, Benjamin. *Developing India*. New Delhi: Oxford University Press, 2005.

Zimmer, Kenyon. *Immigrants against the State: Yiddish and Italian Anarchism in America*. Urbana: University of Illinois Press, 2015.

Zimmerman, Andrew. 'Three Logics of Race: Theory and Exception in the Transnational History of Empire'. *New Global Studies* 4, no. 1 (2010): 1–9.

Zimmerman, Andrew. *Anthropology and Antihumanism in Imperial Germany*. Chicago: University of Chicago Press, 2001.

Index

Aarsonson, Israel. *See* Dayal, Har
acceptable foreigner 62
Acharya, M. P. T. 4, 30–1, 44, 65, 73, 98, 131, 197–8
   Reminiscences of a Revolutionary 98
Afro-Asian Conference, Bandung 109
Agehananda Bharati, Swami 4, 26, 31–2, 36, 41, 73–5
   The Ochre Robe 82, 99
   profession of non-belonging 100
Ahmad, Muzaffar 131 n.98
Alfassa, Mirra (The Mother) 44
Aliluyeva, Svetlana 44
Alipore bomb case 186
Allen, José 155
All-India politics 68, 179
Ambedkar, Bhimrao, *Waiting for a Visa* 175
Anand, Mulk Raj, *The Sword and the Sickle* 97–8
anarchism 83 n.99, 221
anti-capitalism 122
anti-colonial Indian movement 52, 57
anti-imperialism/imperialist 43, 61–2, 108, 122, 158, 183, 217
Aron, Raymond, *The Opium of Intellectuals* 211–12
Aryans 49, 49 n.159, 187–9
Asia and the Americas journal 103
Asian revolutionaries 62, 154
Assemblies of the League of Nations 109
authoritarianism 204
   fear of freedom 205

Bande Mataram 43
Banerjee, Prathama 108
Barakatullah, Maulana Mohamed 20, 41, 64, 73, 92
   Bolshevism and the Islamic Body Politick 191
Barbusse, Henri 135, 135 n.115
Beals, Carleton 21, 119
   Glass Houses 87

Bengali 219
   bhadralok (gentlefolk) 15, 198–9
   intellectuals 11, 14, 107, 110–11, 220
   Marxism 13
   revolutionaries 77, 119, 139
Bengali actors on world stages
   bringing the world to Moscow 120–4
   counter stages 131–7
   humanist international 137–9
   icons of Indian difference 110–19
   representative claims 107–10
   universal aesthetics 124–31
Bengal Renaissance 26, 26 n.40
Berkman, Alexander 72–3
Berlanga, Manuel Aguirre 151 n.33
Berlin 27, 72, 152
   anti-British anticolonialists and Imperial Germany 23
   Free India Centre 28
   Indian revolutionaries 152, 191
   nostalgia 53
Besant, Annie 10 n.39, 113
Bhattacharya, Narendranath. *See* Roy, M. N.
biographical approach 15
birth control 13–14, 19, 21 n.17, 52, 54–5, 71, 221, 226
Bolsheviks 157, 164 n.88, 167, 191
Bombacci, Nicola 28, 28 n.56
Bombay Chronicle newspaper 172
Bonne, Alfred 39 n.113
Borodin, Fanya 25, 72
Borodin, Mikhail 21, 25, 37, 72, 87–8, 120–2, 158–9, 161, 179
Bose, Rash Behari 19–20, 28, 33, 47, 119. *See also* Nakamuraya
Bose, Subhas Chandra 20, 28, 45, 207–8
Bourdieu, Pierre, habitus 8–9
'bourgeois-democratic' nationalist movements 123
Brahmanic purity 37
Brahmo exegesis 183

Brahmo Samaj 139
Brandler, Heinrich 35 n.92
Brincken, Wilhelm von 63-4, 119
Brissaud, André 213-14
    The Meaning of the Divine 213
British Consulate, New York 136
British Imperialism 28, 150 n.31, 196
British Labour Party 172-4, 173 n.121, 208
Brodsky, Isaak 105, 125
Buber-Neumann, Margarete 177, 177 n.143
Burckhardt, Jacob, *The Civilisation of the Renaissance in Italy* 11

Cama, Bhikaji Rustom 42-3, 42 n.131, 45, 125
Carranza, Venustiano 32, 32 n.78, 150 n.31, 152
celibacy 45-6
Chakravarty, Chandra Kanta 83 n.98, 184-5
Chandra, Ram, *India Against Britain* 184
Chatterji, Amarendranath 171
Chattopadhyaya, Harindranath 38
Chattopadhyaya, Kamaladevi 42 n.131
Chattopadhyaya (Chatto), Virendranath 23, 38, 41-2, 44, 51, 62 n.5, 96, 101, 191
    'The Adventurer Unmasked or The Career of M. N. Roy' 144
Chattopadhyay, Suhasini 45
Chaudhuri, Nirad 11 n.43, 76 n.67, 79 n.82
Chen Duxiu 158, 158 n.65
Chettiar, Singaravelu 131 n.98
Chibber, Vivek, *Postcolonial Theory and the Specter of Capital* 215
Chicherin, Georgy 32, 197
Chinese communism 159-60
Chinese Communist Party (CCP) 159
Chinese Socialist Workers Party 125
Chou En-lai 89
Christianity 111-14, 183
Civil Disobedience Movement (1932) 135
clandestinity 61-3, 66, 70, 111, 224
clothes, changing 61, 75-84
colonial and semi-colonial contexts 129, 161
colonial exhibitions and literature 108
Comintern 22-3, 28, 30, 35, 39, 39 n.113, 45, 53, 66, 101, 120, 123, 128-9, 131, 144, 153, 162, 180, 191, 226
    Fifth World Congress 154, 156
    International Colonial Bureau, Paris 154
    Lenin's speech on 105-6
    Pan American Bureau 155
    Second World Congress 67, 129, 194
    Turkestan Bureau of the Comintern 196
    Western European Bureau (WES) 24
Comitati d'Azione per l'Universalità di Roma (CAUR) 109
communism 28, 122, 129-30, 148-9, 157, 167, 175, 191, 207, 209 n.102, 211-12, 217, 223
    China 159-60
    in colonial countries 222
    doctrinaire 99, 166
    as fashion 82
    Indian 131 n.98, 136, 200
    as secular religion 29
Communist International 2, 14, 32, 66, 71, 101, 105, 120, 123, 128, 136, 146-7, 160, 170, 207
Communist Party of Great Britain (CPGB) 72, 98, 133, 156
Communist Party of India 44, 131, 162
communist propaganda, India 175
confinement 89-92
Corey, Lewis 53, 71
cosmopolitan clubs 13, 19-26, 57
    ideological variation 26-9
    precarious elite 29-32
cosmopolitanism 4, 12, 56 n.197, 64, 68, 87, 94, 175, 218
    adventurousness and 70
    distinguished (*see* distinguished cosmopolitanism/cosmopolitans)
    as Eurocentric 5
    physicality and impressions 88
    practising difference 7-11

Dange, S. A. 131 n.98, 174
Das, Taraknath 9, 27, 34, 119, 153
    Free Hindusthan 34
Datta, Bhupendranath 41
Dayal, Har 6, 20, 23, 41, 45-6, 72-3, 79, 85-6, 92, 95, 143-4, 152-3
    Forty-Four Months in Germany and Turkey 85
    Karl Marx, A Modern Rishi 152
Debray, Régis 147-8
Devi, Santi/Shanti. *See* Trent/Roy/Jones, Evelyn
Dey, Sushil 25, 213
Diaz, Juan 52

distant emotional style 8, 224–8
distinguished cosmopolitanism/
    cosmopolitans 4–7, 9, 13, 22, 41,
    57–9, 71, 84, 101, 144, 148, 179,
    182, 218, 220, 224–5, 228
  itinerancy 8
  sociability 19
  value of 14
Doriot, Jacques 28
Draft Constitution of India 173
Dravidians 49 n.159, 187–9
drinks 19, 33, 36–8, 58, 211
  alcohol 35, 211
DuBois, W. E. B. 113–14, 134
Dugan, Ethel Ray 21, 49
Dutta, Sudhindranath 25, 103

Ehrenfels, Rudolf Omar von 73, 82
Einstein, Albert 134–5, 219, 227
El Camino Para la Paz Duradera del Mundo 151
El Heraldo de México newspaper 151, 189
Emmett, Robert 185
emotional regimes 8
Enlightenment 185
equivalences 181–2, 198, 202, 214–15
  assertions of 182, 208, 222–4
  class, struggling with 196–202
  communist categories 190–6
  comparative advantages 183–5
  fascists here and there 202–9
  mixed races 186–90
  totalitarianism 209–14, 209 n.102
Erikson, Agda 46
Etawah Plan 176
Eurocentric, cosmopolitanism as 5
European fascism 97, 184, 203
European Renaissance 170
Evans, Ernestine 23
Evans, Mary 26, 26 n.40

Family of Man 219
famine 34–5, 36 n.96, 37–8, 54, 177 n.141, 219
fascism 28, 144, 173, 202–9, 211, 214, 217, 222, 226
  communism and 212
  European 97, 184, 203
  Italian 209 n.102

Fat Sing 21
fiction, cosmopolitan 92–8
First World War 19–21, 23, 24 n.29, 27, 43, 59, 73, 86, 151 n.33, 152, 196
Fitingof, Rosa 44, 131
food/food practices 19, 33–5, 37, 58, 90, 210, 218, 225
  meat 164 n.85
Ford Foundation 2, 148, 175–8
Foucault, Michel 210
'Foundations for a New Social Philosophy' 137
Fraina, Luis 53, 71, 127
Frankfurt Institute 26
Frankfurt School intellectuals 209
Franklin, Benjamin 184
Freedom: The Anarchist Weekly journal 73
French Revolution 161
Friedman, Thomas L. 15, 181
Friends of Freedom for India (FFI) 80
Fromm, Erich 202–3, 208, 222
  authoritarianism of Reformation 205
  automaton conformity 204
  Escape from Freedom 204, 222
  fear of freedom 205–6
Front National 212

Gadamer, Hans-Georg 118
Gale, Linn 21, 21 n.17, 84 n.100, 121, 151 n.33
  Gale's Magazine 21 n.17, 34, 151, 151 n.33
Gandhian religiosity 205
Gandhi, Mahatma 29–30, 46, 48, 54–5, 78–9, 113, 139–40, 175, 200–2, 205–6, 209
  modernity 207
  non-violence 201
Geissler, Eva 45
Geissler, Louise 24, 48, 53, 59, 159, 226
German Birth Control Committee 24
Ghadarites 184
Ghadar movement 6, 9, 46, 143
Ghadar newspaper 120, 151
Ghose, Sailendranath 21, 153
Glasgow Socialist 194
Goldman, Emma 73
good taste 29, 32–8
Goswami, Manu, insurgent comparison 183–4, 183 n.11

Gottschalk/Roy, Ellen 24, 31, 35, 42, 48–9, 48 n.153, 53–4, 56–8, 67, 83, 91, 102, 134, 164, 166, 171, 176–9, 227
Graefe-Goldebee, Albrecht von 27
Gruzenberg, Mikhail. *See* Borodin, Mikhail
Gupta, Herambalal 21, 41, 52

habitus 8–9, 43, 57, 102, 124, 140, 145, 149, 179, 198, 219
Harper, Tim 62
Hassan, Ismail Hakki. *See* Dayal, Har
Hegel, Georg Wilhelm Friedrich 115, 168
  concrete universal 169
Hill, Christopher, 'generalising universalization' 9 n.33
Hindenburg, Paul von 209
Hindu Conspiracy Trial (San Francisco). *See* Indo-German conspiracy trial
Hinduism 114, 164, 183, 187, 205
  scientific 112
  and universal religion 112
Hindu nationalism 175, 203, 210, 222
Hindustan Times newspaper 68
Hitler, Adolf 209
  'Free India Legion' 74
Hitlerite supermen 214
Ho Chi-Minh 23, 70, 154
humanism 137–40, 168, 209–10, 213–14, 221, 223
humanist movement 55, 74, 177 n.141, 221
human resources 14
Hussain, Ghulam 131 n.98
Huxley, Julian 2, 138

ideologies (ideological) 1–2, 7, 12, 19, 82, 207, 217, 221–2, 228
  differences 12
  globalization 12
  shifts 144–5
  of ultranationalism 109
  uniformity 19
  universal validity 15
  variation 26–9
Immortal India 170
Imperial Germany 20, 63, 152
  anti-British anticolonialists and 23
impression, making 63–9
Indian Federation of Labour (IFL) 171–2, 174

Indian intellectuals 14, 54, 111, 123, 191, 219, 221, 223
Indian National Congress (INC) 135
Indian nationalism 10, 15, 184, 204–5
Indian Radical Humanist Movement 137
Indian Renaissance Institute 25, 31, 36, 38, 176–8
Indian revolutionaries 4, 20–1, 23–4, 26–7, 29, 42–3, 47–8, 51, 63, 83, 94, 152, 156, 184–5, 191, 219. *See also specific Indian revolutionaries*
  in Berlin 191
  in California 49, 153
Indian Revolutionary Association (IRA) 197
Indian spirituality 117, 201, 213, 219
Indo-German conspiracy trial 87, 119, 152, 184
Indonesian War of Independence 155
intellectual independence 144–5
international anti-imperialism 62
International Committee for Political Prisoners (ICPP) 134–6
International Communist Opposition (ICO) 14, 132
International Congress of Orientalists, Rome 114
Internationale Hilfsverein 134
International Humanist and Ethical Union (IHEU) 14, 120, 137–9, 170, 177 n.141
internationalism 125, 138, 144, 145 n.12, 217
  corporeality 220
  Eastern form of 109
  individually driven 13
International Journal of Comparative Civilisation 116
International-Radical-Communist Anarchist Club 46
International Workers of the World 46, 95, 121
International Working Man's Association 4, 131
Irish Republicans 184
Islam 73, 183
  and communism 191, 212
Italian fascism 209 n.102
Italian Renaissance 11, 167

Japan
    fascism 207
    Greater East Asia Co-Prosperity
        Sphere 109
    interracial marriages 47
Jayawardena, Kumari 44 n.137
Jordan, David Starr 20

Kanpur trial 120, 133
Kapp Putsch 30
Kara, Maniben 25, 171 n.112
Karl, Rebecca 108
Karnik, V. B. 25, 171 n.112
Karunovskaya, Lidiya 44
Katayama, Sen 23–4, 64, 85, 125, 125 n.79, 154–5
Kaviraj, Sudipta 192
Kawabata, Yasunari 117
Khankhoje, Pandurang 31
Khilafat movement 196
Kipling, Rudyard, *Kim* 193 n.53
Koestler, Arthur 166–7, 166 nn.95–6, 227
    Darkness at Noon 166
    The God That Failed: Six Studies in Communism 166
Kolariov, Vasil 65
Krishnavarma, Shyamji, *Indian Sociologist* 45
Krupskaya, Nadezhda 146
Kuomintang (KMT) 159

Labour Monthly magazine 72, 200
Lahiri, Shompa 62 n.7
Lal, Chandra 96
Lal, Gobind Behari 79
language 13, 19, 33, 58, 38–42, 91, 128, 161, 182, 218
    Bengali 40
    English 39–41
    German 40
Latin American
    mestizaje 188–90, 222
    racial mixing 15
    whitening 190
Law, Howard. *See* Tan Malaka, Ibrahim Datuk
League Against Imperialism, Brussels 109
Le Bon, Gustav, *Psychology of Crowds* 212
Le Brahmane du Komintern 67 n.24

Lenin, Vladimir 2, 67, 118, 123, 147, 147 n.16, 194, 220
    The Awakening of Asia 122
    Leninism 198
    speech on Second World Congress of the Comintern 105–6
    theory of imperialism 106, 122, 195
    "Theses on the National Question" 139
    What Is to Be Done? 146
Levi, Paul 105 n.1, 106 n.1
life stories, cosmopolitan 98–101
lifestyle radicalism 79
Liu, Lydia 182
Liu Shauzhou 123
Lockean Sensationalism 181
London, Jack, *The Little Lady of the Big House* 95
Lovestone, Jay 45, 70
Lowenhaupt Tsing, Anna 214
Luschan, Felix von 114–15

MacDonald, Ramsay 79
The Mahratta newspaper 98
Majeed, Javed 7
Malik publishing house 24, 26
Manela, Erez 151
Manjapra, Kris 53, 183
    M. N. Roy 183 n.7
Mao Zedong 89
Marshall Aid 36
Martin, Charles Allen. *See* Roy, M. N.
The Marxian/Humanist Way journal 28, 82, 211–12
Marxism 13, 193, 198, 206–7
Marxist intelligentsia 146
Marxist theory 130
Marx, Karl 15, 31, 130, 152, 168, 191, 193
    contemporary India 200
    Theses on Feuerbach 141
The Masses 31
Maugham, Somerset
    Ashenden: Or a British Agent 96
    Giulia Lazarri 96
Mayenburg, Ruth von 23, 38
Mayer, Albert 176
Mayo, Katherine, *Mother India* 54
Meerut Conspiracy Case (1929–33) 99, 134
Mexican Communist Party (PCM) 139, 155

Mexican Revolution 150–1
Mexico City
　anglophone expatriates in 71
　Indians in 65, 123, 221
　night club 13, 17–18
　US radicals in 83
Michaëlis, Karin 51
Michelet, Jules 168–9
　History of the French Revolution 168
migrants / migration 3
　of Indian Muslims 196
Mill, James, *History of British India* 156
Mirza, Bakar Ali 52, 225
mobility 3–6, 12, 29, 42, 48, 66, 80, 144, 218
　spiralists 6
　spiritual 74
Modern Review magazine 72, 152
Mona, Matu 96 n.159
Monnerot, Jules 29, 211–12
　Sociology of Communism 212
muhajirin 196
Mukerji, Dhan Gopal 11, 20–1, 41, 54–5,
　　81, 86–7, 86 n.113, 226
　Caste and Outcast 86
　Rajani: Songs of the Night 20
Mukherji, Abani 44, 65, 123, 131, 192–4,
　　196–7
Münzenberg, Willi 24
Muslims 187, 191, 196
Mussolini, Benito 28
mysticism and Christian esotericism 10–11

Nachman Acharya, Magda 31, 44, 64
Nakamuraya 19–20
Nambiar, A. C. N. 27–8, 41, 45
Nambudiripad, E. M. S. 198 n.68
names, changing 69–75
Narayan, Jayaprakash 162, 162 n.77
National and Colonial Questions 128, 194
nationalism 1, 164, 164 n.87, 196
　colonial 122, 203
　as fascism 203–4
　Hindu 175, 203, 210, 222
　Indian 10, 15, 184, 204–5
Natorp, Paul 118
Nazism 6, 28, 58, 206
　communism and 167
　protestantism and 204
Nehru, Jawaharlal 134, 148, 162, 206–7
Nehru, Motilal 207

New Humanism 167
Nguyen Ai Quoc. *See* Ho Chi-Minh
Noble, Margaret. *See* Sister Nivedita
Non-Cooperation Movement 78
nostalgia 8, 36, 53, 59, 225–6

Ogle, Vanessa 184 n.13
Ohsawa, Georges 47
open applications 150–3
Osman, Mizra. *See* Dayal, Har
outsiders
　independent outsider 144
　model 146–50

Pak Chin-sun 123, 125, 128–9
Palme Dutt, Clemens 156
Palme Dutt, Rajani 156
Pan-Asianism 73, 93, 221
Pan-Asiatic Association, Nagasaki 109
Pan-Islam and khilafatists 200
Pan-Islamic conference, Mekka 109
Pankhurst, Sylvia 121
Parikh, G. D. 11 n.42
Parikh, Indumati 25, 55
Park, Richard 26, 36, 100, 102, 176–8
Partition violence 36
Patjar Merah 96–7
persona 7–9, 12, 51, 56–7, 88, 107, 124,
　　144, 146, 220, 222, 225
Peters, Lana. *See* Aliluyeva, Svetlana
Phillips, Charles 21–2, 70–1, 82, 123, 127,
　　226
Pillai, Chempakaraman 27
politics and aesthetics 64, 77, 84, 107,
　　169–70, 173–4
Postgate, Raymond William, *Revolutions
　　from 1789–1906* 23
Praag, Jaap van 138
practices/practice theory 3, 6–8, 12, 14,
　　58, 102, 182, 222, 224, 226
　distant emotional style 8, 224–8
　racial difference 9–10
　shared tastes and blind spots 19
　social and performative 8, 14–15, 19,
　　62, 224–5, 228
　of translation 182
　writing 63, 102
Pratap, Mahendra 20, 64, 73, 92–3
　The Book of the Religion of Love 73
　My Life Story of Fiftyfive Years 93

professionalism 146–7
professional revolutionaries 14–15, 70, 146–9, 153–7, 223
Prohme, Rayna 25, 33, 72, 88

Quilliam, Abdullah 74
Quit India Movement 171

Rab, Abdur 197–8
  'puriah' class 197
racial difference/discrimination 9–10, 28, 47, 62, 223
racial mixing 15, 43, 186–90, 214, 222
racial passing 62 n.7
Radek, Karl 124, 128, 130
Radical Democratic Party (RDP) 103, 171–4, 208
The Radical Humanist 211
Radical Humanist movement 55, 165, 170, 175, 177 n.141
Rai, Lala Lajpat 9, 20, 143
Rakovsky, Christian 65
Ramkrishna-Vivekananda Mission 20, 112
Ramnath, Maia 92
Ray, Sibnarayan 25, 40, 211
  Selected Works of M. N. Roy 1
Reed, John 35, 127
relationships 3, 42–8, 58, 224
  friends 225
  households 48–54
  interracial love and marriage 13, 43–4, 47, 51–2, 54
  love 225
  reproduction 54–8
  transnational spiritualism 44
renegade 144, 144 n.9, 157, 180
Rivera, Diego 187
Rockefeller Foundation 2, 175–8
Rogers, Marie. *See* Smedley, Agnes
Rolland, Romain 112, 200–2
rooted/vernacular cosmopolitanism 5–6
rootless cosmopolitans 6
Rosmer, Alfred 106 n.1
Rothenstein, William 117
Round Table Conferences 78, 135
Rowlatt Act (1919) 194
Roy, Ellen. *See* Gottschalk/Roy, Ellen
Roy, Evelyn. *See* Trent/Roy/Jones, Evelyn
Roy, M. N. 1–2, 4, 6–7, 10–11, 13, 17, 24, 52, 57–9, 62–5, 67–70, 74, 83 n.99, 90, 97, 101, 107, 119, 125–6, 130, 140, 144–5, 144 n.9, 145 n.12, 147–8, 150, 154–5, 157, 163, 171, 178, 181, 193–4, 202, 214, 217–18, 221–2, 225–6
  abstraction and neutrality 227
  Alternatives to Communism 170
  claim-making abilities 218
  cosmopolitan reputation 3, 170
  cultural criticism 100
  Estudios indostánicos 189
  Europeanization 66
  humanist organization 2, 137
  I Accuse! 135
  If I Were Stalin 103
  India in Transition 78, 192–3
  Indian Labour and Post-War Reconstruction 36 n.96, 172
  international organizations 2, 215
  itinerary 11–13, 29, 47, 71, 101, 150, 228
  Jawaharlal Nehru 205, 222
  khadi 82
  La India; Su Pasado, Su Presente, y Su Porvenir 186–7, 222
  Letters from Jail 90
  Memoirs 37, 83 n.98, 84, 93, 101, 118, 145
  Men I met 88
  My Experiences in China 160
  The Path to Durable Peace of the World 151, 185–6
  The Problem of Freedom 205, 222
  Reason, Romanticism and Revolution 11 n.44, 100, 167, 169
  Revolution and Counter-Revolution in China 160–1
Roy, Rammohun 11 n.43, 183, 187
Russian Revolution 21, 59, 144–5, 152–3

Sanger, Margaret 55
Sankhya system of philosophy 181
Sarekat Islam 159, 195
Sarkar, Benoy Kumar 9
Sartre, Jean-Paul, *Existentialism Is a Humanism* 210–11
Saxena, Baburam 39 n.113
Schenkl, Emilie 45
scientific Hinduism 112
scientific positivism 114

Seal, Brajendranath 11 n.43, 14, 110–11, 110 n.20, 114–16, 140
   'Meaning of Race, Tribe, Nation' 115
   The Positive Sciences of the Hindus 114
   universalist humanism 140
Second World Congress of the Communist International 14, 105–6
Second World War 20, 28, 59, 74, 132, 137, 144, 180, 203, 209
secular religion 29, 210–12
semi-colonial countries 106–7, 106 n.5, 129, 161
Serge, Victor 34, 65–6
Serrati, Giacinto 195
Seth, Sanjay 192
Shaikh, Tayab 25
Shimazu, Naoko 220
   two-tiered conception of race 47 n.150
Sindic, Jeanne 31
Singh, Bhagat 133 n.105
Singh, Brajesh 44
Sino-Japanese war 97
Sister Nivedita 44, 113
Smedley, Agnes 6, 20, 24, 44, 51–2, 55, 55 n.187, 71, 79–81, 94–5, 153, 225
   Daughter of Earth 52, 94
   St Patrick's Day parade 80
Sneevliet, Henk 24, 35, 49–50, 129, 133, 147, 158–9, 195
sociability 5, 13, 19, 26, 29–31
   good taste 33–8
   language 38–42
social and performative practices 8, 14–15, 19, 62, 224–5, 228
social circles 7, 15, 19, 203
Socialism 34, 207
Soma, Tosiko 20, 47
Soong Ching-ling 89
Soong Mei-ling 88–9, 220
Spanish civil war 97
Spencer, Herbert 95
Spionnage-dienst (Patjar Merah Indonesia) 96–7
Spivak, Gayatri 107–8, 108 n.9, 110
Spratt, Philip 25, 25 n.38, 56, 56 n.197, 98, 102–3, 165–6
   Blowing Up India 56 n.197, 98–9
Stalin, Joseph 88, 97, 103, 157, 165, 210
   Great Purge 164, 166, 179
Stolte, Carolien 93

Sultan-Zade, Avetis 123
Sun Yat-sen 61–2, 88–9, 147, 158–9, 220
Dr Sun Yat-sen museum, Hong Kong 61
superiority 29, 104, 199
Swadeshi movement, Bengal 71, 77

Tagore, Rabindranath 14, 41, 77–8, 111, 116–19, 139–40, 187, 219
   Gitanjali 117, 118 n.51
Tan Malaka, Ibrahim Datuk 4, 23–4, 69, 96–7, 132–3, 154–5, 225
   Dari pendjara ke pendjara/From Jail to Jail 89–90
Tenorio, Mauricio 32 n.78, 45 n.140
Thalheimer, August 24, 181
theory of everything 168
Time Out Mexico City 17
Torres-Rodríguez, Laura 190
Trent/Roy/Jones, Evelyn 20–3, 41, 44, 48–50, 65–6, 68, 71–2, 75, 131, 134–6, 150, 189, 194, 196, 224
   Mexico and Her People 22, 189
Trotsky, Leon 35, 81 n.90

ultra-leftist tactics 157
Ulyanova, Maria Ilyinichna 67
Union of South Africa 127
United Front policy 123
the United States 149, 209–10
   antisemitism 71
   discrimination 10, 223
   European colonial powers 153
   Ghadarites 184
   Ramkrishna Missions 20
universalism 115–16
   anti-imperialist 183
   vs. particularism 223
   Roman 109
universality 51, 113, 115, 125, 138–9, 182, 218, 221
universalization 9 n.33, 222, 228
Universal Races Conference, London 113
universal religion
   Christianity 111–13
   Hinduism 112
University of the Toilers of the East (KUTV) 23
Uritsky Palace, Petrograd 67
Usmani, Shaukat 131 n.98, 133

Van Dine, S. S., *The Benson Murder Case* 91, 91 n.135
The Vanguard journal 127, 198
Vasconcelos, José 21, 21 n.18, 186
   cosmic race 189–90
   Estudios Indostánicos 187, 189, 222
   La raza cósmica: Misión de la raza iberoamericana 186, 189
   mestizaje 189–90, 222
Vedanta 187–8
Versailles Treaty for China 158 n.65
Vinci, Leonardo da 11
Villa, Pancho 220
violence 9, 36, 52, 58, 201
Vivekananda, Swami 14, 44, 110–12, 110 n.20, 139–40, 187, 200, 219
   at World Parliament of Religions 110–11
Voitinsky, Grigory 158

Wadia, Homi 26
Wadia, J. B. H. 26, 26 n.39, 37, 83
Wavell, Archibald 104, 173, 209
Webb, Beatrice, *Industrial Democracy* 146
Webb, Muhammad Alexander Russell 74
Webb, Sidney, *Industrial Democracy* 146
Wells, H. G. 129–30, 129 n.93
Wen Yuan Yang 39 n.113
Wijnkoop, David 65, 195
Wilsonian Moment (1919) 151
Wilson, Woodrow 151
Wint, Guy 100
Wolfe, Bertram 53, 59, 65
women 22, 42, 49, 55, 71, 77, 80
World Federation (1929–39) journal 93
World Humanity's League 116

Xin qingnian/New Youth magazine 158

Yeats, William Butler 117
The Young Worker's League of Madras 144
Youth Congresses and Peace Conferences 109
Ypi, Lea 149

Zetkin, Clara 106 n.1
Zhang Guotao 159
Zinoviev, Grigory 67, 81, 106 n.1, 129 n.93, 130, 164 n.88
Zola, Émile 135

www.ingramcontent.com/pod-product-compliance
Lightning Source LLC
Chambersburg PA
CBHW071814300426
44116CB00009B/1318